FOREIGN DIRECT INVESTMENT IN CENTRAL AND EASTERN EUROPE

Transition and Development

Series Editor: Professor Ken Morita
Faculty of Economics, Hiroshima University, Japan

The Transition and Development series aims to provide high quality research books that examine transition and development societies in a broad sense - including countries that have made a decisive break with central planning as well as those in which governments are introducing elements of a market approach to promote development. Books examining countries moving in the opposite direction will also be included. Titles in the series will encompass a range of social science disciplines. As a whole the series will add up to a truly global academic endeavour to grapple with the questions transition and development economies pose.

Also in the series:

Foreign Direct Investment in Central and Eastern Europe

Edited by
SVETLA TRIFONOVA MARINOVA
University of Birmingham, United Kingdom

MARIN ALEXANDROV MARINOV
University of Gloucestershire, United Kingdom
and
University of Umeå, Sweden

ASHGATE

Published by
Ashgate Publishing Limited
Gower House
Croft Road
Aldershot
Hampshire GU11 3HR
England

Ashgate Publishing Company
Suite 420
101 Cherry Street
Burlington, VT 05401-4405
USA

Ashgate website: http://www.ashgate.com

British Library Cataloguing in Publication Data
Foreign direct investment in Central and Eastern Europe :
    theoretical and practical perspectives. - (Transition and
    development)
    1.Investments, Foreign - Europe, Central 2.Investments,
    Foreign - Europe, Eastern
    I.Marinova, Svetla Trifonova II.Marinov, Marin Alexandrov
    332.6'73'0943

Library of Congress Cataloging-in-Publication Data
Foreign direct investment in Central and Eastern Europe / edited by Svetla [i.e. Svetla]
    Marinova and Marin Marinov.
        p. cm. -- (Transition and development)
    Includes bibliographical references and index.
    ISBN 0-7546-3026-9 (alk. paper)
    1. Investments, Foreign--Europe, Eastern. 2. Investments, Foreign--Europe, Central.
    I. Marinova, Svetla. II. Marinov, Marin Alexandrov. III. Series.

    HG5430.7.A3F663 2003
    332.67'3'0943--dc21

                                                                2002038370

ISBN 0 7546 3026 9

Printed and bound by Athenaeum Press, Ltd.,
Gateshead, Tyne & Wear.

Contents

vii

List of Contributors

Emin Akcaoglu, Ankara University, Turkey

Shaukat Ali, University of Wolverhampton, England

Refik Culpan, Pennsylvania State Universty, USA

James W. Dean, Simon Fraser University, USA

Sonia Ferencikova, University of Bratislava, Slovakia

Marian Gorynia, University of Poznan, Poland

Piia Heliste, Helsinki School of Economics, Finland

Inkeri Hirvensalo, Helsinki School of Economics, Finland

Jari Jumpponen, Lappeenranta University of Technology, Finland

Kari Liuhto, Lappeenranta University of Technology, Finland

Carl H. McMillan, Carleton University, Canada

Nadiya Mankovska, Institute for Economic Research, Ukraine

Marin Alexandrov Marinov, University of Gloucestershire, England

Svetla Trifonova Marinova, University of Birmingham, England

Ken Morita, Hiroshima University, Japan

Jarmo Nieminen, University of Sejnioki, Finland

Alojzy Z. Nowak, University of Warsaw, Poland

Jan Nowak, University of the South Pacific, Fiji Islands

Christos N. Pitelis, Cambridge University, England

Josef Pöschl, Vienna Institute of International Economic Studies, Austria

Jeff Steagall, University of North Florida, USA

Valéria Szekeres, Ministry of Education, Hungary

Zsuzsanna Vincze, Turku School of Economics, Finland

Radoslaw Wolniak, University of Warsaw, Poland

PART I

OVERVIEW OF FOREIGN DIRECT INVESTMENT IN CENTRAL AND EASTERN EUROPE

Introduction

MARIN ALEXANDROV MARINOV and SVETLA TRIFONOVA MARINOVA

Foreign direct investment (FDI) is a part of broader activities bringing internationalization and economic integration of businesses worldwide. Trade among nations dates from ancient times. In the recent historic past Dutch, English, French, Portuguese and Spanish firms promoted international trade in their overseas colonies. Gradually, those firms started establishing production facilities in home markets. These activities can be regarded as initial FDI undertakings. Contemporary FDI started in the early 1950s when multinational firms began creating production networks spreading all over the world.

While after World War II the industrialized world got involved in internationalizing activities through FDI, the countries of Central and Eastern Europe (CEE) were developing inward integration within the Council for Mutual Economic Assistance (CMEA) for both trade and investment activities. The economic climate in the CEE region changed after the fall of the Berlin Wall in 1989. Since then there has been a radical change in the flow of capital from developed countries towards countries of the former Soviet Bloc.

Transition CEE countries have adopted different approaches towards the creation and implementation of FDI policies and strategies. The Czech Republic, Estonia, Hungary and Poland, having appreciated FDI as a major stimulus to transition to market as well as a main boost to economic growth, have adopted open and facilitating inward FDI policies at various periods of their early transition to market. Simultaneously, a number of CEE countries started participating in outward FDI activities. In absolute terms Russia and Hungary are among the best performers in this respect (Marinov, 2002).

Taking the investor's perspective, FDI has always been associated with the process of resolving a number of issues. The process of international capital flows is associated with the assumption of a certain degree of risk depending on the environmental characteristics, among others; political, economic, commercial, and financial. Drives that can motivate foreign investors to undertake FDI activities can fall into several categories (Dunning, 1993). They are *access to resources* (natural and labor) unavailable or more expensive in the home country, allowing increase in

1

efficiency; *access to markets* avoiding import restrictions, reducing transportation and transaction costs, quicker and better responding to the signals of host markets; pursuing of *strategic objectives,* among others market domination or establishment of strategic alliances, to *avoid restrictions* that affect the investor's home country.

A Brief Historic Outlook of FDI in CEE

Historically, Russia and some CEE countries like ex-Czechoslovakia, and to a certain extent Hungary and Poland, received substantial FDI inflows before communist governments came to power. For example, Russia attracted substantial inflows of FDI in the last decade of the nineteenth century and immediately before World War I. Those investment inflows brought about fast economic development and internationalization of the Russian economy at the time (Kuznetsov, 1994). There were very limited FDI inflows in ex-Soviet Union between the end of World War I and the beginning of the 1980s. Due to severely limited economic activities within the boundaries of CMEA and lack of legal support, Western FDI in CEE countries was negligible before the start of transition.

The 1980s saw many changes related to the easing of the restrictions for FDI from developed capitalist economies into CEE. Most of the FDI inflow in the CEE resulted in the creation of international joint ventures (IJVs) with the participation of the respective CEE governments and foreign companies as partners. In the majority of cases the foreign companies were of Western European, North American or Japanese origin. Companies, such as Coca Cola, Pepsi Co, Matsushita and British Leyland, penetrated the region through IJV formation and/or licensing agreements.

Foreign Direct Investment Theories and their Relevance to Central and Eastern European Context

Theories and concepts explaining FDI phenomenon have started to appear, develop, be adjusted, refined and modernized since 1960s. There are certain paradigms that can be used in studying, analyzing, developing, implementing and improving FDI policies in both macroeconomic and microeconomic aspects. For a certain period of time the countries from the Commonwealth of Independent States (CIS) and the European part of the Soviet Bloc, the transition countries, were deprived from theoretical and practical development of FDI policies and their application.

Coase (1937) made the first theoretical contribution to international expansion of firms by introducing the notion of the internalization perspective or transaction cost theory. According to him there may be cond 'ions under which a firm may find it more efficient to develop an intern al market rather than penetrating foreign markets. Later, the minimization of transaction cost became a criterion for foreign market entry (Williamson, 1975) to decrease the probability for market failure. This theory is applicable in the CEE context in explaining the behavior of a company entering this regional market by forming a subsidiary on its own (internalization) or going for a collaborative venture formation with a partner or partners, either from the region (mostly when seeking local intelligence) or with a partner or partners from outside the region (principally when wishing to share the risk of undertaking investment).

Hymer (1960) introduced the monopolistic competition and market imperfection theory founded on the assumption that foreign investors need to exploit imperfections because investments in foreign production facilities are associated with more substantial costs and higher risks than investments in production facility creation in the home country. As additional investments are needed to meet the operational and organizational costs of overseas subsidiaries, coupled with higher marketing and business development expenses, the investing company has to possess a monopolistic advantage derived from market imperfections. Hymer's approach was further developed by Kindleberger (1969), Horst (1972), Kimura (1989) and Lall (1980). The contributions of Hymer (1960) have been focused on technology- and innovation-based company-specific advantages. Authors after Hymer studied the specific competitive edges of companies, referring to explanatory variables for making foreign investments, such as size of firm, vertical integration, production differentiation. The monopolistic competition and market imperfection theory of FDI can be useful for the host countries and companies in terms of evaluating the investing company's advantages, corporate assets and capabilities, as well as their suitability for application in the context of CEE.

The product life cycle and investment development path theory considers foreign direct investment based on the transference of skills or advantage, which will be compensated through profit realization. This concept was introduced by Vernon (1966). The idea of various levels of technological development among countries eventually results in geographic relocation of production to host countries where the development of technological capacity and lower production costs account for the competitive advantage of the new production location. Wilkins (1988) has made major contributions to this theory.

Then, in reference to tariff protectionism, Narula (1996) made further contributions. The latter has introduced the notion that he has called Investment Development Path. It expresses the idea that through growth in income, technology and physical capital a country that is a net recipient of inward foreign investment can become a net provider of outward foreign investment at a later stage. This theory provides a valuable explanation for decisions and policies of multinational companies to transfer their production facilities overseas. In addition to the incentives provided by production cycle related location decisions, host government support provided through FDI promotion strategies and investment mechanisms can provide further investment incentives. In the early years of transition such incentives were provided firstly and mostly by Hungary, later by the Czech Republic, Poland and the Baltic countries.

Knickerbocker (1973) has found out that in oligopolistic markets, market leaders who ventured abroad were soon followed by their rivals from the home countries. Graham (1978) has contributed to the oligopolistic market theory through providing explanations of the investment behavior of European and US multinational corporations from strategic perspectives. This means that FDI is not always decided on the basis of tangible economic benefits; rather decisions are most often made on the basis of evaluating major competitors' characteristics. The oligopolistic theory provides an explanation of the motives of the market leader for making introductory investment in the host market. This theory can be used by CEE government policy makers in economic sectors with oligopolistic structures. The results from the oligopolistic analysis can be further applied by policy makers for selection of investing companies.

The network theory, as discussed by Cook and Emerson (1978), Mattsson (1987), Forsgren (1989), Forsgren and Johanson (1991), Blackenburg and Johanson (1992), also analyses the FDI process. The focus of the network theory is mostly relational, i. e., developing mutually reinforcing, long-term relationships based on complementary resources needed to conduct the business process. Therefore, it suggests that parties link up to one another seeking co-operative, mutually beneficial FDI relationships. The glue that binds the entire network together is the elaborate pattern of interdependence and reciprocity also related to resources and collective action over time. The network theory offers opportunities for in-depth processual analysis of FDI relationships in CEE.

Importance of Foreign Direct Investment

Inward FDI represents a significant proportion of total FDI for certain countries in the CEE region while it is insignificant for others (see Table 1). Analyzing the data from Table 1 it is clear that there is a group of countries that have benefited substantially in attracting FDI in relative terms. The clear winners are the Czech Republic, Estonia, Hungary, Latvia and Slovenia. The second group consists of Croatia, Lithuania and Poland. These countries have been relatively successful in attracting FDI to their economies. The group of the laggards comprises Bulgaria, Romania, Russia, Slovakia, and most of all Ukraine.

Table 1   Percentage from the total cumulative inward FDI in CEE by countries by December 31, 2000

Country	% of total inward FDI	% of total population
Bulgaria	1.86	2.67
Croatia	2.92	1.67
Czech Republic	16.16	3.33
Estonia	2.02	0.41
Hungary	15.69	3.32
Latvia	3.16	0.91
Lithuania	1.71	0.77
Poland	25.08	13.35
Romania	4.13	7.67
Russia	15.05	49.68
Slovakia	1.69	1.98
Slovenia	2.43	0.67
Ukraine	2.59	16.67

Sources: Business Central Europe; Authors' calculations.

Some CEE countries have successfully invested abroad both inside and outside the Central and Eastern European region. Table 2 provides data of outward FDI from the most active investing countries of the CEE region. While Russia and Hungary are the main contributors for outward FDI, considering the size of the economies Slovakia and especially Slovenia have done very well, too. The outward FDI going outside CEE is less than one third of total outward FDI. More active than average on relative terms have been Hungary, Poland and Slovenia, whereas on absolute terms the indisputable winner is Russia.

Table 2   Percentage of cumulative outward FDI from the most active CEE investing countries by December 31, 1998

Country	Outward FDI as a percentage of total	Outward FDI as a percentage of total outside the CEE
Czech Republic	5.14	5.01
Hungary	13.19	17.10
Poland	6.38	6.67
Russia	63.91	59.77
Slovakia	3.96	1.56
Slovenia	7.41	9.84

Sources: IMF, UNCTAD and Authors' calculations.

A Brief Overview of the Content of the Book

The book consists of four parts. Part one, containing five chapters, is devoted to an overview of foreign direct investment in CEE.

Chapter 1 analyzes the trends in foreign trade and FDI after one decade of transition to market in CEE. By focusing on macroeconomic issues of transition, foreign trade and FDI in CEE region are studied. The authors have come to the conclusion that a massive re-orientation of foreign trade in CEE and between CEE countries and the rest of the world has taken place. FDI in the region has been insufficient and focused on countries from Central Europe. The participation of Western economies in the process has been uneven. The process of CEE transition has gained various levels of success in different countries because of the substantial variation in FDI inflows in each of them.

The second chapter analyzes the process of attracting FDI into CEE in the first decade of transition to market of the region. This chapter investigates the factors that give reasons for the relative success of the more advanced in their transition to market economies, e.g., Hungary and Poland, in luring FDI to them. The authors apply qualitative and statistical analysis to draw their conclusions.

Chapter 3 studies the patterns and consequences as a result of FDI inflows of FDI in CEE in the period 1990-2000. The authors' conclusion is that FDI has played a crucial role in the transition of CEE. Whereas Hungary has attracted huge amounts of FDI in the start of the transition, now there is a substantial slowdown in the process of FDI inflows in this country. At the same time the Czech Republic and Poland have become a focal point of destination of inward FDI in CEE.

Chapter 4 addresses the issues of motives and investment strategies for FDI in CEE of foreign firms operating in the region. The quantitative research carried out in Bulgaria, Hungary, Poland and Slovenia shows that foreign companies invest in the region mainly because they want to explore the opportunities for building a long-term position in the market, whereas they have mostly achieved the goal of gaining access to the respective domestic markets. The motives of foreign firms for investing in CEE are further analyzed for each particular country and company in which the foreign investor has put capital. In conclusion the chapter provides recommendations to foreign investors for marketing strategy development and implementation that can bring them success in operating in the CEE region.

Chapter 5 investigates the relationships between FDI and trade flows in the context of Ukraine. The empirical study shows that in Ukraine the complementarity relationship between FDI and trade flows in Ukraine is dominant. A number of factors have been found to impact this relationship, e.g., the country of origin of the investor and the degree of similarities between investing and recipient countries. The implications this study may have on FDI and foreign trade policies are analyzed.

Part II of the book pays a special attention to the country of origin effects of the FDI process in CEE.

Chapter 6 investigates the specifics of the Russian outward FDI in and outside CEE. The authors find that there is an ever increasing outflow of FDI from Russia in a very broad variety of countries made in particular industries, e.g., oil and metallurgy. Because of the unstable Russian economy and the political situation in the country the authors develop two types of scenarios for the future, namely optimistic and pessimistic. On the whole the process of Russian internationalization through FDI is studied and some predictions for its future development made.

Chapter 7 studies the characteristics of Japanese FDI in CEE. Through applying retrospective analysis of the Japanese internationalization activities in CEE as well as case studies, the authors make a number of conclusions, e.g., for the participation of Japanese companies, supported by their government, in CEE in the period from the 1960s till the end of the 1980s. Afterwards the participation of Japan in CEE became more risk averse. The relatively small Japanese FDIs in CEE since the start of the transition period have largely been skewed towards Hungary and the Czech Republic and lately towards Poland.

Chapter 8 represents a study of Turkish outward FDI towards CEE and the Commonwealth of Independent States. Although an emerging market itself, Turkey has actively participated as an FDI provider for the transition processes in CEE. Adopting Dunning's eclectic paradigm the authors of the chapter develop it further to explore the reasons behind Turkish outward foreign direct investment in the CEE region.

Part III sheds some light on the impacts of FDI on countries in CEE. The first chapter takes an integrative perspective and analyzes the supply-side strategy for productivity, competitiveness and convergence for the European Union and the CEE countries. Through theoretical and practical reasoning the author makes an analysis of the integrative perspective using FDI as a form of facilitation of the process. The role of such factors as international trade and regional convergence, institution formation and institutional change on the formation of supply-side strategies (resulting in higher productivity, improved competitiveness and convergence in Europe) is critically evaluated. Policy implications are drawn upon on this basis.

Chapter 10 represents an analysis and an evaluation of the roles of international trade and FDI for the globalization of Polish economic activities. The impact of Polish globalization is investigated on a macro and mirco basis. Policy implications are drawn, based on the outcome of the conducted analysis.

Chapter 11 focuses on the impact of foreign capital exercised upon the economic development of Hungary. The author examines and compares various indicators of production of domestic firms against three types of enterprises with the participation of foreign capital. Foreign firms contribute to the restructuring and performance of the Hungarian economy better the domestic companies as far as capital intensity, productivity, export performance and level of wages are concerned. Although that there are some time limitations affecting the validity of the findings, their significance for preliminary judgment of the impact of the foreign capital on the economic activity of Hungary is illustrative.

Chapter 12 features the role of FDI as a driver for the restructuring of the transitional economy of Slovakia from internal and micro external points of view in evaluating change. The author uses the findings from a survey of largest foreign investors in the country. Pointing out to its limitations of the study some important conclusions are emphasized referring to the role of foreign capital in the implementation of transition to market in the Slovakian context.

Part IV of the volume analyzes some of the forms that FDI has taken in CEE. Chapter 13 investigates the strategic orientation of Finnish investors in Russia. The empirical data analyzes the motives of Finnish investors for entering Russia, their approaches towards corporate governance, management of their Russian subsidiaries, and major operational problems.

These factors are discussed at length and some recommendations drawn on the basis of the discussion.

Chapter 14 deals with the issues of organizational learning as a solution for partner conflict resolution in Russian-foreign joint ventures. Learning-related issues such as inability to learn, resistance to learn, imitation, and integrated learning are in focus in this study. Implications are drawn for Western investors in general and Finnish investors in particular and their Russian partners for the improvement of the learning process in general and in the above stated aspects.

Chapter 15 is addressing the foreign market expansion for Finnish companies in the Visegràd countries. The chapter's aim is to find out and analyze the foreign market entry of two middle-sized Finnish manufacturing companies in the Czech Republic, Hungary and Poland. The research and discussion of the findings are based on the grounded theory and emphasize the embeddedness of relationships from historical and developmental perspectives. Using the conceptual part of the chapter researchers can analyze longitudinally the behavioral characteristics of companies entering a foreign market taking into account environmental, strategic and operational issues.

References

Blankenburg, D. and Johnson, J. (1992), 'Managing Network Connections in International Business', *Scandinavian International Business Review*, vol. 1, no. 1, pp. 5-19.

Coase, R. (1937), 'The Nature of the Firm', *Economica*, vol. 5, pp. 386-405.

Cook, K. and Emerson, R. (1978), 'Power, Equity and Commitment in Exchange Networks', *American Sociological Review*, 43, pp. 721-739.

Dunning, J. (1993), *Multinational Enterprise and the Global Economy*, Harlow: Addison-Wesley.

Forsgren, M. (1989), *Managing the Internationalization Process*, London: Routledge.

Forsgren, M. and Johanson, J. (1991), *Managing Networks in International Business*. Philadelphia: Gordon and Breach.

Graham, E. (1978), 'Transatlantic Investment by Multinational Firms: A Realistic Phenomenon', *Journal of Post Keynesian Economics*, 1, pp. 12-26.

Horst, T. (1972), 'The Industrial Composition of US Exports and Subsidiary Sales to the Canadian Market', *American Economic Review*, 62, pp. 37-45.

Hymer, S. (1960), *The International Operations of National Firms: A Study of Direct Investment*, Cambridge: MA: MIT Press.

Kimura, Y. (1989), 'Firm-Specific Strategic Advantages and Foreign Direct Investment Behaviour of Firms: The Case of Japanese Semi-Conductor Firms', *Journal of International Business Studies*, 20, pp. 296-314.

Kindleberger, C. (1969), *American Business Abroad*, New Haven, Connecticut: Yale University Press.

Knickerbocker, F. (1973), *Oligopolistic Reaction and the Multinational Enterprise*, Cambridge, MA: MIT Press.

Kuznetsov, A. (1994), *Foreign Investment in Contemporary Russia: Managing Capital Entry*, London: Macmillan.

Lall, S. (1980), *Monopolistic Advantages and Foreign Involvement by US Manufacturing Industry*, Oxford: Oxford Economic Papers.

Marinov, M. (ed) (2002), *Internationalization in Central and Eastern Europe*, Aldershot and Burlington: Ashgate Publishing Company.

Mattsson, L.-G. (1987), 'Management of Strategic Change in a Markets-as-Networks Perspective', in A. Pettigrew (ed.) *The Management of Strategic Change*, Oxford: Basil Blackwell.

Narula, R. (1996), *Multinational Investment and Economic Structure*, London: Routledge.

Vernon, R. (1966), 'International Investment and International Trade in the Product Cycle', *Quarterly Journal of Economics*, 80, pp. 190-207.

Wilkins, M. (1988), 'The Free-Standing Company, 1870-1914: An Important Type of British Foreign Direct Investment', *Economic History Review*, second series, 41, pp. 259-282.

Williamson, O. (1975), *Markets and Hierarchies: Analysis and Antitrust Implications*, New York: The Free Press.

1 A Decade of Transition in Central and Eastern Europe: Trends in Foreign Trade and Foreign Direct Investment

SHAUKAT ALI, JAN NOWAK and JOSEF PÖSCHL

"It was the best of times, it was the worst of times, it was the age of wisdom, it was the age of foolishness". Charles Dickens, *'A Tale of Two Cities'*

Introduction

The dramatic changes that have occurred in Central and Eastern Europe (CEE) since 1989 have been largely presented in a political context: the abandonment of the leading role of the communist party, multi-party elections, the introduction of Western-style democracy, and the dissolution of the Warsaw Pact and removal of Soviet troops from USSR's satellite countries. However, equally dramatic have been economic transformations that paralleled the political changes: the liberalization of prices and foreign trade regimes, the de-monopolization of internal markets, privatization of state-owned enterprises, openness to foreign investment, and the move towards convertible currencies. Furthermore, at the beginning of the transition period, it was suggested that the desire for economic transformation was the major motivating force behind the political changes in Central and Eastern Europe (Brown, 1990; Sword, 1991).

This chapter focuses on two aspects of the decade-long economic transformation in Central and Eastern Europe since 1989: foreign trade and foreign direct investment. Both aspects are major driving forces in the economic transition.

The fundamental changes in the geographic and sectoral structure of the region's foreign trade over the last decade have had a profound impact on the economic performance of Central and Eastern European countries (CEECs). The changes have either facilitated or impeded the achievement of the desired transition outcomes of these countries.

Likewise, the opening up of CEECs to foreign direct investment (FDI) created a potential for positive contributions to economic transformation, especially in terms of modernization of commercial infrastructure, technology and management processes that, in turn, lead to increased productivity and competitiveness of enterprises. To what extent this potential has been utilized by individual countries depends on their ability to attract the right amount of FDI to the right sectors of the economy. The main purpose of this chapter is therefore to determine the direction (positive or negative) and the extent to which both the changes in foreign trade and foreign direct investment impacted the transition of CEECs since 1990.

The data sets used in this article come from various separate sources. The main components are Research Reports published by the Vienna Institute for International Studies (known by its German acronym – WIIW), UNCTAD's annual World Investment Reports, Economic Commission for Europe Reports and the Transition Reports of the EBRD. The various data sets allow us to study the effect and the role of foreign trade and foreign direct investment (FDI) in explaining transition differences between countries. The transition period covered in the chapter is from 1989 - 2001.

The countries in our analysis fall into four regional groups: Central Europe (the Czech Republic, Hungary, Poland, Slovakia and Slovenia); the Baltic republics (Estonia, Latvia and Lithuania); the Balkans (Albania, Bosnia-Herzegovina, Bulgaria, Croatia, Macedonia, Romania and Yugoslavia); and two members of the Commonwealth of Independent States (CIS) – the Russian Federation and Ukraine.

The Decade of Transition – A Macroeconomic Overview

Moves towards a market-type economy initiated by CEECs in the early 1990s typically consisted of stabilization, economic liberalization and restructuring packages of reforms (Portes, 1990; Hughes and Hare, 1992; Estrin, 1995). Stabilization aimed at reducing inflation and restoring the macroeconomic equilibrium. Economic liberalization involved ending price controls with respect to most, although certainly not all, product markets, leading to price levels dictated by the forces of supply and demand rather than political decisions. Restructuring sought to create the institutions and infrastructure of a market economy (Portes, 1990 and 1992; Hughes and Hare, 1991 and 1992; Estrin, 1995). The reform packages contained also various forms of privatization of state-owned enterprises.

Central European countries started their reforms far earlier than those of the other three groups of countries under study. Poland, Slovenia, Hungary and Czechoslovakia were first to liberalize prices and markets, relax foreign-trade controls, introduce currency convertibility, and initiate ownership changes (World Bank, 1996, pp. 13-14). Moreover, reforms in Poland and Czechoslovakia were introduced in a single package - the 'big bang' or 'shock therapy'. Among early reformers, vigorous stabilization programs paved the way for declining inflation and a resumption of growth. Other countries were either reform laggards or lacked decisiveness and determination in the reform packages implementation.

Although Bulgaria initially introduced a rather radical reform package in the early nineties, strong anti-reform pressures brought about a reversal of the reform process in later years. Similarly, Romania showed a slow and faltering pace of reforms, stalled by former communists and various social groups with vested interests in slowing or stopping the reform process (Howell, 1995, pp. 39-40). Other Balkan countries generally lagged behind Central Europe in the introduction of market-oriented reforms, mostly due to political turmoil besetting parts of the former Yugoslavia. Nevertheless, Croatia managed to introduce a stabilization program and strict monetary policy as early as 1993 (Howell, 1995, p. 41).

The Russian reforms were first introduced in January of 1992. However, right from the beginning the reform process was frustrating and somewhat chaotic, with the reformers striving to secure political clout necessary to push for a radical and comprehensive reform package. Nevertheless, one could point to some early success in the speed of privatization, however isolated and debatable this success was. Another member of the CIS, which is under study Ukraine underwent so much political muddle through in the first years of the country's independence, both internally and externally, that hardly any reforms were started at all at that time (Howell, 1995, pp. 31-32 and 48).

In the Baltic states, on the other hand, rapid and fundamental political change paved the way to more radical economic reforms (Howell, 1995, p. 27). Especially in Estonia and Latvia, reforms started to progress smoothly as early as in 1992 or 1993, while the two economies were being integrated into the Nordic economic sphere.

An important aspect of the reforms undertaken by all Central and Eastern European countries was privatization. Privatization results differed depending on the method used. The voucher mass privatization approach that the Czech and Slovak Republics and, to a lesser degree, the Russian Federation relied upon, brought about a swift change in these countries' economies' ownership structure. For example, by the mid-1990s the Czech Republic had the highest proportion of private ownership share in the economy among the transition countries, boosting this proportion from virtually zero percent at the beginning of the transition process to 70 percent in 1996 (Nowak, 1997). However, the technology and management, and hence productivity and competitiveness, of newly privatized companies remained virtually unchanged. The outcome of this approach to privatization, referred to as 'privatization without restructuring', led to rather poor performance of Czech enterprises, especially banks. In Poland and Hungary, on the other hand, privatization was normally preceded by restructuring and, to a large degree, took the form of the sale of state assets to strategic investors, including foreign investors. The involvement of foreign owners (through FDI) in Polish and Hungarian companies increased the probability of a real change; however, there was significant variation in quality among foreign investors. Some confined themselves to acquisitions without initiating much restructuring or modernization. Furthermore, foreign investors seemed to focus only on a few lucrative sectors of the economy (Nowak and Pöschl, 1999, p. 37). An early sector of interest was the auto-industry, with investments by most of the major players such as Volkswagen, General Motors, Fiat, Renault, and Ford. Not surprisingly, major investors chose only one country to make a significant investment.

Largely irrespective of the privatization method used, several transition champions emerged among CEECs in the second half of the 1990s. They were Poland, Hungary and the Czech Republic, later joined by Slovenia (all members of the CEFTA integration grouping[1]) and the three Baltic republics. The World Bank, in its 1997 Transition report, classified all these seven countries as 'Consolidated Market Economies'. This was in contrast to 'Transitional Economies', the category reserved for the majority of the region's countries, and to 'Consolidated Statist Economies', the term used with respect to a small number of countries that had not even started any transition from centrally-planned to a market economy yet (World Bank, 1997). The term 'Consolidated Market Economies' suggested that the transition in the countries falling into that category was virtually complete.

A crucial indicator of transformation success is the GDP growth rate. In the first years of transformation, all the countries of the region suffered severe declines in the GDP (see Table 1.1). In some countries, the negative growth rate reached staggering magnitudes (in most countries the decline was more than -10 percent a year and by 1992 reached cumulative values in the range of -30 percent).

Estrin (1995) identified four main reasons for this deep decline in output in CEE countries at the beginning of the transition process. They included:

- Demand shock associated with macroeconomic stabilization plans, often entailing a deflation of round 15 percent of GDP or more, to eliminate the budget deficit;

- Restrictive monetary policy associated with macroeconomic stabilization and the introduction of currency convertibility, with high real interest rates and tight credit limits;
- The abolition of CMEA and the former Soviet Union's rouble zone;
- Much of the production in the centrally planned economies was wasteful and rapidly eradicated once market forces started to work (in as much as 20 per cent of industry, value added calculated at world prices was actually negative).

Poland was the first CEE country to experience GDP growing as early as 1992. It was joined by Slovenia and Romania in having positive economic growths by 1993. By the mid 1990s, all CEFTA countries had roughly reached or surpassed EU's growth rates, thus entering a catching-up process (with the exception of Hungary that showed slow, albeit positive, growth rates at that time). This contrasted with Russia and Ukraine, which kept falling behind, as Table 1.1 illustrates.

Table 1.1   Growth of the gross domestic product (GDP) in Central and Eastern European countries, 1990-2001

Real change in percent against the preceding year

Country	1990	1991	1992	1993	1994	1995	1996	1997	1998	1999	2000	2001 (1)	2001 Index (1990 =100)
Czech Republic	-1.2	-11.6	-0.5	0.1	2.2	5.9	4.3	-0.8	-1.2	0.5	3.3	3.3	104.5
Hungary	-3.5	-11.9	-3.1	-0.6	2.9	1.5	1.3	4.6	4.9	4.2	5.2	3.8	112.1
Poland	-11.6	-7.0	2.6	3.8	5.2	7.0	6.0	6.8	4.8	4.1	4.0	1.0	144.6
Slovak Republic	-2.5	-14.6	-6.5	-3.7	4.9	6.7	6.2	6.2	4.1	1.9	2.2	3.3	108.7
Slovenia	-4.7	-8.9	-5.5	2.8	5.3	4.1	3.5	4.6	3.8	5.2	4.6	3.0	123.7
Bulgaria	-9.1	-11.7	-7.3	-1.5	1.8	2.9	-9.4	-5.6	4.0	2.3	5.4	4.0	84.2
Romania	-5.6	-12.9	-8.8	1.5	3.9	7.1	3.9	-6.1	-4.8	-1.2	1.8	5.3	88.3
Croatia	-7.1	-21.1	-11.7	-8.0	5.9	6.8	5.9	6.8	2.5	-0.4	3.7	4.1	90.3
Macedonia	.	-3.2	-8.2	-1.2	-1.8	-1.1	1.2	1.4	3.4	4.3	4.5	-4.6	87.0
Yugoslavia (2)	-7.9	-11.6	-27.9	-30.8	2.5	6.1	5.9	7.4	2.5	-21.9	6.4	6.2	49.4
Russia	-3.0	-5.0	-14.5	-8.7	-12.7	-4.1	-3.4	0.9	-4.9	5.4	9.0	5.0	69.4
Ukraine	-4.0	-8.7	-9.9	-14.2	-22.9	-12.2	-10.0	-3.0	-1.9	-0.2	5.9	9.1	47.1
Estonia	-8.1	-13.6	-14.2	-9.0	-2.0	4.6	4.0	10.4	5.0	-0.7	6.9	5.4	93.8
Latvia	2.9	-10.4	-34.9	-14.9	0.6	-0.8	3.3	8.6	3.9	1.1	6.8	7.6	67.2
Lithuania	-3.3	-5.7	-21.3	-16.2	-9.8	3.3	4.7	7.3	5.1	-3.9	3.8	5.9	72.3

Notes: 1) Preliminary.
             2) Gross Material Product.

Source: WIIW, 2001, p. 2 and 2002, p. 3.

In the second half of the decade, growth continued to be solid in countries such as Poland, Slovenia, Hungary and the Slovak Republic, but proved to be erratic in other countries of the region. Surprisingly, one of the transition champions, the Czech Republic, experienced negative growth rates in 1997 and 1998 and only a meager 0.5 percent growth in 1999. One cause of this poor performance may be attributed to the lack of enterprise restructuring in the first half of the decade and the messy banking situation thereafter.

The economies of Bulgaria and Romania also struggled during that period, slipping into an economic slump for two or three years in a row. The other Balkan countries showed more signs of solid growth (notably Croatia), although Yugoslavia experienced a deep economic decline in 1999 because of political conflicts in the region and the trade embargo imposed by the West. Russia's growth during that period was very erratic, with two years of economic decline, and Ukraine's growth was consistently negative until the year 2000. The Baltic States, on the other hand, showed quite a robust economic performance, except for 1999 when their economies either declined or experienced a recession.

By 2000, all the countries of the region achieved positive growth rates for the first time since the transition began. According to the preliminary data published by WIIW in July 2002, the positive growth continued in 2001, with the exception of Macedonia, which experienced a decline in GDP (see Table 1.1). However, only some of the countries reached or surpassed the 1990 GDP levels in 2001. These included the Czech Republic, Hungary, Poland, Slovak Republic and Slovenia, the so-called CEEC-5 group. By far the strongest growth throughout the decade was shown by Poland. The Polish economy had been growing consistently since 1992 and in 2001 reached a GDP level that was 45 percent higher than that in 1990, as compared to 5 percent higher in the Czech Republic, 9 percent higher in Slovakia, 12 percent higher in Hungary and 24 percent higher in Slovenia. For other countries in our study, the GDP levels in 2001 were still below those for 1990; in some of these countries, notably Yugoslavia and Ukraine, the 2001 level was less than 50 percent of the 1990 level.

One would expect that there would be a clear positive correlation between the progress in reforming the economies and their performance measured by the growth of GDP. However, this correlation is not easily observable in every case. True, Poland's early reform package, implemented with an iron determination, and its stellar economic performance until 2000 can attest to this positive correlation between the reforms and economic performance. The same can probably be said about Hungary.

However, the Czech example raises doubts whether such a correlation can always be valid. In spite of being one of the most advanced countries in transition, the Czech economy was sluggish in the second part of the decade, although its performance improved in 2000 and 2001.

The Czechs seemed to be paying for swift but superficially implemented reforms (notably privatization without restructuring) and the lack of determination in reforming the banking sector.

Slovenia, on the other hand, provides an example of a rather slow reform process (especially privatization) and yet solid and consistent economic growth. However, some favorable external factors may have played a more important role here in boosting the economy than the reforms themselves.

In general, however, countries classified earlier as the 'Consolidated Market Economies' showed much better economic performance in the decade under study than those that are still 'Transitional Economies'.

In the early phase of transition, in most of the countries under consideration, the national currency depreciated vis-à-vis the US dollar and the leading West European currencies. Inflation was high, and nominal depreciation of the currencies supported the corporate sector of the individual countries in their struggle against competition from abroad. Towards the end of the decade, most of the more advanced transition countries developed a tendency towards nominal appreciation.

In the Czech Republic this trend had started already in the first half of 1999. Poland followed the Czech example in mid-1999 (WIIW, 2002).

In 2000, Croatia, Hungary and Slovakia also developed a tendency towards nominal appreciation, which remained, however, less pronounced.

Only Slovenia, in many respects the most developed transition country, did not follow this trend; its currency continued to depreciate. Slovenia's permanent depreciation was homemade – under a regime of managed floating. The country did not follow the other CEE countries in their massive liberalization of cross-border capital flows and did not stimulate the inflow of foreign direct investment. The result was a relatively balanced current account for a number of years. The economy grew during the last five years with an average annual rate of 4.2 percent, without developing any major imbalances.

The countries which liberalized capital flows had trouble keeping the economy balanced. In the case of Poland, exports were negatively affected by the country's currency appreciation, and only the recent stagnation of economic activity has reduced the current account problem. In the Czech Republic, the appreciation did not spoil the current account balance in spite of the strengthening GDP growth. The Czech authorities are trying hard to keep nominal appreciation within limits.

Transition and Foreign Trade

Transition was accompanied by a massive re-orientation of foreign trade. As Table 1.2 indicates, in 2001, the share of the EU-15 in the foreign trade of the vast majority of CEE countries exceeded 50 percent.

Table 1.2   Share of EU-15 countries in foreign trade of CEECs in 1989 and 2001

	Exports percent		Imports percent	
	1989*	2001	1989*	2001
Former COMECON member states, excluding former USSR				
Bulgaria [4]	6	55	12	49
Czech Republic [1]	32	69	32	62
Hungary [2]	34	74	40	58
Poland	40	69	42	61
Romania	34	68	22	57
Slovakia [3]	32	60	34	50
Former Yugoslav republics				
Croatia	42	55	38	56
Slovenia	59	62	66	67
Macedonia	45	49	40	43
Former USSR Countries				
Estonia	49	69	60	57
Latvia	33	61	27	53
Lithuania	17	48	19	44
Russia [4]	33	33	31	38
Ukraine	9	18	9	21

Note: * In the case of Romania and Macedonia data for 1990; in the case of former USSR countries data for 1993.
1) From 1994 according to new methodology.
2) From 1997 including trade of firms with customs-free legal status.
3) From 1998 according to new methodology.
4) Data for 2000 instead of 2001.

Source: WIIW Database incorporating national statistics.

The EU absorbed three-quarters of Hungary's exports and two-thirds of exports coming from the Czech Republic, Poland and Romania. In the more advanced CEECs – the Czech Republic, Hungary and Poland – the EU's share in total exports had been even higher in the late nineties; the increase of the share has come to an end at least for the time being. For former COMECON countries, this was a dramatic change; in 1989 most of them had directed only one third of their exports to EU-15 countries. Bulgaria recorded the biggest change – the EU share in total exports increased from 6percent in 1989 to 55 percent in 2001. In all these countries, the increasing share of EU in total exports occurred at the expense of trade between former COMECON partners. In 2001, the share of Russia in the exports of Poland and Slovenia was around 3 percent and it was even less in the case of Bulgaria, the Czech Republic, Hungary, Romania, and Slovakia.

In former Yugoslav republics, the trade orientation towards EU-15 had already occurred before 1989, courtesy of a more liberal trade regime, completely different from that of COMECON countries. The Yugoslav companies had had the opportunity to enter Western markets, so significant links already existed in 1989.

In the case of imports, the re-orientation towards EU was less dramatic. The individual countries continued to buy a considerable amount of fuels from the CIS region. In 2001, close to 15 percent of Slovakia's imports came from Russia; in other countries under consideration the percentage was below 10.

The trade volume between the CEECs and the EU-15 region grew consistently from the beginning of transition. Correspondingly, it was much higher in 2001 than in 1990, as Table 1.3 shows. The table presents trade figures in euro terms.

In 1990, exports from the five more advanced transition countries – the Czech Republic, Hungary, Poland, Slovakia and Slovenia – to EU-15 amounted to €14.8 billion and exceeded imports by €1.3 billion. In 2001, the exports of these five countries increased to €93.9 billion, while imports climbed to €97.7 billion, leading to a trade deficit of €3.8 billion. Exports were 6.3 times higher than in 1990, while imports were 7.2 times higher. In the Czech Republic and in Slovakia, the export revenues (expressed in euros) were more than nine times higher in 2001 compared to 1990. Czechoslovakia had kept its trade links with the West at a low level, whereas the Czech Republic's building up of these links during the nineties was impressive. We can observe a significant difference between former COMECON countries and former Yugoslav republics. The latter recorded much less increase of trade with the EU-15 region. They had entered the west European markets much earlier. In the trade with the EU, exports from Bulgaria, the Czech Republic, Hungary, Slovakia and Slovenia grew more than imports into these countries, which can be regarded as a success. Poland, on the other hand, had a serious problem of export growth lagging behind that of imports.

Table 1.3   Trade between CEECs and the EU-15, 1990 and 2001

€ billion		1990	2001	2001/1990
Former COMECON members				
Bulgaria (3)	Exports	0.6	3.0	5.1
	Imports	1.2	4.1	3.4
	Balance	-0.6	-1.0	
Czech Republic	Exports	2.7	25.6	9.4
	Imports	3.1	25.2	8.1
	Balance	-0.4	0.5	
Hungary (1)	Exports	3.2	25.5	8.1
	Imports	2.9	22.1	7.6
	Balance	0.2	3.4	
Poland	Exports	5.9	27.8	4.7
	Imports	3.8	34.5	9.0
	Balance	2.1	-6.7	
Romania	Exports	1.5	8.6	5.6
	Imports	1.6	10.0	6.3
	Balance	0.0	-1.3	
Slovakia (2)	Exports	0.9	8.4	9.1
	Imports	1.1	8.2	7.3
	Balance	-0.2	0.2	
Former Yugoslav republics				
Croatia	Exports	1.9	2.8	1.5
	Imports	2.2	5.7	2.6
	Balance	-0.3	-2.8	
Macedonia	Exports	0.4	0.6	1.6
	Imports	0.5	0.8	1.6
	Balance	-0.1	-0.1	
Slovenia	Exports	2.1	6.5	3.1
	Imports	2.5	7.7	3.0
	Balance	-0.4	-1.2	

Note: 1) From 1997 including trade of firms with customs-free legal status.
2) From 1998 according to new methodology.
3) From 1999 according to new methodology.
Comparable data for countries of the former Soviet Union are not available.

Source: WIIW Database incorporating national statistics.

The most surprising feature of the CEECs foreign trade is the evolution of its structure. As shown in Table 1.4, the more developed transition countries have specialized in the export of machinery and transport equipment. In Hungary, the share of this commodity group in total exports was 58 percent in 2001, giving it the leading position among the CEECs in this respect.

Table 1.4   CEE exports: Commodity group with the highest share in 2001

Country	SITC commodity group	Share in 1995	Share in 2001
Bulgaria	Miscellaneous manufactured articles (SITC 8)	9.3	25.3
Czech Republic	Machinery and transport equipment (SITC 7)	30.3	47.3
Hungary	Machinery and transport equipment (SITC 7)	. 25.6	57.6
Poland	Machinery and transport equipment (SITC 7)	21.1	35.5
Romania	Miscellaneous manufactured articles (SITC 8)	31.7	40.2
Slovakia	Machinery and transport equipment (SITC 7)	18.8	38.5
Croatia	Machinery and transport equipment (SITC 7)	16.8	29.4
Macedonia	Miscellaneous manufactured articles (SITC 8)	18.3	28.6[1]
Slovenia	Machinery and transport equipment (SITC 7)	31.4	36.1
Russia	Mineral products (Harmonized System – Gr.5)	42.9	53.8
Ukraine	Base metals and products (Harmonized System - Gr.15)	33.1	41.3

Notes: Total export = 100.
1) Year 2000.
2) Year 1996.

Source: WIIW Database incorporating national statistics.

In the case of less developed transition countries, the most important commodity groups in exports are miscellaneous manufactured articles, mineral products, and base metals and products. Crude oil is dominating Russia's exports. Such a pattern had not been expected. The CEECs' specialization in international trade tends to turn towards more sophisticated products. The general expectation was that production in these countries would specialize in labor and energy intensive products with low content of value added. Now it is clear that cheap labor is not the only or not the main attraction of the CEECs. It may be a combination of cheap labor and skilled labor. There are, however, a few exceptions from that rule, such as R&D departments in Škoda Volkswagen in the Czech Republic and Audi in Hungary.

Compared to other CEECs, Poland was superior in several respects, especially in terms of GDP growth. In trade statistics, the country's performance was less impressive. First, as a percentage of GDP, exports were relatively low, a fact that cannot be fully explained by the size of the Polish economy[2]. In 2001, Poland's exports amounted to 21 percent of GDP, compared to 62 percent for Slovakia, and 59 percent both for the Czech Republic and Hungary. In the same year, export revenues covered over 90 percent of import expenditures in the Czech Republic and Hungary, but only 51 percent in Croatia and 72 percent in Poland. The foreign trade deficit amounted to 22 percent of GDP in Croatia and to 8 percent in Poland.

Several factors play a role in a country's export performance and import intensity. One important factor is the country's price level compared to the main trading partners. Croatia's overall price level amounted to 68 percent of the EU level in 2001, all other countries had lower levels: Slovenia 62 percent, Poland 56 percent, Hungary 47 percent, Czech Republic 44 percent. Possibly, both Croatia's and Poland's price level is too high given the weak competitive position of their manufacturers. In both countries, the current account deficit was much lower than the trade deficit: 4.1 percent of GDP in Poland and 3.1 percent in Croatia (Table 1.5). In Croatia, the enormous difference between the deficit in the trade balance and the gap in the current account stems from the fact that the country's economy is predominantly dependent on tourism.

The current account was in almost all countries negative. In recent years (2000 and 2001) only in Croatia and Slovenia the current account deficit did not exceed 5 percent of GDP. The deficit was, especially in 2001, extremely high in Bulgaria, Slovakia and Macedonia.

In the past, Russia's current account was always positive. Russian expenditures for imports were always below the revenues from exports due to the country's huge crude oil and gas reserves that could be exported in large quantities. The current account surplus shrank to 0.2 percent in 1998, the year of the crisis, but increased again afterwards – thanks to strong currency depreciation. The Ukraine, which followed Russia, achieved similar results.

Table 1.5   Current account of CEE countries, 1997 - 2001

In percent of GDP

	1997	1998	1999	2000	2001
Former COMECON member states (except for Former USSR)					
Bulgaria	10.1	-0.5	-5.0	-5.6	-6.5
Czech Republic	-6.7	-2.2	-2.7	-5.3	-4.6
Hungary	-2.1	-4.9	-4.3	-2.9	-2.1
Poland	-3.0	-4.3	-7.5	-6.3	-4.1
Romania	-6.1	-7.1	-4.1	-3.7	-5.9
Slovakia	-8.6	-9.0	-4.9	-3.6	-8.6
Former Yugoslav republics					
Croatia	-11.6	-7.1	-6.9	-2.3	-3.1
Macedonia	-7.4	-8.6	-3.1	-3.0	-10.3
Slovenia	0.1	-0.8	-3.9	-3.4	-0.4
Former Soviet Union					
Russia	0.5	0.2	12.8	17.9	11.3
Ukraine	-2.7	-3.1	5.2	4.7	3.7

Source: WIIW Database incorporating national statistics.

If a country has a high deficit in the current account, one usually looks at the inflow of foreign direct investment. Not only can such an FDI inflow fill the current account gap, but it can also stimulate exports in the future, thus creating a more permanent solution to the current account deficit problem. Table 1.6 shows the relation between the year's net FDI inflow and the current account deficit. A figure higher than 100 indicates full coverage of the current account gap thanks to the FDI inflow. A figure below 100 may be alarming if the current account deficit is substantial. In 2001, only Bulgaria, Romania and Slovakia had to rely on capital inflows other than foreign direct investment in order to achieve a full coverage of the current account deficit.

Table 1.6   Net annual inflow of FDI into CEE countries as a percentage of current account deficit*, 1997 - 2001

Based on Balance of Payment data

	1997	1998	1999	2000	2001
Former COMECON member states (except for Former USSR)					
Bulgaria	-48	874	126	143	78
Czech Republic	36	296	432	183	186
Hungary	222	89	95	124	221
Poland	114	93	63	94	112
Romania	57	68	71	76	48
Slovak Republic	12	35	40	291	84
Former Yugoslav republics					
Croatia	24	66	118	260	241
Macedonia	6	38	28	163	125
Slovenia	-3.289	168	23	29	661
Countries on the territory of former Soviet Union					
Russia	-239	-419	-13	-6	-7
Ukraine	47	57	-30	-40	-55

Note: *minus indicates a surplus in the current account.

Source: WIIW Database incorporating national statistics.

Trends and Patterns in Foreign Direct Investment

At the beginning of the transition process, Western firms investing in Central and Eastern Europe potentially faced many difficulties and uncertainties unique to the region as summarized in Figure 1.1. However, potential pay-offs from entering the region were also enormous. It was believed progress in macroeconomic reforms would lead to a recovery in economic growth and the emergence of a burgeoning private sector. However, by the mid 1990s, foreign direct investment (FDI), while playing an important part in this process, failed to meet the expectations of the countries in the region, particularly in terms of their integration into the world-wide division of labor (UNCTAD, 1995).

Difficulties and risks of investing in Central and Eastern Europe	Advantages of investing in Central and Eastern Europe
◆Political Risk - Uncertainty about leadership - Uncertain institutional structure - Absence of an accounting system ◆Money Risk - Convertibility of local currency - Unreliable banking system ◆Problems in Corporate Restructuring - A run down infrastructure - Training local management - Training employees	◆Large domestic market ◆Proximity to Western Europe ◆Large undeveloped oil reserves and other minerals

Figure 1.1 Investing in Central and Eastern Europe: Summary of risks and advantages

Recent evidence shows that some countries are now getting enough FDI to transform their economies, bringing in vital expertise, contacts and money. Germany's Volkswagen, for example, is now the biggest exporter in Slovakia, the Czech Republic and Hungary. However, there has been a backlash against foreign investors in several countries, amid claims they repatriate profits and destroy local competition (Business Central Europe, 2001). We divide our exploration of FDI into two halves, the first relates to trends and patterns from the beginning of the transition process to 1995, while the second part examines the latter half of the 1990s and the period 2000 - 2002.

During the first half of the 1990s, total foreign direct investment flows into the CEE countries reached an estimated US$ 6.3 billion in 1993, as shown in Table 1.7, with around US$ 6.5 billion in 1994, increasing the region's FDI stock to an estimated US$ 22 billion (or 5.2 percent of the region's GDP). The growth of inflows slowed down due to continuing economic recession in some countries of Western Europe (the main source of investment flows), combined with the slow transition towards a market economy. Compared with other developing countries and regions, the FDI stock in CEECs remained marginal, being not larger than the stock in

Argentina (UNCTAD, 1995). Estimates by the Economic Commission for Europe (ECE) for 1995 had indicated that over the first six months of 1995 the stock of FDI in the CEE countries grew further by about US$ 1.8 billion, which at the end of June 1995 stood at US$ 25.2 billion (ECE, 1995).

Table 1.7   FDI inflows into Central and Eastern Europe, 1989 - 1994 (in US$ million)

Country	1989	1990	Flows 1991	1992	1993	1994
Bulgaria		4	56	42	55	300
CSFR *	257	207	600	1 103		
Czech Republic					568	862
Estonia				58	168	260
Hungary			1,462	1,479	2,350	1,510
Latvia				14	20	30
Lithuania				10	12	10
Macedonia						19
Poland	11	89	291	678	1,715	1,400
Romania			40	77	94	650
Russian Fed.				700	700	900
Slovak Republic						70
Slovenia				111	112	73
Ukraine				200	200	200
Yugoslavia	9	67	119	64	25	
TOTAL	277	367	2,568	4,536	6,019	6,284
Argentina	1,028	1,836	2,439	4,179	6,305	1,200

Note: * CSFR former Czech and Slovak Republics.

Sources: UNCTAD, World Investment Report, 1995.

The gap between investors commitments and the actual implementation of investments in the region continued to be high. UNCTAD (1995) had suggested that, on average, only about half of all registered FDI projects had, by 1994, actually started operations. In countries such as Belarus and

Estonia, the divergence between the implementation of FDI projects and FDI commitments was even greater (34 and 20 percent, respectively), whereas in Hungary, for example, 75 percent of the foreign registered affiliates were in operation in 1994 (ECE, 1995).

However, in 1995, several countries of the region experienced a substantial surge in the FDI inflow, as Table 1.8 indicates.

Table 1.8   FDI inflows into Central and Eastern Europe, 1995-1998 (in US$ million)

	1995	1996	1997	1998
Bosnia-Herzegovina				100
Bulgaria	98	138	507	537
Croatia	121	516	551	1,014
Czech Republic	2,526	1,276	1,275	2,641
Estonia	199	111	130	574
Hungary	4,410	1,987	1,653	1,453
Latvia	245	379	515	303
Lithuania	72	153	328	921
Macedonia	9	11	16	118
Poland	1,134	2,741	3,041	4,966
Romania	417	414	1,267	2,079
Russia	1,663	1,665	4,036	1,734
Slovak Republic	194	199	84	374
Slovenia	171	188	340	250
Ukraine	267	521	623	743
Yugoslavia			740	113

Notes: Net inflows recorded in the Balance of Payments.
Gross inflows of FDI are in some cases considerably higher than net inflows on account of increasing intra-regional investment flows.

Source: EBRD Annual Reports, 1999, 2000; WIIW/WIFO, 2002; Business Central Europe, 2001.

By 2000, Poland became the regional leader in attracting foreign direct investment having the highest FDI stock. FDI distribution remained uneven, with some countries receiving relatively large amounts of FDI, while others failed to emerge as significant host countries. Such a pattern of cross-country variations has continued to exist to the present time.

According to UNCTAD (1995), by 1994 three clusters of countries had emerged with respect to FDI:

- The founding CEFTA countries: the Czech Republic, Hungary, Poland and Slovakia, which together accounted for 69 percent of the region's stock in 1994;
- The 'next-tier' countries: Bulgaria, Estonia, Kazakhstan, Romania, the Russian Federation, Slovakia, Slovenia, Ukraine and the Federal Republic of Yugoslavia, which together accounted for 29 percent of the FDI stock;
- Those with negligible FDI, such as Albania, Belarus, Latvia, Lithuania, the Republic of Moldova, the Caucasian Republics and Uzbekistan (2 percent in total).

The uneven distribution of inflows reflected the wide variety of countries comprising the group: relatively industrialized countries with well established ties to Western Europe like Hungary, and predominantly primary-commodity producers in Central Asia such as Kazakhstan; large economies such as the Russian Federation and small economies such as Albania. It was also a reflection of the differing speed and success of those countries in approaching a stable, market-orientated, investment-conducive environment through privatization and the establishment of a market system. Another factor was their geographic distance from the Triad, in particular the EU. In addition, the status of negotiation of EU accession agreements and the harmonization of competition policy and environment and other firm-specific legislation in the CEFTA countries was reflected in the larger FDI flows to those countries (UNCTAD, 1995).

During 1994, FDI stocks grew the greatest in Latvia and Moldova, followed by the Ukraine, Estonia, Romania and Bulgaria. However, one has to remember that the small starting volumes of FDI in most of these countries tended to boost the growth rates as compared with those countries that had already accumulated important amounts of FDI (ECE, 1995).

In comparing the structure of FDI stock by host economy, one needs to take into account the methodological differences of the individual country data available. Subject to this, from the transition economies, by 1995, Hungary was by far the most successful in attracting FDI. Although its share in the regional FDI stock decreased during 1994, in January 1995 Hungary still accounted for 40 percent of the total (almost 45 percent in January 1994). Over the same period, Poland became the second regional leader in attracting foreign investment, accounting for 14 percent of the FDI stock, while the Czech Republic's share also tended to increase (12 percent). By contrast, the growth of foreign investment in the Russian

Federation was slower than average and its share decreased marginally (from 13 percent at the beginning of 1994 to 12 percent one year later) (ECE, 1995).

In spite of the limited comparability of the available data, a comparison of the average size of foreign investments in the individual countries was made by the ECE in the mid 1990s. It suggested that at yearly average exchange rates, operational foreign investment enterprises (FIEs) were generally better capitalized than their registered counterparts. At the beginning of 1995, operational enterprises with foreign participation enjoyed an average foreign investment of about US$ 0.6 million in the Russian Federation, US$ 0.4 million in Hungary and Poland, about US$ 0.3 million in Estonia and US$ 0.2 million in Ukraine and Latvia. By the same yardstick, the lowest contributions of foreign capital were among FIEs domiciled in Bulgaria and Moldova about US$ 150,000. Comparable data for other countries was unavailable (ECE, 1995).

Moving towards the second half of the decade, the situation, from a global perspective, had not changed to any significant degree (see Table 1.9). In 2000, for example, Latin America and Asia/Pacific each received over US$ 50 billion in FDI. Central and Eastern Europe, including CIS, received just US$ 19 billion (Business Central Europe, 2001). In terms of FDI per capita, however, the region received more than any other region apart from Latin America and the Caribbean (EBRD, 2001).

Almost 60 percent of FDI into the region in 2000 was destined for the Central European countries, primarily the Czech Republic, Hungary, and Poland. In South-Eastern Europe, Bulgaria, Romania and Croatia were the primary destinations of FDI. At the end of the decade, Hungary, Poland and the Czech Republic, and more recently Russia, emerged as the leaders of the pack in having the largest stocks of FDI (EBRD, Annual Reports, 1999 and 2000). The Czech Republic caught up with Hungary despite earlier neglect as its voucher privatization left little room for direct sales to foreigners. Over the past few years, however, banks and energy companies have been privatized and there have also been greenfield investments. Poland remained the country with the largest stock of FDI of any country in the region over the ten-year period, at just over US$ 29 billion. In Hungary, Poland and the Czech Republic, foreign-owned companies are now driving the economy, mainly by boosting exports. They are also overhauling infrastructure, particularly antiquated telephone systems and polluting water plants. Energy privatization was one of the big themes in 1999, with Poland selling off most of its power plants. Foreign direct investment has also increased among those countries recently invited to begin negotiations on EU accession, particularly Bulgaria and the Slovak Republic.

Table 1.9   FDI inflows into Central and Eastern Europe, 1999 - 2002

	1999	2000	2001	2002 est.
Bosnia-Herzegovina	90	150	130	200
Bulgaria	819	1,2002	689	600
Croatia	1,637	1,126	1,502	1,100
Czech Republic	6,324	4,986	4,916	3,500
Estonia	305	387	542	400
Hungary	1,970	1,649	2,443	1,000
Latvia	348	408	201	400
Lithuania	486	379	446	400
Macedonia	32	176	442	500
Poland	7,270	9,342	8,000	6,000
Romania	1,041	1,040	1,137	1,000
Russia	3,309	2,714	2,540	2,500
Slovak Republic	390	2,075	1,475	3,500
Slovenia	181	176	442	600
Ukraine	496	595	769	500
Yugoslavia	112	25	1656	2000

Note: Based on the Balance of Payments, US$ million.

Source: Extracted from WIIW/WIFO, 2002.

Distribution of Foreign Direct Investment by Source Countries

While the available information on the distribution of foreign investment by source is rather mixed and complex, the data suggests that most of the foreign capital invested in CEE countries throughout the last decade come from developed market economies of Western Europe, more specifically, the EU. In 1995, EU, as a consolidated investor, accounted for 88 percent of the total value of foreign capital in Bulgaria, between 74 - 78 percent in Hungary, Poland and Moldova, 60 - 68 percent in the Czech and Slovak Republics, 50 - 59 percent in Romania, Estonia, Lithuania and Latvia, while in Ukraine and Belarus (38 - 43 percent), and the Russian Federation (20 percent) the weights of this group of investors were the smallest. While generally the shares of the other west European countries did not exceed 5 - 10 per cent, this was as high as 30 per cent in Russia (ECE, 1995).

In 1995, investment by companies from the United States was highest in Poland, the Czech Republic, Russia and Ukraine (about 21 percent), while in Hungary, the Slovak Republic, Lithuania, Latvia and Belarus their share was as high as 13 - 15 percent. Share of US investors was the smallest in Romania, Estonia, Bulgaria and Moldova (5 - 8 percent) and did not exceed one half of a percent in Slovenia (ECE, 1995). Germany was the largest investor in the Czech Republic, Hungary, Slovakia, Bulgaria and Romania. It had invested US$ 5.3 billion among the CEFTA-7 countries, accounting for over 20 percent of the total to these countries. Austria was the largest investor in Slovakia and Slovenia, accounting for over 10 percent of all investment in the above countries. France and the Netherlands had similar levels of investment as Austria, although neither was a dominant investor in any of the countries (EBRD, 1999).

Table 1.10   FDI stock by major investing countries, as of December 2001 shares in percent

	Czech Republic 2000	Hungary 2000	Poland (1)	Slovak Republic	Slovenia 2000	Bulgaria	Romania (2)	CEEC-7
Germany	25.5	25.8	13.4	23.0	12.5	12.5	11.3	17.5
Austria	11.1	12.2	1.5	17.6	45.6	7.8	5.9	7.1
USA	6.5	8.2	14.7	6.0	3.9	6.2	6.4	10.8
Netherlands	30.1	22.5	8.6	20.9	3.9	4.6	16.2	15.2
Switzerland	4.0	2.1	1.7	0.0	3.6	2.4	2.8	2.3
France	4.3	6.5	19.2	1.8	10.7	2.8	6.9	12.4
Italy	0.8	2.7	6.6	10.7	5.4	10.0	7.0	5.3
United Kingdom	3.5	1.1	5.0	3.9	3.6	4.4	4.4	4.1
Japan	0.5	2.1	1.0	0.0	0.2	0.2	0.6	0.9
Other countries	13.7	16.7	28.2	16.1	11.6	49.2	38.6	24.4
EU	84.1	80.2	68.2	81.3	84.0	69.1	61.1	73.5
Total	100.0	100.0	100.0	100.0	100.0	100.0	100.0	100.0
Total, US$ million	21,644	10,310		4,687	2,809	4,494	4,882	101,977

Note: [1] Realized investment with more than US$ 1 million.
        [2] Equity capital given by Chamber of Commerce and Industry.

Source: Extracted from WIIW/ WIFO, 2002.

By 1999, Germany, again, had the largest share in six of the seven CEFTA countries, accounting for 20 percent of the total investment in these countries. Whereas in 1995 Germany was the second largest investor in Poland, by 1999 it had overtaken the US with over 17 percent of total investment as opposed to almost 15 percent by the USA. The US also dropped into third place in terms of total investment into the seven CEFTA countries, being overtaken by little Netherlands. The EU-15 maintained its leading position as a group, accounting for 82.7 percent of the total stock of FDI in the Czech Republic, almost 77 percent in Hungary, almost 64 percent in Poland, just over 71 percent in Slovakia, almost 76 percent in Slovenia, almost 60 percent in Bulgaria, and just under 57 percent in Romania. Almost 70 percent of the stock of FDI in the CEECs came from the EU-15.

As by December 2001, the situation has changed again. As shown in Table 1.10, France became the largest investor in Poland, with the US second and Germany falling to third place. Germany was, however, the largest investor in Bulgaria, the Slovak Republic, and Hungary. In the Czech Republic, Germany was in second place, after the Netherlands, which accounted for over 30 percent of the FDI stock. Unlike the early half of the 1990s, the US no longer had the largest stock of FDI in any of the countries and apart from Poland, where it was the second largest as mentioned before, it was third or fourth highest in most other countries.

Foreign Direct Investment by Industrial Sector Distribution

Data on the industrial sector distribution of foreign investment are available for a limited number of countries. Furthermore, the industrial classifications utilized by statisticians of various host transition economies also differ, thus limiting the scope for comparisons. By the mid 1990s, most sources suggested that in all countries manufacturing invariably was the single largest host sector of foreign investment, accounting for more than 50 percent of FDI in such countries as Poland, the Czech Republic and Ukraine, and being close to 50 percent in many other countries of the region (ECE, 1995). With the exception of Russia, in which the production of fuels accounted for about 17 percent of foreign investment stock at the beginning of 1995, the interest of foreign investor in the mining sector of transition economies had been limited (ECE, 1995).

The proportion of trading activities, another pole of attraction of foreign investors, was highest in the Slovak Republic, Estonia and Bulgaria (21 - 31 percent). In most of the other countries of the region trade intermediation accounted for 12 - 17 percent of total foreign investment stock. Finally, services, the most mixed sector, attracted, at the beginning of 1995, from 6 - 13 percent of cumulative foreign investment in most countries of the region (ECE, 1995). It is clear that the focus of foreign investors in CEE transition economies was demonstrably on the production of goods (manufacturing) and trading activities. At the same time, while individual country experiences differ, their involvement in transport and communications, construction, financial and other services had been limited but changed in the latter half of the decade.

The period from 1995 - 2002 has seen telecom, cars and energy as the main investment sectors. The three biggest investments have been in the telecom sector by TelSource, Deutsche Telekom and France Telecom. Poland raised US$ 4.3 billion when it sold off 35 percent of TPSA in July 2000 the region's biggest ever privatization. The next major sector has been the auto sector, with Germany's Volkswagen being the most prominent due to its acquisition of Škoda and its Audi plant in Gyor, Hungary. In Poland, the big communist-era carmakers went instead to Italy's Fiat and South Korea's Daewoo Motors, though Daewoo has since gone bankrupt. The next sector likely to attract substantial FDI is energy, as the region's electricity monopolies go on sale (Business Central Europe, 2001). Table 1.11 shows some of the main acquisitions in Hungary, Poland and the Czech Republic.

Table 1.11   Main acquisitions in Hungary, Poland and the Czech Republic

Country	Investing company	Local acquired company	Sector	Amount (US$)
Hungary	General Electric (US)	Tungsram	Electricity	1000
	Ferruzzi (Italy) Unilever (NL-UK)	NMW	Food and detergents	160
	IRI (Italy	Gany-Ansaldo	Elect. Eng.	130
	Deutsche Telekom (Germany)	Matav	Telecom	1,727
	Volkswagen (Germany)	Auto Hungaria	Auto	800
	Eridania Beghin-Say)France)	Various	Sugar, Oil	540
	General Motors (USA)	Opel Hungary	Auto	510
Poland	Fiat (Italy)	FSM Bielsko Biala	Automotive	1,540
	Coca-Cola (USA)	Various	Soft drinks	235
	EBRD (International)	Various	Banking	222
	France Telecom (France)	TPSA	Telecom	4,070
	Daewoo (South Korea)	Daewoo FSO motor	Auto	1,552
	Gazprom (Russia)	Various	Energy	1,250
	Vivendi (France)	Elektrim	Telecom	1,204
Czech	Volkswagen (Germany)	Skoda	Automotive	900
Republic	Philip Morris (USA)	Tabak Kutna Hora	Cigarettes	420
	Nestle (Switzerland)	Cokolodovny	Food	100
	TelSource (Holland/Switz)	Cesky Telecom	Telecom	1,460
	IOC (consortium)	Ceska Rafinerska	Petroleum	629
	ABB (Sweden/Switz)	Various	Engineering	450

Source: Charap and Zemplinerova, 1994; Business Central Europe, 2001.

Conclusions and Policy Implications

This chapter has attempted to examine the decade-long transition process in the CEE countries by focusing on transition's macroeconomic issues, foreign trade and foreign direct investment. Given the size of the region and the disparity among countries in terms of their progress towards reforms, the analysis has been broad by necessity. The enormity of the task did not detract us from presenting a balanced overview over the decade-long transition process in several of its manifestations.

Central European countries, which started their transition to a market economy earlier than their Balkan, Baltic and CIS counterparts, were already in 1997 classified by the World Bank as 'Consolidated Market Economies'. This group was contrasted with those of 'Transitional Economies', whose transition was still underway, and 'Consolidated Statist Economies', which hardly started any transition at that time. Early and comprehensive reforms, including privatization, have apparently helped central European countries achieve solid economic growth in the second half of the decade.

Massive re-orientation of trade among CEE economies was a natural phenomenon. Trade diversion took place towards the EU, away from Russian-dominated COMECON arrangements. By the end of the decade, most of the early reforming countries had successfully diverted as much as two-thirds of their trade flows toward the EU. Most have experienced trade deficits, as local firms struggled to compete with better-equipped and more efficient EU competitors. More recently, intra-CEE country trade has increased, seeking comfort, it would seem, among 'old friends'.

In the first part of the decade, FDI inflows into Central and Eastern Europe fell far short of the growth of flows to other developing countries, dampening expectations of the host countries. Flows into the region were similar to flows to Mexico, with accumulated stock similar to that of Thailand. Most of the inflows were concentrated in Hungary, Poland and the Czech Republic. In the first half of the decade, privatization-linked FDI was estimated to account for 35 - 40 percent of the total FDI inflows. In some CEE countries, it was as high as two-thirds. The pattern continued into the second half of the decade, with several high-profile privatizations accounting for the majority of the FDI. Once again, the majority of FDI inflows were located in just three countries Hungary, Poland and the Czech Republic, reflecting their industrial, political and economic superiority over other transition countries.

In all European transition economies, foreign investment is highly concentrated in terms of major source countries. Germany, the Netherlands, France and the US are the top of the list of major investors, followed by

Austria, Italy, the UK, and Switzerland. Also of significance is the emergence of some of the transition economies as relatively important regional investors, namely Poland, Hungary and Russia. The focus of forei: n investors in European transition economies is on the production of good. (manufacturing) and trading activities. However, while individual country experiences differ, most sectors of the economy have now attracted investment. Telecoms and the auto industry have been major beneficiaries.

The challenge for 'Consolidated Market Economies' is to deepen and complete the privatization process as speedily as possible. This is especially so for Poland which has yet to privatize much of its infrastructure. Since these countries are on the threshold of joining the EU, it is imperative that unnecessary delays in opening up their economies are avoided. Reforms in agriculture, for example, are an absolute necessity before any accession to the EU is implemented. At the same time, these countries need to do more in attracting investment in financial services, retailing, transportation, heavy industry and leisure industries. We are of the opinion that FDI and privatization are the best ways of improving the long-run competitiveness of these industries. Subsequent challenges include ensuring that managerial and technical know-how not only enhance the factors of production but are appropriately diffused to lower levels of the industrial and economic infrastructure.

For 'Transitional Economies' the challenges are how to emulate the best practices of the 'Consolidated Market Economies' in ways that enhance their attractiveness to foreign investors. Attempts to insulate their business from competitive pressure will lead to stagnation. Completing the restructuring process for them means political stability, prudent macro-economic management, effective reforms, and transparent and consistent policies. We are of the opinion that countries within this classification can enhance their integration into more mature economies by allowing international bodies such as the EU, the IMF and the World Bank, the EBRD and the OECD to guide the development and implementation of reform packages. We also suggest polices towards privatization of state industries be a priority area.

For 'Consolidated Statist Economies', we do not envisage early progress. Continuing political and economic uncertainty will hinder the introduction of much needed reforms, deterring foreign investment. We suggest priority policies be solid democratic governments, independent financial and legal institutions and free press. Once the basic framework is in place, appropriate restructuring and reforms packages can be designed and implemented.

We end this chapter by referring to the quote from Dickens at the beginning. The decade of transition in Central and Eastern Europe has indeed been the best of times, the worst of times. For many countries the worst is over, and better times lie ahead, for others the worst may yet to come.

Notes

1   CEFTA, or Central European Free Trade Agreement, was established on March 1 1993 by Czech and Slovak Republics, Hungary and Poland. On January 1 1966, Slovenia joined the agreement as the fifth member, and on July 1 1997 Romania become CEFTA's sixth member, to be followed by Bulgaria (Nowak and Pöschl, 1999).

2   If measured in Purchasing Power Parities, Poland's GDP has roughly the same volume as the joint GDP of the Czech Republic, Hungary, Slovakia and Slovenia.

References

Brown, A. C. (1990), 'Eastern Europe: A Dilemma for the Strategic Planner', The *Quarterly Review of Marketing,* Autumn.

Business Central Europe (2001), *The Annual 2001,* The Economist Newspaper Ltd.

Charap, J. and Zemplinerova, A. (1994), 'Foreign Direct Investment in the Privatization and Restructuring of the Czech Economy', Workshop on Legacies, linkages and localities – the social embeddedness of economic transformation in Central and Easter Europe, Berlin, Science Center, September.

EBRD   (1997-2001), *Annual Economic Outlooks,* European Bank for Reconstruction and Development, London.

ECE (1995), *Economic Survey of Europe 1993-1994,* Economic Commission for Europe, UN, Geneva.

Estrin, S. (1995), 'Economic Transformation in Central and Eastern Europe', *The Economic Review,* February.

Howell, J. (1995), *Understanding Eastern Europe. The Context of Change,* Ernst & Young, London.

Hughes, G. and Hare, P. G. (1992), 'Industrial Policy and Restructuring in Eastern Europe', *Oxford Review of Economic Policy,* Vol. 8(1).

Nowak, J. (1997), 'International Market Selection: Developing a Region-Specific procedure for Central and Eastern Europe', *Journal of Transnational Management Development,* Vol. 3(1).

Nowak, J. and Pöschl, J. (1999), 'An Assessment of Progress in Transition, Economic Performance, and Market Attractiveness of CEFTA Countries', *Journal of East-West Business,* Vol. 4(4).

PAIZ (1997). *The List of Major Foreign Investors in Poland,* Polish Agency for Foreign Investment, June.

Portes, R. (1990), 'Introduction to Economic Transformation of Hungary and Poland', *European Economy,* Vol. 43.

Portes, R. (1992), 'Structural Reform in Central and Eastern Europe', *European Economic Review,* Vol. 36.

Sword, K. (1991), *The Times Guides to Eastern Europe*, Times Books, London.
UNCTAD (1992-2001), *World Investment Reports*, United Nations Conference on Trade and Development, New York.
WIIW (2001), *Research Report, No. 275*, The Vienna Institute for Comparative Economic Studies, February.
WIIW (2002), *Research Report, No.* 285, The Vienna Institute for Comparative Economic Studies, July.
WIIW/WIFO (2002), *Research Report, No. 2002/245/S*, The Vienna Institute for Comparative Economic Studies, and the Austrian Institute of Economic Research, July.
World Bank (1996), *From Plan to Market*, World Development Report 1996, Published for the World Bank by Oxford University Press.
World Bank (1997), *Transition*, The Newsletter about Reforming Economies, Vol. 8(3).

2 Attracting Foreign Direct Investment in the First Decade of Transition: Assessing the Successes[1]

CARL H. McMILLAN[2] and KEN MORITA[3]

Introduction

There were strong, initial expectations that foreign private funds, invested directly in productive assets in the economies of Central and Eastern Europe and the former Soviet Union (henceforth referred to as CEE) would play a major role in their post-communist restructuring. Most of these countries quickly adopted laws and regulations intended to attract foreign capital. With few exceptions, however, the early expectations were not realized over the course of the 1990s. Foreign direct investment (FDI) was not attracted in sufficient magnitudes to have a significant impact on the processes of transition to a market-based economic system.[4]

With the benefit of hindsight, we can discern a number of reasons why foreign investors remained cautious despite the potential opportunities afforded by the opening up of a region of Europe whose economies had long been closed to foreign firms. Within the region, there was a good deal of ambivalence towards foreign investment. In part, critical attitudes reflected the years of exposure to communist ideology hostile to FDI. They also reflected genuine concerns that foreign capital could undermine newly gained economic independence. These concerns were exploited by domestic interests that felt threatened by the competition of foreign strategic investors and by populist politicians.

Moreover, the region was plagued by political instability. Inexperienced governments and their frequent turnover created uncertainty with regard to the policy climate for foreign investment. Civil war threatened in Yugoslavia to spill over into neighboring countries and to break out elsewhere as a result of ethnic conflicts. Even in the absence of open conflicts, borders in the region remained uncertain. Czechoslovakia broke into two independent entities; in the former Soviet Union, the continuing independence of some of the new states seemed doubtful. The new Russian Federation, perhaps the great potential magnet to FDI, was plagued by weak government and the resulting political and economic instability. Access to its rich natural resources remained for the most part closed to foreign investors. All of the transition economies experienced deep recessions in the early 1990s, from which most had still not fully recovered. Meanwhile, the early expectation of quick membership in the expanding European Union for some of the countries more advanced in their economic transition continually receded.

As the second decade of transition begins, it seems worth reassessing the prospects for FDI in the region. This chapter attempts to make a contribution to reassessment by examining the experience of the two countries most successful in attracting foreign investors to their economies. We shall explore what seem to be the factors behind the relative success in this respect of Hungary and Poland. If the factors in their success can be identified, we can more easily gauge the prospects that FDI will play a more important role generally in the second decade of transition.

Hungary and Poland themselves contrast in their experience to date. Hungary was the first transition economy to enjoy major inflows of FDI, and continues to lead the others in terms of most measures of the significance of the stock of FDI for its economy. Poland, after a disappointingly slow start, has surged ahead in the second half of the 1990s to dominate in terms of absolute magnitudes of FDI attracted.

We shall proceed as follows. In the next section, we shall sketch the general picture of FDI flows to the transition economies during the 1990s. In reviewing trends, we shall highlight the experience of Hungary and Poland relative to other transition economies over the decade. In a third section, we shall look more closely at the qualitative factors that seem to explain relative success in the two cases, looking first at Hungary, where the experience is richer, and then more briefly at Poland. We shall then undertake a quantitative analysis of the causal factors in the case of the two countries relative to others in the CEE region. Finally, we shall attempt to draw some implications of the FDI experience of the two leading countries for the prospects of others in the second transitional decade.

Trends in Foreign Direct Investment to Central and Eastern Europe

In their decades of industrial development under Soviet-style central planning and state ownership, the CEE economies had been largely closed to foreign direct investment. Only in the last years of communism did they begin to allow inward foreign investment, even in limited forms. Thus, by the end of the 1980s, FDI flows to the area remained negligible, and only two countries (Hungary and Yugoslavia) had received cumulative inflows of any significance.

The opening up of these economies in the post-communist period of transition towards a market-based economy have presented new possibilities for foreign investors. In most cases, however, the barriers posed by the uncertain conditions of the transition caused potential investors to adopt a cautious stance. Over the 1990s, therefore, FDI flows to those economies have varied greatly among them, but on the whole have been much slower to develop than anticipated.

By the end of 1998, the 25 transition economies included in Table 2.1 had received cumulative inflows estimated at over eighty billion US dollars. The bulk of this, almost 85 percent, according to the European Bank for Reconstruction and Development (EBRD) estimates, came after 1993, in the second half of the first decade of transition.

The growth after 1993 was especially pronounced for the Commonwealth of Independent States (CIS) economies, although it is undoubtedly exaggerated by the unexplained absence of EBRD data for Russia before 1994. (UN sources show an inflow of US$ 1.2 billion to the Russian Federation in 1993).[5]

A brief explanation of the discrepancies in FDI statistics for the area is necessary at this point. The most comprehensive, reliable and readily available data are for equity capital investments through the balance of payments, and are reported by the International Monetary Fund (IMF). Other, more statistically problematic, components of total FDI inflows are contributions in kind, reinvested earnings and intra-company loans. Data on these vary among countries in terms of availability and reliability, and this is the major cause of variation in the comparative estimates of international organizations. Nevertheless, principal sources tend to corroborate broad trends and relative magnitudes.[6]

FDI has not been evenly spread across the CEE economies. In the 1990s, three countries in Central Europe, the Czech Republic, Hungary, and Poland, have been the major destinations of FDI flows to the region once formed by the Soviet Union and its European allies. According to the EBRD (see Table 2.1), the three Central European countries received more than a half (51.2 percent) of the US$ 81 billion in cumulative FDI inflows to the 25 transition economies over the period 1989 - 1998 that it records. Almost two-fifths of the FDI inflows to the entire area in this period was concentrated in two countries, Hungary and Poland.

Table 2.1   Cumulative inflows of FDI in CEE in 1989 - 1998 (in US$ million)

Country	As of 1993	As of 1998
Albania	85	423
Bulgaria	138	1,323
Croatia	228	1,997
Czech Republic	1,535	9,997
Estonia	156	1,382
FYR Macedonia	n.a.	242
Hungary	7,302	16,459
Latvia	94	1,604
Lithuania	30	1,534
Poland	981	15,066
Romania	708	4,510
Slovak Republic	374	1,762
Slovenia	39	1,192
CEE without CIS	11,670	57,451
Armenia	n.a.	328
Azerbaijan	20	3,102
Belarus	18	406
Georgia	n.a.	526
Kazakhstan	473	5,661
Kyrgyzstan	10	332
Moldova	31	330
Russia	n.a.	8,901
Tajikistan	9	130
Turkmenistan	79	762
Ukraine	400	2,626
Uzbekistan	48	533
CIS	1,088	23,687
Total	12,758	81,138

Source: Adapted from EBRD Transition Report (1999), London, p. 79.

The EBRD data presented in Table 2.1 reveal a dramatic rise in FDI to Central Europe in the second half of the 1990s. From end-1994 to the end of the decade, combined annual inflows to the Czech Republic, Hungary, and Poland are reported to have risen from US$ 2.4 billion to US$ 11.6 billion. As a result, their combined stock of FDI (as measured by cumulative inflows) increased almost five fold, from US$ 10.7 billion to a projected US$ 53 billion. In the last two years of the decade in particular, inflows to the three leading countries surged; they are estimated to have more than doubled in 1998 alone. Preliminary data for 1999 indicate that the higher levels attained in 1998 have been maintained in 1999. As the Table 2.1 data show, this end-of-decade surge was due to the growth of FDI flows to Poland and the Czech Republic.

Hungary was far ahead of its neighbors in attracting substantial amounts early in the 1990s, and has continued to benefit by significant and stable, annual inflows. As a result, Hungary stands out from most transition economies in terms of measures normalizing FDI stocks and flows to the size of their economies (Table 2.2). This is especially striking on a per capita basis, where the figure for Hungary is more than four times that for Poland. These measures confirm the significance FDI has attained for Hungary's economy compared to its Central European neighbors.

Not surprisingly, the countries of the European Union and the U.S.A. are the major source of FDI flows to the transition economies. Nevertheless, there is considerable variation among the host countries in terms of the sourcing of their FDI stock. Table 2.3 reveals the difference in this regard between Hungary and Poland. Poland has relied on a more diversified set of investment sources than Hungary, which has depended more highly on a few, nearby EU sources.

Hungary[7]

We have seen that Hungary differs from the other transition economies in its early and sustained success in attracting FDI. Beginning in 1991, it has received US$ 1.5 - 2 billion annually in FDI inflows each year.[8] It predominated in the first half of the decade 1989 - 98 covered in Table 2.1, accounting for some 53.2 percent of inflows to the entire CEE region excluding CIS. At the end of the decade Hungary remains among the principal destinations of FDI to the area.[9] As noted, its success is even more striking when we take into account its relative size in demographic and economic terms.

How can Hungary's exceptional performance in these terms be explained? The causes would appear to lie in the legacy of the communist period and in Hungary's post-communist experience. Three factors would seem to have played an especially significant part in its success. They help to explain both its early predominance and the gradual loss of its early lead, as these factors have diminished in relative importance. Let us examine each in turn.

Table 2.2   FDI stocks and flows to CEE economies normalized by various measures

Region/Country	Cumulative FDI inflows per capita in US$ in 1998	FDI stock as a percentage of gross domestic product in 1997	FDI inflow as a percentage of gross fixed capital formation in 1997
CEE without CIS:			
Albania	132	14.7	n.a.
Bulgaria	159	9.4	44.0
Croatia	444	7.5	10.4
Czech R.	967	22.8	8.1
Estonia	953	24.5	21.5
Macedonia	121	1.7	3.0
Hungary	1,627	34.7	20.5
Latvia	642	23.0	48.8
Lithuania	415	10.9	n.a.
Poland	389	11.6	17.1
Romania	200	10.4	18.4
Slovakia	326	8.2	2.4
Slovenia	596	12.1	7.5
CIS:			
Armenia	89	8.4	16.2
Azerbaijan	498	48.8	n.a.
Belarus	45	2.4	6.0
Georgia	98	4.2	n.a.
Kazakhstan	372	27.3	n.a.
Kyrgyzstan	72	15.7	34.3
Moldova	76	9.6	13.8
Russia	61	3.2	7.2
Tajikistan	22	2.2	n.a.
Turkmenistan	57	9.5	n.a.
Ukraine	52	4.2	7.0
Uzbekistan	23	2.6	n.a.

Sources: For column 1, as in Table 2.1; for columns 2 and 3, data from UN World Investment Report 1999, Annex Tables.

Table 2.3   Stock of FDI by country of origin in percent

Source	Hungary (end 1996)	Poland (end 1998)
European Union (of which):	71.2	59.2
Germany	23.8	18.8
Austria	14.5	2.8
France	7.8	8.8
Netherlands	9.5	7.0
United Kingdom	5.8	7.1
Italy	3.8	7.5
Other (of which):	28.8	40.8
U.S.A.	17.1	18.0
Switzerland	2.3	2.4
Japan	1.6	0.7
South Korea	0.8	5.2
Russia	0.8	3.5

Sources: Country national statistics.

The first is the advantages Hungary enjoyed in terms of the initial conditions present as it sought to harness FDI to the aims of the transition. In the preceding decades, Hungary had been in the forefront of attempts to modify and adapt the institutions of the 'classical' Soviet-type economy to its changing needs. The New Economic Mechanism, launched in 1968, and the reforms that followed it over the next two decades, were an important precursor to the post-communist transition. In Hungary, the post-1989 reforms were an expansion and acceleration of a process long underway. This legacy of reform has created a business environment that surveys show investors find more congenial than in other transition economies.

Hungary is also widely regarded as 'the most western of East European economies'.[10] Perhaps even more important is another result of this legacy. FDI is typically the culmination, not the commencement, of investor relations with a host country partner. In the 1970s and 1980s, Hungary was the most open of the Council for Mutual Economic Assistance (COMECON) countries to external trade and other relations with the non-communist world. It was one of the first to permit limited forms of foreign investment from 1972. When, after 1989, the door to FDI in Hungary was opened widely, there was a substantial basis of international, inter-firm relationships to build upon. These legacies of the late communist period also help to explain the importance of small-scale FDI in the Hungarian post-communist transition.

Surveys reveal the importance potential investors attach to constancy and transparency in the regulatory climate of the host country. Political instability generates concern that the rules of the game that investors have gambled upon may change unexpectedly. In the 1990s, Hungary has offered investors the prospect of greater political stability than its major competitors for FDI among the more reformist transition economies. Post-communist Poland experienced a succession of short-term governments and attendant political crises in its first four years. Czechoslovakia split into the Czech and Slovak Republics in 1993. Hungary enjoys the advantages of a more homogeneous population than that of many of its neighbors in Central and Southeastern Europe, and hence the absence of ethnic tensions.

A third factor explains perhaps more than any other Hungary's predominance in terms of FDI flows to the CEE economies. Hungary chose early a method for the large-scale privatization of its state-owned assets (direct sale) that allowed foreign bidders a major role. Moreover, it moved relatively quickly to implement its policy choice. Acquisitions by foreign investors accounted for the bulk of the sales by the State Property Agency in the early transition years (1991 - 93) of Hungary's large-scale privatization program. The take-off in FDI inflows to Hungary coincided with the initiation and acceleration of the privatization program in these years. Direct sale of a controlling interest in them resulted in the acquisition by foreign investors of some of Hungary's largest and best known firms: Tungsram (lighting equipment), Chinoin (pharmaceuticals), Ganz-Mavag (transport equipment), Lehel (refrigerators), Matrav (telecommunications), Budapest Bank (financial services), etc. An important determinant of this approach was Hungary's heavy foreign debt.[11] The imperative need to service this debt was a crucial argument in overcoming opposition to foreign acquisitions.

While direct sale of state assets provided an early boost to FDI in Hungary, it had by its nature a one-time effect. Together with the factors cited above, however, it created a climate for *de novo* entry to the private sector in Hungary. As the program of large-scale privatization neared completion, greenfield investments grew in relative importance. By the end of the 1990s, greenfield investment accounted for some two-thirds of the stock of FDI in Hungary. In terms of numbers of foreign-owned companies, the share of newly formed companies is even higher.

Hungary is one of a handful of transition economies that is on the 'fast track' to membership in the European Union. The others, the Czech Republic, Estonia, Poland, and Slovenia are all leading CEE recipients of foreign direct investment. EU countries have been a major source of FDI inflows (Table 2.3). The prospect of EU membership in the medium term and the actions of these countries to bring their commercial laws and regulations in line with EU standards have clearly encouraged foreign investors to prefer these locations. This has no doubt been a significant factor in the rapid growth of FDI to the region at the end of the 1990s. It has helped Hungary to maintain the level of inflows as the factors outlined above have declined in relative significance.

Hungary's early and sustained intake of significant magnitudes of foreign direct investment makes it a unique 'laboratory' to study the impact of FDI on the processes of transition in a post-communist economy. Comprehensive data on the degree of foreign ownership in the major sectors of the Hungarian example are not available. The data presented in Table 2.2 suggest its overall significance. In some sectors (banking and finance, automotive industry), foreign ownership predominates.

Analysis of the impact of FDI on a host economy is inevitably a complex task. There are a variety of measures; some subject to quantification, many not. The data for measuring even the quantifiable variables are often inadequate. The effects are widespread, can be positive and negative, short-term and long-term. A well-known illustration is the impact on the balance of payments, positive in the short run as capital flows in, but with growing negative effects in the longer run as foreign investors repatriate profits. This latter effect has already begun to become significant for Hungary's current account.[12] Finally, there is the problem of weighing the net effects revealed by the different indicators, in order to come up with an overall assessment.

Analysis of the impact of FDI on a host economy in transition requires broader approaches from those customarily employed in analyzing the host economy effects of FDI. Foreign direct investment in an economy in transition can bring with it more than the capital, technology and know-how with which it is traditionally associated. In addition to the traditional subjects of analysis, it is important to assess its impact on the processes of transition to a market-based economy. A clear example in the case of Hungary's transition, is the role already mentioned of foreign direct investment in Hungary's privatization program, designed to achieve a more balanced structure of ownership in the economy.

Hungarian economists have tackled the problem of analyzing the impact of foreign direct investment and have produced a substantial body of work, addressing various aspects of the problem.[13] They have shown that FDI has contributed to important economic dimensions of the transition in addition to privatization of state assets. It has mitigated the effects of the transitional recession, assisted the reorientation of foreign trade, contributed to a more balanced and competitive economic structure, helped to develop the institutional infrastructure of a market economy, including the requisite attitudes, values, and patterns of behavior.

The results of the analyses have not always been unambiguous, and FDI has its critics in Hungary, among economic analysts as well as politicians. There is in particular some dispute over whether FDI has raised value-added in Hungarian exports, contributed to indigenous technological capability, improved environmental standards in Hungarian industry. There are even some questions about whether FDI has had a net positive effect on the balance of trade or whether foreign controlled firms are more efficient than national firms.

The consensus among Hungarian economists, however, appears to be that FDI has been an important, positive factor in Hungary's comparatively successful progress along the transition path. They have found substantial evidence that it has contributed in significant ways to Hungary's economic recovery, to the restructuring of its economy and to the marketization and privatization of its economic institutions.

Poland

The case of Poland presents us with something of a paradox. Poland is frequently cited as the East European 'tiger' economy (DeBroeck and Koen, 2000). It was the first country to recover from its transitional recession (in 1992) and has since enjoyed higher rates of growth than its Central European neighbors. As we have seen, however, this performance did not ensure it a similar, leading position with regard to inflows of FDI. Only towards the end of the 1990s did Poland begin to attract foreign investment in the magnitudes that one would have expected.

How can we explain these trends? Two reasons for Poland's lag in this regard suggest themselves. The first is the factor of relative political stability that surveys indicate to be a major consideration for foreign investors. In the first half of the 1990s Poland was plagued with political instability as one short-term government succeeded another. Although the rapid turnover of governments did not in fact lead to Poland's abandonment of the economic reforms launched at the beginning of the decade, we would argue that coming so soon in Poland's post-communist history, the uncertainty it created did adversely affect the initial climate for foreign investment. By the latter part of the decade, government terms had lengthened, and the election process had demonstrated its strength, although Polish politics remained fractious.

It also contributed to the delays in implementing Poland's privatization program. Poland, like Hungary, has relied principally on the direct sale approach to the privatization of state-owned companies, in contrast to the give-away/voucher distribution of state property pursued by the Czech and Slovak Republics and Russia.[14] In contrast to Hungary, however, Poland was slow to get the program fully underway. The political economy of privatization in Poland is a subject beyond the scope of this chapter, but certainly the ideological opposition of important elements in the Solidarity and Peasants parties that led early post-communist governments played a role. Somewhat surprisingly, it was the advent in early 1995 of a social-democratic (SLD-led) government (including former communists) that heralded an acceleration of the privatization program. The same year saw a doubling of FDI flows to Poland and ushered in a trend that accelerated through the remainder of the decade. Happily for Poland, this improvement in the domestic conditions coincided with an economic boom in the West that boosted FDI generally.

It is clear from all this that FDI did not play the same role in Poland's economic recovery that it did in Hungary's. Nevertheless, the growth of the private sector in Poland is generally regarded to have been a major factor in Poland's economic dynamism after 1991 This private sector growth was due, however, to the increase in new, small and medium-sized firms rather than to the privatization of state enterprises. Although FDI played a role in the development of the *de novo* private sector, it did so through inflows of relatively small magnitudes.

A final factor to note is that German investments have been less significant in Poland than in other CEE economies. The share is rising, however. As Table 2.3 shows it was 18.8 percent at the end of 1996, while at the end of 1994, it was only 12.7 percent. As Germany is Poland's largest neighboring economy and has been the primary source of investment flows to other Central European economies, the initial obstacles to flows of German FDI to Poland are another plausible explanation of Poland's slow start.[15]

A Quantitative Analysis of the Determinants of FDI in CEE

In this section, we examine the difference of FDI inflows in the Czech Republic, Hungary and Poland from the experiences in five other CEE countries, namely, Bulgaria, Croatia, Romania, Slovak Republic and Slovenia, and then comparatively investigate Polish and Hungarian cases.

First, we attempt to identify a critical factor explaining trends and relative success of the three countries by a statistical analysis.[16] Our statistical investigation was done with regression analysis that tried to recognize which variable could significantly explain the FDI inflows. The variables used to explain the FDI inflows here are the following:

- GDP growth rate in percentage;
- GDP per capita in PPP expressed in US$;
- Budget balance as percentage of GDP;
- Current account balance in US$ billion;
- Industrial production growth rate in precentage;
- Unemployment rate in percentage;
- Inflation in percenatge;
- Foreign exchange reserves in US$ billion;
- Foreign debt in US$ billion;
- Exchange rate of a respective CEE currency to the US$.

We first tried a unit root test for the 10 variables and FDI inflow (expressed in US$ million) to avoid a wrong statistical calculation of mixing variables with a unit root and variables without a unit root. Then we tested the 10 explanatory variables for multicollinearity.

Poland

The results of our regression analysis for Poland are as follows. Of the 10 variables, GDP growth rate and budget balance as share of GDP do not have a unit root and were eliminated from the calculation. Also some variables were not included to avoid multicollinearity. The estimation equation is:

$$x1 = a1 + a2\,x2 + a3\,x3 + a4\,x4 + a5\,x5 + a6\,x6 + e$$

Here x1, x2, x3, x4, x5 and x6 indicate respectively FDI inflow, unemployment rate, inflation, foreign exchange reserves, foreign debt and dummy. The results of the calculation, shown in Table 2.4, indicate that foreign exchange reserves are the only one significant variable.[17]

Table 2.4   Poland

a1	-643.7	(-0.201)
a2	240.7	(2.901)
a3	2.3	(0.216)
a4	294.3	*(6.188)
a5	-70.3	(-1.193)
a6	-531.6	(-0.766)
R2	0.977	

The figures in parenthesis are the t-values.
* significant at the 0.05 level.

Hungary

Among the 10 variables, the GDP growth rate and the unemployment rate were excluded because they have no unit root. After checking and adjusting the multicollinearity, the estimation equation is:

$$x1 = a1 + a2\ x2 + a3\ x3 + a4\ x4 + a5\ x5 + a6\ x6 + a7\ x7 + a8\ x8 + e$$

The above x1, x2, x3, x4, x5, x6, x7 and x8 express respectively FDI inflow, budget balance of GDP, current account balance, industrial production growth rate, inflation, foreign exchange reserves, foreign debt, and dummy. The results of the calculation (Table 2.5) again show foreign exchange reserves to be the only significant explanatory variable.

Table 2.5   Hungary

a1	-5753.3	(-4.067)
a2	-106.3	(-2.638)
a3	523.9	(3.077)
a4	115.9	(3.827)
a5	98.5	(3.1)
a6	352.8	*(6.554)
a7	176.2	(1.729)
a8	-2322.2	(-4.03)
R2	0.949	

The figures in parenthesis are the t-values.
* significant at the 0.05 level.

The Czech Republic

By a unit root test, GDP growth rate and inflation were excluded. Also after testing to avoid multicollinearity, the estimation equation is:

$$x1 = a1 + a2\ x2 + a3\ x3 + a4\ x4 + a5\ x5 + a6\ x6 + a7\ x7 + e$$

Here x1, x2, x3, x4, x5, x6 and x7 show respectively FDI inflow, budget balance as percentage of GDP, current account balance, industrial production growth rate, foreign exchange reserves, exchange rate and dummy. The calculation result are presented in Table 2.6. In the Czech case only foreign exchange reserves are significant to explain FDI inflow into the Czech Republic.

Table 2.6   Czech Republic

a1	-12611.0	(-2.271)
a2	-504.5	(-3.691)
a3	217.8	(1.907)
a4	33.0	(1.002)
a5	272.9	*(6.401)
a6	428.3	(2.171)
a7	-2380.7	(-2.079)
R2	0.928	

The figures in parenthesis are the t-values.
* significant at the 0.05 level.gg

Thus, in the case of all three Central European countries one significant variable emerges to explain FDI inflows, which is foreign exchange reserves.[18] Other variables and dummies are not significant. When we investigated the other five CEE countries with the same method of calculation, no variable was found to be significant to explain FDI inflows into any of them.[19]

What might be the major difference among Poland, Hungary and the Czech Republic in the statistical investigations with macro-economic indices? If we split the 1990s into a first half and a second half and apply a simple regression analysis (because sample size was very small) examining whether explanation of FDI inflow by foreign exchange reserves was significant, a difference is found for Poland in comparision with Hungary and the Czech Republic.

The estimation equation is:

$$x1 = a1 + a2 \ x2 + e$$

In the equation, x1 and x2 are respectively indicated as FDI inflow and foreign exchange reserves.

As far as the first half of 1990s was concerned, the three countries had no significant result. Concerning the second half, Poland had a significant result (as shown in Table 2.7). Neither Hungary nor the Czech Republic had a significant result (see Table 2.8 and in Table 2.9).[20]

With the above consideration, we could speculate particularly in the cases of Poland, Hungary, and the Czech Republic that FDI inflow can be explained by foreign exchange reserves. The significance of the second half of the 1990s in Poland is compatible with our expectation, which is that Poland has become a leading country of attracting FDI inflow into CEE countries. The main reason coming from this section's statistical study is foreign exchange reserves closely related with the financial risk.[21]

Table 2.7   Poland (1995-1999)

a1	194.4	(0.355)
a2	234.1	(9.324)*
R2	0.956	

The figures in parenthesis are the t-values.
* significant at the 0.05 level.

Table 2.8   Hungary (1995-1999)

a1	-2834.5	(- 0.740)
a2	517.4	(1.375)
R2	0.182	

The figures in parenthesis are the t-values.

Table 2.9   Czech Republic (1995-1999)

a1	-2653.4	(- 0.638)
a2	409.1	(1.222)
R2	0.110	

The figures in parenthesis are the t-values.

Statistical investigations in this section have been limited to macro-economic indices although we did examine a dummy variable. As it was mentioned in the previous sections, however, some non-economic indices might be also important. As far as the correlation of FDI inflows with foreign exchange reserves is concerned, factors like internal political stability, external relations, the legal framework, all contributed effectively to the financial risk.

Conclusions

This chapter has explored the factors that appear to explain the relative success of Hungary and Poland in attracting foreign direct investment in the first decade of the post-communist transition in CEE. Of course, success often breeds success, just as failure can breed failure. This may well lead to greater divergence among the transition economies in their capacities to attract FDI.

Our qualitative analysis showed that the transition strategy followed and in particular the reliance on a more organic development of the private sector, including direct sale of privatization of state-owned enterprises were the most important determinants. It not only helps to explain the relative success of Hungary and Poland in attracting FDI into the two countries. Hungary's early success in attracting FDI is linked to its relatively prompt implementation of its privatization program. Poland, on the other hand, experienced major delays in the implementation of its privatuzation program, which help us to understand its late start in attracting significant magnitudes of foreign direct investment. It is logical that direct-sale privatization should be such an important determinant of FDI, given the opportunities that it opens up to foreign investors for the acquisition of major assets.

As statistical analysis, with macro-economic indices, has rather strict limitations, it is more difficult to apply than qualitative analysis. Our statistical investigations indicate primarily the importance of foreign exchange reserves for attracting FDI, which we interpret as closely related with the financial risk for foreign investors. Such a risk is presumably linked to the 'imperfect' information coming from such factors as political instability that was revealed in our qualitative analysis.

Hungary and Poland provide us with interesting 'laboratories' to analyze the impact of FDI on the processes of transition. Hungary's longer and richer experience has already prompted a significant analytical literature. If inflows to Poland continue at their current rates, it too will have a stock of FDI large enough to be a significant factor in its economic restructuring. We shall expect to see a growth in the Polish literature on the subject analogous to that of Hungary.[22]

Intercountry comparisons of the structure of FDI have also been beyond the scope of this chapter. Certainly FDI has generally helped to correct one of the most glaring disproportions of the communist period the underdevelopment of the 'unproductive' service sector.

Notes

1   This chapter is based on a paper presented at the VI World Congress of Central and Eastern European Studies in Tampere, Finland, in August 2000. The authors are grateful for the constructive comments and suggestions made by the assigned discussant, Professor Stefan Hedlund from the University of Upsalla, Sweden and other participants in the session. At the same time, they assume responsibility for all remaining errors of fact and interpretation.

2   Affiliation Carleton Univers 'y, Canada.

3   Affiliation Hiroshima University, Japan.
4   For a review of the potential linkages between FDI and the transition processes which underlay these expectations, see McMillan (1993).
5   World Investment Report 1999, p. 480.
6   The principal comparative sources are the EBRD and the UN (UNCTAD). UNCTAD estimates the stock of FDI at the end of 1998 for the 25 CEE countries covered in Table 1.1 at US$ 100.2 billion.
7   This section is based in part on McMillan and Hakogi (1998).
8   In 1995, thanks to a large privatization in telecommunications, the inflow was almost US$4.5 billion.
9   The National Bank of Hungary Monthly Report, 3/2000, reports inflows of US$ 1,567 million in 1999 and a stock at the end of 1999 of US$ 19.1 billion (equity capital and inter company loans).
10   Cf. *The Economist*, 16 May 1998, p. 52.
11   FDI inflows in the 1990s have ranged from 100 percent to over 200 percent of Hungary's current account deficit.
12   According to PlanEcon Report, Washington, D.C., 28 April 2000 profit repatriation by foreign investors could produce some unpleasant surprises for Hungary's balance of payments in 2000.
13   Cf. Farkas (1997), Hunya (1997), Szanyi (1997), Szanyi and Szemler (1997), Szekeres (1999).
14   Janos Kornai refers to these as transition strategies A and B in his thoughtful retrospective piece, Kornai (2000).
15   President Walesa's much quoted 1993 remark that 'any foreign investment is welcome in Poland, so long as it is not German' is reflective of Polish attitudes at the time (cited in Wielgus, 1995). These attitudes were also reflected in bureaucratic and regulatory barriers to German investment.
16   The calculations in this section were fundamentally based upon Business Central Europe Database.
17   When we have the regression analysis in Poland and the Czech Republic (not in Hungary because FDI inflow and GDP growth rate was not compatible from a unit root test) to examine if GDP growth rate could explain FDI inflow in 1990s. In neither Poland nor the Czech Republic was the GDP growth rate significant enough to explain FDI inflow as indicated in Table A (Poland) and in Table B (Czech Republic). Estimation equation in Poland is:

$$x1(t) - x1(t-1) = a1 + a2\ x2(t) + a3\ (x3(t) - x3(t-1)) + a4\ x4(t) + e$$

(Where: $x1$ = FDI inflow, $x2$ = GDP growth rate, $x3$ = Foreign debt, $x4$ = Dummy)

Table A   Poland

a1	671.5	(2.237)
a2	77.0	(1.285)
a3	155.5	(2.311)
a4	-60.2	(-0.114)
R2	0.446	

The figures in parenthesis are the t-values.

Estimation equation in Czech Republic is:

$$x1(t) - x1(t-1) = a1 + a2\ x2\ (t) + a3\ (x3\ (t) - x3(t-1)) + a4\ x4\ (t) + e$$

(Where: x1 = FDI inflow, x2 = GDP growth rate, x3 = Budget balance of GDP, x4 = Dummy).

Table B   Czech Republic

a1	748.9	(0.421)
a2	-82.6	(-0.515)
a3	418.4	(0.516)
a4	103.9	(0.062)
R2	-0.440	

The figures in parenthesis are the t-values.

18   As FDI directly increases foreign exchange reserves, we have a test asking whether FDI inflow explains foreign exchange reserves. With the test, in Poland it is significant, but in Hungary and the Czech Republic it is not significant. Results of the test might mean that FDI would be one of the factors to increase foreign exchange reserves.

19   Other five CEE countries cases are as follows:

1. Bulgaria

$$x1 = a1 + a2\ x2 + a3\ x3 + a4\ x4 + a5\ x5 + a6\ x6 + a7\ x7 + a8\ x8 + a9\ x9 + e$$

(Where: x1 = FDI inflow, x2 = GDP growth rate, x3 = Current account balance, x4 = Industrial production growth rate, x5 = Unemployment rate, x6 = Inflation, x7 = Foreign exchange reserves, x8 = Foreign debt, x9 = Dummy).

Table C   Bulgaria

a1	-3488.6	(-8.101)
a2	-29.0	(-6.278)
a3	0.7	(8.020)
a4	44.6	(4.901)
a5	-451.0	(-7.128)
a6	4.4	(1.529)
a7	37.7	(7.212)
a8	0.5	(10.364)
a9	79.1	(1.014)
R2	0.988	

The figures in parenthesis are the t-values.

2. Romania

$$x1 = a1 + a2\ x2 + a3\ x3 + a4\ x4 + a5\ x5 + a6\ x6 + a7\ x7 + a8\ x8 + e$$

(Where: x1 = FDI inflow, x2 = GDP growth rate, x3 = Current account balance, x4 = Unemployment rate, x5 = Inflation, x6 = Foreign exchange reserves, x7 = Foreign debt, x8 = Dummy).

Table D   Romania

a1	248.5	(1.330)
a2	-2.223	(-0.191)
a3	-34.3	(-0.474)
a4	18.6	(0.624)
a5	1.6	(1.207)
a6	-942.6	(-4.342)
a7	35.7	(1.093)
a8	2547.5	(6.596)
R2	0.988	

The figures in parenthesis are the t-values.

3. Slovakia

$$x1 = a1 + a2\,x2 + a3\,x3 + a4\,x4 + a5\,x5 + a6\,x6 + e$$

(Where: x1 = FDI inflow, x2 = Current account balance, x3 = Industrial production rate, x4 = Unemployment rate, x5 = Foreign exchange reserves, x6 = Dummy).

Table E   Slovakia

a1	-535.7	(-2.657)
a2	-160.7	(-4.864)
a3	35.1	(5.007)
a4	63.5	(4.093)
a5	-102.9	(-3.375)
a6	-120.9	(-1.650)
R2	0.838	

The figures in parenthesis are the t-values.

4. Slovenia

$$x1 = a1 + a2\,x2 + a3\,x3 + a4\,x4 + a5\,x5 + e$$

(Where: x1 = FDI inflow, x2 = Industrial production growth rate, x3 = Unemployment rate, x4 = Foreign exchange reserves, x5 = Dummy).

Table F   Slovenia

a1	132.0	(0.891)
a2	5.3	(0.701)
a3	5.3	(0.464)
a4	-5.8	(-0.124)
a5	118.6	(0.892)
R2	0.170	

The figures in parenthesis are the t-values.

5. *Croatia*

$$x1 = a1 + a2\,x2 + a3\,x3 + a4\,x4 + a5\,x5 + a6\,x6 + e$$

(Where: x1 = FDI inflow, x2 = GDP per capita, x3 = Current account balance, x4 = Inflation, x5 = Exchange rate, x6 = Dummy).

Table G   Croatia

a1	-1781.6	(-0.999)
a2	0.5	(1.793)
a3	165.3	(1.093)
a4	-0.6	(-0.528)
a5	224.6	(0.99)
a6	-1968.1	(-1.208)
R2	0.814	

The figures in parenthesis are the t-values.

20   The simple regression analysis of the whole 1990s (from 1990 to 1999) said that the three countries had significant explanation of FDI inflow by foreign exchange reserves.
21   Concerning the financial risk, see Morita 1997b.
22   An early example is Witkowska (1997).

References

DeBroeck, M. and Koen, V. (2000), *The 'Soaring Eagle': Anatomy of the Polish Take-Off in the 1990s*, IMF Working Paper/00/06, Washington, D.C.: International Monetary Fund.

EBRD (1999), *Transition Report 1999*, London: European Bank for Reconstruction and Development.

Farkas, P. (1997), *The Effect of Foreign Direct Investment on Research, Development and Innovation in Hungary*, Working Paper No. 81, Institute of World Economy, Budapest, Hungary.

Hunya, G. (1997), 'Large Privatisation, Restructuring and Foreign Direct Investment', in S. Zecchini, (ed), *Lessons from the Economic Transition: Central and Eastern Europe in the 1990s*, OECD: Kluwer Academic Publishers.

Kornai, J. (2000), 'Ten Years after: The Road to a Free Economy. The Author Self-Evaluation', in B. Pleskovic and N. Stern (eds) *Annual World Bank Conference on Development Economics 2000*, Washington, DC: World Bank, pp. 49-66.

McMillan, C. (1993), 'The Role of Foreign Direct Investment in the Transition from Planned to Market Economies', *Transnational Corporations*, Vol. 2, No. 3, pp. 97-120.

McMillan, C., and Hakogi, M. (1998), 'Foreign Direct Investment and Economic Transition: Assessing the Impacts on the Hungarian Economy', *Journal of the Graduate School of International Cultural Studies*, Vol. 6, pp. 101-116.

Morita, K. (1997a), 'On a Weakness of Japan's FDI into East European Countries', *South East European Monitor*, Vol.4, pp. 3-16.

Morita, K. (1997b), 'An Economic Analysis of Foreign Direct Investment into Eastern Europe: A Case of Japan's FDI into Poland', Paper presented at the Conference on Transition to Advanced Market Institutions and Economies, Warsaw, Poland, June 18-21.

Morita, K., and Stuglik, D. (1998), 'Nihon no tai Poland Chokusetsu Toushi: Genjou to Kettei Youin' ('Japan's Foreign Direct Investment into Poland: Current Situation and Determinants'), *Hiroshima Daigaku Keizai Ronsou* (*The Hiroshima Economic Review*), Vol.21, No.4, pp. 21-40.

Morita, K. (1998), 'On Determinants of Japan's Foreign Direct Investment in East Europe: The Case of Poland', *Journal of East-West Business*, Vol. 4, Nos. 1/2, pp. 141-148.

Szanyi, M. (1997), *Experience with Foreign Direct Investment in Eastern Europe: Advantages and Disadvantages*, Working Paper No. 85, Institute of World Economy, Budapest, November.

Szanyi, M. and Szemler T. (1997), *Investment Patterns in Hungary 1989-95*, Working Paper No. 79, Institute of World Economy, Budapest.

Szekeres, V. (1999), *Comparative Studies of Foreign and Indigenous Enterprises in the Hungarian Manufacturing Industries*, Paper presented at the 40th Annual Convention of the International Studies Association, Washington, D.C., December.

United Nations (1999), *World Development Report 1999*, Geneva.

Wielgus, A. (1995), *Is Poland Emerging from the Periphery of Foreign Direct Investment Flows to Central and Eastern Europe? An Examination of the Evidence*, M. A. Thesis, Carleton University, Canada.

Witkowska, J. (1997), 'Foreign Direct Investment as a Factor of Structural Change in the Polish Economy', *Osteuropa Wirtschaft*, Vol 42, pp. 418-436.

3 Foreign Direct Investment in Central and Eastern Europe in the Period 1990 - 2000: Patterns and Consequences

ALOJZY Z. NOWAK and JEFF STEAGALL

Introduction

International investment flows come in two forms. The largest share derives from flows of financial capital seeking the highest returns. While financial investments are important to economic development, they are too fickle to be a reliable source of sustainable economic development. The negative aspects of relying on financial investment were clearly evidenced by the financial flight experienced by such varied nations as Mexico, Thailand, Indonesia, South Korea, the Philippines, Russia, and Brazil at various times between late 1994 and 1998. Moreover, researchers are now studying the so-called contagion phenomenon, in which instability that generates capital flight in one country can spread quickly to other nations throughout the globe, even if these other nations are relatively free of the economic shortcomings of the country that initially experienced capital flight.

Therefore, the most-desired form of international investment from the recipient country's viewpoint is a direct investment into physical assets, including productive facilities, infrastructural improvements, education and training, supply chains, etc. Such investment is known as foreign direct investment (FDI), and is the focus of this article. Both FDI flows, which represent annual movements of FDI into (i.e., inflows) and out of (i.e., outflows) a country, and FDI stocks, which track the cumulative FDI inflows (net of outflows) over a given time period are important. FDI stock thus measures the accumulated foreign-owned assets at a point in time.

FDI has become increasingly important, having grown more rapidly than either global trade volumes or world output during the last fifteen years. Developing nations worldwide, particularly in Southeast Asia and in Central and Eastern Europe, have received significant FDI inflows. Such investment is due to the political changes and the economic restructuring that these nations undertook in the 1980s and 1990s. Thus, it is important to understand the forces that move FDI and the benefits that FDI provides to the recipient nations.

This chapter investigates the FDI inflows to the Central and Eastern Europe (CEE) region during 1990 - 2000. For the purposes of this study, CEE is defined as including Bulgaria, Croatia, the Czech Republic, Estonia, Hungary, Latvia, Lithuania, Poland, Romania, the Slovak Republic, Slovenia and the Ukraine, because comparable FDI data are available for all of them. Since the transition to market-oriented economies began at different times in different nations, early data are not always comparable across countries. This problem sometimes restricts the analysis to 1993 - 2000.

In order to understand the FDI pattern, the next section describes the typical determinants of FDI, with an emphasis on CEE-specific issues. It then summarizes the specific FDI needs of the CEE region, distinguishing between the needs at the beginning of the period and those that remain today. The next section provides an empirical overview of the FDI pattern for the region, explaining why most FDI went to Poland, the Czech Republic, and Hungary while other CEE nations received virtually none. A more detailed analysis of the three main recipient countries follows. The chapter concludes with a look into the future of the FDI in CEE.

Determinants of FDI

International investors make their FDI decisions by identifying the highest available expected returns. The expected return on any investment is simply the sum of likely returns under a variety of scenarios, each weighted by the probability that the scenario will be realized. Clearly, such calculations are imprecise. They were particularly difficult for investors considering investments in the CEE region during the early 1990s, because investors had to make such predictions in the unique environment of the post-Soviet transition from socialism to capitalism. However, the possibility of huge returns in the new markets did lure some FDI even in the early 1990s.

In order to evaluate the risks of making FDI in any country, investors consider a variety of issues. Among these are variables that would normally be considered even in making a decision on domestic investment. These include the skill, educational and productivity of the workforce; the cost of labor, including the regulatory environment (e.g., health and safety rules, the right to hire and fire); the cost of purchasing raw materials and getting them to the productive facility; the reliability of inputs, including electricity; and the tax burden, including unemployment insurance, etc.

In considering FDI, a number of additional variables must be considered. First, the political stability of the potential recipient country is paramount. This item refers to both stability of the form of government and to the stability of the nation's policies that relate to foreign-owned production and profits. The form of government is of less importance than the stability of that form. Firms prefer environments of certainty, because they can develop profitable business strategies and tactics, whether the government is autocratic, democratic, or some intermediate form. However, the risk of switching from one form of government to the other can prove costly for foreign firms, which are often viewed by the incoming government as symbols of what was wrong with the old government. Such firms are thus easy, high-profile targets for retaliation and plunder by the new government. The stability of policies is equally important. Many firms have lost 100 percent of their FDI when governments shifted toward the political left and embraced nationalization of industries as policy. Similarly, firms have invested heavily in FDI-friendly environments only to have subsequent governments restrict the repatriation of profits to the home country. Such restrictions have varied from prohibitions against repatriation to allowing it only under extremely unfavorable government-imposed exchange rates. In CEE nations, both types of political stability were in question for all countries during the early 1990s, and remain so to varying degrees for many of those nations even today. In 1990, it was unclear that the privatization and other market reforms underway in many CEE countries would be sustained. Indeed, there was some risk of a return to Russian domination, and firms had to consider that. However, by 1993, several nations had made significant progress toward convincing international investors that enduring systematic changes had been made. These included political freedom, free press, and representative democratic discussion of problems. With regard to the stability of policies, markets were heartened by the establishment of clear private property rights and a sensible regulatory environment, both backed by the rule of law.

Second, currency risk is important. An unexpected devaluation or depreciation in the currency of the FDI recipient country can render an impressive local currency profit virtually worthless in the source-country currency that matters to the investor. Even modest, predictable weakening of the host country currency can undermine the incentive to invest in a nation. For the CEE, especially early in the period under analysis, exchange rate issues presented a special problem. A significant portion of pre-1989 CEE trade had in fact been countertrade, or barter, between east-bloc nations. Although there are additional explanations for why countertrade occurred, one reason was certainly the inconvertibility of the national currencies. Firms considering investing in the region were forced to predict the currency values for nations that had had no experience with market-driven exchange rates.

Third, access to markets is important. The current trading environment is dominated by trading blocs like the North American Free Trade Area (NAFTA) and the European Union (EU). Moreover, the short-term evolution of the trading environment is likely to be increasingly bloc-oriented. The World Trade Organization (WTO) has been unable to launch its scheduled 'Millennium Round' of trade talks because of disruptive violence at its meetings for that purpose in Seattle and elsewhere. In addition, the trade blocs are seeking both to expand themselves For example, EU expansion to include up to a dozen CEE countries seems imminent, while the US is likely to bring Chile into NAFTA while simultaneously pursuing a trans-Pacific free trade area known as the Asia-Pacific Economic Cooperation (APEC) Forum. Because trade is (relatively) free across national borders within a given trading bloc but faces significant tariff and, increasingly, non-tariff barriers when exports are sourced in non-member nations, firms have a strong incentive to make foreign direct investments in each major bloc, in order to serve each regional market without facing trade restrictions. In the case of the CEE, geopolitical strategies made it clear early in the period that accession of at least some CEE nations, certainly to include Poland, to the EU provided an obvious incentive for FDI in Poland for American, Canadian, Japanese, and other non-EU firms. This would allow access to the EU market from a source of well-educated, skilled workers.

The CEE presented additional challenges beyond those faced elsewhere by FDI sources. While none of the CEE nations was particularly ready to compete with import competition from abroad, much less to compete in the international marketplace, some countries were certainly better positioned than others. Until prices had been rationalized (reset by market mechanisms), investing firms could not hope to predict future profits accurately. In addition, the institutional infrastructure that supports efficient markets had to be established. It includes the rule of law; sensible, enforceable and enforced regulation; relatively complete privatization; elimination of the barriers against entrepreneurial activity; liberalization of the rules of exchange domestically and the trade rules internationally; currency convertibility and a stable exchange rate; sound fiscal policies, including small central government deficits, restrained spending with an adequate social safety net, and reasonable tax rates; pro-FDI policies (including the method of privatization used) and incentives; and sound monetary policies including low, stable interest rates; and a return to economic growth. Later sections address these issues directly for the CEE.

Koźminski (1995) has identified the Eight S Formula, which concisely describes the benefits of FDI in CEE markets for multinational corporations (MNCs) (see Table 3.1).

Table 3.1   Koźminski's eight S formula

Eight S	Summary	Favors FDI into
- Size of market	Large present market and high future growth imply higher returns to FDI	Poland
- Strong margins	Novelty appeal of western goods and services, especially in early 1990s; some governments awarded exclusive contracts to firms	Less stable, less advanced CEE
- Stability	Political, legal, monetary	Czech Republic, Estonia, Hungary, Poland, Slovenia
- Skilled workers	High educational levels at low wages	All countries
- Support	Infrastructure, business services (e.g., consulting, auditing, legal, financial)	Czech Republic, Estonia, Hungary, Poland, Slovenia
- Suppliers	Well-developed and privatized suppliers are needed	Czech Republic, Estonia, Hungary, Poland, Slovenia
- Safety	Operations safety implies well-developed legal structures (regulations and enforcement)	Czech Republic, Estonia, Hungary, Poland, Slovenia
- Springboard	Use initial FDI as a platform for penetrating other (usually less developed) markets	Czech Republic, Estonia, Hungary, Poland, Slovenia

Source: Koźminski, A.K. (1995).

Need for Regional Inward FDI in Central and Eastern Europe

In 1990, the uncertainty regarding the political and economic future of the region was exacerbated by the dire need for FDI from the west. Obviously, the CEE lacked both the physical and financial capital needed to drive its restructuring and stimulate economic growth. However, FDI also generates additional benefits to the recipient nation. In the case of the CEE, these were arguably more important than the capital itself.

Most obviously, FDI is likely to bring in certain technological advances from abroad, including new physical plant and equipment, as well as modern production processes. The purchase of state-owned enterprises (SOE) by firms from advanced economies resulted in the modernization of the plants. This typically resulted in enhanced worker productivity (which was further supplemented through firm-sponsored training programs), resulting in higher real wages for some sectors.

Perhaps more important, however, was the transmission of management know-how, which in the Soviet-era CEE had lagged several decades behind the practices utilized in the rest of the world. Standard management practices such as incentive systems and the motivation of workers were largely absent. A comprehension of the principles of competition (both domestic and international) was sorely needed, while marketing practices such as attractive, differentiated packaging and appealing advertising campaigns were virtually non-existent. More recent management best practices were even less apparent. Logistics and supply-chain management were unheard of. Attention to quality in the production process and a focus on customer service in both the manufacturing and service sectors were lacking. FDI brought all of these processes to the CEE, although ingraining them into the management and workforce has occurred only slowly. The new management practices emphasized competition as both an opportunity for success and a threat to the firm's existence. Entrepreneurial attitudes and skills followed shortly.

Foreign exchange was important because it allowed for the purchase of both imported industrial inputs and imported consumer goods. Fortunately, FDI tended to occur in the most promising export industries, providing critical foreign currency to the CEE nations.

Regional Macroeconomic Overview, 1990 - 2000

The socioeconomic transition from socialism to capitalism met with varying success in CEE nations. Many countries in the region had stable and relatively fast economic growth, falling inflation, and controlled government spending. Other countries experienced significant negative economic fluctuations. The latter countries often also suffered from high inflation and large central government budget and current account deficits. As a result, countries' readiness for FDI inflows differed significantly. This section therefore provides macroeconomic information about all CEE countries during 1990 - 2000, in order to explain variations in inward FDI.

The twelve-nation CEE analyzed in this chapter ranges in population from 1.5 million in Estonia to 49.3 million in the Ukraine, with an aggregate population of 158.3 million in the year 2000. However, Poland (38.6 million) is the dominant economy in the group, with its 2000 purchasing power parity (PPP) GDP of US$ 364.38 billion representing 25.2 percent of regional income. As this chapter demonstrates below, the Czech Republic, Hungary, and Poland account for nearly 70 percent of cumulative inward FDI over this period, although they represent just 37.2 percent of the population and 43.5 percent of the real GDP in the region (see Table 3.2).

Table 3.3 shows the severe economic problems that CEE countries experienced during the 1990s. All twelve economies contracted significantly in both 1990 and 1991, as privatization, foreign competition, and price rationalization that forced firm closures resulted in huge layoffs. Only Poland grew in real terms during 1992, and just by 2.6 percent after shrinking by nearly 18 percent in the previous two years. By 1993, five countries were experiencing positive growth, and by 1995, only the Ukraine, which contracted in every year until 2000, saw real GDP growth in at least one year, indicating a general return to economic stability. The Ukraine had lost 60 percent of its real GDP during 1990 - 2000.

Fortunately, economic growth was more widespread and more robust during the second half of the decade, as countries emerged from their transition shocks. However, despite the higher real GDP growth rates in the second half of the decade, most CEE countries still have lower real GDP levels than before transition started (Figure 3.1). In fact only four (Hungary, Poland, the Slovak Republic, and Slovenia) of the twelve CEE countries had higher real GDP in 2000 vis-à-vis 1990. Poland grew fastest, experiencing a net growth of 43.6 percent over the period (see Figure 3.1).

Many of the economic difficulties in the early 1990s were generated by price rationalization. Soviet-era prices had been set by technocrats, who dictated prices in order to fulfill political goals, without regard to market forces. Typically, prices on the essential goods that citizens could afford were set far below market levels. When the transition required the releasing of government control over prices, in order to provide economic agents with market-based incentives and signals, significant inflation was the unavoidable result. Inflation in consumer prices averaged 155.5 percent across the region in 1990.

The Ukraine initially avoided widespread price rationalization, suffering only a 4.8 percent inflation rate in 1990. However, its strategy of procrastination came back to haunt it in 1993, when consumer prices rose by 4,725 percent. On the other hand, countries that carried price releasing processes gradually and in addition had relatively flexible structure of supply side of economy did not suffer from high level of inflation. The best examples of such countries are Czech Republic, which suffered the lowest inflation over the period, and Hungary, which had no single-year inflationary spike. Almost all countries had stabilized their price levels by 2000, when the average inflation rate was 13.9 percent. In fact, only Romania (45.7 percent) and the Ukraine (28.2 percent) had uncontrolled inflation rates in 2000, with double-digit rates only in Poland (10.1 percent) and the Slovak Republic (12.1 percent). The Czech Republic and Estonia even experienced developed-country inflation rates near 4 percent (see Table 3.4). Inflation has been brought under control through two accomplishments. First, price rationalization and other necessary structural reforms had largely been accomplished by 1995. Second, CEE nations learned to conduct sound monetary policy.

In addition to learning to run monetary policy, CEE governments had to learn to practice fiscal restraint, particularly with respect to the central government budget balance, called internal balance in the jargon of economics. Transition processes, mostly financed by internal sources, put enormous strains on central government budgets. As economies adjusted to the transition, the associated pressures to spend declined. Moreover, those countries that aspire to join the European Union, have begun to apply the Convergence Criteria, which include restrictions that budget deficits do not exceed 3 percent of GDP and that accumulated government debt does not exceed 60 percent of GDP. In 1999, the latest year for which complete data are available, only Hungary and Latvia failed to meet the 3 percent ceiling, with deficits at 3.8 percent of GDP in each nation. Only Bulgaria boasted a budget surplus in 1999. Most nations for which data are available experienced higher deficits in 2000, though Estonia, Hungary, and Latvia improved their balances, while Slovenia posted a 1.4 percent surplus (see Table 3.5).

A related and extremely important problem for CEE economies is the current account deficit, which summarizes the net flow of currency out of the country due to trade in goods and services, net repatriation of profits, and net private remittances. A sustained current account deficit (known as external imbalance), unless offset by net capital inflows, implies downward pressure on the national currency. The International Monetary Fund (IMF) recommends that the current account deficit be less than 7 percent of GDP in order to be sustainable. Every country except Slovenia experienced a current account deficit that level exceeded this 7 percent target during at least one year. Bulgaria, Croatia, Estonia, Latvia, Lithuania, the Slovak Republic and the Ukraine experienced current account deficits that exceeded 10 percent of GDP at least once. While single-year anomalies can be tolerated, repeated deficits in excess of 7 percent can generate severe currency problems. For example, Lithuania's deficit exceeded 10 percent of GDP in five consecutive years (1995 - 1999). Such a situation indicates the high level of external imbalance, which can lead to a currency crisis. Even the potential of a currency crisis is sufficient to deter all FDI. Fortunately, all countries for which 2000 data were available had current account deficits of less than 6 percent of GDP, except for Poland at 6.2 percent (see Table 3.6).

Because of the potential for serious economic consequences, including capital flight, that can result from a currency crisis, exchange rate policy is a critical determinant of FDI. CEE countries have adopted a variety of exchange rate regimes. Most CEE countries operate either with a managed float regime, in which the government sometimes intervenes to alter the value of an otherwise floating currency, or peg their currencies to other developed-country currencies. On the one hand, Bulgaria and Estonia have euro-based currency boards. Having a currency board ensures that each euro's worth of national currency in circulation is backed by a euro held in reserve by the currency board. In effect, a currency board credibly pegs the value of the national currency to the value of the euro, so long as international markets believe that the currency board can maintain the required euro balance. The result is an extremely stable exchange rate, at the expense of completely deferring to the monetary policy set by the European Central Bank. At the other hand, Poland, the Ukraine, the Slovak Republic, and Slovenia allow their currencies to float virtually freely in the international marketplace, ensuring some control over monetary policy but potentially opening the nations to currency runs.

Table 3.7 shows the exchange rate for each national currency against the US dollar. Every country has experienced some degree of weakening against the dollar during 1990 - 2000. The list of countries with seemingly stable exchange rates includes Bulgaria, Estonia, Latvia, Lithuania, Poland, Slovak Republic, and the Ukraine. Much of the weakening of currencies between the end of 1998 and 2000 can be explained by the dramatic weakening of the euro vis-à-vis the dollar. Since CEE nations are more closely tied to the eurozone nations than to the US, it is unsurprising that their currencies have also weakened against the dollar.

Table 3.2   Real GDP (PPP), 1990-2000 (US$ bn) and population, 2000 (in millions)

GDP in bn US$	1991	1992	1994	1995	1996	1997	1998	1999	2000	Population mln
Bulgaria	52.76	48.91	49.04	50.07	44.61	41.53	42.99	44.02	46.00	8.2
Croatia	31.18	27.53	26.82	28.64	30.36	32.34	33.14	33.01	34.20	4.5
Czech Republic	127.34	126.70	129.62	137.27	143.86	142.42	139.29	138.17	141.63	10.3
Estonia	8.52	7.31	6.52	6.80	7.07	7.82	8.18	8.09	8.61	1.5
Hungary	99.68	96.59	98.80	100.28	101.58	106.25	111.46	116.48	122.30	10.0
Latvia	15.40	10.03	8.58	8.52	8.80	9.55	9.93	10.04	10.54	2.4
Lithuania	22.24	17.51	13.23	13.67	14.31	15.36	16.37	15.68	16.14	3.7
Poland	235.97	242.11	264.37	282.88	300.14	320.85	336.25	350.03	364.38	38.6
Romania	148.91	135.80	143.22	153.39	159.37	149.65	141.57	137.04	139.78	22.4
Slovak Republic	49.44	46.23	46.70	49.83	52.92	56.20	58.50	59.61	60.80	5.4
Slovenia	25.53	24.12	26.11	27.18	28.13	29.43	30.55	32.07	33.58	2.0
Ukraine	367.85	317.45	209.73	184.14	165.73	160.76	157.70	157.07	166.50	49.3

Source: European Bank for Reconstruction and Development - Country Investment Profiles 2001; Business Central Europe Magazine; Authors' calculations.

Table 3.3   Real annual GDP growth rates, 1990 - 2000 (percent)

GDP (percent change)	1990	1991	1992	1993	1994	1995	1996	1997	1998	1999	2000	Total 1990-2000
Bulgaria	-9.1	-11.7	-7.3	-1.5	1.8	2.9	-10.1	-7.0	3.5	2.4	5.0	-23.01
Croatia	-7.1	-21.1	-11.7	-8.0	5.9	6.8	5.9	6.8	2.5	0.4	3.5	-13.45
Czech Republic	-1.2	-11.5	-3.3	0.1	2.2	5.9	4.8	-1.0	-2.2	-0.2	3.1	-1.68
Estonia	-8.1	-13.6	-14.2	8.5	-2.0	4.3	3.9	10.6	4.7	-1.1	6.4	-12.70
Hungary	-3.5	-11.9	-3.1	-0.6	2.9	1.5	1.3	4.6	4.9	4.5	5.3	8.09
Latvia	-3.5	-10.4	-34.9	-15.0	0.8	-1.0	3.3	8.6	3.9	0.1	na	-38.71
Lithuania	-6.9	-5.7	-21.3	-16.2	-9.8	3.3	4.7	7.3	5.1	-4.2	2.9	-31.58
Poland	-11.6	-7.0	2.6	3.8	5.2	7.0	6.0	6.8	4.8	4.1	4.1	43.61
Romania	-5.6	-12.9	-8.8	1.5	3.9	7.1	3.9	-6.9	-5.4	-3.2	1.6	-18.24
Slovak Republic	-2.5	-14.6	-6.5	-3.7	4.9	6.7	6.2	6.2	4.4	1.9	2.2	5.03
Slovenia	-4.7	-8.9	-5.5	2.8	5.3	4.1	3.5	4.6	3.8	4.9	4.7	19.85
Ukraine	13.0	-8.7	-9.9	-14.2	-22.9	-12.2	-10.0	-3.2	-1.7	-0.4	6.0	-59.99

Source: European Bank for Reconstruction and Development - Country Investment Profiles 2001; Business Central Europe Magazine; Authors' calculations.

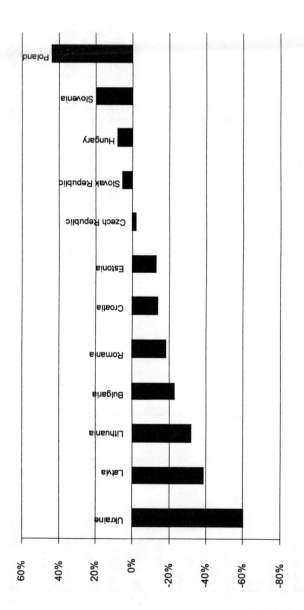

Source: European Bank for Reconstruction and Development - Country Investment Profiles 2001; Business Central Europe Magazine; Authors' calculations.

Figure 3.1   **Real GDP changes, 1990 - 2000 (PPP)**

Table 3.4   Consumer prices – annual percent changes

Inflation (percent)	1990	1991	1992	1993	1994	1995	1996	1997	1998	1999	2000
Bulgaria	23.8	338.5	91.2	72.8	96.0	62.1	123.0	1,082.0	22.3	0.3	9.9
Croatia	609.5	123.0	665.5	1,149.0	-3.0	2.0	3.5	3.6	5.7	4.2	6.2
Czech Republic	9.7	56.6	11.1	20.8	10.0	9.1	8.8	8.5	10.7	2.1	3.9
Estonia	17.2	211.0	1,076.0	89.8	47.7	29.0	23.1	11.2	8.2	3.3	4.0
Hungary	28.9	35.0	23.0	22.5	18.8	28.2	23.6	18.3	14.3	10.0	9.8
Latvia	10.5	172.0	959.0	9.2	35.9	25.0	17.6	8.4	4.7	2.4	na
Lithuania	8.4	225.0	1,161.0	188.8	45.1	35.7	12.1	8.4	2.4	2.5	na
Poland	585.8	70.3	43.0	35.3	32.2	27.8	19.9	14.9	11.8	7.3	10.1
Romania	5.1	170.2	210.4	256.1	136.8	32.3	38.8	151.4	40.6	45.8	45.7
Slovak Republic	10.4	61.2	10.0	23.2	13.4	9.9	5.8	6.1	6.7	10.5	12.1
Slovenia	551.6	115.0	207.3	32.9	21.0	13.5	9.9	8.3	7.9	6.2	8.9
Ukraine	4.8	91.2	1,210.0	4,735.0	891.0	376.8	80.2	10.1	20.0	22.7	28.2
Average	155.5	139.1	472.3	553.0	112.1	54.3	30.5	110.9	12.9	9.8	13.9

Source: European Bank for Reconstruction and Development - Country Investment Profiles 2001; Business Central Europe Magazine; Authors' calculations.

Table 3.5   Central government budget balances, 1990 - 2000 (as percent of GDP)

Budget balance	1990	1991	1992	1993	1994	1995	1996	1997	1998	1999	2000
Bulgaria	-4.9	-3.7	-5.2	-10.9	-5.2	47.2	-10.9	-3.9	1.5	1.8	na
Croatia	na	-4.8	-3.9	-0.8	1.9	-0.7	-0.1	-0.9	0.9	-1.8	-3.9
Czech Republic	na	-1.9	-3.1	0.5	-1.3	-1.2	-1.8	-2.2	-1.6	-1.7	-2.3
Estonia	na	5.2	-0.3	-0.6	3.3	0.0	-1.6	2.6	-0.2	-3.0	-2.8
Hungary	0.4	-2.9	-6.8	-5.5	-9.2	-5.5	-1.9	-4.0	-3.7	-3.8	-3.5
Latvia	na	na	-0.8	0.6	-1.9	-2.9	-1.3	1.8	0.1	-3.8	-2.8
Lithuania	-5.4	2.7	0.5	-3.3	-1.7	-1.6	-2.8	-0.7	-3.4	-2.3	-3.3
Poland	3.1	-6.7	-6.7	-3.1	-2.4	-2.4	-2.4	-1.3	-2.4	-2.0	-2.7
Romania	1.0	3.3	-4.6	-0.4	-2.0	-4.1	-4.9	-3.6	-2.8	-2.6	-3.6
Slovak Republic	na	Na	na	-7.0	0.0	-1.6	-4.4	-2.6	-2.7	-1.9	na
Slovenia	-0.3	2.6	0.2	0.3	-0.3	0.0	0.3	-1.2	-0.8	-0.6	1.4
Ukraine	na	Na	-25.4	-16.2	-9.5	-7.4	-4.4	-6.6	-1.9	-1.3	na

Source: European Bank for Reconstruction and Development - Country Investment Profiles 2001; Business Central Europe Magazine; Authors' calculations.

Table 3.6   Current account balances, 1990 - 2000 (percent of GDP)

Current account balance (percent of GDP)	1991	1992	1993	1994	1995	1996	1997	1998	1999	2000
Bulgaria	-5.4	-9.3	-12.8	-2.1	-0.5	1.2	4.3	-0.5	na	-5.8
Croatia	-3.2	3.2	5.6	5.7	-7.7	-5.8	-11.6	-7.1	-7.6	-4.2
Czech Republic	1.2	-1.0	0.3	-0.1	-2.6	-7.4	-6.1	-2.4	-2.0	-3.7
Estonia	na	3.3	1.3	-7.3	-4.4	-9.1	-12.1	-9.2	-5.8	na
Hungary	0.8	0.9	-9.0	-9.4	-5.6	-3.7	-2.1	-4.9	-4.2	-3.7
Latvia	na	1.7	14.4	-0.2	-3.6	-4.2	-6.1	-10.6	-10.2	na
Lithuania	na	10.6	-3.2	-2.2	-10.2	-9.2	-10.2	-12.1	-11.2	na
Poland	-2.6	1.1	-0.7	2.5	4.6	-1.0	-3.1	-4.4	-7.6	-6.2
Romania	-4.5	-7.8	-4.7	-1.7	-4.9	-7.3	-6.2	-7.2	-3.8	-2.5
Slovak Republic	na	na	-4.7	4.6	2.1	-10.6	-9.6	-9.7	-5.5	-3.7
Slovenia	1.0	7.4	1.5	4.0	-0.5	0.2	0.1	-0.8	-3.9	-3.2
Ukraine	-33.1	-2.4	-2.4	-3.1	-3.1	-2.7	-2.7	-3.1	2.7	5.0

Source: European Bank for Reconstruction and Development - Country Investment Profiles 2001; Business Central Europe Magazine; Authors' calculations.

Table 3.7   Exchange rates, 1990 - 2000 (Currency Units per US$)

Exchange rate (/US$)	1990	1991	1992	1993	1994	1995	1996	1997	1998	1999	2000
Bulgaria	na	na	na	na	0.1	0.1	0.2	1.7	1.8	1.8	2.1
Croatia	na	na	0.3	3.6	6.0	5.2	5.4	6.2	6.4	7.1	8.3
Czech Republic	18.0	29.5	28.3	29.2	28.8	26.6	27.1	31.7	32.3	34.6	38.6
Estonia	na	na	12.7	13.2	13.0	11.5	12.0	13.9	14.1	14.8	16.9
Hungary	63.2	74.8	79.0	92.0	105.1	125.7	152.6	186.8	214.5	237.2	282.2
Latvia	na	na	0.7	0.7	0.6	0.5	0.6	0.6	0.6	0.6	0.6
Lithuania	na	na	1.8	4.3	4.0	4.0	4.0	4.0	4.0	4.0	4.0
Poland	1.0	1.1	1.4	1.8	2.3	2.4	2.7	3.3	3.5	4.0	4.4
Romania	24	76	308	760	1,655	2,033	3,083	7,168	11,233	15,338	21,693
Slovak Republic	18.0	29.5	28.3	30.8	32.0	29.7	30.7	33.6	35.2	41.4	46.2
Slovenia	11.3	27.6	81.3	113.2	128.8	118.5	135.4	159.7	166.1	181.8	222.7
Ukraine	na	na	na	0.1	0.3	1.5	1.8	1.9	2.5	4.1	5.4

Source: European Bank for Reconstruction and Development - Country Investment Profiles 2001; Business Central Europe Magazine; Authors' calculations.

Table 3.8   CEE currencies and exchange rate regimes

Country	Currency	Currency code	Exchange rate regime
Bulgaria	Lev	BGL	Currency board (fixed to the euro)
Croatia	Kuna	HRK	Managed float
Czech Republic	Czech Koruna	CZK	Managed float
Estonia	Estonian Kroon	EEK	Currency board (fixed to the euro)
Hungary	Forint	HUF	Pegged to the euro
Latvia	Latvian Lat	LVL	Pegged to the SDR
Lithuania	Litas	LTL	Pegged to the US$
Poland	Zloty	PLN	Float
Romania	Leu	ROL	Managed float
Slovak Republic	Slovak Koruna	SKK	Float
Slovenia	Tolar	SIT	Managed float
Ukraine	Hryvnia	UAH	Float

Source: European Bank for Reconstruction and Development - Country Investment Profiles 2001;
Central Intelligence Agency – The World Factbook 2001.

In summary, the CEE region, as well as the majority of its constituent countries, has made remarkable macroeconomic progress during its decade of transition. Foreign direct investment has certainly played a role in that progress, and should be an even more significant factor in the CEE's economic future, since the macroeconomic and underlying structural reforms, together with the certain expansion of the EU to include most of these countries, should increase the incentive for FDI to flow into CEE nations. The remainder of this chapter summarizes the FDI pattern to date and draws some conclusions about its efficacy in fostering the transition and economic growth.

Regional FDI Pattern

As previously mentioned, data availability restricts the FDI analysis to the 1993 - 2000 time period. Also, initial flows were sporadic and not indicative of rational FDI strategies, so that drawing conclusions from 1990 - 1992 FDI is likely to lead to erroneous conclusions. It is appropriate to begin with a view of global FDI flows prior to and during this period, in order to put CEE FDI into perspective.

Table 3.9   FDI annual average inflow (billions of US$)

FDI inflow (US$ bn)	1985-1995	1997	1998	1999	2000
CEE	3.2	19.2	21.0	23.2	25.4
South, East and Southeast Asia	29.8	98.5	86.0	96.2	137.3
Latin America and the Caribbean	15.3	71.2	83.2	110.3	86.2
Developing countries	50.7	187.4	188.4	222.0	240.2
World	180.3	477.9	692.5	1,075.0	1,270.8

Source: United Nations Conference on Trade and Development, World Investment Report 2001, Author's calculations.

Table 3.9 shows that world FDI increased dramatically during the late 1990s. The annual global inflow of FDI in 2000 increased to US$ 1.270 trillion, compared with US$180 billion during 1985 - 1995. The world's stock of FDI in 2000 accounted for over US$ 6.314 trillion, of which just 18.9 percent flowed into developing nations. Asia, despite its recent economic crisis, remains the biggest recipient of the FDI in the developing world, having attracted over 10 percent of the world's FDI in 2000. The second biggest recipient is the Latin America and Caribbean region, with over 6.7 percent. Central and Eastern Europe attracted only 2 percent of global FDI in 2000. However, this FDI totaled US$ 25.4 billion, representing more than 10 percent of FDI directed to developing countries, even though the CEE represents a much smaller percentage of both developing country population and GDP. Measured in a different way, CEE received approximately 1.7 percent of real GDP in year 2000 FDI.

Therefore, despite the difficult and sometimes unpredictable economic situation in CEE countries during the last decade, the region attracted significant foreign direct investment. Figure 3.2 illustrates the gradual rise of CEE FDI inflows during 1993-2000 from US$ 4.38 billion to US$ 21.50 billion.

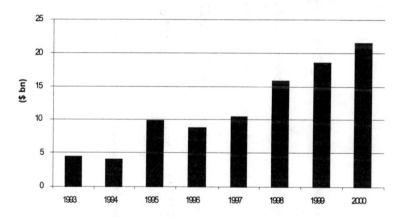

Source: European Bank for Reconstruction and Development – Country's Investment
Profile 2001, Business Central Europe Magazine, Author's calculations.

Figure 3.2   FDI inflow to CEE, 1993 - 2000 (in US$ billion)

The increased FDI inflow during the latter part of decade was probably driven by the more stable economic situation in the region as well as its more dynamic privatization process. Cumulative CEE FDI inflow for 1993 - 2000 equals US$ 93.25 billion, or US$ 589 per capita (see Table 3.10).

Table 3.10 FDI inflow, cumulative inflow and per capita cumulative inflow in CEE

	1993	1994	1995	1996	1997	1998	1999	2000
FDI inflow (US$ billion)	4.38	3.99	9.85	8.76	10.33	15.84	18.60	21.50
FDI cumulative inflow (US$ billion)	4.38	8.37	18.22	26.98	37.31	53.15	71.75	93.25
FDI cumulative inflow per capita (US$)	27.00	51.79	113.03	168.00	232.90	333.44	451.54	589.00

Source: European Bank for Reconstruction and Development – Country's Investment Profile 2001; Business Central Europe Magazine; Authors' calculations.

These aggregate FDI figures, however, obscure the essential fact that 68.52 percent of the US$ 93.25 billion went into three countries Poland (30.76 percent), the Czech Republic (19.77 percent), and Hungary (17.99 percent) that together represent just 37 percent of the region's population and 55 percent of its GDP (see Figure 3.3).

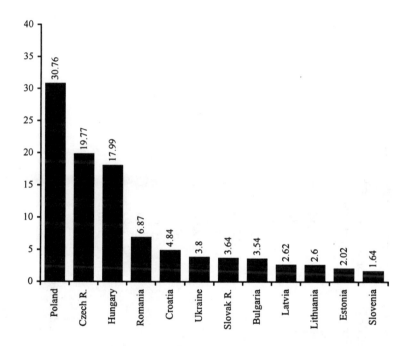

Source: European Bank for Reconstruction and Development – Country's Investment Profile 2001; Business Central Europe Magazine; Author's calculations.

Figure 3.3   Distribution of cumulative FDI inflow in percentages, 1993 - 2000

In dollar terms, these three nations had received US$ 28.68 billion, US$ 18.44 billion, and US$ 16.78 billion, respectively, between 1993 and 2000. These dollar figures are misleading, however, since Poland received less than half as much FDI per capita (US$ 743) as did the Czech Republic (US$ 1,790) or Hungary (US$ 1,678). As a percentage of the GDP in year 2000, Poland received 7.9 percent, the Czech Republic 13.0 percent, and Hungary 13.7 percent in FDI during 1993 - 2000 (see Table 3.11).

Table 3.11 Cumulative FDI breakdown by country, 1993 – 2000

Country	Accumulated FDI (US$ million)	Share in CEE FDI (percent)	Accumulated FDI as a percentage of GDP (2000)	Accumulated FDI per capita (US$)
Bulgaria	3,206	3.44	6.97	390.98
Croatia	4,515	4.84	13.20	1,003.33
Czech Republic	18,442	19.78	13.02	1,788.54
Estonia	1,881	2.02	21.85	1,254.00
Hungary	16,779	17.99	13.72	1,677.90
Latvia	2,447	2.62	23.22	1,019.58
Lithuania	2,428	2.60	15.04	656.22
Poland	28,690	30.77	7.87	743.26
Romania	6,406	6.87	4.58	285.98
Slovak Republic	3,395	3.64	5.58	628.70
Slovenia	1,528	1.64	4.55	764.00
Ukraine	3,545	3.80	2.13	71.91
Totals	93,262	100		

Source: European Bank for Reconstruction and Development – Country's Investment Profile 2001; Business Central Europe Magazine; Authors' calculations.

FDI in the Czech Republic, Hungary, and Poland

Why did these three nations receive the lion's share of FDI inflows to the CEE during the 1990s? First, together with Slovenia, these countries were by far the most prepared to begin competing on international markets. Each country had been able to export some of its products to Western Europe even during the Soviet era, attesting to the efficiency of production and the quality of goods in those sectors. Slovenia's receiving the smallest share (1.64 percent) of 1993 - 2000 CEE FDI despite having perhaps the best such credentials of any country can be explained by the ethnic unrest and violence in the other regions of former Yugoslavia. Foreign investors simply considered Slovenia to be too high a risk given three roughly similar economies that lay out of harm's way.

Second, and by no means least important, were geopolitical considerations. It was clear early in the 1990s that the Czech Republic, Hungary, and Poland would be admitted as a group to the North Atlantic Treaty Organization (NATO). Furthermore, it was obvious that no other country would be offered admission. The stated purpose of adding these nations to NATO in April 1999 was to ensure that any renewal of Soviet aggression stopped well short of the former Iron Curtain, and that these three countries in particular would forever be part of the West, rather than the East. Joining NATO provided potential investors a much more substantial guarantee of the safety of their investments than any other individual country could match.

Third, each of these countries had specific characteristics that indicated a readiness to turn west. The geographic predecessors of the Czech Republic had played an integral role in Western Europe for centuries, for example. More importantly, however, this western culture was due to the relatively recent and never fully accepted inclusion of these countries under Soviet influence. The Ukraine, for example, has suffered (and continues to suffer) from living for generations under a socialist system. One result is that entrepreneurship had thereby been largely eliminated from the culture. In contrast, certain sectors in the Czech Republic, Hungary, and Poland had retained some degree of entrepreneurial activity. For example, Polish farms had never been collectivized. The Czech Republic (1968) and Hungary (1956) had both rebelled enough to have Soviet forces move in to suppress unrest. Poland's Solidarity movement is well documented.

Fourth, Poland and Hungary both passed legislation allowing 100 percent repatriation of profits at market exchange rates, providing the investors with the assurance that any returns from the investment would be available for use. Moreover, all three nations rank high in all of the so-called globalization drivers identified by Koźminski and Yip (2000), including favorable trade policies, favorable FDI rules, likelihood EU admission, freedom from government intervention, legal protection, compatible technical standards, and common marketing regulations. Only Slovenia can compare across the board - in fact, Slovenia outperforms all three of these countries on all globalization drivers except favorable FDI rules, in which it ranks one category behind Hungary and equal to both the Czech Republic and Poland (see Table 3.12).

Koźminski and Yip also identify a set of globalization drivers affecting costs. Poland ranks high in these categories because of its size and shared border with Germany, scoring top marks for global and regional scale economies, sourcing efficiencies, and favorable logistics, though overall infrastructure is problematic. Hungary and the Czech Republic, on the other hand, have very good physical infrastructure (and logistics in the Czech case), but suffer from small size (see Table 3.13).

The remainder of this section describes the temporal patterns, country sources and industry targets of FDI in Poland, the Czech Republic, and Hungary.

Poland

As indicated before, Poland attracted over 30 percent of the CEE's FDI inflow during 1993 - 2000. At US$ 28,690 billion, Poland's aggregate FDI ranks first. However, in *per capita* terms, Poland ranks only seventh, following the Czech Republic, Hungary, Estonia, Latvia, Croatia, and Slovenia, respectively (see Table 3.11). Table 3.14 presents the FDI inflow to Poland in 1993 - 2000. FDI grew steadily from US$ 580 million in 1993 to US$ 9.3 billion during 2000.

Poland's FDI comes mainly from EU countries, with six of ten top investing nations being EU members. According to the Polish Agency for Foreign Investments, by 2000, France had invested most heavily, having invested an accumulated US$ 7.9 billion in Poland. A large share of the French investment resulted from its huge investment in TP SA, the Polish telecommunications company. American investment is a close second to France at US$ 7.35 billion, with Germany, the Netherlands, and Italy rounding out the top five investors. Russian investment in the Polish economy amounted to US$ 1.3 billion, making it the tenth largest investor (see Table 3.15).

Table 3.12   Evaluation of globalization drivers[1]

Country	Favorable trade policies	Favorable FDI rules	Role in regional trade blocs	Freedom from government intervention	Absence of government owned competitors	Legal protection	Compatible technical standards	Common marketing regulations
Germany	*****	*****	*****	****	*****	*****	*****	*****
Hungary	****	****	***	***	****	***	****	*****
Poland	***	***	***	***	***	***	*****	*****
Czech R.	***	***	***(*)	***	***	***	****	*****
Slovakia	**(*)	***	***	**(*)	**(*)	***	*****	*****
Slovenia	****	***	***	***	****	****	*****	*****
Baltic S.	***	***	*	***	****	***	****	****
Romania	***	***	***	****	**	**(*)	***	*****
Bulgaria	***	**	***	**	*	**	***	***
Ukraine	**	*(*)	*(*)	*	*	*(*)	***	*****

Note: *= very low, ***** = very high; ratings vary somewhat by industry.

Source: Kozminski, A.K. and Yip G.S. (eds) (2000).

Table 3.13   Cost globalization drivers[2]

Country	Global scale economies	Regional scale economies	Sourcing efficiencies	Favorable logistics	Good infrastructure (overall)	Financial infra-structure	Physical infra-structure	Business country	Favorable country costs	Technology role
Germany	*****	*****	***	*****	*****	*****	*****	*****	*	*****
Hungary	**	***	***	***	***	***	****	***	***	***
Poland	***(*)	****	****	****	**	***	***	***	***	***
Czech R.	**	***	***	***(*)	*(*)	**(*)	***(*)	***	**(*)	**(**)
Baltic S.	*	**	**	****	**	**	***	***	***	**
Slovakia	**	***	***	***	***	**	***	***	***	**
Slovenia	*(*)	**	***	****	****	***	****	****	**	**(**)
Romania	**	***	***(*)	***	**	**	**	**	***	**
Bulgaria	*	**	**	***	**	*	**	**	***	**(*)
Ukraine	**	***	****	**(*)	*	*	**	**	****	**

Note: * = very low, ***** = very high

Source: Kozminski, A.K. and Yip G.S. (eds) (2000).

Table 3.14   FDI in Poland, 1993 – 2000

	1993	1994	1995	1996	1997	1998	1999	2000
Foreign direct investment inflow (US$ million)	580	542	1,134	2,741	3,041	4,966	6,348	9,338
Foreign direct investment stock (US$ million)	580	1,122	2,256	4,997	8,038	13,004	19,352	28,690
Foreign direct investment per capita (US$)	15	29	58	129	207	336	500	743

Source: European Bank for Reconstruction and Development – Country's Investment Profile 2001; Business Central Europe Magazine; Authors' calculations.

Table 3.15   FDI in Poland by country of origin, 2000 stock

	Country	FDI (in US$ million)	Number of companies that invested over US$ 1 million
1	France	7,901.0	70
2	USA	7,350.3	130
3	Germany	5,903.7	209
4	Netherlands	4,224.9	66
5	Italy	3,417.6	65
6	International	2,296.7	21
7	United Kingdom	2,181.1	35
8	Sweden	2,027.9	53
9	South Korea	1,617.4	5
10	Russia	1,286.4	2

Source: The Polish Agency for Foreign Investment.

As elsewhere in CEE, a large share of Poland's FDI originated from privatization process that accompanied economic transition. With Polish privatization nearly complete, it is useful to draw conclusions about the Polish industry sectors that attracted the most FDI (see Table 3.16).

Table 3.16   Distribution of FDI in Poland across main recipient industries

Industry	FDI (in US$ million)	As a percent of total FDI
Financial services	10,392.7	21
Automotive	5,167.7	10
Food, beverages and tobacco processing	4,961.9	10
Trade and other services	3,962.0	8
Construction	2,490.6	5

Sources: The Polish Agency for Direct Investment; European Bank for Reconstruction and Development 'Country Investment Profile: 2001'; Authors' calculations.

The most attractive industry for foreign investors was the financial sector. Due mostly to the completed bank privatization process and the opening insurance and pension businesses to foreign investors, the financial sector received over US$ 10 billion of accumulated FDI, accounting for 21 percent of total FDI invested in Poland. The main financial sector investors are UniCredito Italiano, Bayersiche Hypo- und Vereinsbank and Citibank. The automotive industry received over 10 percent of Polish FDI inflows at US$ 5.16 billion. The main automotive sector investors are Daewoo, Fiat and General Motors. The food, beverage and tobacco processing industry also received over 10 percent of FDI, or US$ 4.96 billion, with the main investors being Reemstma, Coca-Cola Beverages and Philip Morris. Trade and other services attracted US$ 2.49 billion, 5 percent of the total FDI.

Czech Republic

The Czech Republic received 19.78 percent of FDI inflow in CEE in 1993 - 2000. At an accumulated US$ 18.4 billion, Czech FDI ranks second place in the region, although its US$ 1.8 billion in FDI per capita leads the CEE (see Table 3.17).

Table 3.17   FDI in the Czech Republic, 1993 - 2000

	1993	1995	1996	1997	1998	1999	2000
Foreign direct investment inflow (US$ million)	563	2,526	1,276	1,275	2,641	4,912	4,500
Foreign direct investment stock (US$ million)	563	3,838	5,114	6,398	9,030	13,942	18,442
Foreign direct investment per capita (US$)	55	373	496	621	877	1,354	1,789

Source: European Bank for Reconstruction and Development – Country's Investment Profile 2001; Business Central Europe Magazine; Author's calculations.

Czech FDI came mostly from European countries, especially the Netherlands (US$ 6.4 billion), Germany (US$ 5.7 billion), and Austria (US$ 2.7 billion). American FDI totaled US$ 1.4 billion, with Belgium, France, Switzerland, and Sweden following in rank (see Table 3.18).

Table 3.18   FDI in Czech Republic by country of origin, 2000 stock

	Country	FDI (in US$ million)
1	Netherlands	6,392.5
2	Germany	5,677.6
3	Austria	2,715.5
4	USA	1,388.4
5	United Kingdom	1,018.0
6	Belgium	985.8
7	France	946.2
8	Switzerland	576.6
9	Sweden	386.6
10	Others	2,062.0

Source: CzechInvest – Impact Statement 2001.

Although financial services FDI was strong in the Czech Republic, its recipient industries differed from those in Poland. Among the Czech industries that received the highest level of FDI were trade and repairs (16.8 percent), financial services (16 percent) and the transport and communication sector (10.6 percent) (See Table 3.19).

Table 3.19   Distribution of FDI in Czech Republic across main recipient industries

Industry	FDI in US$ million	As a percent of total FDI
Trade and repairs	3,730.9	16.8
Financial services	3,546.6	16.0
Transport and communication	2,347.0	10.6
Other non-metallic mineral products	1,620.5	7.3
Real estate and other business activities	1,569.4	7.1

Source: CzechInvest – Impact Statement 2001.

Hungary

Hungary received the third-largest FDI inflow in the CEE (US$ 16.8 billion), but ranked second in per capita FDI. In 1993, Hungarian FDI inflows dominated, with Hungarian FDI of over US$ 2.3 billion being more than double the combined inflows to Poland and the Czech Republic. However, unlike the Polish and Czech patterns, Hungarian FDI fell by more than half in 1994 before peaking at US$ 4.4 billion in 1995. Hungarian FDI has decreased every year since then, except for a small increase from US$ 1.56 billion in 1998 to US$ 1.7 billion in 1999. Year 2000 receipts fell to US$ 1.65 billion (see Table 3.20).

Table 3.20   FDI in Hungary, 1993 - 2000

	1993	1995	1996	1997	1998	1999	2000
Foreign direct investment inflow (US$ million)	2,339	4,410	2,280	1,740	1,560	1,700	1,650
Foreign direct investment stock (US$ million)	2,339	7,849	10,129	11,869	13,429	15,129	16,779
Foreign direct investment per capita (US$)	227	769	993	1,175	1,329	1,497	1,677

Source: European Bank for Reconstruction and Development – Country's Investment Profile 2001; Business Central Europe Magazine; Author's calculations.

Like the previous cases, FDI in Hungary came mostly from European Union nations, with Germany providing 28 percent and the Netherlands providing 15.5 percent of FDI. US funds accounted for 12.2 percent of FDI stock in 2000, with Austria (11.7 percent) following closely in fourth place. Other major investors included the United Kingdom, France, Italy, Switzerland, Belgium, and Japan (see Table 3.21).

By far, the lion's share (38.4 percent) of Hungarian FDI flowed into the manufacturing sector. Utilities received nearly 15 percent, with the wholesale/retail trade and repairs sector earning 12.3 percent. Hungarian financial services lagged behind in fourth position, accounting for just 10.9 percent of FDI inflows, as compared to 16 percent in the Czech Republic and 21 percent in Poland (see Table 3.22).

Table 3.21   FDI in Hungary by country of origin, 2000 stock

Country	Percent of total FDI
Germany	28.0
Netherlands	15.5
USA	12.2
Austria	11.7
United Kingdom	6.4
France	6.1
Italy	3.2
Switzerland	2.9
Belgium	2.7
Japan	1.9
Other	9.4

Source: European Bank for Reconstruction and Development – Country's Investment Profile 2001.

Table 3.22   Distribution of FDI in Hungary across main recipient industries, 1998 stock

	As a percent of total FDI
Manufacturing	38.4
Electricity, gas, steam and water supply	14.8
Wholesale, retail trade and repairs	12.3
Financial services	10.9
Real estate, renting and other business activities	9.8

Source: European Bank for Reconstruction and Development – Country's Investment Profile 2001.

Conclusion

Foreign direct investment has played a key role in the transition of CEE economies during the 1990s. In addition to providing the capital needed to modernize plant and equipment, FDI has led to technology transfer in production, as well as in modern business practices. While FDI inflows are increasing at respectable rates in countries such as Poland and the Czech Republic, other once-favored nations like Hungary have seen significant declines in FDI during the latter half of the decade. Moreover, the FDI pattern has been skewed dramatically in favor of those three nations, with other nations receiving very little FDI.

Nations of Central and Eastern Europe require continued and increased FDI to ensure their economic growth. A more detailed analysis of the causes of changing FDI patterns is needed. In the meantime, CEE nations can only work to foster favorable investment environments through continued market-oriented reforms; the creation of sound, well-regulated financial markets; and open, transparent economies.

Notes

1   *Favorable trade policies:* Extent to which the country has favorable trade policies, including both tariff and non-tariff barriers and how these are changing.
Favorable foreign investment rules: Extent to which the country has rules that favor foreign direct investment, including currency regulations, repatriation of capital and foreign ownership.
Role of regional trade blocs: How the country's participation in the trade blocs effects the opportunities for multinational companies.
Freedom from government intervention: Sensitivity of the country's government to foreign dominance of key industries, and response via intervention.
Absence of state-owned competitors: Extent to which industries of interest to foreign MNCs are dominated by government-owned competitors or customers.
Reliable legal protection of contracts, trademarks, and intellectual property: Extent to which contracts, trademarks and intellectual property are protected from imitation.
Compatible technical standards: Extent to which the country uses global technical standards.
Common marketing regulations: Extent to which the country has similar marketing regulations to the rest of the world (for example, rules on television advertising).

2   *Global and regional scale economies:* Extent to which the country has markets that
        can contribute sales volume to MNCs needing to achieve global or regional scale
        economies (is the local market large enough to support a minimum efficient scale
        plant? If not, are there sufficient exports to support a minimum efficient scale
        plant?).
        Sourcing efficiencies: Extent to which the country can provide critical factors of
        production in efficient volumes.
        Favorable logistics: Extent to which the country has favorable logistics
        (transporting goods and services to and within the country) as either a production
        site or market or both.
        Good infrastructure:
        • Financial (banking system, credit, insurance, and so on).
        • Physical (roads, power, communications, and so on).
        • Business (advisory services, investor support, and so on).
        Favorable country costs (including exchange rates):
        • Extent to which the country offers low production costs, taking into account not
          just labor wage costs, but also overhead costs and productivity.
        • Summary statistics on country's labor rates, hourly and with benefits/social
          charges.
        Technology role: Extent to which the country can be used as a base for developing
        technology.

References

Central Intelligence Agency (2001), *The World Factbook*.
CzechInvest (2001), *Impact Statement 2001*.
European Bank for Reconstruction and Development (2001), *Country Investment Profiles*.
Koźmiński, A.K. (1995), 'Lessons from the Restructuring of Post-Communist Enterprises,'
        in D.P. Cushman and S.S. King (eds) *Communicating Organizational Change: A
        Management Perspective*, State University of New York Press, Albany, NY, pp. 311-328.
Koźmiński, A.K. and Yip G.S. (eds) (2000), *Strategies for Central and Eastern Europe*.
        Macmillan, London.
United Nations Council on Trade and Development (2001), *World Investment Report*.

4 Motives and Strategies for Foreign Direct Investment in Central and Eastern Europe

SVETLA TRIFONOVA MARINOVA and MARIN ALEXANDROV MARINOV

Introduction

The countries of Central and Eastern Europe (CEE) are undergoing a process of transformation from centrally planned command economies towards a market orientation. During a period of forty-five years or more, CEE countries were isolated from the rest of the world trying to develop cohesion and interdependence with each other. These countries are now reversing their inward-looking legacy of central planning as they want to benefit from globalization. For CEE countries, the inflows of foreign direct investment (FDI) are of crucial importance for their integration into the world economy as globalization has a positive impact on the volume of FDI.

The process of reintegrating CEE economies into the global marketplace is a challenging task for investors. The potential gains for foreign investors include access to new markets, exploitation of relatively cheap factor inputs, and the acquisition of strategic assets (Quelch, Joachimsthaler and Nueno, 1991; Culpan and Kumar, 1994; Healey, 1994; Tietz, 1994; Haiss and Fink, 1995).

In CEE countries, economic and political instability, together with complex privatization practices, make FDI particularly challenging (Geringer and Herbert, 1989; Lyles and Baird, 1994; Szanyi, 1994). It is by no means ensured, therefore, that motives for undertaking FDI in CEE will be achieved. Neither is it assured that the motives of the host governments and host companies will be met through FDI ventures.

In assessing the prospects for and the impact of FDI, it is critically important to consider the motives and strategies of the foreign investors and to identify the degree to which their motives are achieved and strategies realized (Shapiro, 1987; Beamish, 1988; Holstius, 1990; Hill, 1990; Ring and Van de Ven, 1992; Zajac and Olsen, 1993; Madhok, 1995; Ghauri and Holstius, 1996).

This chapter explores the motives of foreign investors in the CEE and their achievements. This is done for the region consisting of four countries in general, and for each of these countries in particular, namely Bulgaria, Hungary, Poland and Slovenia. These are related to the strategic priorities of the investors and the way they are realized. Some recommendations for foreign investors' behavior in CEE are drawn. Bulgaria has been somewhat slower in encouraging and attracting FDI than the 'tiger' economies of the region (Poland and Hungary). Slovenia is a special case, a small and new country that came into existence in 1991 after the start of the disintegration of former Yugoslavia.

Conceptual Framework

Motives are the key drivers of foreign investors in the FDI process. They can give insight into what investors seeks from the involvement in a new venture. In the context of FDI deals, success or failure often hinges on whether or not investors have realized from the venture the benefits they expected (Porter and Fuller, 1986). Foreign investors want to satisfy their initial motives, although those might undergo changes. Nevertheless, the achievement of the originally stated motives largely determines the outcome of the FDI process in CEE.

Johanson and Vahlne (1977) see learning about the foreign market and closing the psychic distance as major motives for engaging in international joint ventures, and in particular, when the desire for control can motivate acquisitions. Root (1994) has classified motives into two general groups: market-seeking and factor-seeking. Low-cost production-seeking motives can assist investors in an overall global sourcing strategy (Brouthers *et al.*, 1996) and increase their ability for exports (Phongpaichit, 1990). Dunning (1977, 1993) points out that a prime motive for FDI is assumed to be the acquisition and internalization of assets and capabilities that can then be exploited in the marketplace.

Investor Motives for Foreign Direct Investment

Substantial literature exists on the internationalization of enterprises providing theoretical explanations of investors' motives for undertaking FDI. These theories are rooted in trade theory, most notably market imperfections theory, internationalization theory and the eclectic paradigm (see Dunning, 1977; Buckley and Casson, 1988; Buckley, 1988). Classical trade theory explains the existence of international trade in terms of absolute and comparative advantages. While trade theory offers explanations as to why nations trade with each other, it does not provide an explanation for why individual firms engage in FDI. Hymer (1960) proposed that in addition to the search for financial returns, foreign investment is driven by a need to control foreign operations more directly. He posited that multinational companies (MNCs) inherently suffer from disadvantages compared with local competitors when operating in foreign markets (see Hymer, 1960; Caves, 1971). According to this theory, motives for FDI will include building a more intimate knowledge of the market.

A number of studies in CEE (e.g., OECD, 1994; Paliwoda, 1995; Svetlicic and Rojec, 1994; EBRD, 1994) confirm that although there can be four main groups of motives for FDI in that region, these are mostly dominated by market-seeking motives. For example, Gatling (1993) reveals a clear pattern of investors' motives across all CEE countries: to establish a market share in the host market; tap into the regional market; tap into the EU market; and low-cost sourcing. A study in OECD countries (OECD, 1994) shows that motives have been ranked by 162 companies investing in CEE as follows: access to large domestic markets; gaining market share; low cost of production; and source of raw materials. Essentially, the acquisition of market assets is a means of reducing psychic distance between the investment country and the investor's home base.

This chapter develops the approach suggested by Dunning and Rojec (1994) examining the strategic assets sought by investors in the FDI process. The assets sought by foreign investors can be identified as physical assets (including economic ones), human assets, and marketing assets (Marinova *et al.*, 1997).

Foreign Direct Investment in Central and Eastern Europe

FDI can potentially play a vital role in the globalization process of CEE companies. There has been a constant trend of increases in FDI inflows in the region since 1989. In 1996, due to various reasons, partly due to the relative slowdown in foreign privatization transactions, FDI into CEE declined to approximately US$ 11 billion compared to US$ 13 billion in 1995.

The cumulative inflow of FDI-based capital into CEE in the period 1990 - 1998 was estimated at approximately US$ 78 billion. On the whole, all CEE economies attracted substantially less FDI than the other regions in the world (e.g., South-East Asia and South America). For example, the cumulative FDI inflow in the period 1991 - 1996 was less than 4 percent of the GDP in CEE countries. For the East Asian developing countries, the respective figure in the same period was 13 percent.

Two major reasons, related to the supply and demand side of foreign investment, account for the insignificant FDI inflow in CEE countries (Sinn and Weichenrieder, 1997). From the investors' point of view, the high level of insecurity and risk associated with investing in CEE has increased with the return to power of former communist parties in a number of CEE countries. EU restrictions on trade and 'sensitive industrial sectors' have also contributed to the discouragement of FDI in CEE. On the other hand, from the demand side, certain CEE countries have demonstrated resistance to FDI inflows, fearing political and economic dependability on other nations.

Table 4.1   FDI inflows into CEE countries in the period 1989 - 1999

Country	Cumulative FDI inflows (US$ billion)	Cumulative FDI inflows per capita (US$)	Percentage FDI inflows to GDP in 1995
Bulgaria	2.3	285	0.8
Czech Republic	17.5	1,720	5.6
Estonia	2.5	1,950	7.5
Hungary	19.3	1,990	10.2
Latvia	3.9	1,695	2.3
Lithuania	2.1	595	0.9
Poland	28.0	740	1.3
Romania	5.4	240	1.0
Slovakia	2.1	395	1.1
Slovenia	3.0	1,590	10.0
Ukraine	3.2	60	0.5

Sources: Business Central Europe (2001), UN/ECE, World Bank, EBRD.

According to the values of cumulative FDI inflows, FDI inflows per capita, and percentage FDI inflows to GDP, CEE countries are divided into two groups by most international financial institutions. The group of countries more advanced in transition consists of the Czech Republic, Hungary,

Estonia, Poland, Slovakia, Croatia, Latvia, Slovenia and Lithuania. All of the rest from the CEE region are in the group of less advanced transition countries. Across the countries more advanced in transition FDI cumulative inflows per capita and FDI as a percentage of GDP are higher than in the rest of the countries in the region (see Table 4.1).

The geographical, sectoral, in economic terms and temporal distribution of FDI in CEE has been uneven. In value terms Hungary is in the lead, followed by Estonia and the Czech Republic. Most recently, there has been a reverse trend in FDI in Hungary, while Poland and the Czech Republic have become the major attractions for foreign investors.

In terms of country-of-origin, Austria, Germany and the United States have been by far the major investors accounting for more than 70 percent of the investment into CEE economies in 1994 and for almost two thirds of the cumulative investment inflow in the region in the period 1989-1998 (Business Central Europe, 2001). In terms of sectoral composition, in the early years of transition, a large share of FDI was put in sectors focused on supplying the domestic market; for example, trade and distribution sectors, manufacturing, food and beverage industries and the tobacco processing industry (Hunya and Stankowsky, 1996).

Privatization of former state-owned companies and greenfield investments have both been used by foreign investors in CEE as modes of entry. Privatization through FDI accounts for more than 60 per cent of the cumulative FDI inflow in CEE in the period 1989-1996 (Rolfe and Doupnik, 1996; Sinn and Weichenrieder, 1997).

The following common patterns of FDI in the CEE region can be defined:

- FDI inflows have been higher in countries more advanced in their transition process;
- The attitude of host governments has largely influenced the mode of entry and timing of FDI;
- The bulk of FDI has come from neighboring countries or those with historical, cultural and business linkages with CEE countries;
- FDI has been largely motivated by the opportunity to gain a first mover advantage in CEE markets.

Research Methodology

The data have been gathered through fieldwork in Bulgaria, Hungary, Poland, and Slovenia as a part of a two-year international research project funded by the European Commission. In the first phase, quantitative data were collected. Case studies were developed in the four countries. They examined the experience of FDI companies with different forms of ownership, consisting of firms created or privatized through foreign capital.

The main purpose of the FDI case studies has been to investigate foreign investment motives and achievement issues and to identify obstacles and benefits experienced by the researched firms. Between five and seven face-to-face interviews were conducted with CEOs and functional managers in each FDI company.

The second phase of the project started with analyzing the results from the case studies followed by the creation of a structured questionnaire. The questionnaire was designed to study a number of issues relating to the macro and micro-elements of the business environment and their impact on the motives of the foreign investors in the FDI companies. The degree of motive achievement was also assessed. The questionnaire was pilot tested in each country and changes were made to its content. It was used in three subsequent mail surveys.

The third phase represented mail surveys and personal interviews. In each country, a sample was created to be representative among other sets of criteria also in terms of flow and stock of FDI, both for participation in privatization and greenfield investment. The questionnaires were mailed in three waves to CEOs and functional managers (expatriate and local) in each country. In some cases, personal interviews were undertaken, mainly in Bulgaria.

Research data were tested separately for non-response bias. The tests showed no systematic differences for FDI companies in the four countries by type of foreign investment (privatization or greenfield), industry sector, and ownership structure (fully or partly foreign owned). The slight tendency for marginally better responses from larger companies reflects their greater importance and influence in the economies of the respective countries.

Analysis of Results

The motives of foreign investors for investing in the CEE region as a whole and in the individual countries studied are presented in Table 4.2 and Table 4.3, respectively.

As most important motives for investing in the CEE region, investors point out the opportunity for building a long-term position in that market.

This suggests that most of the investors do not view CEE as a market, offering them 'cherry picking' in the short run. Investors perceive the region with potential for performing business operations in the long run that adds a new dimension to the internationalization and globalization strategies of investing companies.

The economic, financial and political turbulence of the CEE markets and the relatively lower purchasing power of the population, compared to Western standards, do not appear to be a deterrent for the commitment of investors to entrench in the region and have a long-lasting presence there. This also shows that local politicians and media fears of short-term profit appetite of investors in CEE can be hardly justified. If this motive is further compared to 'taking advantage of government grants and tax concessions' ranking last in importance, investors' drive to establish themselves in the region seems not only pioneering, but underlines their willingness to work in CEE in spite of tax and grants relief not being in place. That is largely valid for Bulgaria, followed by Poland, then Hungary and Slovenia. In the whole CEE region the degree of achievement of this motive has been low, especially in Poland and Slovenia.

Table 4.2   Investor motives for investing in the CEE region

Investor Motives for Investing in the CEE Region	Importance (Mean*) (N=217)	Achievement (Mean*) (N=196)
Gaining access to the domestic markets	2.60	2.57
Using CEE countries to as a gateway to provide access to other markets in the region	2.22	1.90
Taking advantage of low labor costs	2.48	2.37
Taking advantage of skilled labor force	2.49	2.44
Taking advantage of raw material sources	1.70	1.67
Taking advantage of government grants and tax concessions	1.86	1.78
Using the opportunity to make good short-term profits	2.08	2.01
Exploring the opportunity to build a long-term position in the market	2.79	2.31

* Means are calculated on a three-point scale. Results are significant at .05.

Table 4.3   Importance (A) and achievement (B) of investor motives

Investor Motives	Bulgaria Mean* (Number) S.D.		Hungary Mean* (Number) S.D.		Poland Mean* (Number) S.D.		Slovenia Mean* (Number) S.D.	
	A	B	A	B	A	B	A	B
Access to market	2.76	2.85	2.48	2.70	2.86	2.40	1.19	2.16
	(41)	(41)	(90)	(90)	(69)	(68)	(32)	(32)
	.5376	.4220	.5850	.4558	.3546	.5502	.6445	.8839
Gateway to the region	1.85	2.00	2.23	1.91	2.46	1.82	2.16	1.91
	(41)	(41)	(88)	(87)	(67)	(65)	(32)	(32)
	.7925	.7746	.7067	.6404	.6815	.5560	.7666	.8561
Labor costs	1.93	2.10	2.60	2.51	2.72	2.51	2.31	2.07
	(41)	(41)	(92)	(89)	(71)	(69)	(32)	(32)
	.8772	.9697	.6123	.6053	.5394	.5847	.7378	.7594
Skilled labor	2.34	2.76	2.44	2.34	2.66	2.27	2.53	2.72
	(41)	(41)	(91)	(90)	(69)	(68)	(32)	(32)
	.8249	4348	.6533	.5831	.5376	.5630	.8713	.6342
Raw materials	1.29	1.41	1.79	1.69	2.06	1.75	1.25	1.78
	(41)	(41)	(85)	(84)	(65)	(61)	(32)	(32)
	.5120	.7062	.7574	.5803	.6818	.5673	.4399	.7507
Tax concessions	1.02	1.02	2.11	2.08	2.21	1.71	1.43	2.04
	(41)	(41)	(90)	(90)	(70)	(66)	(32)	(32)
	.1562	.1562	.7256	.7378	.8146	.6740	.6690	.8608
Short-term profits	2.51	2.47	1.89	2.00	2.21	1.95	1.81	1.59
	(41)	(41)	(90)	(89)	(66)	(63)	(32)	(32)
	.5967	.6363	.7256	.6571	.6449	.6332	.7387	.7121
Long-term opportunities	3.00	2.93	2.75	2.39	2.86	1.14	2.47	1.69
	(41)	(41)	(89)	(88)	(71)	(65)	(32)	(32)
	.0000	.3457	.5283	.5956	.4241	.4961	.5671	.7378

* Means are calculated on a three-point scale. Results are significant at .05.

In compliance with other studies mentioned above, the market-seeking motives of investors in the CEE region also rank high. This is mostly true for access to the local domestic markets, which have been largely underdeveloped and protected within the boundaries of the former Council for Mutual Economic Assistance (CMEA). These markets offer opportunities not only for overall development and expansion, but also for creating new market segments with spurring consumer demand. Some of the domestic markets, especially the Polish, represent a large growth potential for investors in terms of size and growth rate. The Hungarian and Bulgarian markets are smaller than the Polish, however the Hungarian market consists of customers with relatively high purchasing power for the CEE region. Some East Asian companies, like the South Korean Daewoo and Japanese Suzuki, find CEE an excellent entry platform to the Western European, Russian, Middle East and all CEE markets. The motive for getting access to adjacent markets is highest in priority for Poland, followed by Bulgaria and Hungary, whereas strangely enough, in Slovenia it is with almost no significance.

Third and fourth ranked motives related to the labor characteristics of the region, namely, the opportunity for access to skilled labor that can bring the gains of low labor costs. These investor motives for tapping into CEE reveal one of the major advantages of the region its human potential. International comparisons of educational and training systems rank those of the former Soviet Bloc countries among the best in the world.

Communist regimes have always stressed the need for developing individual intellectual power. They did their best to get rid of illiteracy and to educate their nations according to high educational standards. That effort resulted in a highly educated population, with highly respected technical expertise and creativity. However, as the overall economic development and living standards of CEE have remained far behind those of the West, labor costs are still very low. This provides enormous opportunity for foreign investors to reduce the overall costs of production and the unit costs of the product. Labor motives have proved to be very important for investing in Poland and Hungary, and to some extent in Slovenia. However, although not a highly rated motive for Bulgaria, in terms of its achievement, investors are happiest with the skilled labor force in Bulgaria.

If the initial investor motives for investing in CEE are compared with the degree of their achievement, it seems that investors have been mostly satisfied with the access they could gain to the domestic markets. Obviously, the international market experience of investors together with local support and well managed relationships have provided them an exciting role in the CEE market.

Foreign investors think they have also greatly achieved the benefits they expected from the human capital in CEE, not only in terms of lower labor costs, but as far as the utilization of knowledge and skills is concerned. It is worth mentioning that the competition for jobs with foreign investment companies has become very severe due to the high level of unemployment, favorable payment conditions and feeling of well being offered by such companies. In turn, CEE employees try to offer investors knowledge, skills and expertise if not always commitment. It is interesting to note that the extent of achieving the first most important motive of foreign investors the opportunity to build long-term position in the market has not wholly matched the expectations of the investors. That can be a result of underestimating the conditions and impediments in the region's markets, as well as not being where investors expect to go because of growing competition, lack of government support, economic difficulties, and the loss of first mover advantages.

Table 4.4   Investor motives for investing in a particular CEE company

Investor Motives for Investing in a Particular CEE Company	Importance (Mean) (N=211)	Achievement (Mean) (N=198)
To use the firm's existing distribution network	1.99	1.95
To use the business relationships the firm already has in the domestic and CEE markets	2.22	2.22
To explore the domestic reputation of the firm and/or its existing brands	2.09	2.19
To use the physical resources of the firm	2.08	2.09
To use the human resources and expertise of the firm	2.39	2.45
To use the technological assets of the firm	1.84	1.94
To rationalize its production operations	1.81	1.87
To improve the efficiency of its operations	2.18	2.01
To explore the potential to market the firm's products in the investor's home market	1.76	1.70

* Means are calculated on a three-point scale. Results are significant at .01.

Table 4.5 **Importance (A) and achievement (B) of investor motives in a particular company**

Investor Motives for Investing in a Particular Company	Bulgaria Mean* (Number) S.D.		Hungary Mean* (Number) S.D.		Poland Mean* (Number) S.D.		Slovenia Mean* (Number) S.D.	
	A	B	A	B	A	B	A	B
Using the distribution network	1.59	1.65	2.00	2.12	2.02	1.89	2.47	2.03
	(37)	(37)	(80)	(76)	(59)	(54)	(32)	(29)
	.8887	.7623	.8715	.7297	.8609	.7689	.6148	.8230
Using the relationships of the host company	2.62	2.54	2.23	2.22	2.13	2.07	1.91	2.10
	(37)	(37)	(79)	(77)	(60)	(54)	(32)	(28)
	.5940	.5575	.7152	.6412	.8329	.5208	.7771	.8751
Domestic reputation of the company	2.11	2.62	2.11	2.17	2.10	2.07	2.05	1.97
	(37)	(37)	(79)	(78)	(61)	(58)	(32)	(30)
	.9656	.5452	.7843	.6726	.8889	.8348	.9112	.8899
Physical resources	2.05	2.03	2.04	2.05	2.00	2.11	2.41	2.02
	(37)	(370	(79)	(75)	(59)	(54)	(32)	(30)
	.9112	.9276	.7586	.6757	.8305	.7687	.6652	.7279
Human resources	2.67	2.59	2.58	2.40	2.51	2.42	1.35	2.50
	(37)	(37)	(81)	(78)	(63)	(60)	(31)	(30)
	.4746	.5507	.5887	.5886	.6690	.7200	.6607	.7311
Technological assets	2.03	2.00	1.89	1.97	1.95	1.90	1.29	1.87
	(37)	(37)	(78)	(76)	(59)	(51)	(31)	(30)
	.8971	.9129	.7488	.6527	.8184	.7281	.5287	.7761
To rationalize production	1.73	1.68	1.88	1.93	1.82	1.83	1.73	2.07
	(37)	(37)	(78)	(75)	(57)	(52)	(30)	(30)
	.7691	.8516	.8055	.7229	.8477	.8336	.6915	.8277
Improve efficiency	1.70	1.75	2.44	2.26	2.18	2.02	2.09	1.66
	(37)	(37)	(79)	(77)	(60)	(55)	(31)	(29)
	.8454	.9251	.7116	.6570	.8129	.7575	.5975	.7689
Re-import potential	1.62	1.54	1.75	1.75	1.85	1.75	2.00	1.73
	(37)	(37)	(72)	(67)	(60)	(51)	(31)	(30)
	.9235	.8691	.8517	.7852	.8796	.8206	1.000	.7397

* Means are calculated on a three-point scale. Results are significant at .05.

Table 4.4 presents the motives of investors for investing in a particular company as an average for the CEE region, while Table 4.5 gives the data for each of the countries researched.

When considering a specific company as an investment target, foreign investors have largely focused on the use of the human resources and expertise of the firm, its business relationships in the CEE region and in any local country market, and on efficiency improvement gains. It is confirmed once again that the wealth of the CEE nations is their human capital that can make the difference between companies within one and the same industry. In choosing a host company to invest in, foreign investors have mostly been interested in the skilled workforce. Investors have been aware that the initial investment in training the workforce need not be substantial, but rather directed to encouraging responsibility and decision-making capabilities, marketing and management skills, and entrepreneurial thinking. Experience shows that by far the most successful FDI in CEE are those that have managed to incorporate the local employees into the innovation, product and marketing strategy design and implementation of the foreign investment ventures. The technical expertise is available, but it has to be gradually tuned to using new advanced technologies. This goal has been evaluated as greatly achieved in all the four countries, even surpassing the mean for initial motives. That research result further supports the understanding that if the local labor force has been carefully used and directed, foreign investors can enjoy low-cost, highly skilled and committed workforce. In some privatization deals with FDI that imply restrictions on layoffs, problems between the investor and local staff have appeared when the investor has attempted to trim down the company in a drive to make it leaner and more efficient.

Another very important goal considered by foreign investors in their choice of host company is the potential for using the domestic and CEE business relationships of the host firm. This motive is much more valid for acquisitions of former state-owned enterprises and for different types of joint ventures, than for greenfield, wholly-owned subsidiaries. It should be mentioned that relationships and networks in CEE are of great importance for establishing and running a business. In many cases, there are old and new networks that have intertwined with government and political interests, the in-depth knowledge of which and of the ways they can contribute to the success/failure of a foreign investment venture in CEE can be crucial for the investor. That motive has been most important for investing in specific companies in Bulgaria, and to a lesser extent in Hungary and Poland. Surprisingly, the degree of achievement of this motive is exactly corresponding to the mean of its importance. It can be suggested that on the one hand foreign investors have been mostly well aware not only of the significance of relationships, but have also tried to make the best use of them. On the other hand, local companies receiving FDI, as well as consulting organizations, have helped investors find their way in the maze of local relationships. Data show that although investors have been very keen in achieving increased efficiency, they have done it on an average basis far less than expected. This has been mostly true for Slovenia. This may be partly due to an irrational organization of production operations, outdated technology or lack of overall strategy for achieving this motive. Investors report greater achievement than initially envisaged exploring the domestic reputation of the firm and its existing brands. This is valid mostly for Bulgaria and Hungary. That is supposed to be more significant for companies different from greenfield operations. The phenomenon is much in line with the rise of nationalism, local pride and consumer protectionism feelings in the post-communist countries. It also speaks about the need for keeping local brands and sustaining local companies' reputation as a part of the overall investment strategy. This is mostly true for investment operations targeting the local (country) or regional (CEE) markets. Data show that this is with far less significance and importance of achievement if the foreign investor targets export markets own or third ones. In such cases, it is mostly the investor's own brands and reputation that are most important.

By contrast, the access to the physical resources of the firm and its technological assets has been rated low in significance by foreign investors across the CEE region with the exception of Slovenia. It is largely determined by the perception of most CEE technologies as of lower quality and outdated by Western standards. However, the achievement of these goals has been according to the expectations or even higher. It appears that although technological level in CEE was lower than in the industrialized countries, many of the former state-owned companies, especially those in Poland and Hungary, possessed relatively good technologies that, combined with more efforts in product quality improvement, met the requirements of the local consumers.

Strategic Priorities and Approaches of FDI Companies in CEE

Investors Strategic Priorities

In compliance with the motives of foreign investors, data show that the strategic priority of FDI companies in the CEE region for investing in each country in the past was long-term market positioning. Therefore, investors describing long-term market positioning in the CEE as a major motive have designed and implemented a strategy for achieving that motive. That is confirmed for the four countries studied.

Only in Slovenia companies investing for the benefits of labor costs and looking for long-term benefits focused on survival issues. The major priority of FDI companies for the future is again long-term market positioning, but the percentages have risen significantly. Very few of the firms focus on survival strategies. The results are consistent with the attempts of foreign investors to step firmly in the four CEE countries to stay there in the long run.

When comparing the motives for investing in individual companies with the strategy developed and applied, the strategic priority of the investors in the last two years was predominantly long-term market positioning. However, in Slovenia investors who were seeking to use the domestic reputation of the acquired firm and to improve efficiency through acquisition were mostly with survival strategy. The strategic priorities for the next two years are, again, dominated by long-term positioning in the market. Those results confirm that FDI has mostly come to specific CEE companies with a long-term vision and a strategic interest in developing the companies.

Approaches of Strategy Implementation

The way of strategy implementation has been studied in terms of cost reduction and efficiency, expanding the total market and attacking selected market segments. During the last two years the long-term market position of companies investing in Hungary, Poland and Bulgaria was mostly achieved through expanding the total market. This was related to the degree of market development and the attempts of companies to get the benefits of expanding markets. Many firms have realized they could set prices that the markets could stand in as many market segments as possible. Attracting more customers was also a question of building and keeping the competitive position in the country marketplace.

In Slovenia, the case was somewhat different. FDI companies tried to achieve survival through cost reduction and efficiency. This may, to some extent, be due to the relatively higher labor cost of producing in Slovenia compared to the other three CEE countries. For the next two years, the foreign investors in two of the four countries Poland and Hungary have decided to preserve the predominant way of strategy implementation existing in the last two years. This speaks about the big potential offered by the markets in those two countries in terms of size (mostly valid for Poland) and of potential increase of purchasing power and overall economic recovery.

In Bulgaria, in the next two years, due to the difficulties in the macroenvironment and the reduced purchasing power of consumers, the major way of strategy implementation is thought to be winning market share from competitors for establishing and maintaining long-term market position. That implies market tensions and increased competition not only between foreign-owned and domestically-owned companies but also among FDI companies that are much better off compared to their local rivals. FDI companies in Slovenia plan to move closer to the strategic characteristics of their counterparts and competitors in Hungary and Poland.

Marketing Objectives

The strategic objectives of FDI companies in CEE translate into marketing objectives that define the goals FDI firms want to achieve in the marketplace. Those are supposed to be in compliance with the motives of foreign investors. The marketing objectives of foreign investors in CEE and by country as a percentage of all companies studied are presented in Table 4.6.

One of the major motives of foreign investors in the CEE is gaining access to local markets. It relates to the marketing objective dominant in the region – 'to achieve steady sales growth', supported by 67.9 percent of all companies researched.

Table 4.6   Marketing objectives of FDI companies in CEE

Marketing Objectives	Percentage in CEE	Percentage in Bulgaria	Percentage in Hungary	Percentage in Poland	Percentage in Slovenia
To Achieve Steady Sales Growth	67.9	68.3	57.2	81.8	60.6
To Defend Current Position	18.0	4.9	28.3	8.3	27.3
To Dominate the Market	14.1	26.8	14.5	9.9	12.1

Statistically significant at .000.

Most FDI companies in Poland (81.8 percent), 68.3 percent of FDI firms in Bulgaria, 60 percent of those in Slovenia and more than half of all studied in Hungary state that they want to achieve steady sales growth. That objective is also supported by the motive for achieving long-term presence in CEE. Although only 18 percent of all FDI companies try to defend their current position, the percentage is significantly higher for Hungary and Slovenia.

That can be explained with the strong presence of FDI in the economies of those two countries that are relatively small in terms of market size. Meanwhile, the competition FDI companies face there is much stronger and constantly growing, forcing some firms into a defensive strategy. About 14 percent of all FDI companies direct their efforts to dominating the market. That percentage is significantly higher for Bulgaria where a number of FDI companies operate in a virtual monopoly or duopoly (Marinov and Marinova, 1997). That is especially valid for former state-owned companies privatized through FDI.

Approaches to Market

Marketing objectives are achieved through various approaches to the market. The most important approaches for the CEE region appear to be attacking the whole market, attacking selected market segments and targeting individual customers. About sixty percent of all FDI companies studied reported that they apply targeting selected market segments as a major approach to the market. It allows them not only to increase their presence in selected market segments, but also to expand the whole market through developing new, previously undefined segments and penetrating existing ones. This approach is most important for Bulgaria, followed by Hungary, then by Slovenia.

The big potential of the Polish market in terms of market size and growth rate makes FDI companies there (about 30 percent of all Polish companies) seriously consider attacking the whole market. Individual customers are targeted mostly in Poland, Hungary and Slovenia where the markets are much more advanced, compared to the market in Bulgaria.

Product and Branding Strategies

Data show that more than a half of the FDI companies in applying their approach to the market think the quality of their product compared to that of major competitors is about the same. The percentage for Bulgaria is much higher more than 70 percent of the firms studied. About 40 percent of the companies with FDI in Hungary, Poland and Slovenia agree that they have better quality products. Offering products of better quality shows the degree to which customers realize the need for such and their ability to buy them due to higher purchasing power.

More than 58 percent of all respondents use the same prices as their major competitors. At the same time, more than 40 per cent of the FDI firms in Bulgaria price their products lower than their competitors, while that value is much less for the other three countries (for Poland it is 4 times smaller). Hence, in Bulgaria FDI companies go with product quality almost the same or higher than that of competitors, but price the same or lower.

In Slovenia and Poland, FDI companies offer predominantly higher product quality, charging the same or higher price.

In terms of product/service offered by FDI companies more than two thirds of them for the whole region offer superior service for their product aiming at building closer relationships with customers. This is mostly true for Hungary (89 percent of all companies studied), followed by Bulgaria 73 percent, and Poland 68 percent. This seems not very important for FDI companies in Slovenia.

The basic approach to the product/service used by 69 percent of all FDI companies in CEE is product/service modification in accordance to different market needs and wants. In Bulgaria, that approach is valid for 93 percent of all the respondents. For Poland and Hungary, it is true for about two thirds of all FDI firms in each country. By contrast, only 34 percent of FDI companies in Slovenia apply the above approach to products/services offered. Next in significance comes the product/service customization to meet the requirements of individual target customers 65 percent of the companies in CEE region, mostly adopted by FDI companies in Slovenia.

More than seventy per cent of all respondents in the region focus on investing in the creation of strong and well recognized brands in the minds of customers. That seems to be of utmost importance for Bulgaria and Poland, where product and brand sensitivity is higher and customers demonstrate trust in company reputation. In new product/brand development, 78 percent of FDI companies in CEE actively develop new products/brands to lead and dominate the market. This is again more true for Bulgaria and Poland rather than for Hungary and Slovenia.

Pricing Strategies

Almost two thirds of the FDI companies in CEE set prices that the market is prepared to pay. This pricing strategy is adopted by 83 percent of the studied FDI firms in Bulgaria and 72 percent in Hungary. This accounts for higher sensitivity of Bulgarian and Hungarian markets to pricing than those in Poland and Slovenia.

Cost plus pricing on the basis of production cost plus a fixed margin allowing for profit is pursued by 40 percent of the studied FDI companies in CEE. This pricing is more typical for the companies in Bulgaria (58 percent) and Poland (54 percent) than for those in Slovenia (44 percent). It is least applied by FDI companies in Hungary (only 23 percent). Premium pricing is used by 33.5 percent of the researched FDI companies in CEE. This is particularly true for Poland (59 percent), less so for Hungary (32 percent). By contrast only 15 percent of FDI companies in Slovenia and 12 percent in Bulgaria charge more for their products because they offer higher customer value compared to the products of the competitors. This again emphasizes the higher purchasing power of Hungarian and Polish customers compared to the Bulgarian as well as the more sophisticated customer expectations in Hungary and Poland.

Distribution Strategies

Most of FDI companies in CEE predominantly distribute their products directly to customers. Seventy per cent of the companies in the whole region apply this approach. Next in importance is the distribution on the basis of special relations with distributors and building one's own distribution network. This is more significant for the companies in Bulgaria and Poland, while for Hungary and Slovenia it is not a priority.

Promotion Strategies

Companies with FDI use a variety of promotional forms that are almost evenly spread. Amongst them direct marketing is especially stressed in Bulgaria and Poland whereas in Hungary and Slovenia it is not very much preferred. Second factor in significance is public relations. Public relations is mostly applied in Bulgaria and Poland. Third in importance is media advertising, being much favored in Bulgaria and Hungary.

Competitive Advantage

When analyzing the achievement of their motives and the success of their strategic approaches in CEE, FDI companies focus on the competitive edges they have established in Bulgaria, Poland, Hungary, and Slovenia (see Table 4.7).

A high percentage of companies from Bulgaria, Hungary and Poland believe they have competitive edge in company and/or brand reputation, rating first in Bulgaria and second in Hungary and Poland. This is much in line with the high brand sensitivity of customers in those countries. It is also directly related to the product/brand strategy of FDI companies there already discussed.

Table 4.7   Percentage of FDI companies in CEE admitting having a competitive advantage

Competitive Advantage	Percent in CEE	Percent in Bulgaria	Percent in Hungary	Percent in Poland	Percent in Slovenia
Company and/or Brand Reputation	37.2	39.1	36.9	34.5	26.2
Product Performance	34.8	33.1	35.8	32.6	29.2
Technical Product Quality	34.2	24.4	39.8	36.1	26.5
Close Links with Customers	31.8	29.4	34.2	33.1	27.8
Understanding of Customer Needs	31.0	28.8	36.4	31.2	28.0
Competitive Pricing Based on Cost Advantage	26.2	38.9	26.4	29.3	32.1

Statistically significant at .001.

More than one third of FDI companies in Bulgaria, Hungary and Poland believe they have competitive advantage in terms of product/service performance, closely related to product quality coming first for Hungarian and Polish FDI companies. This competitive edge, although smaller in percentage terms, ranks second for Slovenian companies with FDI.

It has been well recognized that relationships play a major role in the business environment and operation in CEE. Hence, establishing and maintaining close relationships with customers is stated to be of utmost importance for Hungary and Poland, less important for the other two countries. The advanced development of the Hungarian market and the experience gained by FDI companies there shows that highest percentage of those firms have competitive advantage in understanding customer needs and wants.

Not surprisingly competitive pricing is the most important edge for FDI companies in Bulgaria underlying the severe restrictions of the low purchasing power of the population in that country.

Marketing Strategy Recommendations for Foreign Investors

Competitive Advantage

The analysis of the literature on foreign investment in CEE advocates that a clear focus on *cost leadership* is the most important competitive advantage in the present business environment in the region (see for example, Nowak, 1996; Stara, 1994). Research findings of the present study also support this strategic marketing approach.

The low purchasing power of the average customer in CEE will not reach the Western level in the foreseeable future. In some already competitive markets for consumer goods in the CEE, as the ones producing fast moving consumer goods (FMCG), *quality advantage* can also be of significant importance (Marinov and Marinova, 1997).

Focus and Features of Marketing Strategies

Marketing strategies of foreign investors should be mostly focused on *differentiation* through separate strategy development (Douglas and Wind, 1987) for each CEE country. This means separate positioning and segmentation and marketing mix development for every country. Developing separate marketing strategy is justified by the dynamic divergence processes taking place in the region with constantly increasing differences in political, economic, and socio-cultural aspects.

The divergence process for the region can be interpreted as a precondition for the convergence towards Western economies of the countries more advanced in their transition to market. This can create conditions for adopting Western-like approaches to marketing strategy. development of foreign investors in the CEE countries.

Market penetration strategy with current products into current markets is most appropriate for CEE taking into consideration the technological gap that existed between the West and the former Soviet Bloc countries, and the present low purchasing power of the average customer in the transition economies. Timing of market entry through foreign investment would bring more benefits if combined with the first mover advantage. This is understandable as competition from local firms is low and many opportunities can be found in all industry sectors, especially in services.

Marketing Mix Strategic Characteristics

Products and packaging should differentiate by country as mentioned above. The products offered should not be the last word of technology. As CEE customers are technically minded their expectations for products are that they should be exceedingly reliable. Because of the legacy from the communist past when virtually no product servicing was available, CEE expect to buy products needing as little servicing as possible. Similar customer characteristics have been previously observed in developing markets from other parts of the world (Simon-Millar, 1984).

Product development has to follow the product selection strategic approach. Therefore, Western products should be adapted to local needs, wants, and expectations in various countries. Brand awareness and brand recognition of both local and Western brands are low. Because of the increasing strong nationalism significant adaptation of Western brands produced in CEE region is advisable.

Pricing strategies supporting the best achievement of preset motives of foreign investors can be summarized as 'what the market can stand'. On the whole low prices are suitable for large market segments. Premium prices for the high-end market segments can be charged bearing in mind its very limited size. Country-of-origin effects in relation to product and brand name although significant at present (Nowak, 1996) are constantly becoming less important reducing the opportunities for premium pricing.

Western promotion approaches need adaptation to the CEE context with the input of local experts under the supervision of expatriate marketers. The adaptation should be in aspects of content and form of presentation. In content terms, the advertisement should be informative rather than persuasive. Word of mouth, networking and relationships can play crucial roles in the successful implementation of promotional strategies in CEE.

Distribution should be done through establishing direct control of channels or through designing and developing of one's own distribution network. The major aim in implementing distribution in CEE has to be performed with low cost and aiming at high cost-efficiency.

References

Beamish, P. (1988), *Multinational Joint Ventures in Developing Countries*, London and New York: Routledge.

Brouthers, L., Werner, S. and Wilkinson, T. (1996), 'The Aggregate Impact of Firms' FDI Strategies on the Trade Balances of Host Countries', *Journal of International Business Studies*, vol. 27, no. 2, pp. 359-373.

Buckley, P. (1988), 'The Limits of Explanation: Testing Internationalization Theory of the Multinational Enterprise', *Journal of International Business Studies,* vol. 19, pp. 181-194.

Buckley, P. and Casson, M. (1988), *The Future of the Multinational Enterprise*, London: Macmillan.

Business Central Europe (2001), General Statistics.

Caves, R. (1971), 'International Corporations: The Industrial Economics of Foreign Investment', *Economica,* vol. 38, pp. 1-27.

Culpan, R. and Kumar, N. (1994), 'Co-operative Ventures of Western Firms in Eastern Europe: The Case of German Companies', in P. Buckley and P. Ghauri (eds) *The Economics of Change in East and Central Europe*, London: Academic Press.

Douglas, S. and Wind, Y. (1987), 'The Myth of Globalization', *Columbia Journal of World Business,* Winter, pp. 19-29.

Dunning, J. (1977), 'Trade Location of Economic Activity, and the Multinational Firm. A Search for an Eclectic Approach', in B. Ohlin, P. Hesselberger and P. Wijkman (eds) *The International Allocation of Economic Activity*, London: Sage Publications.

Dunning, J. (1993), *Multinational Enterprises and the Global Economy*, Wokingham: Addison-Wesley.

Dunning, J.and Rojec, M. (1994), 'Foreign Privatization in Central and Eastern Europe', The Central and Eastern European Privatization Network (CEEPN) *Technical Paper Series* No. 2.

EBRD (1994), *Report on Investment in CEE.*

Gatling, R. (1993), 'Foreign Investment in Eastern Europe: Corporate Strategies and Experience', EBRD, *Paper* 7, London.

Geringer, J. and Herbert, L. (1989), 'Control and Performance of International Joint Ventures', *Journal of International Business Studies,* vol. 20, pp. 235-254.

Ghauri, P. and Holstius, K. (1996), 'The Role of Matching in the Foreign Market Entry Process in the Baltic States', *European Journal of Marketing* vol. 30, pp. 75-88.

Haiss, P. and Fink, G. (1995), 'Western Strategies in Central Europe', *Journal of East-West Business,* vol. 1, pp. 37-46.

Healey, N. (1994), 'The Transition Economies of Central and Eastern Europe: A Political, Economic, Social and Technological Analysis', *Columbia Journal of World Business*, vol. 29, pp. 62-70.

Hill, C.W.L. (1990), 'Cooperation, Opportunism, and the Invisible Hand: Implications for Transaction Cost Theory', *Academy of Management Review*, vol. 15, pp. 500-513.

Holstius, K. (1990), 'The Matching Concept and its Application to International Joint Ventures', Lappeenranta University of Technology, Department of Industrial Engineering and Management. *Research Report* 29, Lappeenranta.

Hunya, G. and Stankowsky, J. (1996), 'Foreign Direct Investment in Central and Eastern European Countries and the Former Soviet Union', Vienna: Vienna Institute for Comparative Economic Studies.

Hymer, S. (1960), *The International Operations of National Firms: A Study of Direct Foreign Investment*, Cambridge MA: The MIT Press.

Johanson, J. and Vahlne, J.-E. (1977), 'The Internationalisation Process of the Firm - A Model of Knowledge Development and Increasing Foreign Market Commitments', *Journal of International Business Studies*, vol. 8, pp. 23-32.

Lyles, M. and. Baird, S (1994), 'Performance of International Joint Ventures in Two Eastern European Countries: The Case of Hungary and Poland', *Management International Review*, vol. 34, pp. 313-329.

Madhok, A. (1995), 'Revisiting Multinational Firms' Tolerance for Joint Ventures: A Trust Based Approach', *Journal of International Business Studies*, vol. 26, pp. 117-137.

Marinov, M. and Marinova, S. (1997), 'Acquisitions in Central and Eastern Europe: Learning through Experience: The Case of Interbrew', Paper presented at the *23rd European International Business Academy Conference*, December 14-16, Stuttgart, Germany.

Marinova, S., Hooley, G., Marinov, M. and Cox, A. (1997), 'Host and Investor Marketing Related Motives, Promises and Actions in Explaining the Success and Failure of Privatizations through Foreign Direct Investment in Bulgaria', *Proceedings of 26th EMAC Conference*, vol. 2, pp. 824-843.

Nowak, J. (1996), 'Marketing Strategies for Central and Eastern Europe', *Journal of Euromarketing*, vol. 5, no. 2, pp. 101-125.

OECD (1994), *Foreign Investment in Eastern Europe*,Report.

Paliwoda, S. (1995), *Investing in Eastern Europe: Capitalizing on Emerging Markets*, London: Addison-Wesley and EIU.

Phongpaichit, P. (1990), *The New Wave of Japanese Investment in Asia*, Singapore: Institute of Southeastern Asian Studies.

Porter, M. and Fuller M. (1986), 'Coalitions and Global Strategies', in M. Porter (ed.) *Competition in Global Industries*, Boston, MA: Harvard Business School Press, pp. 315-343.

Quelch, J., Joachimsthaler, E. and Nueno J. (1991), 'After the Wall: Marketing Guidelines for Eastern Europe', *Sloan Management Review*, Winter, pp. 82-93.

Ring, P. and Van de Ven, A. (1992), 'Structuring Cooperative Relationships Between Organisations', *Strategic Management Journal*, vol. 13, pp. 483-498.

Rolfe, R. and Doupnik, T. (1996), 'Going East: Western Companies Invest in East/Central Europe', *Multinational Business Review*, Fall, pp. 1-12.

Root, F. (1994), *Entry Strategies for International Markets*. New York: Macmillan.

Shapiro, S. (1987), 'The Social Control of Impersonal Trust', *American Journal of Sociology*, vol. 93, pp. 623-658.

Simon-Millar, F. (1984), 'African Marketing: The Next Frontier', in G. Kindra (ed.) *Marketing in Developing Countries*, New York: St. Martin's Press, pp. 115-129.

Sinn, H.-W. and Weichenrieder, A. (1997), 'Foreign Direct Investment, Political Resentment and the Privatization Process in Eastern Europe', *Economic Policy*, April, pp. 179-210.

Stara, F. (1994), 'Henkel Austria. Aufbruch in den Osten - Strategien und Erfahrungen', *Werbeforschung & Praxis*, vol. 3, p. 117.

Svetlicic, M. and. Rojec, M (1994), 'Foreign Direct Investment and the Transformation of Central European Economies', *Management International Review*, vol. 34, pp. 293-312.

Szanyi, M. (1994), 'Experiences with Foreign Direct Investment in Hungary', Institute for World Economics, Hungarian Academy of Sciences, *Working Paper* No. 32, April.

Tietz, B. (1994), 'The Opening up of Eastern Europe: The Implications for West European Business', in P. Buckley and P. Ghauri (eds), *The Economics of Change in East and Central Europe*, London: Academic Press.

Zajac, E. and Olsen, C. (1993), 'From Transaction Cost to Transaction Value Analysis: Implications for the Study of Interorganizational Strategies', *Journal of Management Studies*, vol. 30, pp. 131-145.

5 Relationships between Foreign Direct Investment and Trade Flows in a Transition Economy: The Case of Ukraine[1]

NADIYA MANKOVSKA and JAMES W. DEAN

Introduction

This chapter examines the relationships between the inflows of foreign direct investment (FDI) into Ukraine, as well as the level of imports to and exports from the country. Theoretically, FDI and international trade can be regarded as substitutes or complements. Empirically, the chapter reveals that FDI from the European Union (EU) into Ukraine in extractive industries is mostly export-oriented and consequently complements trade, whereas FDI into manufacturing industries tends to substitute for imports. It is argued that primary-industry FDI from the EU is motivated by Ukraine's comparatively abundant and cheap natural resources, whereas secondary-industry FDI is motivated by cost factors in Ukraine such as low labor cost and on the revenue side by its large and relatively untapped domestic market. Secondary-industry FDI thus has the potential for import-substitution, although tests of this hypothesis at aggregate levels were inconclusive.

By contrast, FDI from countries of the former Council for Mutual Economic Assistance (CMEA) complements trade in secondary products. We support the notion that FDI from the former CMEA countries is motivated by the potential for economies of scale, including those that might arise from resuming production links which existed during the Soviet times. This is supported by evidence of the relationships between FDI from CMEA countries and intra-industry trade between CMEA countries and Ukraine.

Although FDI is crucial for the Ukrainian economy, the level of FDI remains rather insignificant in comparison with other transition countries.[2]

Several surveys of current investors in Ukraine (Flemings/CAPS Consortium, 2000; Dean and Kudina, 1999; Moellers, 1998) show that the dominant factor motivating current FDI inflows is the possibility of expansion into the domestic market. Low wages or other potential sources of comparative advantage do not seem to be important motivators, nor does the prospect of export markets. Ukraine still imposes substantial trade barriers. They may impede export-oriented FDI, and stimulate FDI inflows that lead to the production of import-substitutes.

In this chapter, we analyze the relationship between FDI and trade flows within Ukraine. In particular, the question whether FDI into Ukraine is a complement or a substitute for trade flows is addressed.

A large body of literature analyses both substitutability and complementarity between FDI and trade (Fontagné and Pajot, 1997; Chunlai, 1997; Razin, Yuen and Sadka, 1999). Theories that rationalise substitutability are primarily based on the Heckscher-Ohlin model of international trade, where *differences in factor endowments* are the major causes of trade between countries (Mundell, 1957; Goldberg and Klein, 1999; Brainard, 1997). Dropping key assumptions of the Heckscher-Ohlin model leads to inferences of complementarity rather than substitutability. Capital may complement trade when there are *technological differences* between countries (Markusen *et al*., 1995; Purvis, 1972), or when countries base their trade relations on *economies of scale* (Ethier, 1982). The first might be applicable to Ukraine since we could consider differences in natural resource endowments as a proxy for differences in production technologies. The second might also apply since scale economies were widespread in the planned economies of the former CMEA countries.

Empirical evidence for transition countries like Poland, Hungary and the Czech Republic shows strong complementarity between FDI and international trade (Guerriery, 1998; Kaminski, 1998). Aggregate Ukrainian data also weakly supports the complementarity thesis. During transition, while GDP levels decreased, the level of foreign trade as well as the share of exports in Ukrainian GDP increased substantially. We argue that these observed changes in trade might be partially explained by FDI inflows. However, our preliminary estimates with aggregate data did not reveal a strong linkage between FDI and international trade. Therefore we formulated more dis-aggregation questions:

(1) Does FDI flowing into production of primary products have a different relationship to trade than FDI destined for the production of secondary products? We raise this question on the basis of theories of international trade that treat FDI and trade flows in primary products as potential complements, but FDI and trade in secondary products as potential substitutes (Schmitz and Helmberger, 1970). In fact, financial

difficulties in transition countries often induce policies stimulating export-oriented production in order to generate foreign currency inflows. Natural resources are one of the few assets of these countries that attract foreign partners. Therefore, we suspect that FDI into primary industries in Ukraine might be a complement to trade.

(2) Is the relationship between FDI inflow in Ukraine and Ukrainian trade with the EU different from the relationship of FDI inflow and Ukrainian trade with countries from the former CMEA market? There could be different motives as well as impediments facing investors from these two groups of countries. The relationship between FDI and trade seems to depend upon certain similarities or differences between investing and recipient countries (Somwaru and Bolling, 1999). Cheap labor or undeveloped internal markets in Ukraine may attract investors from developed countries but not from the former CMEA market member states since investors from transition economies have similar conditions in their own countries. At the same time the former CMEA investors may have advantages over Western investors due to their strong historical links and may be interested in recapturing the lost markets and re-establishing the former CMEA's production chains (Goloven, 2000).

(3) Does FDI have an impact on the level of intra-industry trade in Ukraine? If FDI into Ukraine were oriented toward the establishment of vertical production, it would raise the level of intra-industry trade (Hoekman and Djankov, 1996) and support an inference of complementarity.

Answers to these three questions may be useful to policy-makers to focus and fine-tune their policies concerning FDI toward particular industries from particular countries of the world. The answers can also add to our understanding of the host country's competitiveness and long-term growth potential.

Peculiarities of FDI Inflows in Ukraine: Initial Evidence

A preliminary analysis of Ukrainian data allows us to distinguish two groups of investing countries. The first is comprised of the EU countries, which, as of December 31 2000, have invested about 29 percent of the cumulative FDI into Ukraine. The second group is comprised of transition countries former members of the CMEA market that have invested 15 percent of total FDI. Our evidence is that FDI from countries of the former CMEA market member countries, mostly from Russia, is distributed differently from the FDI that came from the EU. Table 5.1 shows that the major recipient of FDI in Ukraine is the food industry. However, this industry is mostly attractive to investors from advanced countries: some 44 percent of FDI from the EU was directed into food, as compared to only 4 percent of FDI from the former CMEA countries.

Table 5.1   Cumulative FDI into Ukraine as of December 31, 2000 (constant 1996 prices)

	Total FDI inflows		FDI from EU countries		FDI from the former CMEA countries	
	Total US$ mln	% of total	Total US$ mln	% of total	Total US$ mln	% of total
All sectors	3275.0	100.0	946.0	100.0	492.0	100.0
Industry	1680.0	51.0	704.0	74.0	242.0	49.0
Power sector	204.0	6.0	9.0	0.9	141.0	29.0
Ferrous metal	127.0	4.0	7.0	0.8	18.0	4.0
Non-ferrous metal	27.0	0.8	13.0	1.0	0.8	0.2
Chemicals	137.0	4.0	47.0	5.0	9.0	2.0
Machine-building	294.0	9.0	103.0	11.0	17.0	3.0
Wood-processing	68.0	2.0	44.0	5.0	11.0	2.0
Construction materials	49.0	2.0	14.0	1.0	10.0	2.0
Light industry	37.0	1.0	24.0	3.0	6.0	1.0
Food industry	657.0	20.0	417.0	44.0	20.0	4.0
Medical industry	19.0	0.6	10.0	1.0	6.0	1.0
Agriculture	67.0	2.0	18.0	2.0	4.0	0.9
Transport and telecommunications	196.0	6.0	54.0	6.0	28.0	6.0
Internal trade	617.0	19.0	183.0	19.0	56.0	11.0
External trade	39.0	1.0	9.0	0.9	0.9	0.2
Health and tourism	107.0	3.0	7.0	0.7	90.0	18.0
Finance sector	210.0	6.0	85.0	9.0	35.0	7.0

Sources: Derzhkomstat and authors' own calculations.

Industries of the Ukrainian economy, such as machine-building, ferrous metals, chemicals, and wood-processing, are also attractive for foreign investors, and again they attract quite different proportions of FDI from the former CMEA countries and from the EU. It can be hypothesized that

CMEA investors have different motives for sending FDI into Ukraine than EU investors do.

The external trade line in Table 5.1 shows that substantial investments were made in the development of trade infrastructure in Ukraine, supporting the complementarity hypothesis. At the same time, much higher figures for FDI into internal trade sector suggest that domestic market expansion is an important motivator for investing.

Main Hypotheses

We hypothesize that FDI inflows from the transition countries and the EU member countries have different impacts on trade flows because the investment motives are different. In addition, we suggest that industry specifics may predetermine incentives for FDI inflows and the relationship between FDI and trade flows. Thus, we propose the following:

For FDI into Ukraine that comes from the EU member countries:

- If it flows into industries that produce primary products, it is mostly export-oriented, and should have a positive impact on the exports of such industries (complementarity).
- If it flows into industries that produce secondary products, it is oriented towards internal market expansion and is induced either by possibilities to produce more efficiently within the country and/or by opportunities to avoid trade barriers. Such FDI acts as a substitute for trade, particularly for imports.

FDI that comes into Ukraine from former CMEA member countries can be regarded as follows. Whether it flows into industries that produce primary products or secondary products, it is motivated by the potential for economies of scale, including those that might arise from resuming production links which existed during the Soviet times. Consequently, this FDI will cause an increase in trade flows, both for export and import (complementarity).

Empirical Study

We have constructed export supply and import demand functions for Ukraine as functions of FDI and several control variables. The model (based on Thursby and Thursby, 1987; Ethier, 1973) takes the following forms:

$$EX_{it} = a_i + \beta_1 \cdot FDI_{it} + \beta_2 \cdot DIF\_GDPPC_{it} + \beta_3 \cdot ER\_VAR_t$$
$$+ \beta_4 \cdot IND\_OUTPUT_t + \varepsilon_{it} \tag{1}$$

and

$$M_{it} = \lambda_i + \gamma_1 \cdot FDI_{it} + \gamma_2 \cdot DIF\_GDPPC_{it} + \gamma_3 \cdot ER\_VAR_t$$
$$+ \gamma_4 \cdot POP\_INCOME_t + \upsilon_{it} \tag{2}$$

where *i*   country index;
       t   index for the year, 1996-2000;
       EX, M   exports, imports from Ukraine to country *i;*
       FDI   FDI inflows;
       DIF_GDPPC   absolute difference between GDP per capita of Ukraine and of country *i;*
       IND_OUTPUT   output for industries analyzed;
       POP_INCOME   net real income of the Ukrainian population;
       ER_VAR   exchange rate variability;
       ε_{it}, υ_{it} error terms.

All data are real and expressed in thousands of US dollars.

We ran pooled regressions on the basis of the available panel data. We used the official yearly Derzhkomstat data for FDI, trade,[3] and industrial output. TACIS/UEPLAC (December 2000) is the data source for net real population income. The bilateral data for per capita GDP differences between Ukraine and other countries was obtained from the IMF (2001).

Available data do not allow the use of lag variables. Not willing to ignore past FDI inflows, we tested two types of models: with FDI flows per year and with FDI stocks. Also, the empirical analysis of this paper was conducted for both bilateral and aggregate flows of exports and imports.

Two groups of industries were analyzed: (1) industries that produce secondary manufacturing products (food and machine building) and (2) industries that mostly produce primary products (ferrous metals, chemicals, and wood). Conclusions concerning the relationship between FDI and trade can be drawn from the estimated coefficients β_1 and γ_1 presented in Table 5.2 and Table 5.3.

The coefficient estimates show that the hypothesis concerning FDI flows into primary industries from the EU is supported quite strongly. However, this relationship is not observed on the bilateral level. Thus, this FDI cannot be explained by the relatively high demand for primary products in the investing country. Most likely, profit opportunities on world wholesale markets (especially for ferrous metals) are the reason for FDI flows into Ukrainian primary industries.

Our evidence rejects the hypothesis concerning complementarity between FDI from transition countries into Ukrainian primary industries and trade in correspondent products. This may be due to limited interest of investors from these countries in cheap natural resources, compared to investors from the EU (as can be seen from Table 5.2).

Table 5.2   Relationship between FDI and export flows

	Primary products		Secondary products		
	0.03	11.76	0.005	-0.24	FDI
European	(0.98)	(0.09)	(0.92)	(0.91)	flows
Union	-0.27	14.50	-0.01	-3.13	FDI
	(0.73)	(0.17)	(0.51)	(0.21)	stocks
	-3.30	38.77	7.28	152.95	FDI
Former	(0.30)	(0.19)	(0.37)	(0.14)	flows
CMEA	2.09	11.93	4.43	-82.40	FDI
	(0.40)	(0.38)	(0.34)	(0.25)	stocks
	Bilateral trade	Aggregate trade	Bilateral trade	Aggregate trade	

Note: p-value in parentheses.

FDI inflows to Ukrainian secondary industries do not explain the export volumes of these industries' products. Rather, these investments are either induced by lower cost local production, and/or are motivated by local markets for selling the final products. These findings support the results by Dean and Kudina (1999) and by the Flemings/CAPS Consortium (2000) conducted on micro levels.

On the basis of the results for the import demand function (Table 4.3) we accept our hypothesis concerning different patterns of relationship between FDI and trade for the two groups of investing countries. Indeed, the estimated coefficients differ for the different types of investors.

However, on the basis of our estimations we cannot accept the hypothesis about substitutability between FDI from the EU into secondary industries and imports of corresponding products. The negative coefficient on the FDI variable signifies that secondary-industry FDI has the potential for import in general and imports of corresponding products in particular. The negative coefficient on the FDI variable signifies that secondary-industry FDI has the potential for import-substitution, although tests of this hypothesis are inconclusive. However, the substitutability effect is not strong enough to outweigh other effects, for example the process of external liberalization that has simultaneously taken place in Ukraine.

Table 5.3   Relationship between FDI and import flows into Ukraine

	Primary products		Secondary products		
	0.22	2.16	0.02	3.37	FDI
European	(0.56)	(0.61)	(0.90)	(0.17)	flows
Union	0.19	0.60	-0.04	0.95	FDI
	(0.51)	(0.80)	(0.49)	(0.39)	stocks
	0.18	-3.03	9.17	109.91	FDI
Former	(0.74)	(0.64)	(0.09)	(0.001)	flows
CMEA	-0.15	-0.92	6.31	37.87	FDI
	(0.76)	(0.75)	(0.05)	(0.19)	stocks
	Bilateral trade	Aggregate trade	Bilateral trade	Aggregate trade	

Note: p-value in parentheses.

The significance of our results for imports of secondary products supports the hypothesis regarding reintegration processes among former CMEA countries although it cannot be accepted with certainty since we cannot observe this for trade in primary products.

To find additional evidence for reintegration we turn to the analysis of intra-industry trade in Ukraine. This allows us to trace the impact of FDI on trade diversification, which surely should be the result of intensified bilateral economic interrelations. A positive relationship between FDI inflows and the country's intra-industry trade level for corresponding industries would support our inferences on complementarity of trade and FDI (Markusen *et al.*, 1996).

Impact of FDI on Trade Diversification

In transition economies, FDI flowing into the production sector can be considered as a source of innovation and might lead to an increase in diversity of output and trade. EBRD (1995) reports that countries that are more successful with reforms export and import a higher diversity of products. However, in Ukraine the Grubel-Lloyd (GL) index, which is the measure of the intra-industry trade level, has being decreasing during transition (Table 5.4).

Table 5.4   Grubel-Lloyd index calculated for Ukraine

Year	1994	1995	1996	1997	1998	1999	2000
GL Index	0.153	0.143	0.118	0.196	0.090	0.086	0.085

Source: Ministry of Economy, Department of Statistics; authors' calculations.

Theory predicts that intra-industry trade arises when economies of scale are the major motivator of trade (Ethier, 1982; Helpman and Krugman, 1985). Another explanation is vertical production relations: countries may export some products for assembling or further processing and then re-import these products again (Markusen *et al.,* 1995).

Figure 5.1   Intra-industry trade between Ukraine and other major investing countries by 2000

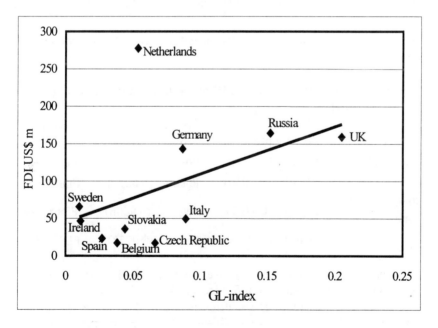

Sources: Derzhkomstat and Ministry of Economy.

In the empirical literature, FDI inflows are found to be highly correlated with intra-industry trade. In particular, transition countries that managed to attract the largest investment inflows rely more heavily on intra-industry trade and vertical specialization (Hoekman and Djankov, 1996). However, taking into account the decreasing levels of intra-industry trade in Ukraine, we might suspect that FDI into Ukraine does not positively influence trade diversification.

To clarify this phenomenon we analyze the relationship between FDI and intra-industry trade between Ukraine and other countries at bilateral levels. Our evidence (presented in Figure 5.1) suggests that although the GL-index for the aggregate trade of Ukraine has decreased, it has increased at the bilateral level between Ukraine and major investing countries.

For empirical testing we use our equations of trade volumes, however, this time our dependent variable is the value of the GL index:

$$GL_{it} = \delta_i + \xi_1 \cdot FDI_{it} + \xi_2 \cdot DIF\_GDPPC_{it} + \xi_3 \cdot ER\_VAR_t$$
$$+ \xi_4 \cdot IND\_OUTPUT_t + \xi_5 \cdot POP\_INCOME_t + \eta_{it} \quad (3)$$

where all variables have the same meaning as before (η_{it} is the error term).

Table 5.5 presents the signs of coefficient ξ_1 as well as p-values (in parentheses).

Table 5.5   Relationship between FDI and bilateral intra-industry trade

Sources of FDI	Primary products	Secondary products	FDI
EU member countries	Positive (0.9076)	Positive (0.6206)	FDI flows
	Negative (0.8255)	Positive (0.0671)	FDI stocks
Former CMEA states	Positive (0.4181)	Negative (0.9606)	FDI flows
	Positive (0.0000)	Positive (0.0758)	FDI stocks

On the basis of the estimation results we conclude that FDI inflows into the Ukrainian economy positively influence the level of intra-industry trade between Ukraine and investing countries. For FDI inflows from the former CMEA this result appears to be significant for both types of industries. This finding is quite important as it supports our hypothesis about the reestablishment of broken economic links between countries of the former

CMEA countries since the GL-index to some extent also measures the overall level of cooperation between countries.

As for the EU, we observe a positive impact of FDI on intra-industry trade only for secondary products.

Conclusions

Studying the peculiarities of the external sector in transition economies should help to develop reform strategies and even to conduct foreign policy. External sector policy is made yet more complex by the reintegration processes taking place alongside large-scale institutional and structural changes.

Our research has shown that for Ukraine, as for other transition countries, the complementarity relationship between FDI and trade flows dominates. However, the relationship between FDI and trade flows depends on the type of investors, or more specifically on the extent of similarities between investing and recipient countries. Moreover, our research has revealed that different groups of industries, primary and secondary, show different relationships between FDI and trade.

Our results might have implications for FDI and foreign trade policies. In particular, differences between the FDI motives and trade patterns of former CMEA countries and countries of the EU suggest that optimal policies for enhancing FDI and trade with CMEA countries might differ from those designed for EU countries.

Notes

1   We would like to record our thanks to the EERC Research and Outreach Center, which provided financial support for this research to be conducted under Research Project EERC RP01-02. We wish to express our sincere appreciation to those who reviewed this paper and supplied valuable comments: Roy Gardner, Charles Steele, Ghaffar Mughal, Ihor Burakovsky and Victor Goloven. Special thanks to Serhij Kovaliov who was extremely kind and patient in supplying extensive statistical data sets that were critical for conducting this investigations, and also to Stepan Mankovskyy who was of great help with processing our statistics.

2   According to the State Statistical Committee (Derzhkomstat), as for December 31 2000, the cumulative net FDI stock to Ukraine since independence (August, 1991) totaled about US$ 3.3 billion.

3   The data provided by Derzhkomstat is nominal in terms of US dollars. We got real values through the value of USA GDP deflator (source: IMF, 2001). As for the trade data, a 4-digit level of dis-aggregation is available.

References

Brainard, L. (1997), 'An Empirical Assessment of the Proximity-Concentration Trade-off Between Multinational Sales and Trade', *American Economic Review*, vol. 4, no. 87, pp. 66-83.

Chunlai, C. (1997), 'Foreign Direct Investment and Trade: an Empirical Investigation of the Evidence from China', *Working Paper 97/11*, Chinese Economies Research Centre, University of Adelaide, Australia.

Dean, J. and Kudina, A. (1999), 'Incentives and Disincentives for Foreign Direct Investment in Ukraine', Paper Presented at the Academy of Business and Administrative Sciences Conference, November 1999, Barcelona, Spain.

Ethier, W. (1973), 'International Trade and the Forward Exchange Market', *American Economic Review*, vol. 63, pp. 87-99.

Ethier, W. (1982), 'National and International Returns to Scale in the Modern Theory of International Trade', *American Economic Review*, vol. 72, no. 3, pp. 123-138.

EBRD (1995, 1998, 1999), *Transition Report*.

Flemings/CAPS Consortium (2000), 'Determination of Interests and Abilities of Direct Foreign Investors in Ukraine', Report on Survey Results, Kyiv.

Fontagné, L. and Pajot, M. (1997), *How Foreign Direct Investment Affects International Trade and Competitiveness: an Empirical Assessment*, Paris: CÉPII.

Goldberg, L. and Klein, M. (1999), 'International Trade and Factor Mobility: an Empirical Investigation', *Working Paper 7196*, NBER.

Goloven, V. (2000), 'Determinants of Capital Flows into Ukraine from Countries of Former Soviet Union and the Rest of World and Application for Trade Diversification', *Scientific Journal of NaUKMA*, vol. 3, Kyiv.

Guerriery, P. (1998), 'Trade Patterns, Foreign Direct Investment, and Industrial Restructuring of Central and Eastern Europe', *Working Paper 124*, BRIE.

Helpman, E. and Krugman, P. (1985), *Marker Structure and Foreign Trade*, Cambridge, MA: The MIT Press.

Hoekman, B. and Djankov, S. (1996), 'Intra-Industry Trade, Foreign Direct Investment and the Reorientation of East European Exports', *Discussion Paper 1377*, CEPR, London.

International Monetary Fund (2000), *World Economic Outlook* (www.imf.org/external/pubs/ft/weo).

Kaminski, B. (1998), 'Foreign Trade and Foreign Direct Investment in Hungary and Slovenia: Different Paths – Different Outcomes', *Transition Report*, Washington, DC: World Bank.

Markusen, J., Melvin, J., Kaempler, W. and Maskus, K. (1995), *International Trade: Theory and Evidence*, New York: McGraw-Hill, Inc.

Markusen, J., Venables, A., Konan, D.A. and Zhang, K. (1996), 'A Unified Treatment of Horizontal Direct Investment, Vertical Direct Investment, and the Pattern of Trade in Goods and Services, *Working Paper 5696*, NBER.

Moellers, F. (1998), 'Foreign Direct Investment in Ukraine – Experiences Taken from Reality', in German Advisory Group (eds) *Ukraine at the Crossroads: Economic Reforms in International Perspective*, Berlin: Physica.

Mundell, R. (1957), 'International Trade and Factor Mobility', *American Economic Review*, vol. 47, no. 3, pp. 193-236.

Purvis, D. (1972), 'Technology, Trade and Factor Mobility', *Economic Journal*, vol. 82, no. 337, pp. 69-96.

Razin, A., Sadka, E., Yuen, C.-W. (1999), 'An Information-based Model of Foreign Direct Investment: The Gains from Trade Revisited', *Working Paper 6884*, NBER.

Schmitz, A. and Helmberger, P. (1970), 'Factor Mobility and International Trade: The Case of Complementarity', *American Economic Review*, vol. 60, no. 4, pp. 127-139.

TACIS/UEPLAC (2000), *Ukrainian Economic Trends*, Kyiv.

Thursby, J. and Thursby, M. (1987), 'Bilateral Trade Flows, the Linder Hypothesis, and Exchange Risk', *Review of Economics and Statistics*, vol. 69, no. 3, pp. 68-79.

PART II

FOREIGN DIRECT INVESTMENT IN CENTRAL AND EASTERN EUROPE: COUNTRY OF ORIGIN EFFECTS

6 Russian Outward Foreign Direct Investment: Windows Open to the West, Doors not Closed to the East

KARI LIUHTO and JARI JUMPPONEN

Introduction

Russian foreign direct investment (FDI) abroad has substantially increased. In 2000 the recorded outward FDI stock of Russia amounted to almost US$ 12 billion. The majority of the outward FDI flow has taken place during the past few years, i.e., almost US$ 9 billion of Russian capital has been invested abroad during the period 1997 - 2000.

Russian foreign direct investment has not flown only to the West, but to a large extent to Central Eastern European countries and to the former Soviet republics. Russian companies have invested considerably in Poland, Hungary and in the Baltic States. Moreover, the Russian involvement in the Ukraine, Kazakhstan and other Commonwealth of Independent States (CIS) countries seems to have strengthened during the past few years.

Even though the energy sector dominates the Russian outward FDI, other sectors are also internationalizing rapidly. One could anticipate the speeding expansion of the Russian metal companies outside their domestic playground. The most powerful Russian banks also seem to eye foreign markets, especially those of CIS.

Another observation worth mentioning is the fact that Russian companies aim at acquiring a control stake in their foreign business units, if not immediately, then in the longer run. A strategy of obtaining a control stake, which used to be the main investment strategy during the Soviet era, seems to be a common investment pattern among Russian corporations.

Should business objectives dominate in their internationalization strategies, the Russian corporations will easily find an appropriate place in the global business. Especially, the role of Russian energy companies in strengthening the energy collaboration between Russia and the European Union (EU) would be important. Russia would benefit directly from the advantages of enlargement through the Russian investments in the current and enlarged EU. Moreover, the Russian investments in the EU would support EU-Russian trade. Increasing EU-Russian trade would ultimately strengthen stability in Europe and beyond. On the other hand, should the internationalization of Russian corporations be used as instruments of foreign policy, the attitudes towards the expansion of the Russian companies will become reserved.

Foreign Direct Investment to and from the East

Foreign firms have clearly become more active in their operations in the transition economies since the mid-1990s. A clear indicator of a growing interest is that of expanded foreign direct investment inflow to transition economies (TEs).

According to the United Nations Conference on Trade and Development (UNCTAD, 2001), the FDI inflow to all TEs was approximately US$ 7 billion in 1994, whereas half a decade later the annual FDI inflow exceeded US$ 25 billion. In 2000, the FDI inward stock in the former centrally planned economies amounted to over US$ 150 billion.

Poland, Hungary and the Czech Republic account for one half of the FDI inward stock, i.e., over US$ 75 billion. Russia with her giant natural resources and population of approximately 2.5 times the combined population of these three Central East European countries (CEECs) has been able to attract FDI worth less than US$ 20 billion, i.e., just as much as Hungary alone.

The FDI inflow analysis suggests that Western companies have not entered Russia and the CIS to the same extent they have penetrated the CEECs. The statistics indicate that the CEECs have been integrated via Western FDI more intensively towards global business than Russia or the rest of the CIS.

If Western corporations have not been able to integrate Russia and the CIS as tightly as the CEECs into the world economy, what is the opposite direction of the FDI flows, i.e., to what extent have the Eastern enterprises become integrated into the world of global business? (See Figure 6.1.)

As the Russian statistics are deficient, the researchers aimed at producing a more detailed picture of Russian direct investments abroad. This has been mainly achieved through intensive data collection using primary and secondary sources. The authors have been given access to a variety of data sources offered by independent bodies and also publicly available non-confidential information supplied by managers and company-

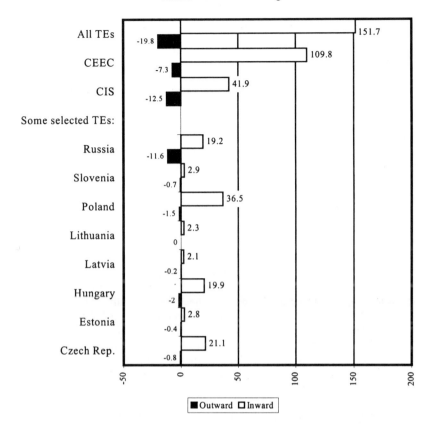

Figure 6.1   Outward and inward FDI stocks of transition economies by 2001 in US\$ billion

Source: UNCTAD, 2001.

level data on the international operations of Russian corporations. Since thousands of Russian firms have already been registered abroad, it is not possible to describe their activities comprehensively within this chapter, and thus the authors considered it appropriate to focus on the international operations of the largest Russian business units, and by investigating them to answer the four questions:

• What is the driving force behind the Russian companies' internationalization?
• In which countries has Russian capital landed?

- Which industries are dominant amongst the Russian corporations?
- What are the main operational modes?

Internationalization of Russian Corporations: A Historical Approach

A description of the historical development of Russian/Soviet internationalization offers a reader some background information, which may be useful in anticipating the motives, directions and modes of the Russian corporations' expansion abroad in the future.

Bulatov (1998, 69-70) describes aptly the early stages of the internationalization of Russian corporations as follows

> Russian firms started to invest abroad in the last decades of the 19th century. Capital was exported primarily to China and Persia, as well as to Mongolia. During the period 1886 - 1914, Russian capital exports amounted to about Russian roubles 2.3 billion, (equivalent to US$ 33 billion at 1996 prices). Between the two World Wars, the Union of Soviet Socialist Republics did not withdraw all outward investment, although it radically diminished it. To support trade with Turkey, Iran, Afghanistan and Mongolia, a whole net of trading companies was established and operated in those traditional partner countries. Trading affiliates in Western Europe were added later. Also, various banks, transport, insurance and other types of firms were established abroad with Soviet capital. In the post-war period, the number of companies abroad increased somewhat.

Even if the number of the Soviet business units abroad grew after the Second World War, their number remained modest. In spite of their small amount, it is necessary, due to a different business environmental reality, to divide the international operations of the Soviet enterprises into two main categories: (1) Soviet companies in socialist countries and (2) Soviet companies in non-socialist countries.

Soviet companies in socialist countries   met hidden resistance from small countries in the Council for Mutual Economic Assistance (CMEA) towards intensifying collaboration with the Soviet Union and various economic difficulties kept inter-enterprise co-operation rather modest. By the mid-1980s, only a handful of CMEA joint enterprises with the participation of the USSR were established. Matejka (1988) names eight CMEA joint enterprises with Soviet participation: the Ulan-Bator Railway (activity: railway network, location: Mongolia, year of establishment: 1949), Wismut AG (uranium mining, German Democratic Republic, 1954), Erdenet (copper mining, Mongolia, 1973), Mongolsovtsvetmet (gold mining, Mongolia, 1973), Petrobaltic (prospecting for Baltic petroleum and gas, Poland, 1975), Interlichter (Danube-Maritime freight, Hungary, 1978), Robot (scientific cooperation, Czechoslovakia, 1985), and Bulgarian-Soviet enterprise (the manufacturing of electronic parts, Bulgaria, 1986).

Perestroika expanded foreign trade rights in the USSR and joint venture legislation improved in Eastern Europe in the second half of the 1980s, and as a consequence, the number of the enterprises with Soviet participation within the CMEA multiplied. By 1990 at least 175 Soviet-owned joint ventures were registered in the European CMEA countries: sixty eight in Poland, 50 in Hungary, 38 in Bulgaria, 21 in Yugoslavia and four in Czechoslovakia (Cheklina, 1991).

Soviet companies in non-socialist countries   Operations   of   Soviet companies were also rare in non-socialist countries. USSR firms had around 30 subsidiaries in developing countries and 116 subsidiaries in the OECD countries at the end of 1983. Most of them, over 60 percent, operated in the current EU member states. For example, nine Soviet-owned enterprises, such as Suomen Petrooli (oil trading), Teboil (gasoline filling stations), Konela (sales of Soviet automobiles), and the Saimaa Lines (transportation), were established in Finland[1]. Five were registered in the U.S.A.: the Amtorg Trading Corp. in New York, Morflot America Shipping Incorporation in Clark, the Marine Resources Company in Seattle, Sovfracht Ltd. in New York and Belarus Machinery Inc. in Milwaukee (Zaleski, 1986; McMillan, 1987).

The overwhelming majority of the Soviet subsidiaries in the West operated in the marketing of oil, metals, timber, chemicals, machinery and vehicles. In addition to this export promotion, Soviet subsidiaries serviced the foreign trade activities of the USSR as they operated in transportation, banking and the insurance business. Besides those foreign trade related activities, Soviet organizations operated in tourism and traveling (Hill, 1986).

Soviet parent companies usually possessed a majority ownership in their Western-based units. The Soviet parent company had a majority stake in nine firms out of ten. Pursuing majority ownership was a natural investment strategy, since the Soviet corporations wanted to maintain direct control over their business activities rather than only act as a profit-seeking investor.

To summarize, the number of Soviet corporations outside the Soviet Union was less than 500 before the dissolution of the USSR but despite the relatively small amount, their importance in supporting the Soviet exports cannot be neglected since they were selling about 40 percent of Soviet oil and oil product supplies abroad, 60 percent of the timber, paper, and cellulose exports and more than 50 percent of the exports of civilian-use manufactured goods (Sokolov, 1991a; 1991b). When evaluating the role of Soviet enterprises abroad, it should not be forgotten that the foreign operations of these Soviet firms were not motivated by business logic alone, but the Soviet firms abroad also served the goals of the USSR's foreign policy (Hamilton, 1986).

Another observation worth noticing is the fact that Russian firms controlled most of the Soviet corporations abroad. Soviet corporations having their headquarters located in any Soviet republic other than Russia, established just a handful of foreign subsidiaries. This is one explanation why Russian companies inherited the Soviet business units abroad after the dissolution of the Soviet Union.

Russian Companies Finding Their Way Westwards

Oil and Gas

The Russian gas sector is practically a monopoly of Gazprom, which produced 523.2 billion cubic meters (bcm) in 2000, some 90 - 95 percent of Russia's natural gas. The company owns some 70 percent of Russia's gas reserves (EBRD, 2001). The next largest Russian gas producers have rather modest production numbers, even though in a global comparison these companies cannot be neglected. Surgutneftegaz has an annual production of 11 bcm, Rosneft 5.5 bcm, LUKoil 3.5 bcm and Tyumen Oil Company (TNK) 2.5 bcm (Liuhto, 2001). The predecessor of Gazprom, the Ministry of Gas Industry, started its internationalization as early as 1966, when the USSR exported gas to Poland (Cullison and Bahree, 1999). When Gazprom was established in the late 1980s, it inherited the foreign customers, the majority of the Russian gas reserves and the pipelines from the Ministry of Gas Industry. The internationalization of Gazprom began within the CMEA and the former Soviet republics. When taking into account the fact that Gazprom represents intertwined relations of both the business and political life, it has to be emphasized that the internationalization of the company may not necessarily follow the theories of internationalization only, but also those of international politics.

Today, the company exports approximately one-third of its production, and a wide price gap between the Russian and the world market motivates Gazprom to deliver even a bigger share of its gas production abroad, especially to solvent West European countries. The company now exports to 25 European countries and wants to keep adding foreign clients, because they are more reliable in paying their bills than domestic customers. In order to strengthen its position abroad, Gazprom has made some equity investments. Currently Gazprom owns equity stakes, for example, in Finland, Germany, Greece, Hungary, and Poland. Besides these countries, Gazprom has shareholdings also in the Baltic States and other ex-Soviet republics. Recently, Gazprom has been examining possibilities to set up marketing and distribution operations in China, which is expected to have an ever-increasing demand for energy. Gazprom has already opened a representative office in China and intends to set up a joint venture (*New Europe*, 2001c; 2001d). The summary of Gazprom's investments abroad is presented in Table 6.1.

While the Russian gas sector is dominated by Gazprom, the country's oil industry is made up of a dozen vertically integrated companies. The most significant of them are LUKoil, Yukos, Surgutneftegaz, TNK, Rosneft, Tatneft, Sibneft, Basneft and Slavneft.

LUKoil is the largest oil company in terms of production. Even though about 30 percent of the company's oil reserves are located abroad, only a small percentage of oil production occurs outside the Russian borders. However, the production abroad is growing rapidly. The company has been purchasing stakes in oil fields, especially in the Caspian Sea region and in Iraq. Besides participating in the development of oil fields, LUKoil has acquired controlling shares in refineries abroad, in Romania, the Ukraine and Bulgaria.

As in the case of Gazprom, it has also been rational for LUKoil to expand sales to foreign markets, since the prices of oil products are considerably higher abroad. Currently, some 40 percent of the company's production is exported. In addition to exports, oil production and refining, LUKoil has been involved in gas retailing as well.

At the end of 2000 LUKoil acquired a 60 percent share of Getty Petroleum Marketing, which was a first step in its expansion into the US market and also the first time when a Russian firm acquired a publicly traded US company. Up to now the company has had gas filling stations mainly in the ex-CMEA markets, but the acquisition of Getty shows that the company is not only directed towards the post-socialist markets.

Later on, LUKoil has expressed its interest to acquire an oil refinery in the U.S.A. (*New Europe*, 2001e). The company is also said to be looking for retail networks in Canada, Mexico and Austria. In July 2001 LUKoil proved that it has truly become an active player in the global oil business: the company acquired a Canadian exploration and production company, Bitech Petroleum, which has been operating in Russia, Egypt, Morocco, Tunisia and Colombia.

Table 6.1   Major stakes of Gazprom in European gas joint ventures

Country	Joint Venture	Stake	Activities
Germany	Wingas	35%	Gas transportation and storage
	Wintershall Erdgas Handelshaus (WIEH)	50%	Gas trading company. Single trader of all the gas exported by Gazeksport until 2012.
	Zarube gas Erdgashandel	100%	Gas trading
	Verbundnetz Gas (VNG)	5%	Gas transportation and marketing
	Ditgaz	49%	Gas trading
UK/ Belgium	Interconnector	10%	Pipeline which connected Bacton (UK) with Zeebrugge (Belgium)
Poland	Gas Trading	35%	Gas trading
	Europol Gaz	48%	Gas transport
Italy	Volta	49%	Gas trading and transport
	Promgaz	50%	Gas trading and marketing
France	FRAgaz	50%	Gas trading
Austria	GHW	50%	Gas trading company
Serbia	Progress Gas Trading	50%	Gas trading
Slovenia	Tagdem	8%	Gas trading
Greece	Prometheus Gaz	50%	Marketing and construction
Finland	Gasum Oy	25%	Gas transportation and marketing
	North Transgas Oy	50%	Construction of a pipeline beneath the Baltic Sea
Estonia	Eesti Gaas	31%	Gas trading and transport
Latvia	Latvijas Gaze	25%	Gas trading and transport
Bulgaria	Topenergo	100%	Gas trading and transport
Romania	WIROM	25%	Gas trading. The stake of Gazprom is hold by WIEH
Hungary	Panrusgas	50%	Gas trading and transport
Turkey	Turusgaz	45%	Gas trading
Yugoslavia	JugoRosGaz	50%	Gas trading and transport
Slovak Republic	Slovrusgaz	50%	Gas trading and transport

Source: Heinrich (2001).

The second biggest Russian oil producer, Yukos, ranks among the world's largest oil companies in terms of reserves. The export/production ratio increased to over 40 percent. The company has had drilling operations in Peru since 1995, when it signed an agreement to explore and develop and oil and gas field there for over 30 years.

Yukos have subsidiaries in the Baltic States and in the U.S.A. In Lithuania Yukos agreed to buy a 26.9 percent stake in a local refinery, Mazeikiu Nafta (BCE, 2001). Through this foothold Yukos is expected to increase its exports to other countries in the region (*The Russia Journal*, 2001). Yukos' long-term internationalization strategy has recently focused towards China and Southeast Asia, where the company is aiming to raise its exports.

The third largest oil company in Russia, Surgutneftegaz, is the most cost-efficient of all Russian oil companies, having the highest share of export revenues in total turnover. On the other hand, the high export orientation could make Surgutneftegaz more vulnerable to future decreases in world oil prices (EBRD, 2001). So far, the company has not made investments outside Russia.

TNK is partially owned by the Renova and Alfa Group, a powerful financial and industrial holding company. In September 2000 TNK acquired the state-controlled Onako oil company.

Through the acquisition the company hopes to enhance its attractiveness to foreign investors, which suffered in 1999 as a result of its purchase of a key part of the Russian Sidanko oil company (EBRD, 2001). TNK and the American oil giant, Texaco, have an agreement over cooperation in the retail sector, which includes establishing a joint venture and operating service stations around Moscow and Kiev, the capital of the Ukraine. The company also has two refineries in the Ukraine.

Rosneft, the state-owned oil company, already participated in international operations during Soviet times. In June 2001 Rosneft signed a contract with Colombia's state oil company Ecopetrol and two other Colombian companies to launch oil extraction at a block in the south of Colombia. The contract will aim to increase production by updating technology (*New Europe*, 2001b).

In Algeria, Rosneft initialed an agreement with a local state-run oil company Sonatrach on the development of oil fields under production-sharing terms.

Table 6.2   Some foreign operations of the Russian oil companies

Company	Markets	Operations
LUKoil	Various countries	Oil exports
	Azerbaijan, Kazakhstan, Uzbekistan, Iraq, Egypt	Oil production
	Morocco, Tunisia, Colombia, Bulgaria, Romania, Ukraine, Czech Republic and Lithuania	Oil refining
	Baltic countries, Czech R., Kazakhstan, Azerbaijan, Moldova, Ukraine, U.S.A.	Gas retailing
	UK	Sales office
Yukos	Planning a pipeline to China and Southeast Asia	Oil exports
	Drilling operations in Peru	Oil production
	Share in Lithuanian refinery	Oil refining
	Subsidiaries in Latvia and the U.S.A.	Marketing
TNK	Various countries	Oil exports
	Ukraine	Oil refining
	Ukraine	Gas retailing
Rosneft	Various countries	Oil exports
	Azerbaijan, Iraq, Kazakhstan, Vietnam, Algeria, Colombia	Oil production
	Bulgaria, Romania	Gas retailing
Surgutneftegaz	Various countries	Oil exports
Slavneft	Bulgaria, Romania	Gas retailing
	Plans to operate in Azerbaijan, Iran and Iraq	Oil production
Tatneft	Various countries	Oil exports
Sibneft	Various countries	Oil exports
Bashneft	Various countries	Oil exports
Onako	Various countries	Oil exports

Note: In September 2000 TNK acquired the formerly state controlled Onako for US$ 1.8 billion.

Source: Väätänen and Liuhto (2001).

In addition, the company has ongoing or is considering, foreign operations in Azerbaijan, Kazakhstan, Vietnam and Iraq. For instance, in Kazakhstan, Rosneft has agreed to form an oil and gas extracting holding in cooperation with Florida-based Itera and American First International Oil Corporation. In Iraq, Rosneft has signed an agreement to develop oil fields, but carrying the deal into effect is dependent on the sanction policy of the United Nations.

Furthermore, Rosneft has expressed its interest in further expanding its international operations in South America. Participating in oil production in Vietnam is under consideration.

The other Russian major oil companies, Tatneft, Sibneft, Basneft and Slavneft have not been so active in their internationalization except for export activities. However, Slavneft has recently announced its plans to carry out operations in Azerbaijan, Iran and Iraq. This far, the company has been operating jointly with Rosneft a petrol station network in Bulgaria and Romania. Tatneft, in turn, received permission from the UN sanctions committee to carry out a contract to drill 33 wells in Iraq (*New Europe*, 2001a). The foreign operations of the Russian oil companies abroad are summarized in Table 6.2.

Energy

In the energy sector, Russia suffers from inefficient energy production, which is causing the wastage of raw materials. It has been estimated that annual investments of some US\$ 5 - 7 billion are needed during the next 10 - 15 years in order to arrest the decline in power output (EBRD, 2001).

The world's largest centrally managed integrated power system, RAO UES (United Energy System of Russia) directly or indirectly controls the production, transmission and distribution of electricity in Russia. Currently the federal government owns over 50 percent of the company.

The tariffs of the energy sector are strictly state-regulated, so exporting energy is a rather attractive alternative to RAO UES in order to boost cash flows. The exports to the former Soviet republics have been declining as a result of several unpaid deliveries (Trofimenko, 2001). Therefore, the company has started to focus on non-CIS countries, as financially they are a more attractive target area for exporting. Although the share of these countries is expected to increase, only some 10 percent of the total electricity exports were delivered to non-CIS countries in 1999. The future orientation of electricity exports is likely to lay its emphasis more and more to both Western European and Asian countries, for example, Japan and China, as Table 6.3 indicates. However the plans considering further cooperation, such as establishing joint companies, are scheduled to happen within the former Soviet states. This indicates that these states are not likely to lose their importance in the internationalization process of RAO UES.

Table 6.3   Some Foreign Operations of RAO UES

Operations	Countries
Production	Moldova
Sales	Ukraine, Kazakhstan, Belarus, Georgia, Finland, Latvia, Turkey
Agreements on exports	Germany, Poland, France, Switzerland, Japan, China
Plans to establish a joint venture	Georgia, Kazakhstan, Tajikistan, Kyrgyz Republic

Source: Trofimenko (2001).

Metals and Mining

Alrosa (Almazy Rossii-Sakha, Diamonds of Russia and Sakha) is one of the world's leading diamond mining companies, with 21 percent of world output. In the Soviet era, the company was operating as the state's diamond monopoly. In 1992 Alrosa was re-established to explore and mine diamond fields and to market and sell rough diamonds. In addition to exports, Alrosa has representative offices in Israel, Belgium, the UK and Angola. Alrosa is an equity partner in the Catoca diamond mine in northern Angola, which proposed programs for exploration and technical cooperation in the diamond sector in Angola, Namibia, Botswana and Tanzania.

Until the end of 2001 Alrosa had an agreement with South Africa's De Beers, which was guaranteeing sales to Russian diamond producers. According to this agreement, De Beers was committed to purchase Russian diamonds for US$ 550 million annually. However, Russia could not export more than 26 percent of De Beers' annual sales and therefore, the deal was an obstacle to the development of the diamond industry in Russia. After long-lasting negotiations, both parties are agreeing the new terms for further cooperation. It is likely that Alrosa will continue to cooperate with

De Beers, but will also establish new relations with Russian and foreign diamond sellers so as to enter the world market smoothly.

In the non-ferrous metals sector Norilsk Nickel is the largest producer in Russia controlling 70 percent of world palladium supplies, 25 percent of platinum, 20 percent of nickel and 40 percent of rhodium. Its operations consist of mining, concentrating, smelting, and refining these metals. The company's exports currently represent about 2 percent of Russia's total exports, so the importance of the company to the Russian economy is evident. The company has announced having two major investment strategies: (1) to upgrade its current production facilities and (2) to start producing new products. With these actions the company aims at becoming one of the most efficient producers of nickel in the world by 2005 (EBRD, 2001). The company has also planned to create own sales network abroad, which materialized in 2000 by setting up a joint venture with a Belgian company Sogem. The joint venture is planned to sell all of Norilsk's cobalt output with the support of worldwide sales network of the Belgian counterpart (*Business Central Europe*, 2000).

The high world market prices for palladium have made exporting an extremely attractive option for Norilsk Nickel for a long time. However, for a long time exports were blocked by state decree. From the beginning of 2001, Norilsk Nickel has been allowed to ship palladium to Japan.

Last year, Norilsk Nickel announced to complete the construction of a nickel mine and plant, the project that started in 1983, had been left unfinished as a result of the fall of the Soviet Union. Recently, the company announced to establish a joint venture with a Canadian company, Argosy Minerals, in order to study cooperation in New Caledonia, Australia (see Table 6.4).

Table 6.4   Some foreign operations of Alrosa and Norilsk Nickel

Company	Markets	Operations
Alrosa	Angola, Namibia, Botswana, Tanzania	Diamond exploration
		Diamond exploration
	Israel, Belgium, UK, Angola	Representative office
Norilsk Nickel	Cuba	Building a nickel plant
	Japan	
	New Caledonia, New Guinea	Exports (palladium)
	Belgium	Planned production
		Cobalt trading unit

Metallurgy

The Russian steel industry enjoys self-sufficiency in raw materials accounting for almost 10 percent of the world's effective capacity. Measured by output, Russia is the fourth largest steel producer in the world and 60 percent of this total steel output is exported. Even though Asia and Western Europe, with a combined share of 70 percent, are dominating destinations for Russian steel exports, the exports to CIS countries experienced strong growth in 2000. While the exports to countries outside the CIS increased by 20 percent, the respective growth in the case of CIS countries was 60 percent (EBRD, 2001).

The largest of the Russian steel producers, by both production and market capitalization, is Severstal. After privatization, which started in 1993, Severstal has been transformed from an inefficient Soviet behemoth into one of Russia's best managed and most efficient companies (EBRD, 2001). The company has expanded sales, especially in North America and Asia, focusing particularly on the export of specialized and value-added steel products in order to avoid anti-dumping disputes. Currently the company exports its products to almost a hundred countries.

Russia's position as the world's biggest exporter of aluminium is supported by the world's second largest aluminium producer, Russian Aluminium (Russkiy Aluminiy). This company is owned by the market leader Siberian Aluminium and the oil company Sibneft, and it controls about three-quarters of Russian aluminium production and one-tenth of global primary aluminium production with annual sales of about US$ 3.4 billion (EBRD, 2001).

Asia has become the main market for its products with 50 percent share of the company's exports, while the U.S.A. receives 30 percent and Europe 20 percent. The company also has several production units abroad. It is expanding control across national borders to facilities that were once integrated under the ex-USSR. For example, Russian Aluminium has production units in Armenia and the Ukraine, where it owns three-quarters of the aluminium plant Nykolayev. It has also purchased a refinery in Romania and is planning to acquire a production unit in the Czech Republic and Yugoslavia. In addition, Russian Aluminium plans to purchase bauxite mines in Italy and Venezuela. Russian Aluminium managed to acquire production facilities in a local bauxite company in Guinea (Liuhto, 2001).

The raw-material suppliers have been active in raising their role in Russian automotive industry. The second largest company of the sector, GAZ, has nowadays the aluminium company Siberian Aluminium as its majority shareholder. Also the third biggest automotive company UAZ experienced a respective takeover, which was carried out by Severstal, the aforementioned steel producer. The largest automotive manufacturer, AvtoVAZ, has been a very active exporter, having its cars sold to 70 countries, including Canada, Finland, France, Germany and Hungary. Some of the foreign operations of Russian aluminium companies are presented in Table 6.5.

Table 6.5 Some foreign operations of Severstal and Russian Aluminium

Company	Markets	Operations
Severstal	Various countries	Exports
Russian Aluminium	Romania, Ukraine, Armenia	Refineries
	Czech Republic, Yugoslavia	Planned to buy a production unit
	Guinea	Bauxite mine
	Italy, Venezuela	Planned to buy bauxite mines

Table 6.6 Some operations of Russian banks abroad

Company	Markets	Operations
Alfa Bank	Luxembourg, Ukraine, Kazakhstan	Branches
	United Kingdom, the U.S.A. and the Netherlands	Subsidiaries
Vneshtorgbank	Switzerland, Luxembourg, Cyprus, Austria	Subsidiaries
	Italy, China	Representative offices
	Securities license for a London based subsidiary	Brokerage

Banking Sector

Internationalization has been taking place in the Russian banking sector as well (see Table 6.6).

Alfa Bank has become Russia's largest privately owned bank. Today, the Bank has more than 60 branches in Russia, Ukraine and Kazakhstan and subsidiaries in the United Kingdom, the United States and the Netherlands. Recently, Alfa Bank has also widened its operations to other branches of the economy by acquiring stakes in about 30 companies operating, for instance, in the telecommunications, oil and gas, trading, chemicals and food processing sectors (Alfa Bank, 2001).

Vneshtorgbank, owned by the Central Bank of the Russian Federation with a share of 99.9 percent, has been increasing its domestic banking activities and is further expanding its foreign network. Currently the bank has subsidiary banks in Switzerland, Luxembourg, Cyprus and Austria, and representative offices in Italy and China (Vneshtorgbank, 2001).

Discussion

The economic relations between the independent states play an increasingly important role in integrating the goals of the countries, and the well-integrated economic ties are assumed to provide benefits to all the parties involved in the economic collaboration, which none of the partners would be able to gain by acting alone. In addition to these economic advantages, mutual economic interests are an essential source of mutual understanding, and hence, economic integration forms an effective means for building and sustaining stability.

When the role of FDI inflow to Russia is examined, it becomes apparent that the foreign direct investments have not been able to integrate Russia as closely as the CEECs into the Pan-European economic collaboration. The modest FDI inflow to Russia is mainly due to the harsh business environment characterized by deficient business legislation, non-consistent law enforcement, overwhelming bureaucracy, high corruption, and organized crime, which have kept many potential foreign investors outside the Russian borders (see Figure 6.2).

If foreign firms have not succeeded in integrating Russia into the global business, the Russian corporations, via their outward FDI, have managed to integrate their country into foreign markets more successfully than companies of any other transition economy. The Goskomstat data suggests that the Russian corporations have expanded especially in the U.S.A. and the EU.

Alternative A.   Globalizing Russia

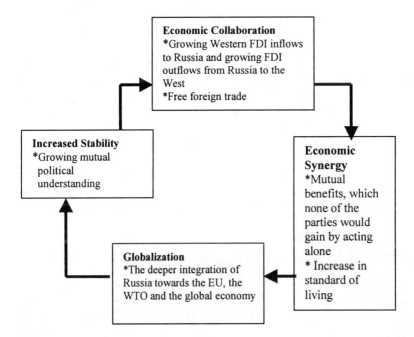

Alternative B.   Blocalizing Russia

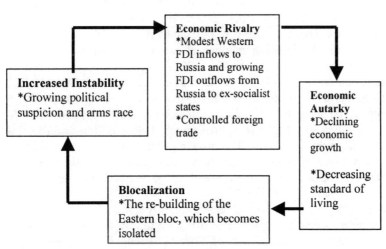

Figure 6.2   The two 'extreme' alternatives of the expansion of Russian corporations abroad

The direction of the expansion towards the ex-CMEA bloc has created some suspicion concerning the ultimate goal of integration, which to a large extent defines whether the expansion of the Russian companies abroad either leads to the closer integration of Russia in the global economy or to new 'blocalization'.

Figure 6.2 above describes the two extreme outcomes of the Russian corporations' expansion abroad. Most probably, neither of the alternatives will be realized as such, but the outcome will likely be the mixture of the two, i.e., it is not an excluded alternative that both Western and Eastern integration would occur simultaneously.

Should the Russian corporations, especially those involved in energy and other strategic raw materials, act like business units, a globalizing Russia seems to be a dominating alternative. However, if the Russian corporations will be used as tools to reach the objectives of Russian foreign policy, the blocalization is a more likely alternative than the globalization.

Summary

At the end of the 1980s, less than 500 Soviet enterprises operated abroad. A decade later, a multitude of Russian companies have been established outside the Russian borders. According to the Russian Ministry of Internal Affairs, some 60,000 firms with Russian capital have been registered in these taxation havens. In addition to these taxation paradise firms, thousands of other Russian companies have been founded elsewhere. For example, over 1,500 joint stock companies with Russian management participation have been registered in Finland alone.

Along with the growing number of these registered business units, Russian FDI abroad has increased. In 2000 the recorded outward FDI stock of Russia amounted to almost US$ 12 billion. The majority of the outward FDI flow has taken place during the past few years, i.e., almost US$ 9 billion of Russian capital has been invested abroad during the period 1997 - 2000. According to UNCTAD, approximately US$ 3 billion floated away from Russia in the year 2000. The growing FDI outflow suggests that the financial position of some Russian companies has significantly improved, and hence, Russian corporations have become increasingly interested in expanding abroad.

In this context, it needs to be remembered that the recorded FDI outflow forms only a fraction of the total Russian capital abroad. It can be estimated that the Russian outward FDI stock is roughly 5 - 10 percent of the total Russian capital stock abroad as the capital flight from Russia was roughly US$ 80 - 200 billion during the 1990s.

Various sources indicate that Russian direct investment has not flown only to the West but, to a large extent, to Central and Eastern European countries, and to the former Soviet republics. Russian companies have invested considerably in Poland, Hungary and in the Baltic States. Moreover, the Russian involvement in the Ukraine, Kazakhstan and other CIS countries seems to have strengthened during the past few years.

The available data suggests that the oil and natural gas business form the lion's share of the Russian investments abroad. Gazprom, with its US$ 1.25 billion investment in Poland alone, gives a good indication of the dominance of energy-related investments[2]. The foreign assets of the major Russian oil companies, especially LUKoil's foreign assets worth some US$ 2.3 billion, confirm the conclusion on the dominating role of the energy sector in the internationalization of Russian corporations. Even though the energy sector dominates the Russian outward FDI, other sectors are also internationalizing rapidly. One could anticipate the speeding expansion of the Russian metal companies, such as Russkiy Aluminiy and Norilsk Nickel, outside their domestic playground. The most powerful Russian banks seem to eye foreign markets, especially those of the CIS.

The empirical evidence shows that Russian foreign direct investments are not always very direct. For example, when Gazprom wanted to acquire TVK, a Hungarian petrochemical factory, it used both Austrian and Irish face companies to purchase this Hungarian factory. Some other Russian corporations have also been detected using face companies when they have tried to finalize international acquisitions. These incidences, often related to the privatization of a company in the CEECs, show that the Russian investment outflow statistics describe only a fraction of the real acquisition potential of Russian companies abroad.

Another observation to be considered is that Russian companies aim at acquiring a control stake in their foreign business units, if not immediately then in the longer run. The approach of obtaining a control stake, which used to be the main investment strategy during the Soviet era, seems to be a common investment pattern among Russian corporations nowadays.

All in all, Russian corporations are currently more active abroad than during the Soviet period, and most probably, the expansion of Russian businesses abroad will continue. However, there is a general question of how to react to the active involvement of Russian corporations in operations outside Russia.

The answer to this question depends to a large extent on the ultimate goals of the Russian internationalization. Should business objectives dominate in their internationalization strategies, the Russian corporations will easily find an appropriate place in the global business. Especially, the role of Russian energy companies in strengthening the energy collaboration between Russia and the EU would be important. Through the Russian investments in the current and enlarged EU, Russia would benefit directly from the advantages of enlargement. Moreover, the Russian investments in the EU would support EU-Russian trade. Increasing EU-Russian trade would ultimately strengthen stability in Europe and worldwide.

On the other hand, should the internationalization of Russian corporations be used as a means of imposing Russia's foreign policy, the attitudes towards the expansion of the Russian companies will become reserved. To date, the attitudes towards the international operations of Russian firms have been generally positive. However, in a few formerly socialist countries, the political and public opinion on the penetration of the Russian firms has been rather suspicious. This is mostly due to the fact that Russian corporations have tried to acquire ex-socialist enterprises via face firms or shadow operations. Further studies would most probably be able to reveal whether the internationalization of Russian corporations signifies a new era in global business or a return to history.

Notes

1   By the beginning of 2001, over 1500 joint stock companies with Russian management participation have been established in Finland (Jumpponen, 2001). During the Russian Prime Minister's visit in Finland in July 2001, it was announced that the cumulative Russian FDI in Finland – US$ 260 million is higher than the Finnish FDI in Russia – US$ 230 million.

2   According to the Polish Agency for Foreign Investment (Jelonkiewic, 2001), the five largest investors in Poland are the following: Daewoo (US$ 1.55 billion), Fiat (US$ 1.54 billion), Gazprom (US$ 1.25 billion), Vivendi (US$ 1.2 billion) and United Pan-European Communication (US $1.2 billion).

References

Alfa Bank (2001), http://www. alfa-bank.com (referred 25.7.2001).

Bank of Finland (2001), *Russian Economy: The Month in Review 5/2001*, Institute for Economies in Transition, Helsinki: Bank of Finland.

Business Central Europe (2001), July/August, vol. 8, no. 83 p. 14.

Business Central Europe (2000), The Economist Intelligence Unit, October 23, p. 10.

Bulatov, A. (1998), 'Russian Direct Investment Abroad: Main Motivations in the Post-Soviet Period', *Transnational Corporations*, vol. 7, no. 1, pp. 69-82.

Cheklina, T. (1991), 'Joint Ventures in Eastern Europe', *Foreign Trade,* vol. 8, pp. 25-27.

Cullison, A. and Bahree, B. (1999), Gazprom's Dilemma, *Central European Economic Review*, September, pp. 10-13.

European Bank for Reconstruction and Development (2001), *Russian Federation Investment Profile in 2001*, London: EBRD.

Goskomstat (2000), *Россия и страни мира*, Статистический сборник, Москва: Госкомстат России.

Hamilton, G. (ed.) (1986), *Red Multinationals or Red Herrings? - The Activities of Enterprises from Socialist Countries in the West*, London: Pinter.

Heinrich, A. (2001), 'Internationalisation, Market Structures and Enterprise Behaviour - The Janus-faced Russian Gas Monopoly Gazprom', in K. Liuhto (ed.) *East Goes West - The Internationalisation of Eastern Enterprises*, Lappeenranta: Lappeenranta University of Technology, pp. 51-87.

Hill, M. (1986), 'Soviet and Eastern European Company Activity in the United Kingdom and Ireland', in G. Hamilton (ed.), *Red Multinationals or Red Herrings? - The Activities of Enterprises from Socialist Countries in the West*, in London: Pinter, pp. 17-87.

Hunya, G. (2000), *Recent FDI Trends, Policies and Challenges in South-East European Countries*, Vienna, The Vienna Institute for International Economic Studies (WIIW), No. 273.

Hunya, G. and Stankowsky, J. (2001), 'Foreign Direct Investment in Central and East European Countries and the Former Soviet Union', WIIW-WIFO Database, June.

International Monetary Fund (2000), *World Economic Outlook 2001*, Washington: IMF Publications.

Jelonkiewicz, W. (2001), 'Foreign Direct Investment Fuelling Transformation', *The Polish Voice*, January, pp. 12-13.

Jumpponen, J. (2001), '"Made in Russia" in Finland - Some Preliminary Findings', in K. Liuhto (ed.) *East Goes West - The Internationalisation of Eastern Enterprises*, Lappeenranta: Lappeenranta University of Technology, pp. 223-232.

Liuhto, K. (ed.) (2001), *East Goes West - The Internationalisation of Eastern Enterprises*, Lappeenranta: Lappeenranta University of Technology.

Matejka, H. (1988), 'More Joint Enterprises within CMEA', in J. Hardt and C. McMillan (eds) *Planned Economies - Confronting the Challenges of the 1980s*, Cambridge: Cambridge University Press, pp. 171-189.

McMillan, C. (1987), *Multinationals from the Second World - Growth of Foreign Investment by Soviet and East European State Enterprises*, London: Macmillan Press.

New Europe (2001a), Number 409, p. 46.

New Europe (2001b), Number 422, p. 47.

New Europe (2001c), 'Gazprom says will work on Chinese gas market', Number 424, p. 47.

New Europe (2001d), 'Gazprom to build unified gas multi-pipeline system in Asia', Number 426, p. 23.

New Europe (2001e), 'LUKoil mulls over US refinery acquisition', Number 426, p. 23.

The Russia Journal (2001), 'YUKOS Buys Nafta Stake, Posts Results', vol. 4, no. 24, pp. 22-28.

Sokolov, S. (1991a), 'Companies Set up Abroad with Soviet Capital', *Foreign Trade*, vol. 10, pp. 15-17.

Sokolov, S. (1991b), 'Sovetskiy Kapital za Rubezhom', *Ekonomika i Zhizn*, vol. 14, p. 1.

Trofimenko, O. (2001), 'In Search of the New Lights – Internationalisation of RAO UES' in K. Liuhto (ed.), *East Goes West - The Internationalisation of Eastern Enterprises*, Lappeenranta: Lappeenranta University of Technology, pp. 113-133.

UNCTAD (2001), *World Investment Report 2001*, New York: United Nations.

Vneshtorgbank (2001), http://www.vtb.ru (referred 24.7.01).

Väätänen, J. and Liuhto, K. (2001), 'The Internationalisation of Russian Oil Companies - LUKoil and Its Princes', in K. Liuhto (ed.) *East Goes West - The Internationalisation of Eastern Enterprises*, Lappeenranta: Lappeenranta University of Technology, pp. 88-112.

Zaleski, E. (1986), 'Socialist Multinationals in Developing Countries', in G. Hamilton (ed.) *Red Multinationals or Red Herrings? – The Activities of Enterprises from Socialist Countries in the West*, London: Pinter, pp. 156-184.

7 Characteristics of Japanese Foreign Direct Investment in Central and Eastern Europe

MARIN ALEXANDROV MARINOV, KEN MORITA and
SVETLA TRIFONOVA MARINOVA

Introduction

The internationalization of multinational corporations (MNCs) in Central
and Eastern Europe (CEE) has been intensifying since the start of
transition. One of the most important modes of penetrating the CEE market
has been foreign direct investment (FDI). The supply of FDI has been
mainly provided by Western European MNCs, Germany being the major
player, and MNCs from the USA (Culpan and Kumar, 1994; Jain and
Tucker, 1994; Peng, 2000; Marinov and Marinova, 2001).

The behavior of the MNCs already operating in CEE through an
investment mode of market entry would seem to contradict the Uppsala
internationalization model (Johanson and Wiedersheim-Paul, 1975;
Johanson and Vahlne; 1977) suggesting processes of gradual and
incremental international growth. The actions of MNCs that moved early
into CEE can be explained using the network model of internationalization
(Johanson and Mattsson, 1987) only for a limited number of cases (Davis *et
al.*, 1996; Lehtinen, 1996; Salmi, 2000). The 'first mover' behavior of
foreign MNCs can be better accounted for using the transaction cost
analysis model (Coase, 1937) of the internationalization process
(Williamson, 1975) as emphasizing among others the factors of
opportunism and asset specificity.

All existing internationalization models refer to environments where
change is characterized as slow and with high level of predictability. CEE
markets are generally perceived as turbulent with quick and sometimes
unpredictable environmental changes. Hence, investments in CEE markets
involve assumption of certain level of risk, higher than in relatively more
stable and predictable markets.

The international recognition of Japanese MNCs can be traced back to
the early 1960s. At that time they performed mainly exports of

155

transportation and electronic equipment. The export activities intensified in the 1970s. Starting in the 1970s, but most typical for the 1980s and 1990s, production activities centralized in Japan have been spreading worldwide through FDI.

According to the official statistics of IMF, UNICAD and JETRO, Japan was the fourth largest world investor in 1994 and 1995 with FDI of US$ 18.1 billion and US$ 22.5 billion respectively.

Despite the increase of FDI in absolute figures Japanese MNCs could not keep the pace of increase as demonstrated by the world largest investing countries and went to sixth place in the world ranking in 1996 and 1997 with FDI of US$ 23.4 billion and US$ 26.1 billion respectively. In 1998 there was a decrease in Japanese FDI by 5.8 percent compared to its level in 1997. Consequently, Japan went to seventh place in the world ranking of FDI by country-of-origin.

Japanese investment has shown a strong tendency of preferential allocation. From being a negligible investor in the USA in the 1960s, by late 1980s Japan became the second largest investor there with more than 20 percent share of all FDI in the country (Lipsey, 1994). Japan is a leading provider of FDI for the Asian countries (Anand and Delios, 1996).

However, Japanese MNCs did not rush to take advantage of the investment opportunities in CEE (Artisien *et al.*, 1993; Bakos, 1992). Apart from some incidental acquisitions and greenfield investments in the period 1989 - 1997 Japanese MNCs did not engage in substantial FDI activities in CEE. According to official JETRO statistics in the period 1990 - 1995 FDI inflow from Japan into CEE including the Commonwealth of Independent States was US$ 763 million whereas in the countries of Taiwan, Thailand and Singapore the FDI inflow from Japan for the same period was more than six times bigger (JETRO Annual Bulletin, 1996). Initially, instead of investing in CEE some Japanese MNCs, for example Nissan, have given a strategic priority to creating extensive sales and distribution networks across the region expecting those to be instrumental in gaining large shares in the CEE market.

In the first years of transition this strategy proved successful providing a 25 - 35 percent annual increase of Japanese exports to CEE on a year-on-year basis. Since 1992 the export strategy has proved unsuccessful across the region. All the same Japanese MNCs have demonstrated hesitant behavior in engaging themselves in substantial FDI activities in CEE. In this respect Japanese MNCs have been more risk-averse than many of their Western European and North American rivals. Perceived uncertainties in the CEE region and substantial psychic distance between CEE and Japan may be accountable for this behavior. At the same time during the 1990s Western Europe was very much in the focus of Japanese MNCs, who assumed that CEE could be left for future consideration.

Japanese MNCs in CEE: Pre-Transitional Perspective

Before the start of the transition in CEE in the late 1980s Japan had good economic and business relationships with the countries of the region (Hutchings, 1999). For instance, by August 1989 Japan had nineteen joint ventures in the Russian Federation as a part of the former Soviet Union.

In the 1970s intergovernmental agreements on economic, industrial, scientific, and technological cooperation were reached between Japan and most of the CEE countries. Throughout the pre-transition period some of the most important active Japanese MNCs participating in trade and investment activities with and in CEE were: Ataka & Co., Itochu Co., Hitachi, Honda Motor, Kanebo, Matsushita Eclectic Industrial, Mitsubishi, Mitsui, Nissan Motor, NEC, Nissho-Iwai, Sony, Sumitomo Co., Toyota Motor (Horaguchi, 1992).

Economic cooperation between Japan and CEE started in the 1960s. In the 1970s many licensing agreements were concluded between Japanese MNCs and CEE governments for providing mostly technology, patents, and technical know-how from Japan to CEE countries and from some CEE countries to Japan. Former socialist countries most active in the process were Bulgaria, ex-Czechoslovakia, former German Democratic Republic, Hungary, Poland, and ex-Yugoslavia. In the 1980s many international joint ventures were created between Japanese MNCs and various CEE governments. For example, in Bulgaria Japan was the most important international joint venture partner of the Bulgarian government outside the Soviet Bloc (Wolf and Razvigorova, 1991).

Japanese MNCs in CEE: Post-Transitional Perspective

After the start of transition the FDI inflows into CEE started to grow mostly because of investments by Western European and US MNCs. Most substantial growth of investment since 1996 has been indicated in Poland and recently in the Czech Republic, while FDI in Hungary has been leveling.

Initially, the investments made by Japanese MNCs in CEE were primarily as joint ventures and channeled mainly through Japanese affiliates based in Europe. Starting in 1996, signs of full-scale investments

by Japanese MNCs in manufacturing industries have begun to appear such
as the creation of wholly owned subsidiaries by Matsushita Electric in the
Czech Republic, Sanyo Electric Co. in Hungary, and Isuzu Motors Ltd. in
Poland.

The inflow of capital from Japanese MNCs into CEE has been
irregular and on a small scale. Table 7.1 provides data of the total FDI
inflow in several CEE countries and the share of Japanese MNCs in it in
the period 1990 - 1997.

Table 7.1   Inflow of FDI in CEE Countries and Share of Japanese FDI in US$ million

Country	1990	1991	1992	1993	1994	1995	1996	1997	1990-1997
FDI in the Czech R.	72	523	1,003	568	862	2,559	1,428	3,325	10,340
FDI from Japan	0	232	0	2	0	1	134	179	548
FDI in Hungary	990	1,614	1,641	2,481	1,320	4,570	2,524	1,147	16,287
FDI from Japan	29	181	4	72	41	33	13	42	415
FDI in Poland	100	300	978	1,563	1,280	2,511	5,196	3,137	15,065
FDI from Japan	3	2	0	7	3	3	10	13	41
FDI in Romania	107	149	307	156	568	313	609	1,235	3,444
FDI from Japan	0	0	0	0	0	2	5	5	12
Total FDI in Russia	n.a	n.a.	n.a.	809	549	2,445	2,060	5,721	11,584
FDI from Japan	0	2	44	22	19	30	18	139	274

Note: Japanese investment in the Czech Republic till 1993 represents total
investment from Japan in ex-Czechoslovakia.

Sources: National Statistics of individual CEE countries.
Statistics of the Japanese Ministry of Finance.
Vienna Institute for Comparative Economic Studies.

Japanese FDI in Hungary

Before the start of transition in 1989 Japanese MNCs had six investments in Hungary made in the period 1979 - 1989. The pre-transition cumulative Japanese FDI in Hungary was approximately US$ 11 million. The most important part of the investment was in the financial and manufacturing sectors. With the creation of Magyar Suzuki Hungary became on top position in CEE in terms of attracting Japanese FDI. By the end of September 1992 the number of Hungarian companies with Japanese capital increased to 25 and the cumulative FDI reached US$ 221 million.

When Suzuki started its production several other Japanese MNCs invested in Hungary for supplying Suzuki's operations. In late 1993 the then Daikin Corporation (now Exedy Corporation) started clutch production for the manufacturing of Suzuki's cars in Hungary. In 1993 and 1994 the inflow of Japanese FDI into Hungary was mainly in the manufacturing sector.

After the investments in 1996 and 1997 Hungary reinforced its leading position in attracting Japanese FDI in the CEE region. By the end of 1999 almost half of total number of the Japanese FDI projects in Hungary were in services, predominantly finance and banking. In value terms Japanese investment in manufacturing was almost two thirds while the number of manufacturing projects was less than 25 percent.

The overall evaluation of the Japanese FDI in Hungary shows that Japan had only 2.55 percent of the total FDI inflow in the period 1990 - 1997. Due to some recent trends of intensification of Japanese FDI in Hungary its cumulative value has reached US$ 1 billion at the end of year 2000 to get to 5.1 percent share of all FDI into the country. Most of the investments have been greenfield. By the end of 1999 there were 75 companies in Hungary with Japanese investment of US$ 750 million. The types of investments are presented in Table 7.2.

Table 7.2   Types of Japanese FDI in Hungary 1990 - 1999

Type of Investment/Subsidiary	Number	Capital Invested in US$ million	Percent of Number/Capital
Greenfield	63	560	84/75
Acquisitions	12	190	16/25

Source: Hungarian National Statistics.

Japanese FDI has followed the general trend of foreign investment inflows in Hungary. Initially, Japanese FDI went into joint venture formation with Hungarian private investors or the government. The importance of greenfield investments has gradually increased since 1992 because of the success of previous investments and the introduction of government incentive programs.

Japanese FDI in Poland

Until the start of transition Japanese FDI in Poland was in only one company set up in mid-1989. Japan lagged far behind the US, Western Europe and South Korea in terms of investment in the country (Morita, 1998; Morita and Stuglik, 1998).

By the end of 1991 there were eight Japanese FDI cases in Poland with a total value of US$ 3 million. All of them were trade representative offices, three of which were wholly owned by Japanese MNCs, as for example Toyota Motor Poland. In 1992 there were another six FDI transactions with investment of more than US$ 2 million.

The first more substantial Japanese investments in Poland were made by Matsushita-Philips and Marubeni (Morita, 1995). Altogether Japanese investment was on a much smaller scale in comparison to that made in the Czech Republic, Hungary and Russia in the period 1990 - 1997 (see Table 7.1). In two and a half years, from January 1998 till June 2000, Japanese MNCs invested eight times more than in the previous nine years (PAIZ Annual Bulletin, 2000).

The amount of cumulative Japanese FDI in Poland at the end of year 2000 is estimated to be US$ 450 million. Table 7.3 presents information of the amounts Japanese MNCs invested in Poland specifying the industry sector and type of investment.

Most of the investments have been made in the manufacturing sector with approximately 60 percent in the automotive industry. Interestingly enough, this is the only investment in manufacturing that resulted in the formation of a wholly owned subsidiary of Isuzu Motors Limited. Most of the other investments went for the formation of international joint ventures with either Polish private and state capital or other foreign capital participation.

The contribution of Japanese capital to the total investment inflow in Poland has been negligible. Table 7.4 shows that Japanese MNCs have invested seventeen times less than their German counterparts, eleven times less than French MNCs, and nine times less than their Dutch rivals.

Table 7.3   Japanese FDI in Poland from 1989 up to July 2000

Investing Corporation	Capital Invested (US$ mln)	Industry	Type of investment
Isuzu Motors Limited	192.7	automotive	wholly owned subsidiary
Bridgestone Corporation	45.0	rubber and plastics	joint venture
NSK-RHP Europe Ltd.	39.2	machinery and equipment	joint venture
Tohoku Pioneer Electronic Corporation	35.7	electrical machinery	joint venture
Matsushita Electric	22.5	electrical machinery	joint venture
Nichimen Corporation	5.6	machinery and equipment	joint venture
Nomura	5.0	wholesale trade	n.a.
Toyota	5.0	wholesale and retail trade	joint venture
Nissho Iwai	4.5	wholesale trade	joint venture
Sumitomo Corporation Europe	4.4	trade and repair	trade representative office
Itochu	1.0	wholesale trade	trade representative office
Kanematsu	1.0	wholesale trade	trade representative office

Source: Panstwowa Agencja Inwestycji Zagranicznych (PAIZ), Poland.

Table 7.4   Cumulative FDI by major investing countries and Japan in Poland in the period January 1, 1990 - December 31, 1999

Rank	Country of Origin	Capital Invested (US$ million)	Percent of Total Investment
1.	Germany	6,077.3	15.62
2.	U.S.A.	5,152.9	13.25
3.	France	3,854.7	9.90
4.	Netherlands	3,233.2	8.31
5.	Italy	3,208.1	8.25
16.	Japan	374.3	0.92

Source: Panstwowa Agencja Inwestycji Zagranicznych (PAIZ), Poland.

Japanese FDI in the Czech Republic

The first post-transition recorded Japanese FDI in ex-Czechoslovakia was contracted in 1990 by SSB-ANTI for the creation of a shopping center with dedication of US$ 300,000. However, the investment partnership dissolved in the early 1991.

The first successful case was that of Summit Motors Czechoslovakia made in 1991 for the creation of a wholly owned subsidiary. The first big successful Japanese investment in the Czech Republic (then Czechoslovakia) after the start of the transition was contracted in 1991. It amounted to US$ 232 million for the acquisition of a large glass-making plant.

By the end of 1992 there were altogether 30 Japanese subsidiaries, 10 of which were representative sales offices as the ones of Toyota and Nissan. Several joint ventures were created in 1993, most important of which was the one set by Nissho Iwai.

By the end of June 1999 the cumulative post-transition Japanese FDI in the Czech Republic reached US$ 579 million, representing 4.7 percent of the total FDI inflow in the country.

By the end of 1999 almost 80 percent of Japanese FDI in the Czech Republic went into the manufacturing sector.

Since the second half of 1996 Japanese FDI in the Czech Republic has started to grow (see Table 7.1). By the end of 1999 Japanese MNCs had invested almost US$ 620 million (CzechInvest, 2000). Large-scale greenfield FDI in the Czech Republic was undertaken by Mastushita

Electric Industrial Corporation, Toray Industries, Mitsubishi Electric Corporation and Showa Aluminum Corporation.

Table 7.5 contains data of the FDI in the Czech Republic made by varic is Japanese MNCs in different industrial sectors specifying the type of in restment. Only three of the investments resulted in the creation of international joint ventures with the participation of Czech private or state capital. The Japanese participation in the joint ventures is small in value and insignificant for the Czech economy.

Table 7.5   Japanese FDI in the Czech Republic in 1990 - 2000

Investing Corporation	Invested Capital (US$ mln)	Industry	Type of Investment
Matsushita Electric	254.5	electronics	greenfield
Asahi Glass	232.0	glass production	acquisition
Toray	150.0	textiles	greenfield
AVX/Kyocera	54.0	electronics	greenfield/acquisition
Mitsubishi Electric	32.0	automotive	greenfield
Showa	28.0	automotive	greenfield
Daiho	10.0	engineering	greenfield
Nippon Kayaku	10.0	automotive	joint venture
Nissho Iwai Co.	2.5	metal industry	joint venture
Euro-Matsushita	1.7	electrical	greenfield
Tatsuno	1.3	engineering	joint venture
Toyoda	1.2	textile machinery	technical cooperation
Denon	1.0	electronics	technical cooperation

Source: Czech Invest, Czech Republic.

Comparison of Japanese FDI in the Czech Republic and Poland

Table 7.6 presents data showing the concentration of Japanese FDI in the Czech Republic and Poland using the system of the Standard Industrial Classification (SIC). While the Japanese FDI in the Czech Republic is made in seven industries, it is more concentrated in Poland, encompassing five industrial sectors. In four sectors investments have been made in both countries.

Table 7.6   Comparison by industry of Japanese FDI in the Czech Republic and Poland in the period 1990 - 1999

Industry	SIC	Percent of total volume of Japanese FDI in the Czech R.	Percent of total volume of Japanese FDI in Poland
Textile Mill Products	22	0.15	0.0
Apparel and Other Textile Products	23	19.20	0.0
Rubber and Plastics	30	0.0	12.44
Stone, Clay and Glass Products	32	29.81	0.0
Industrial Machinery and Equipment	35	0.32	12.39
Electrical and Electronic Equipment	36	39.99	16.10
Transportation Equipment	37	8.99	53.29
Trade		1.54	5.78

Source: CzechInvest, Czech Republic; PAIZ, Poland.

The most significant investment in the Czech Republic has been made in electrical and electronic equipment industry, while in Poland it is in transportation equipment. The traditionally strong industrial sectors in the two countries have received sole investments, in the Czech Republic - apparel and other textile products, in Poland - rubber and plastics industry.

Japanese FDI in Slovakia

The first Japanese FDI in Slovakia was made in 1994 by Yazaki Corporation. It amounted to US$ 62,000. By the end of June 1995 JAIDO-OLIGO made a second investment for more than US$ 1 million. In April 1996 Sony created a wholly owned subsidiary in Slovakia. In the period 1996 - 1998 investments were made by United Electronics, Mastishita Electric and Sony.

By the end of March 1999 Japan has invested in Slovakia more than US$ 12 million representing 1.8 percent of the total FDI inflow in the country. The most substantial Japanese FDI in Slovakia was made in 1997.

Japanese FDI in Romania

According to the official JETRO and Romanian state statistics there was no Japanese FDI registered in Romania before the start of transition. By the end of October 1991 there were seven FDI cases in Romania all of which were for the establishment of sales representative offices, including the investment by Panasonic Distribution.

At that time Japanese MNCs were trying to establish strategic alliances in the form of joint ventures with Romanian investors. The lack of domestic capital turned out to be a substantial deterrent for Japanese FDI in Romania. New sales representative offices were created in 1992.

In 1993 new auto sales offices were opened by Honda, Mazda, Itochu, Nissan and Sumitomo. By the end of 1993 there were five Japanese auto sales subsidiaries representing more than 70 percent of Japanese FDI in Romania.

By the end of 1996 the cumulative FDI from Japan into Romania reached US$ 7 million mainly due to the investment by Kokusai Boeki for the production of colored TV sets. According to official Romanian statistics by the end of year 2000 the cumulative Japanese FDI in Romania reached US$ 13.5 million for 75 projects. This investment ranked Japan in 39th place among the other investors in Romania with a share of 0.3 percent of total investment in the country. Hence, Japanese MNCs' position in Romania is very weak. Japanese investors perceive Romania as a promising market. However, from their point of view the major obstacles for investing in the country have mostly been the lack of domestic capital to participate in joint investment, unstable environment, and underdeveloped infrastructure.

Japanese FDI in Bulgaria

Before 1989 Japanese MNCs have established five international joint ventures with the Bulgarian government. After the start of transition two of them withdrew in 1990 because of the unstable political and economic environment. By the end of 1990 there were three joint ventures in Bulgaria with the participation of Japanese capital. They were Fanuc-Masinex with the participation of Fanuc established in 1981, SOMICO with the participation of Tokyo Maruichi Corporation, created in 1982, and Medicom Systems, again with Tokyo Maruichi Corporation founded in 1986. In the three cases the Bulgarian government partnered the Japanese MNCs.

In 1992 an auto sales representative office was created as a joint venture set up by Nissan and Tokyo Maruichi Co. on the Japanese part, and Techno-Import-Export on the Bulgarian part. This was the first Japanese FDI in Bulgaria after the transition started amounting to US$ 165,000.

In 1994 three new sales representative offices were created as a joint venture with the participation of K&B International and two wholly owned subsidiaries by TM Auto and Sony. One new wholly owned sales representative office was established in 1995 by Sumimoto. Thus, by the end of 1995 there were seven Japanese FDIs in Bulgaria (Marinov and Marinova, 1997) with cumulative investment of US$ 502,000. Eleven more small sales representative offices were created in 1996 with investment of US$ 678,000.

According to the Bulgarian Investment Agency, by the end of 1998 the cumulative Japanese FDI in Bulgaria reached almost US$ 5 million which ranked Japan on 23rd place among all foreign investors in Bulgaria with 0.97 percent contribution. The largest investment by a Japanese MNC in Bulgaria is the investment by Sumitomo Co. in the wine plant Vinprom Svishtov amounting to US$ 1.86 million.

Bulgaria was one of the strongest CEE partners of Japan before the start of transition. Since then this position weakened significantly as transitional Bulgaria has been perceived as turbulent and very unstable both politically and economically.

Japanese FDI across CEE

The short outlook of Japanese FDI in six CEE countries shows a general trend of low level of participation. Three CEE countries, the Czech

Republic, Hungary, and Poland, have received the bulk of Japanese FDI in the region amounting to almost 90 percent.

There is also a common trend among those three countries for recent increase in the level of Japanese FDI. This may be due to the improved economic conditions in those countries and the good perspectives they have for joining the European Union in the near future.

The sluggish FDI inflow from Japan into Poland till 1996 was due to several causes. In the early 1990s two Japanese investments failed that possibly exercised negative impact on next Japanese FDIs. Daihatsu was overcome by the Italian Fiat for investing in FSO, Asahi Glass was overcome by the British Pilkington for the acquisition of Sandomierz factory.

On the other end Japanese FDI into Bulgaria, Romania, and Slovakia was exceptionally small. Those three economies with the approximate size of Poland attracted less then US$ 30 million in the period 1990 - 1999, while the FDI inflow in Poland for the same period was more than 12 times bigger. Almost all Japanese investments in the three countries were for the creation of sales representative offices with some occasional investments in production subsidiaries.

Short Case Studies on Japanese FDI into CEE countries

The Cases of Daihatsu and Asahi Glass in Attempting FDI in Poland

As mentioned above, the Daihatsu case might have had a serious negative impact on potential Japanese investors for entering Poland. The Daihatsu case is presented from the point of view of the Japanese corporation.

The Polish company FSO started a process of modernization in the early 1980s. To make the process happen the Polish government began negotiations with several foreign car producers in 1983. Sixteen automotive companies were considered for partnership. The Japanese candidates were Daihatsu and Sumitomo Co. Daihatsu presented its offer for partnership through Itochu Co. that had previously exported automobiles produced by FSO to third countries. Since 1970s Sumitomo Co. had imported Daihatsu-made passenger cars made in Poland. Daihatsu, Itochu, and Sumitomo joined in a consortium that allowed them to make one proposal for partnership with the Polish government for the modernization of FSO.

In the 1980s Poland was considering the launch of a new model passenger car to be manufactured in cooperation with an outstanding automotive company. The new model would be a five-seat car with initial annual output of 120,000 units per year. One fourth of output was planned for export. The project was for US$ 850 million at least half of which amount was expected to be invested by the foreign partner.

According to Japanese sources of information, Japan had shown strong interest in the project. The existing consortium got one more member, Mitsui Co. The Japanese offer was supported at ministerial level and by the Japan-Poland Economic Committee, initiated by Mr. Toshikuni Yahiro, president of Mitsui Co. The strongest rival to the Japanese consortium was the Italian automotive maker Fiat.

The visit of then Japanese Prime Minister Yasuhiro Nakasone in Poland in 1987 was undertaken to make a positive impact on the negotiations between the Japanese consortium and Polish government. Before his visit to Poland, a specially made program on the Polish National TV took the position that the visit was expected to have an important impact on the national passenger car project. Although initiated by private Japanese companies the opportunities for economic cooperation between Japan and Poland were a high priority for the Japanese government.

The possible cooperation between Poland and Japan was looked upon very favorably by the Polish President and government. The visit to Japan of the then First Communist Party Secretary and Polish President, Mr. Jaruzelski, in 1987 had also very positive influence on the prospects of Polish-Japanese cooperation. According to a Japanese source of information, a major focus of the talks was the allocation of a medium-sized car production project to Daihatsu and a possible small-sized car production project to the Italian Fiat.

At this stage the position of the Japanese consortium seemed stronger than that of Fiat. This situation was reflected in a very pessimistic statement by Mr. Govanni Agnelli, the President of Fiat, concerning future prospects of Fiat in Poland. Mr. Agnelli officially admitted that Fiat had apparently lost the Polish contract to Japanese Daihatsu in a bid to build a modern car plant in Poland. He also admitted that the Japanese consortium had offered superior technology and better financial terms.

A private credit was offered to Daihatsu before government support could be obtained for the Polish project. However, the Japanese consortium did not consider the bridge credit favorably. At the same time the Japanese consortium was also in sharp conflict with the Japanese government concerning whether or not MITI would give Daihatsu a definite written promise of export insurance for the project. Meanwhile in the middle of October 1987, officials of the Polish Ministry of Foreign Affairs and Polish Ministry of Foreign Trade gave their opinion that Daihatsu would win against Fiat.

At the same Poland was engaged in multilateral and bilateral negotiations concerning rescheduling of its enormous foreign debt. Those negotiations had negative impact on the position of Daihatsu. When the agreement for the rescheduling of the debt was reached, on August 19, 1988, Mr. Tomohiro Eguchi, the president of Daihatsu, declared his pessimistic expectation concerning the severe competition with Fiat.

On September 8, 1988, just after the successful agreement on the rescheduling talks of the Polish foreign debt, the Polish government requested that the Japanese government start new negotiations on interest rates in the first and the second rescheduling plan, which had already expired. However, the Japanese Ministry of Finance immediately rejected this request.

After the rejection of the Polish request by the Japanese government Mr. Pietrzek, the President of FSO, announced on the National TV that Fiat won the contract without previously informing the Japanese consortium about this decision.

A year later when the drastic Polish transition toward a market-led economy began, the Italian involvement in the project had become uncertain; however the Japanese consortium had already withdrawn definitely from it.

Japanese investors thought that the failure of Daihatsu in 1980s was over. They believed in new opportunities in Poland with the introduction of democratic reforms and transition toward market-oriented system. However, in 1993 Asahi Glass was unexpectedly turned down by the Polish government at the very final stage just before the opening ceremony of establishing a joint venture with Sandomierz factory for float glass production. That contract was given to the British Pilkington.

The failures of Daihatsu and Asahi Glass in attempting FDI in Poland have distracted many Japanese potential investors from entering Poland. Instead they gave preference to the Czech Republic and Hungary.

The Case of Toyota

Toyota has developed and implemented an important strategy toward expansion of European market mainly through its Belgian subsidiary Toyota Motor Europe Marketing and Engineering (TMME) established in 1990.

Toyota finalized its strategy for the European market in 1997. The strategic priorities included the creation of a second car production factory in Europe starting production in 2001, introduction of a new car model, initial production capacity envisaged 10,000 cars a year. The probable investment sites were in France, because of easy access for local contents and in Poland, because of low labor cost.

The UK was also considered for a possible production site. In terms of labor cost Poland had a clear advantage. However, the CEE market was considered small in size and with limited potential due to the small purchasing power of population. However, transportation costs from Poland to Western European markets would be approximately the same as from France or the UK. France had the advantage of a better location for export in Western European countries, the larger size of the domestic market, and in providing good supply of spare parts. Production sites in France included the disadvantages of high labor cost and short working hours. The major advantage of UK production location through the expansion of the factory in the UK would be to benefit of economies of scale. The major disadvantage of the UK location was the high value of the pound sterling and British reluctance to join the EMU, which might result in foreign exchange instability.

In 1997 the Polish government expressed publicly enthusiasm for attracting Toyota investment in Poland and offered Katowice for a possible investment site. Preferential treatment included ten years exemption from corporation tax. The Polish government also emphasized the successful transition toward a market-oriented system resulting in expanding the car market in Poland. This brought about 46 percent increase in car sales in 1996 compared with the volume sold in 1995. The sale of new Toyota cars in Poland in 1996 reached the amount of 5,559 that gave Toyota only 1.3 per cent of the Polish car market. Toyota lagged far behind its mayor competitors Fiat and Daewoo with 42 per cent and 28 percent of the Polish market respectively.

Meanwhile, Mr. Hiroshi Okuda, the then President of Toyota, officially announced that the new Toyota factory in Europe was decided, the production site would be found by mid-1998, and the new plant would start production in 2001. To consider possible production sites the corporation officials would visit Reims and Cherbourg in France and a city in Poland.

In the second half of 1997 Toyota announced the final decision of production sites in three countries for making automobiles, engines, and transmissions. The second car production factory of Toyota would be located in France. The corporation would expand its production capacity of producing engines in the UK. The enlarged UK engine production of Toyota would be used for the manufacturing of the new small-sized car in the new production site in France. Toyota decided to locate its new transmission making factory in Poland. The total investment for the expansion of Toyota's operations in Europe would amount approximately US$ 2 billion. The main reason for the selection of France was that the French small-sized car market was one of the largest in Europe. France and Italy account for more than 65 of the European small car market. Poland was selected as a production location because of the perceived big potential growth of domestic and CEE market.

In 1998 Toyota finally decided on the transmission production site in Poland near the borders with the Czech Republic and Germany.

What attracted Toyota into Poland and the town of Walbrzych? Three main reasons accounted for the choice of the country: the large size of the constantly growing market, the government incentives for ten years exemption from corporation tax and the favored treatment on duties after Poland joins the EU. Walbrzych was chosen because of its favorable geographic position close to car makers, high unemployment rate in the region of 25 percent, and the availability of abundant subterranean water needed for industrial production. Toyota's official announcement of FDI in Poland was made on September 10, 1999. The contracted investment was around 10 billion Japanese yen for initial employment of 300 workers. The transmissions produced in Poland would be exported to France, the UK, and Turkey for Toyota car production in the three countries.

By late 1999 Toyota had plans to establish a company for car sale in Poland through its wholly owned subsidiary Toyota Credit Bank in Cologne, Germany.

By early 2001 Toyota has considered establishing a diesel engine factory in Poland with approximately the same amount of investment as the transmission production factory. Toyota's initial decision on a production site for the factory was the UK. However, the corporation reconsidered it due to the unfavorable exchange rate of the British pound sterling making UK production incompatible. It is still an uncertain case, but we could recognize that Poland may be a rather attractive country for Toyota.

In contrast to the failure cases of Daihatsu and Asahi Glass, Toyota's FDI in Poland has been successful accounting for the diminished risk factor for potential Japanese investors.

The Case of Magyar Suzuki Rt.

Suzuki Corporation Ltd. is a horizontal *keiretsu* with relatively low level of vertical integration. The corporation is controlled by Tokai Group and affiliated with Toyota. General Motors owns a minority share of Suzuki. To increase the international strength of the corporation and its bargaining power towards suppliers Suzuki has entered into strategic alliances with Fuji Heavy Industries (Subaru) and Daihatsu-Toyota. Presently, Suzuki has achieved limited internationalization towards core markets. The corporation has targeted peripheral markets and production sites to gain stronger bargaining position towards suppliers and host governments. For example, Suzuki has used Canada to penetrate the US market, and Spain and Hungary to establish presence in the overall European market.

As far back as the late 1970s the Hungarian government was interested in attracting investments from Japanese car producers in general and Suzuki in particular. Suzuki started negotiations with the Hungarian government to set up a production plant in Hungary in early 1985. In 1989 the strategic priority of Suzuki's investment shifted from producing car models in Hungary for the CEE market to producing car models for the Western European market. The pressure from the intended investments in Hungary by Audi and General Motors/Opel, intensively searching at that time for favorable locations for production facilities in Hungary and market opportunities in the CEE, made Suzuki reconsider its strategic priority and a compromise was reached to produce car models for both CEE and West European markets. The major motives for investing in Hungary were to make use of the cheap production base and utilize Hungary as a second springboard, apart from Spain, for penetrating the East and West European markets. Although Suzuki enjoyed a stronger bargaining position in its negotiations with the Hungarian government the negotiation process continued for almost six years. Together with the negotiations with the Hungarian government Suzuki held talks with the Austrian and Spanish governments for creating production sites in the respective countries. The Japanese corporation targeted these three European countries aiming at overcoming trade barriers and getting easier access to the European markets. While the negotiations with the Austrian government were not successful those with the Hungarian and Spanish governments succeeded. The Hungarian government refused Suzuki's demand for a ten-year tax holiday, but the corporation got strong support from the local government that became a major incentive for Suzuki to create a production site in Hungary.

Suzuki established its European car manufacturing base on a Hungarian production site in the town of Esztergom in 1990. It is Suzuki's European principal production site manufacturing Suzuki Swift and Suzuki Sedans. The plant cost Suzuki HUF40 billion (US$ 190 million). It is still the largest Japanese investment in Hungary. The company is supplied by more than forty local firms and employs 1,500 people.

Suzuki selected a greenfield approach to the creation of its Hungarian plant, relying on a well developed independent exclusive supply infrastructure mostly consisting of small weak local companies. The relationships between Suzuki and its suppliers are problematic because of the low capacity of the Magyar Suzuki Rt. and the incompatibility of Suzuki's components, being of Japanese design, with the components generally used in the car industry. So Suzuki is faced with the dilemma of exporting Hungarian-made components to other Japanese car producers in Europe or sending them to Japan for car production there.

Magyar Suzuki Rt. was created as an international consortium. Its initial capital was HUF 5.5 billion, with 40 percent participation of Autokonszern Rt., 40 percent of Suzuki Motor Corporation, 11 percent invested by the Japanese commercial house C. Itoh and 9 percent share of IFC. In 1996 Autoconszern Rt. seized its existence and its shares were transformed into Magyar Suzuki Rt. shares. The current ownership structure is 83.7 percent owned by Suzuki, 14.2 percent - by Itochu Corporation and 2.1 percent - by Suzuki's Hungarian supplying companies.

The first investment priority of Suzuki was export to Western European markets. Its second investment priority was the domestic market. However, initially the Hungarian car market proved to have a more limited potential than expected. Consequently, it became necessary for Magyar Suzuki Rt. to increase exports in the first years of its existence. In 1996 Magyar Suzuki Rt. exported more than 38,000 cars to become the largest Hungarian exporter in terms of revenue. The highest level of export was reached in 1997 amounting to 47,702 cars. Since then the number of Magyar Suzuki's total sales have increased. However, this has been due to the constant increase of sales in the Hungarian market and decrease in the number of exported cars (see Table 7.7).

Table 7.7   Sales of cars produced by Magyar Suzuki Rt. 1997 – 1999

Market sales	1997	1998	1999
	Number of cars	Number of cars	Number of cars
Domestic	17,679	23,788	30,800
Export	47,702	42,001	37,305
Total	65,381	65,789	68,105

Source: Hungarian Trade Office.

The export of Suzuki Swift to the former Soviet Union started in the second half of 1993. The first deliveries were to Russia and Ukraine. There was also great interest in the Baltic countries and Middle East. The long-term strategy of Magyar Suzuki Rt. has been to expand car exports in Europe including the whole CEE region. To facilitate its CEE sales Suzuki relied on the already established Japanese trade networks in the Czech Republic and Poland.

Magyar Suzuki Rt. has followed a single sourcing strategy. To avoid export tariffs for its exported cars the value of local components should be more than 60 percent of the value of the assembled car. Magyar Suzuki has successfully met this requirement posed by the Hungarian government as since 1997 more than 70 percent of the parts and components for the Suzuki cars produced in Hungary have been made in the country. Suzuki requires from its local suppliers to use Japanese technology. Magyar Suzuki's local suppliers have 2.1 percent stake in the company.

In 1996 Suzuki sold more cars than General Motors/Opel and had become the best selling trademark in Hungary. In the same year Suzuki had 20.5 percent market share in the country. In 1999 the Hungarian market for new cars expanded by almost 25 percent. Magyar Suzuki Rt., seizing this opportunity, increased sales in the domestic market by 28.5 percent. This has allowed the company to reinforce its leading position on the Hungarian passenger car market and cross-country vehicle market. In 1999 Suzuki increased its market share in Hungary by 1 percent compared to 1998. In sales volume in 1999 Suzuki was followed by General Motors/Opel with 15.06 percent of the Hungarian market. Among all other manufacturers of cars in Hungary only Suzuki has managed successfully to sustain its market share growth in the domestic market since the creation of its Hungarian subsidiary.

The Case of Denso Corporation

The President of Denso Corporation, Mr. Hiromu Okabe, opened the corporation's new production facility, Denso Manufacturing Hungary Kft's in Szekesfehervar in August 1999 with registered capital of Hungarian forints equivalent of DM 100 million. For the creation of the Hungarian company for the production of diesel injectors the Japanese MNC invested US$ 100 million through its European subsidiary Denso International Europe B.V. The construction project has been supported by a loan of DM 35 million granted by the European Bank for Reconstruction and Development. Denso's decision to invest in Hungary came on the basis of

Suzuki's successful operations in the country. The Hungarian subsidiary of Denso employs more than 500 people.

Created more than 50 years ago, Denso Corporation, one of the world's leading motor industry suppliers, has widespread international activities. Apart from Hungary, Denso has four other subsidiaries in Europe.

The capacity of the Hungarian plant is 230,000 injectors a year. The major client is the Isuzu plant in Katowice, Poland. Other customers comprise car factories in Hungary and other CEE countries. Denso has also started to sell the injectors to Western European automotive manufacturers, mainly to plants owned by BMW and General Motors.

The Case of Bridgestone/Firestone Corporation

Bridgestone/Firestone Poland Sp. z.o.o. was officially registered as an international joint venture in July 1998. The Japanese Corporation Bridgestone, the world's third largest car tire producer, has a 71.2 percent stake in the company and the state-owned Stomil Poznan S.A. owns 28.8 percent of the shares. Previously, Stomil had experience in producing tires for industrial vehicles, large size and plane tires. The new joint venture has focused exclusively on manufacturing of car tires. The joint venture capital amounts to US$ 63.2 million. The Japanese MNC invested US$ 45 million and promised additional investment of US$ 31 million by 2002. The Polish joint venture is Bridgestone's first investment in CEE.

The strategy of the investor is to meet demand for car tires in Poland and CEE. Three quarters of the production volume is exported in Europe. During the first years export has been mostly to the dynamic markets of the Czech Republic and Hungary. The biggest customer is the Polish operations of General Motors in Gliwice for the production of Opel Astra. In the fist year of its existence the joint venture produced 5,000 tires daily. Since its establishment, production has almost doubled and employment has been constantly increasing from the initial 300 employees.

The Case of AVX/Kyocera

The Kyocera Group is one of Japan's fifty largest corporations. It is based in Kyoto, established in 1956 for the production of ceramic and electrotechnical products. It is one of the world's top 500 corporations. The Kyocera group has production facilities and sales offices worldwide, employing more than 40,000 people.

The US-based AVX Corporation is one of the world's largest producers of passive electronic components. It is a part of Kyocera

Corporation, Japan. AVX Corporation has 31 subsidiaries worldwide employing more than 11,000 people. The company expands its activities to meet the constantly growing demand for electronic components. It has made substantial investment worldwide since early 1990s. Sales increased reaching US$ 1.1 billion in 1997, 22.5 percent higher than in the previous year.

AVX Czech Republic s.r.o. is a wholly owned subsidiary of AVX corporation, rapidly expanding its production at two Czech sites. Expansion of one of the production sites is in progress. AVX Czech Republic currently employs 3,000 people with further expansion of 450 by the end of 2001. The motives of AVX/Kyocera for their investment in the Czech Republic were the availability of highly skilled labor force, labor force flexibility and willingness to work 12-hour shifts for continuous production, availability of local technicians and toolmakers capable of designing, building and installing equipment for the production sites, the strong R&D skills in Czech universities, good capabilities of technicians for in-company product design.

AVX/Kyocera began operations in the Czech Republic in the beginning of 1990 with small-scale operations for simple product testing. In 1991 factory space was purchased from a producer of plastic and electrotechnical capacitors. In 1992 AVX/Kyocera signed a long-term lease of large production facilities that was fitted as the new AVX plant by mid 1993. By the end of 1993 this production site employed almost 1,000 workers. In the period 1994-1998 the Czech subsidiary obtained quality certification by meeting the requirements of ISO 9002 and QS 9000. By 1996 the construction of a second plant was completed and by the end of the year it employed 1,000 people. Through continuous re-investment in the first production site by the end of 1997 AVX employed more than 2,000 workers. In 1998 the two production sites produced 20 per cent of the global world annual supply of tantalum chip capacitors. AVX Czech Republic is the second largest Czech exporter operating 'ship-to-store' to the distribution centers of AVX in Northern Ireland, Singapore and the USA, also performing direct sales to major end user clients worldwide.

The Case of Matsushita

Matsushita Group is one of the largest consumer electronic producers in the world having 27 production facilities for making Panasonic television sets in 25 countries all over the world. In June 1996 Matsushita announced its first US$ 66 million greenfield investment in the Czech Republic to establish Matsushita Television Central Europe Ltd. as a wholly owned subsidiary. A year later production began in the city of Plzen. By mid-1998 Matsushita announced its second investment to assemble digital television sets. The Czech government provided the company with investment incentives for US$ 72 million during the second phase expansion of the plant. Currently the production site employs 1,400 people. Matsushita has decided to expand the existing production of color TV sets of the Panasonic brand enriching them with a new production of stereo and digital sets on the site creating additionally 1,500 new jobs by the end of 2005.

Matsushita's motives for investment in the Czech Republic were:

- Political and economic stability, making the Czech Republic a low investment risk country;
- Key geographic location, reducing logistic costs as most of the production is for export;
- The crucial assistance by the local government for obtaining a licensing permit;
- The availability of skilled, educated and cheap labor force;
- The personal commitment and dedication of the Mayor of the town of Plzen.

The initial production of 300,000 units in 1997 increased to 900,000 in year 2000. This output represents almost one third of the annual production of television sets in Europe. The new production lines introduced in late 1998 represent the latest generation of digital television sets. More than 85 per cent of the production output is exported, one-third to Western Europe, one third to North America and one third to CEE markets. Initially, half of the export was planned for the CEE markets. That figure was reduced because of the severe economic collapse in Russia in 1998. Matsushita had the idea to develop a network of local component suppliers. However, the Czech producers have had difficulties in meeting quality standards and volume requirements. Hence, only up to 10 percent of supply come from the Czech Republic and about 20 percent from CEFTA member countries. The management of Matsushita have set a target for developing the local supply system in the Czech Republic and CEFTA so that almost all supplies come from the region.

The Matsushita project in the Czech Republic is the most substantial Japanese investment in the country and one of the largest in the CEE. In early 1999 Matsushita Group opened its second plant for the production of electromagnetic relays, employing 100 people. In October 2000 Matsushita announced the joint establishment by Matsushita Electric Industrial Co.

and Matsushita Communication Industrial Co. of a new company in the Czech Republic to manufacture mobile telephones and car audio equipment. The new company, Matsushita Communication Industrial Czech s.r.o. was set up in the city of Pardubice and was scheduled to start production in October 2001. The initial investment was of 3.27 billion Czech korunas (8.5 billion Japanese yen) and the company employed about 550 people.

Conclusion

Japanese FDI in CEE has been disproportionately small in comparison to the size and significance of the Japanese economy, and the participation of Japan in the world FDI outflow. The overall FDI inflow from Japan into CEE has been estimated US$ 2.8 billion at the end of year 2000. This amount is more than fifteen times less than the German investments in the region for the same period representing a mere 0.8 percent of the total FDI inflow. This may be due to the low level of interest shown in the early years of transition by Japanese MNCs for undertaking investment mode of market entry in the CEE region. On a later stage their investment behavior has been very cautious, hesitant, and risk-averse as their perception of the CEE market was as one of high level of uncertainty and volatility.

The CEE countries where Japanese MNCs have shown some interest can be divided into two groups. The first group comprises the Czech Republic, Hungary, and Poland. These three countries have attracted US$ 1.8 billion Japanese investments by the end of 1999. They have been perceived as less risky and more promising because of their inclusion in the first wave of countries that would join the EU by year 2003. While the Czech Republic and Hungary have attracted some large Japanese investments in the early years of transition, Poland lagged somewhat behind. This was due to the negative investment experience of Daihatsu and Asahi Glass during that period. Recent successful large investments in Poland undertaken by Isuzu and Toyota seem to have changed the trend. Greenfield type of Japanese investment strongly prevails in the three countries. While in the Czech Republic and Hungary Japanese FDI has resulted mostly in the creation of wholly owned subsidiaries, in Poland joint ventures are the norm.

The second group consists of Bulgaria, Romania, and Slovakia. Investments in these countries are perceived as riskier. As a rule Japanese MNCs have invested in the creation of sales representative offices in the three countries. Incidental investments have been made in production, for example in the wine industry in Bulgaria, TV production in Romania, and electronic sector in Slovakia.

Recent Japanese investments in CEE have been undertaken mostly on the basis of good relationships between Japan and respective CEE countries in the pre-transition period. While Hungary has been benefiting from the good pre-transitional relationship between the two countries, the favorable previous development of relationships between Bulgaria and Japan has been largely damaged in the post-transitional period. This may be explained with the more stable environment and better progress towards transition to market orientation of the economy in Hungary than in Bulgaria.

In the last years there has been a clear trend of gradual increase in the amount of Japanese FDI in CEE. They show a high level of gravitation towards the Czech Republic, Hungary, and Poland. The expected membership of these countries in the EU may be the major drive for Japanese FDI as since the mid-1980s Japan has had as a strategic priority in attaining a significant business presence in the EU.

In the production sectors Japanese FDI in CEE has shown a strong tendency of vertical integration among Japanese MNCs. An example is the automotive industry where vertical integration has been achieved within and across national borders inside and outside the CEE region.

References

Anand, J. and Delios, A. (1996), 'Competing Globally: How Japanese MNCs Have Matched Goals and Strategies in India and China', *The Columbia Journal of World Business.* Fall, pp. 50-62.

Artisien, P., Rojec, M., and Svetlicic, M. (1993), *Foreign Investment in Central and Eastern Europe*, New York, St. Martin's Press.

Bakos, G. (1992), 'Japanese Capital in Central Europe', *Hitotsubashi Journal of Economics*, 33, pp. 149-168.

Coase, R. (1937,) 'The Nature of the Firm', *Economica,* vol. 4, pp. 386-405.

CzechInvest (Annual Bulletin 1996-2000), *Foreign Direct Investment in the Czech Republic,* Prague.

Culpan, R. and Kumar, N. (1994), 'Co-operative Ventures of Western Firms in Eastern Europe: The Case of German Companies', in P. Buckley and P. Ghauri (eds.) *The Economics of Change in East and Central Europe*, London: Academic Press.

Davis, J. H., Patterson, J. D. and Grazin, I. (1996), 'The Collapse and Re-Emergence of Networks within and between Republics of the former Soviet Union', *International Business Review*, vol. 5, no. 1, pp. 1-21.

Horaguchi, H. (1992), *Nihon Kigyo no Kaigai Chokusetsu Toushi (Foreign Direct Investment of Japanese Companies)*, Tokyo, Tokyo University Press.

Hutchings, R. (1999), *Japan's Economic Involvement in Eastern Europe and Eurasia*, London: Macmillan Press Ltd.

Jain, S. and Tucker, L. (1994), 'Market Opportunities in Eastern Europe: MNC's Response', in P. Buckley and P. Ghauri (eds), *The Economics of Change in East and Central Europe*, London: Academic Press.

JETRO (Annual Bulletins 1993 - 2000), *Sekai to Nihon no Kaigai Chokusetsu Toushi (Foreign Direct Investment of the World and Japan)*, Tokyo.

Johanson, J. and Mattsson, L.-G. (1987), Interorganizational Relations in Industrial Systems: A Network Approach Compared with the Transaction-Cost Approach', *International Studies in Management and Organization*, vol. 17, no. 1, pp. 34-48.

Johanson, J. and Vahlne, J.-E. (1977), 'The Internationalization Process of the Firm - A Model of Knowledge Development and Increasing Foreign Market Commitments', *Journal of International Business Studies*, vol. 8, pp. 23-32.

Johanson, J. and Wiedersheim-Paul, F. (1975), 'The Internationalization of the Firm - Four Swedish Cases', *Journal of Management Studies*, October, pp. 305-322.

Lehtinen, U. (1996), 'Relationship Marketing Approaches in Changing Russian Markets', *Journal of East-West Business*, vol. 1, no. 4, pp. 35-49.

Lipsey, R. (1994), *Outward Direct Investment and the U.S. Economy*, Working Paper No. 4691, Washington: National Bureau of Economic Research.

Marinov, M. and Marinova, S. (1997), 'Privatization and Foreign Direct Investment in Bulgaria: Present Characteristics and Future Trends' *Communist Economies and Economic Transformation*, vol. 9, no. 1, pp. 101-116.

Marinov, M. and Marinova, S. (2001), 'Foreign Direct Investment in the Emerging Markets of Central and Eastern Europe: Motives and Marketing Strategies', *Advances in International Marketing*, vol. 10, pp. 21-52.

Morita, K. (1995), 'Japan's Foreign Direct Investment in East European Countries', in I. Zloch-Christy (ed.) *Privatization and Foreign Investments in Eastern Europe*, London: Praeger, pp. 183-195.

Morita, K. (1998), 'On Determinants of Japan's Foreign Direct Investment in East Europe: The Case of Poland', in V. Samonis (ed.) *Enterprise Restructuring and Foreign Investment in the Transforming East: The Impact of Privatization*, The Haworth Press, pp. 141-148.

Morita, K. and Stuglik, D. (1998), 'Nihon no Tai Poland Chokusetsu Toushi: Genjou to Kettei Youin (Japan's Foreign Direct Investment into Poland: Current Situation and Determinants)', *Hiroshima Economic Review*, vol. 21, no. 4, pp. 21-40.

PAIZ (Polish Agency for Foreign Investment) Annual Bulletins (1992 - 2000), *Foreign Investments in Poland*, Warsaw.

Peng, M. (2000), *Business Strategies in Transition Economies*, London: Sage Publications.

Salmi, A. (2000), 'Entry into Turbulent Business Markets: The Case of a Western Company on the Estonian Market', *European Journal of Marketing*, vol. 34, nos. 11/12, pp. 1374-1390.

Williamson, O. (1975), *Markets and Hierarchies: Analysis and Antitrust Implications. A Survey in the Economics of Internal Organizations*, New York: The Free Press.

Wolf, G. and E. Razvigorova (eds) (1991), *East-West Joint Ventures: The New Business Environment,*. London: Blackwell.

8 An Examination of Turkish Direct Investments in Central and Eastern Europe and the Commonwealth of Independent States

REFIK CULPAN and EMIN AKCAOGLU

Introduction

The opening-up of Central Eastern Europe (CEE) and Commonwealth of Independent States (CIS) markets since 1989 has created new opportunities for investors. The common characteristic of these countries is that they are all still in a state of transition, moving from a centrally planned economy to an open market economy. Nevertheless, this has given an ample opportunity to Turkish companies to invest in these countries to which Turkey has geographical proximity and with some of those it has even cultural proximity. In the past, like many other developing countries, a limited number of Turkish companies had invested abroad and the total amount of Turkish direct investment (TDI) was negligible.

This study aims at identifying patterns of the TDI into 19 of the former centrally planned economies during the period of 1995 - 2001. The countries covered are the former Soviet Republics of Azerbaijan, Belarus, Georgia, Kazakhstan, Kyrgyzstan, Moldova, Russia, Tajikistan, Turkmenistan, Ukraine and Uzbekistan, and the nine Central and Eastern European countries including Albania, Bulgaria, Bosnia, the Czech Republic, the Slovak Republic, Macedonia, Hungary, Poland, and Romania.

Our purpose is to explore the TDI in the CEE and CIS countries, which has not been studied previously. Because of unavailability of relevant data, this study is a pioneering work for ground building for further empirical studies. Nevertheless, it provides a systematic picture of investments by Turkish firms in a conceptual framework to understand their internalization process.

The first part of the chapter reviews the theories of foreign direct investment (FDI) in general. The second part deals with specifically FDI by firms in developing countries. The third part discusses the patterns of TDI in CEE and CIS countries while the fourth part analyzes the type of TDI. The last part offers an overall assessment and draws a conclusion.

Theories of FDI

The theoretical foundations of FDI are rooted in two main streams in the literature. These are the theory of industrial organization (Hymer, 1976), and the theory of international trade (Vernon, 1966). The later research focused on (1) the sources of firm (ownership) specific advantages, (2) the location of production and (3) the reasons for integrating different business units in a single firm. There were also other attempts at explaining the activities of multinational corporations (MNCs) in the mid-1970s. The internalization theory of MNCs is micro-economic and behavioral explanations of international production. On the other hand, the macro theory of FDI attempts to explain types of investments in different countries rather than analyzing the business engagements from the standpoint of MNCs. Recent contributions to the study of international trade and production include the integration of MNC into trade models and the rediscovery of economic geography. In this regard, one of the popular theories of FDI is the eclectic paradigm of international production, which is also known as Ownership-Location-Integration (OLI) paradigm (Dunning, 1980; 1981; 1988; 1993) combining different theories into a general eclectic framework.

The eclectic paradigm suggests that FDI depends upon three advantages. The MNC has some specific ownership advantage (O) as compared to the domestic/local firm making it more competitive. There has to be a location advantage (L) of production in the foreign country rather than producing at home for export. There also has to be some internalization advantage (I) meaning risks sharing and scale economy benefits. Moreover, it asserts two types of market imperfections must be present. Structural market failure discriminates between firms in their ability to gain and sustain control over property rights or to administer multiple and geographically dispersed business activities. Failure of intermediate product markets to transact goods and services at a lower cost than within the enterprise also has to occur.

Ownership advantages or firm-specific assets can be such assets as patents, trademarks, human capital, managerial superiority or reputation for quality. These confer cost advantages and market power sufficient to overcome the costs of producing abroad. Such advantages are endogenous to the firm (Buckley and Casson, 1991; Caves, 1996). It must be more beneficial for the firm possessing these firm-specific advantages to exploit them internally rather than through licensing-type agreements by foreign firms. These incentives depend on such factors as the form of corporate governance, internal transaction costs versus market costs, and the specific characteristics of the knowledge to be transferred and the cost of transferring it (Rugman, 1986; Markusen, 1995). Indeed, this approach explains the emergence of MNC as a result of market failures.

Location advantages, which are external to the firm, depend on host country economic characteristics. They can be analyzed in three categories, namely economic, social and cultural, and political. Economic factors include the quantity and quality of the production factors, size and scope of the market, transport and telecommunication costs. Social and cultural factors consist of psychic distance between the home and host country. Psychic distance implies the geographical, cultural, political and linguistic distance between the home and host country. Political factors include the government policies that affect inward FDI flows, international production and intra-firm trade. For instance, foreign markets may become attractive when they provide abundant and cheaper production factors (e.g., labor) that allow the firm to increase efficiency. Gains may also be achieved through the utilization of the scale in a large market (Dunning, 1993).

Dunning (1993) identifies four different types of motives for investment: resource seeking, market seeking, efficiency seeking, and strategic asset (or capability) seeking. The first motive means acquiring some particular resources at a lower cost in the host country than at home. These resources mainly consist of primary products. The second motive depends on the expectation of new sales opportunities from the opening of markets, to which investing companies previously had no access. The third motive of efficiency seeking refers to utilizing the specific comparative advantages of a host economy. The fourth type of investment motive is related with long-term strategic considerations such as gaining an important stake in the market in the long run.

FDI from Developing Countries – Motivations for Internationalization

Although the theoretical explanations provided in the previous section have been originally developed for the multinationals of developed countries, they are also useful to analyze the multinational activities of developing country firms. Multinationals from developing countries first emerged in the late 1960s. As a result of industrial development of numerous developing countries, many indigenous firms have grown to expand production beyond their national frontiers, mostly to neighboring developing countries. Research on developing country multinationals can be grouped in three areas (Ghymn, 1980; Lall, 1982; Wells, 1983; Kumar and Kim, 1984; Khan, 1986; Lecraw, 1993): (1) the firm-specific advantages that allowed these firms to compete with both domestically owned firms and other multinationals abroad; (2) the factors that motivated them to invest abroad; and (3) the factors that influenced the geographical location of their investments.

A well-known argument on MNCs from developing countries is that developing country multinationals possess a number of unique characteristics, which distinguish them from their counterparts from developed countries (Lall, 1982; Wells, 1983; Lecraw, 1993). One such difference refers to the relative appropriateness of their technology to host developing countries. On the basis of this presumption, the conventional wisdom on multinationals from developing countries holds that the technology of these firms is more appropriate to the relative labor and capital costs in the host developing country. In other words, these firms have come to acquire or have been able to develop smaller scale, more labor-intensive, multipurpose operating technologies that use locally available inputs. In most cases, they operate in industries using standard or traditional technologies. Their output might be generally of lower quality than that of developed country multinationals, but they compete more on low price than on product differentiation. The capital resources of these firms are also generally limited. These MNCs tend to export less of their productions from their foreign subsidiaries than other multinationals or domestically owned firms do. Their exports are most often to markets other than those in their home countries (Lecraw, 1993).

Several factors have been identified as motivating developing country multinationals to invest abroad. They fall primarily into three categories. The first motivation can be an actual or perceived need by the firm to protect overseas markets previously developed through export activity. This can be caused by market protection and/or development in host countries. As developing country firms generally produce standardized, low technology products; and use less sophisticated marketing activities, they may be in need of protecting their overseas markets by direct investment. Wells (1983) and Khan (1986) point out that majority of the subsidiaries created were preceded by exports to the countries concerned. As will be shown in the following sections, this is also the case for Turkey's FDI in CEE and CIS countries.

The second motivation refers to cost factors. Developing country firms are forced to invest in other developing countries as those may provide low-wage and cheaper input prices. This does not refer only to the wage-differences between the home and host countries, but also the favorable cost advantages to be competitive in international markets (Wells, 1983; Kumar and Kim, 1984; Khan, 1986). For instance, some textile products provided by such countries as China and India at very low prices have forced Turkish firms to find cost-saving production locations. In this regard, CEE and CIS countries provide cheaper wages and skilled labor for Turkish investors. In addition, the steady availability and lower cost of energy sources (e.g., electricity) in CEE and CIS should be particularly mentioned. Moreover, the privatization trend in many developing and former socialist countries has played a role in investment decisions of MNCs from developing countries. This is a relatively recent matter concerning FDI by developing country firms. After the opening-up of CEE and CIS countries, privatization programs in those countries provided opportunities to foreign firms to acquire existing plants at bargain prices. This is certainly one of the motivations to invest in such countries (Lansbury, Pain and Smidkova, 1996; Jermakowicz and Bellas, 1997; Voinea, 2001). Another major motive for firms from developing countries to invest abroad is to avoid import quotas imposed by developed countries and to diversify their business risk by locating assets outside their home countries (Lecraw, 1993).

The foregoing reasons for FDI by developing country firms are accountable for productions investments, but do not cover investments in service sectors such as financial services (banking and insurance), tourism (hotels) and trading. Nevertheless, some of these same reasons are valid for investments in services as well.

We would also like to point out a paradox concerning FDI from developing countries. While developing countries in the need of FDI themselves try to attract foreign investments, a number of domestic firms make investments abroad. This presents a paradox for home country governments. Then the critical question is whether home country governments should encourage FDI outflow while they promote FDI inflow. Here there might be a contradiction between macro economic (development economic) and micro economic (firm behavior) perspectives.

A Conceptual Model for FDI by Developing Countries

In this chapter, we used the eclectic paradigm, also known as OLI (Ownership-Location-Internalization) paradigm of Dunning (1980; 1981; 1988; 1993) to explain the investment behavior of Turkish firms in post-communist countries in Europe and Euro-Asia. Although the OLI paradigm is able to describe host-country specific and firm-specific conditions concerning investment of multinational firms in foreign countries, it does not fully explain non-production investments by firms and home-country related factors. Thus, we added two more dimensions, 'geographic/cultural proximity' and 'home country conditions' to the OLI paradigm (see Figure 8.1). Each dimension of the new model is defined as follows. The OLI dimensions are adopted from Dunning (1980; 1981; 1988; 1993) and defined in their original terms while additional dimensions of the model are described below.

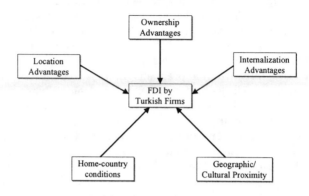

Figure 8.1   Enhanced OLI Model for FDI

Ownership-specific advantages Principal factors of ownership (simply O) advantages include rapidity of new O-advantages development, rapidity of existing O-advantages exploitation, higher flexibility, O-advantages based on the combination of complementary, but not similar assets, O-advantages based on the supply of a complete range of systemic and compatible products, O-advantages based on products with dominant standards.

Location-specific advantages Dunning defines them as follows: access to complementary assets based on the nations' competitive advantages, access to main world markets for the inputs and outputs.

Internalization factors Sharing the risk of spreading the risks in high certainty situations, transaction costs less important because of the technological diffusion rapidity, benefits from scale economies, the launching projects with high sunk costs, and new oligopolistic reactions to replace the traditional oligopolistic strategies.

Geographic and/or cultural proximity An extension of the Swedish school of internationalization theory to FDI suggests that firms start initial investments into countries which are geographically closer to and/or present similar cultural characteristics to the home country of investing firms (Johanson and Vahlne, 1977; Johanson and Wiedersheim-Paul, 1975). In fact, this dimension is covered in the Dunning's OLI paradigm under location-specific advantages, however, we thought it would be more appropriate to present them as an additional dimension because of its importance for the Turkish case.

Home-country-specific conditions They include market conditions in the home country of investing firms. Conditions, whether positive like liberalization of exchange rate system or negative such as economic instability and recession, can stimulate firms to look for business opportunities abroad. In other words, they can be considered as push factors for FDI. We believe that the Enhanced OLI model introduced above can best explain FDI by Turkish firms in CEE and CIS countries. Therefore, we will use this framework in analyzing TDI in a subsequent section below.

Regional and Sectoral Patterns of Turkish FDI in CEE and CIS

Turkey has become not only a recipient of FDI, but also has become a donor of FDI. The country now has a noticeable place among a group of developing countries such as Argentina, Brazil, Hong Kong, India, Korea, Mexico, and Taiwan, whose firms have been investing in foreign countries. According to the unpublished official statistics of the Republic of Turkey, Treasury Undersecretary (2002), the total number of overseas joint ventures and subsidiaries established by Turkish multinationals is 1,160 as of the end of 2001, and the total amount of overseas investment is over US$ 4.7 billion. Turkish multinationals have invested in financial services (banking and insurance), manufacturing, trade, telecommunication, mining, tourism, construction, energy, and transportation sectors. Financial services investments account for nearly 48 percent of the total of FDI by Turkish multinationals; manufacturing accounts for nearly 29 percent and, trade accounts for approximately 14 percent (see Table 8.1).

Table 8.1   Sectoral distribution of Turkish direct investments

Sectors	Turkish Direct Investments	
	US$ million	% in Total
Financial Services	2,281	47.87
Manufacturing	1,381	28.99
Trade	650	13.63
Telecommunication	142	2.98
Mining	115	2.42
Tourism	86	1.79
Construction	70	1.47
Energy	11	0.23
Transport	6	0.13
Miscellaneous	24	0.50
Total	4,765	100.00

Source: Republic of Turkey Treasury Undersecretary (2002).

Table 8.2   Turkish direct investments in host regions

Host Regions	US$ million	% in Total	No. of Firms
Western Europe	3.414	71.64	352
CIS Countries	638	13.38	382
Central & Eastern Europe	230	4.83	173
North America	187	3.92	50
Off-shore Centers	130	2.73	43
Northern Cyprus	79	1.65	98
Middle East	36	0.75	19
Africa	24	0.50	22
Latin America	15	0.33	1
East Asia	13	0,27	20
Total	4.765	100.00	1160

Source: Republic of Turkey Treasury Undersecretary (2002).

As shown in Table 8.2, the overwhelming majority of these investments, amounting to US$ 3.4 billion by 352 Turkish firms, accounts for 72 percent of the total Turkish FDI in developed countries of Western Europe. This is not surprising because the European Union is the largest trading partner of Turkey. Next, the CIS countries have attracted about 13 percent of the total Turkish FDI while the CEE countries have attracted nearly five percent of the total. The number of the Turkish firms investing in the CIS and CEE countries are 382 and 173 respectively. Other regions follow these with relatively small amounts.

As shown in Table 8.3, Turkey's FDI in the CEE and CIS countries increased from US$ 116.3 million in 1995 to US$ 866.1 in 2001. Along with this increase Turkish firms gained a remarkable share in these markets, particularly in Russia, Kazakhstan, Azerbaijan, and Romania. Despite Turkey's limited financial capabilities, this is a notable accomplishment.

When we look at the FDI flows by Turkish firms into these countries, there is no distinctive pattern. The year 2001 was, however, the worst year for Turkish FDI as the country experienced a severe economic and financial crisis in the spring of 2001. This economic recession was followed by devaluation of the Turkish lira against major hard currencies. Therefore, firms had to postpone their earlier investment plans due to serious financial difficulties.

As Table 8.3 demonstrates, the most of TDI went to the Russian Federation and then to Kazakhstan, Azerbaijan, and Romania. The sheer size of the Russian market justifies the bulk of inflow of TDI into this country.

Table 8.3   Turkish direct investments in CEE and CIS (in US$ thousand)

Host Countries	Cumulative at end-1995	1996	1997	1998	1999	2000	2001	Total
Russian Fed	12,027	36,865	47,398	25,458	41,111	6,273	12,249	181,380
Kazakhstan	18,832	11,521	10,976	50,173	47,064	10,197	21,782	170,545
Azerbaijan	11,498	47,676	10,579	43,644	19,579	18,792	4,865	156,634
Romania	41,176	12,834	18,757	13,951	7,606	21,618	1,907	117,849
Hungary	3,545	-	-	-	40,000	-	70	43,615
Bulgaria	256	-	188	10,999	10,004	19,334	844	41,625
Georgia	126	3,489	6,099	8,182	8,655	10,200	1,113	37,864
Kyrgyzstan	8,064	8,406	2,130	4,118	346	-	728	23,793
Ukraine	3,224	3,599	4,660	2,107	1,169	5,624	608	20,992
Bosnia	-	-	6,751	48	8,447	-	-	15,246
Turkmenistan	640	32	417	2,928	834	1,955	126	6,933
Albania	35	-	-	-	-	6,000	-	6,035
Poland	214	3	-	1,037	482	-	806	2,542
Macedonia	-	163	-	13	48	308	-	531
Moldova	10	322	-	-	-	100	-	433
Czech Republic	10	85	145	-	-	27	93	361
Slovakia	-	-	-	-	-	333	5	338
Belarus	-	-	-	-	-	25	80	105
Total	116,324	126,574	108,760	170,477	188,816	108,071	47,113	866,137

Source: Republic of Turkey Treasury Undersecretary (2002).

Table 8.4   Turkish direct investments in CEE and CIS – sectoral distribution (in %)

Host Countries	Manu-facturing	Financial Services	Trade	Mining	Telecom	Tourism	Cons-truction	Energy	Trans-port	Miscell-aneous	Turkish FDI in US$ million	Turkish FDI % in Total	No. of Investing Firms
Russian Fed.	25.97	48.01	21.82	-	-	0.05	4.15	-	-	-	181,380	20.94	66
Kazakhstan	25.20	20.38	9.17	13.18	7.55	22.73	0.03	-	1.76	-	170,545	19.69	64
Azerbaijan	17.21	4.01	5.68	56.60	14.81	-	-	1.69	-	-	156,634	18.08	112
Romania	39.12	33.26	18.66	0.47	-	6.03	2.44	-	-	0.01	117,849	13.61	101
Hungary	94.02	5.96	0.01	-	-	-	-	-	-	-	43,615	5.04	8
Bulgaria	16.42	51.14	31.95	-	-	0.10	-	0.38	-	-	41,625	4.81	33
Turkmenistn	83.27	7.05	1.27	1.27	-	7.13	-	-	0.01	-	39,316	4.54	23
Georgia	43.97	10.16	0.01	-	44.27	-	1.58	-	-	-	37,864	4.37	17
Kyrgyzstan	69.74	7.57	22.69	-	-	-	-	-	-	-	23,793	2.75	16
Uzbekistan	50.31	15.59	34.08	-	-	-	-	-	0.02	-	20,992	2.42	54
Bosnia	0.31	98.78	-	-	-	-	0.91	-	-	-	15,246	1.76	3
Ukraine	18.78	-	47.18	-	-	-	0.72	32.47	-	0.85	6,933	0.80	28
Albania	-	99.42	-	-	-	-	0.58	-	-	-	6,035	0.70	4
Poland	93.09	-	6.87	-	-	-	0.04	-	-	-	2,542	0.29	8
Macedonia	88.64	2.39	-	-	-	-	8.97	-	-	-	531	0.06	5
Moldova	74.43	-	2.37	-	23.10	-	-	-	0.10	-	433	0.05	5
Czech Rep.	-	-	28.75	-	-	71.25	-	-	-	-	361	0.04	4
Slovakia	1.58	-	98.42	-	-	-	-	-	-	-	338	0.04	2
Belarus	38.10	-	61.90	-	-	-	-	-	-	-	105	0.01	2
Total	33.83	25.81	13.42	12.93	6.10	5.66	1.31	0.58	0.35	0.01	866,137	100.00	555

Source: Republic of Turkey Treasury Undersecretary (2002).

Kazakhstan and Azerbaijan with their Turkic ethnic origins attracted considerable Turkish investments. Also, Romania, despite its relatively small size, because of its closeness to Turkey and its receptiveness for foreign investments received a significant portion of TDI.

Table 8.4 shows the sectoral composition of Turkey's FDI in CEE and CIS countries in 2001. Although the amount of TDI varies across countries, it is concentrated in four industries: manufacturing (33.8 percent), financial services (25.8 percent), trade (13.4 percent) and mining (12.9 percent). Together these four sectors account for more than 85 percent of Turkey's FDI in the CEE and CIS countries. The composition of the Turkish FDI in the CEE and CIS countries is significantly different from the sectoral distribution of the total Turkish FDI in general. While nearly half of the total (47.9 percent) is in financial sector, it is about 25 percent in CEE and CIS, but more, about 34 percent, in manufacturing.

Analysis of Turkish Direct Investments

After describing the enhanced OLI model and the picture of TDI in the CEE and CIS countries, we would like to analyze Turkish investments in the region within the context of the model. We will portray the characteristics of the markets and determinants of Turkish firms in reference to each dimension of the model.

Ownership Advantages

Turkish firms possessed both tangible and intangible assets such as capital, strategic leadership, talented and skilled human resources, and domestic and overseas experience to penetrate these emerging markets. These resources combined with Turkey's geographic and/or cultural proximity to CEE and CIS gave Turkish firms a great leverage against even Western European companies which envied Turkish firms' success in the region. These ownership advantages largely involved the privileged possession of intangible assets (e.g., talented but inexpensive engineers, Western educated business leaders and managers) as well as those gained as a result of their previous business activities in the Middle East, Libya, and Pakistan. Because of Turkish construction firms' earlier involvements in the Russian Federation, Kazakhstan and Azerbaijan, these countries are listed in the top three in receiving TDI.

Basically, sustainable ownership-specific advantages of Turkish firms vis-à-vis firms of other nationalities served them well. These ownership advantages and their effective utilization have increased the capabilities of Turkish firms and hence the value of their assets.

Location-specific Advantages

As shown in Table 8.4, the sectoral distribution of TDI reflects that the receiving countries needed investments in manufacturing, financial services, trade and mining (i.e., petroleum listed under mining). The CEE and CIS countries during and after transition to market economy were eager to attract FDI in many of their major industries. That is to say the local markets were ripe for FDI. Many Turkish firms with experiences in the domestic market or other foreign countries felt confident to exploit opportunities in these emerging markets. This demonstrates that, as stated by the original OLI model, the location-specific advantages just were there. The TDI in each country can be summarized as follows.

In Russia 48 percent of Turkey's FDI was invested in the financial services sector and approximately 26 percent in the manufacturing sector. The trading sector comes just after with almost 22 percent of the total investment. Russia is one of the largest consumers of Turkish goods and construction services. In 2001 the officially recorded Turkish exports to Russia were over US$ 922 million. Since 1992, Russia has become the best market for Turkish construction services. According to the Turkish Contractors Association, between 1989 and 1997 CIS accounted for 63 percent of the overseas contract portfolio of Turkish builders and developers. As pointed out earlier, Turkish contracting firms moved to the commercial property sector after establishing their presence in the country. In addition, many other industries received Turkish investments. For instance, Efes Beverage Group is now one of the biggest Turkish investors in Russia. Koc, the biggest industrial conglomerate in Turkey, is also building a strong presence in Russia and other CIS countries in home appliances, retailing and food distribution. Utilizing its expertise in retailing, Koc is in the process of setting up the CIS's first supermarket chain. In 1997, together with construction company Enka, Koc opened Moscow's then largest shopping mall and hypermarket. The cost of this project was US$ 35 million. This was followed by a second one in 1998.

In Kazakhstan, 25 percent of Turkey's FDI was in the manufacturing sector, approximately 23 percent in the tourism sector and 20 percent in the financial services sector. The biggest hotels in the country were constructed and are being operated by Turkish firms.

In Azerbaijan, most FDI has taken place within the oil and natural gas sector. The state-owned Azerbaijan International Oil Company is involved in alliances with firms from Russia, Norway, Japan, Saudi-Arabia and Turkey through production-sharing arrangements. The Turkish Petroleum Company has held the Turkish stake of this investment. Therefore, the share of the mining (petroleum) sector in the Turkish investments consisted of over 56 percent of the total. In addition, similar to the Russian market, there is a chain of Koç-operated supermarkets in Azerbaijan.

In Romania, the main target of the Turkish companies has been the manufacturing (39.1 percent) (e.g., textile, chocolate, biscuits, glass, plastic and petrochemical industries) and financial sector (33.3 percent) (operating bank branches or joint-ventures in banking such as Turkish-Romanian Bank, Demirbank, Finansbank and UGBI). Other investments have been made in retailing (e.g., Bucharest Mall). Recently, Erdemir, the biggest iron and steel company in Turkey, has bought Cost S.A. from the Privatization Agency of Romania. The cost of the deal was US$ 15 million for Erdemir. Cost S.A. produces a special type of flat steel strengthened with silicon. The capacity of the plant is large enough to satisfy both the Romanian and Turkish markets and even to export to other countries.

Table 8.4 also indicates that in Bulgaria, a little more than half of the Turkish investments (51.1 percent) were in the financial sector. The trading sector investments were in the second place (32 percent) followed by the manufacturing sector investments (16.4 percent) in the third place. Bulgaria is the country which attracts the second biggest portion of Turkey's FDI in the Balkans after Romania. Although, the Turkish official statistics indicate that the amount of Turkish investments in Bulgaria was US$ 41.6 million with 33 investors, it is argued that this does not reflect the complete picture. According to the Bulgarian Chamber of Commerce and Industry, there are 1,215 Turkish-owned companies in Bulgaria and 814 joint ventures have been set up with Bulgarian partners, and Turkish investment in Bulgaria since 1992 has reached US$ 128 million (Xinhua News Agency, 2002).

It seems that the Turkish official FDI statistics do not reflect the true picture. This is true not only for the Bulgarian market, but it is also the case for all CEE and CIS countries. There are strong reasons for this argument. For example, as explained in the following section, the Turkish foreign exchange market has been fully deregulated since 1989, and, therefore, it had been very difficult for the Turkish official agencies to follow and record the type of capital movements (whether for portfolio investment or direct investment) between Turkey and other countries. As a result, it is not known exactly the amount of Turkish capital invested in overseas markets. Furthermore, it is a fact that some Turkish firms invested abroad through firms registered in other countries, such as Germany and Switzerland. Through this mechanism Turkish firms can access to developed countries' insurance schemes and financing, which are scarce or difficult to secure in Turkey. In this respect, although the official statistics indicate that the amount of total Turkish investments is about US$ 866 million in all CEE and CIS countries, there are estimates in the Turkish business press claiming more than US$ 1 billion invested in only the Russian Federation. Overall, it is a common belief that the total TDI in CEE and CIS is more than the official statistics reflect.

For the governments of Central and Eastern Europe (CEE), attracting foreign direct investment (FDI) has been an important component of their strategies to privatize their productive resources and create market economies. They thought FDI would also generate hard currency to maintain debt service, balance of payment stability, introduce modern technology and management methods, and supply local markets with quality products.

Internalization Advantages

Turkish firms in CEE and CIS mostly established businesses or undertook projects independently (through wholly-owned subsidiaries), but occasionally they preferred joint ventures and consortiums with Western firms. To control supplies and conditions of sale of inputs, they heavily relied on their own sources including technology. They tended to control market outlets (e.g., supermarket chains). In addition, they were able to engage in practices such as cross-subsidization, predatory pricing, and transfer pricing as a competitive strategy. Most importantly to avoid broken contracts and ensuing litigation, they established very good relationships with the host governments. Moreover, to ensure quality, they used key expatriate personnel throughout the projects. This helped Turkish firms to transfer their 'company culture' to new environments.

Turkish firms first entered into the CIS market through construction projects. Turkish construction firms had well-established experience in the Middle Eastern and North African countries before moving to the former Soviet Union in 1980s. The former Soviet Union opened its construction market to Turkish builders for such projects as hotels, health care centers, trade centers, housing, and industrial facilities and allowed the imports of a variety of products from Turkey for these projects (Kaynak and Dalgic, 1991). About a half of the public contracts in Russia and other CIS countries have been undertaken by Turkish firms, which have been predominant in the region since 1991 (Munir, 1998). These construction engagements have paved a way for Turkish firms to exploit other business opportunities in these markets. For example, after completion of their construction projects, the firms engaged in areas related with real estate such as tourism and commercial property business. The liberalization of both host and home country economies enabled many Turkish firms to consider overseas investment as an attractive alternative to domestic expansions.

Most of the large Turkish manufacturers traditionally produced goods under licenses with Western companies. This restricted their ability to export and invest abroad. However, many licensing multinationals have relaxed such restrictions via entering joint ventures with Turkish partners to take advantage of Turkey's strategic position in accessing particularly the newly emerging markets of Central Asia (Passow, 1994).

It must be also noted that some Turkish companies have been pushed into business abroad for strategic motives like investing in foreign countries to defend their home markets as a result of the customs union with EU together with the liberalization of the FDI regulations. For instance, Ilker Keremoglu, chief executive of the Efes Beverage Group, one of the biggest Turkish investors in the CIS, claims 'In the brewery sector we had reached the limits in Turkey and were at risk of being swallowed by foreigners. We ran as fastest as we can because we felt potential acquisitions were a great danger for us' (Munir, 1998).

Geographic/Cultural Proximity

As confirmed by the literature, FDI is largely influenced by the earlier trade relations and by the geographical and cultural proximity to host countries (Johanson and Wiedersheim-Paul, 1975; Johanson and Vahlne, 1977; Altzinger and Winklhofer, 1998). Turkey has been geographically close to CEE and CIS while it has ethnic ties with some of them including Azerbaijan, Kazakhstan, Turkmenistan, and Kyrgyzstan. Consequently, in 1995 the largest proportion of the Turkish FDI was in Romania with over US$ 41 million. Romania was followed by Kazakhstan and the Russian Federation with over US$ 18 million and US$ 12 million respectively, and Azerbaijan was in the fourth place. However, currently the largest Turkish FDI recipient is the Russian Federation, followed by Kazakhstan, Azerbaijan and then Romania. Together these four countries account for over 72 percent of Turkey's FDI in CEE and CIS countries. The total number of Turkish firms invested in these countries is 555 in 2001. The number of investing firms is 66 in Russia, 64 in Kazakhstan, 112 in Azerbaijan and 101 in Romania.

Turkey has an advantageous location along the straits that link the Black Sea to the Aegean, which means it has geographical proximity to both CEE and CIS countries. In addition, Turkey has historical and/or cultural ties to TDI-receiving countries. For instance, the Turkish people share racial, linguistic and cultural ties with the peoples of Azerbaijan, Kazakhstan, Kyrgyzstan and Turkmenistan. Their languages are derived from Turkic and their religion is predominantly Muslim. For example, Turkish is spoken in both Turkey and Azerbaijan. Therefore, Turkey was the first country to recognize these newly independent republics. Turkish Airlines was the first carrier to establish direct flights to the capitals of the Central Asian Republics. Furthermore, Turkey has had also close relations with the CEE (particularly the Balkans) countries such as Romania and Bulgaria as well as Russia since the era of Ottoman Empire. It should also be noted that Turkey has pioneered the Black Sea Economic Cooperation

Agreement, which envisages the establishment of a free trade zone in line with the European Union accord.

It should be noted that unlike their Western European or U.S. counterparts, Turkish firms were not deterred by the uncertain legal framework, bureaucratic redtape, and delays in obtaining licenses and permits that are an inevitable part of doing business in CEE and CIS countries, because they have experienced similar problems at home as well. Therefore, Turkish firms are more adaptable to the market conditions in these emerging markets. This situation reflects the importance of cultural proximity, or similarities between the home and host countries.

The brief outline of the regional and sectoral patterns of Turkish FDI in the CEE and CIS countries reveals the importance of geographical and cultural proximity. This can be considered as an important factor for Turkish firms' investments in the region.

Home Country Conditions

In order to grasp the Turkish FDI in CEE and CIS, a brief description of the Turkish economy and industrial structure will be useful. From the 1930s until 1980, Turkey held a relatively closed economy, with a reliance on large state enterprises and high tariff barriers. Turkey's development strategy for the pre-1980 era, based mainly on the industrialization drive and an inward looking import substitution strategy, was supported by a high degree of protectionism. The foreign exchange bottleneck arose basically from the low level of exports and the heavy dependence on imports of raw materials and investment goods by the manufacturing sector. As a result of long-lasting economic crisis, the government was committed to liberalize the economy and to pursue an export-led growth policy on January 24, 1980 (Uygur, 1993; Sak, 1995). As a result, the country embarked on an economic development program that included the liberalization of import restrictions, fostering greater domestic competition, privatization of state enterprises, and the reduction of taxes.

The deregulation of interest rates, establishment of organized financial markets for money, foreign exchange, stocks and securities, liberalization of capital movements and reforms in the banking sector are some of the major economic policy changes during this period. In this regard, there has been substantial liberalization of external capital movements since 1984. In 1984, a partial deregulation of external financial flows was adopted. Major changes in this area have been in effect since 1989. A decree on the protection of the value of the Turkish currency, which was issued in 1989, has been a very important step for foreign direct investment activities of Turkish firms. With these changes, Turkish residents were allowed to transfer the foreign exchange required to purchase securities abroad. In addition, Turkish commercial banks were allowed to extend foreign currency credits. Currently, the Turkish lira is fully convertible without any restrictions on transfer of capital, profits, fees, and royalties (Uygur, 1993; Sak, 1995).

Moreover, Turkey entered into a customs union with the Europe Union (EU) in January 1996. This union has brought Turkey into the single European market and extended most of the EU's trade and competition rules to Turkish economy (*Financial Times*, 1996). Turkey's once heavily protected markets were opened following the abolition of tariffs and levies against goods from the EU. In the current framework, the customs union includes only industrial products, but it will be extended to services and agricultural sectors in the future. In addition, the Turkish government has liberalized foreign direct investment regulations to encourage FDI inflows.

The export-led growth strategy of the early 1980s was quite successful. The average annual growth rate of the real GDP was an impressive 5.8 percent between 1981 and 1988 without experiencing any economic recessions. In 1988, however, the economy entered into a new phase. Since then the growth performance has been highly volatile with a 'boom-bust' behavior. There have been five recessions in the years of 1989, 1991, 1994, 1999 and 2001. The 1991, 1994 and 2001 recessions were preceded by a substantial increase in the real exchange rate (Selcuk and Ertugrul, 2001).

All these domestic conditions provided a stimulus for Turkish firms to expand beyond their national borders and take advantage of emerging market opportunities. On the one hand, the domestic market was reaching a sort of saturation point so that Turkish firms started to envision new markets. On the other hand, they had been stimulated by the economic liberalization in their home country, which constrained their international expansions for many years.

Conclusion

The total amount of Turkish direct investments in the CEE and CIS countries has reached US$ 866 million with 18.2 percent of its total investments. These investments have been realized by 555 firms. This picture reflects that more firms invested in the post-socialist countries than invested in Western Europe. However, the total amount of TDI in CEE and CIS is less than that in Western Europe. This may mean that smaller sized firms invested in the post-socialist countries than those invested in Western Europe. In other words, capital-intensive Turkish firms with market knowledge and experience have invested in Western Europe while more risk-taking smaller firms have invested in the CEE and CIS countries. This could be a typical firm behavior given the differences in the market infrastructure and competitive environments in these two different regions.

Our study suggests that both home-country conditions and location-specific advantages have contributed to the FDI by Turkish firms in the region in the last decade. The home-country conditions include the radical liberalization of the foreign exchange regulations, economic slow-down in Turkey, and the customs union agreement between the European Union and Turkey. On the other hand, the location-specific advantages are the economic liberalizations in the CEE and CIS countries and the emerging consumer demand for quality goods and services. As a result of all these developments, Turkish companies have exploited the emerging markets of CEE and CIS countries to maintain and enhance their competitiveness. Our analyses based on the Enhanced OLI model reveal that market access as well as productivity are the primary motives of Turkish firms for their investments in the CEE and CIS countries.

In summary, a number of factors have contributed to TDI in the CEE and CIS countries as explained within the context of Enhanced OLI model. They are the attractive markets of CEE and CIS, the strategic motives and readiness of Turkish firms, with the opening-up of the Turkish economy and export-led growth strategies in Turkey from the beginning of the 1980s and the geographic and/or cultural proximity of Turkey to those emerging markets.

We believe that the Enhanced OLI model used in this study can also be used for other studies on FDI by developing countries. It offers a sound conceptual framework by expanding the existing knowledge with additional dimensions to capture the realities and dynamics of FDI by firms in developing countries. We hope that this study stimulates further conceptual and empirical research on the subject.

References

Altzinger, W. and Winklhofer, R. (1998), 'General Patterns of Austrian FDI in Central and Eastern Europe and a Case Study', *Journal of International Relations and Development*, vol. 1, pp, 65-83.

Buckley, P. and Casson, M. (1991), *The Future of Multinational Enterprise*, London: Macmillan.

Caves, R. (1996), *Multinational Enterprise and Economic Analysis*, Cambridge: Cambridge University Press.

Dunning, J. (1980), 'Toward an Eclectic Theory of International Production: Some Empirical Tests', *Journal of International Business Studies*, vol. 11, pp. 9-31.

Dunning, J. (1981), *International Production and the Multinational Enterprise*, London: Allen and Irwin.

Dunning, J. (1988), *Explaining International Production*, London: Unwin Hyman.

Dunning, J. (1993), *Multinational Enterprises and the Global Economy*, New York: Addison Wesley.

Financial Times (1996), 'Turkey: The Customs Union with Lupe', January 22, Monday.

Ghymn, K. (1980), 'Multinational Enterprises from the Third World', *Journal of International Business Studies*, vol. 11, pp. 118-122.

Hymer, S. (1976), *The International Operations of National Firms: A Study of Direct Investment*, Cambridge, MA: MIT Press.

Jermakowicz, W. and Bellas, C. J. (1997), 'Foreign Direct Investment in Central and Eastern Europe: 1988-1993' *International Journal of Corporate Management*, vol. 7, pp. 33-55.

Johanson, J. and Vahlne, J.-E. (1977), 'The Internationalization Process of the Firm', *Journal of International Business Studies*, vol. 8, pp. 23-32.

Johanson, J. and Wiedersheim-Paul, F. (1975), 'The Internationalization of the Firm: Four Swedish Cases', *Journal of Management Studies*, vol. 12, pp. 305-322.

Kaynak, E. and Dalgic, T. (1991), 'A Lesson for Third World Countries? Internationalization of Turkish Construction Companies', *Columbia Journal of World Business*, vol. 26, pp. 60-76.

Khan, K. M. (1986), 'Multinationals from the South', in K. M. Khan (ed.), *Multinationals of the South: New Actors in the International Economy*, New York: St. Martin's Press.

Kumar, K. and Kim, K. Y. (1984), 'The Korean Manufacturing Multinationals', *Journal of International Business Studies*, vol. 15, pp. 45-61.

Lall, S. (1982), 'The Emergence of Third World Multinationals: Indian Joint Ventures Overseas' *World Development*, vol. 10, pp. 127-146.

Lansbury, M., Pain, N. and Smidkova, K. (1996), 'Foreign Direct Investment in Central Europe Since 1990: An Econometric Study', *National Institute Economic Review*, May, pp. 104-114.

Lecraw, M. (1993), 'Outward Direct Investment by Indonesian Firms: Motivations and Effects', *Journal of International Business Studies*, vol. 24, pp. 589-600.

Markusen, J. R. (1995), 'The Boundaries of Multinational Enterprises and the Theory of International Trade', *Journal of Economic Perspectives*, vol. 9, pp. 169-180.

Munir, M. (1998), 'Controlling the Crossroad', *Euromoney*, issue 353, pp. 353-359.

Passow, S. (1994), 'Turkey: Positioned for Growth', *Institutional Investor*, vol. 17, pp. 4-9.

Republic of Turkey Treasury Undersecretary (2002), *Unpublished Statistics on Turkey's FDI*.

Rugman, A. M. (1986), 'New Theories of the Multinational Enterprise: An Assessment of Internalization Theory', *Bulletin of Economic Research*, vol. 38, pp. 101-118.

Sak, G. (1995), *Public Policies Towards Financial Liberalization: A General Framework and an Evaluation of the Turkish Experience in the 1980's*, Ankara: Capital Markets Board Press.

Selcuk, F. and Ertugrul, A. (2001), 'A Brief Account of the Turkish Economy, 1980–2000', *Russian and East European Finance and Trade*, vol. 37, pp. 6-30.

Uygur, E. (1993), *Financial Liberalization and Economic Performance in Turkey*, Ankara: CBRT Publication.

Vernon, R. (1966), 'International Investment and International Trade in the Product Cycle', *Quarterly Journal of Economics*, vol. 80, pp. 190-207.

Voinea, L. (2001), *SEE the Difference: Romanian Regional Trade and Investment*, mimeo, December.

Wells, L. (1983), *Third World Multinationals: The Rise of Foreign Direct Investment from Developing Countries*, Cambridge, Mass.: MIT Press.

Xinhua News Agency (2002), 'Turkey may become Bulgaria's No. 1 trading partner in the Balkans', March 19.

PART III

IMPACT OF FOREIGN DIRECT INVESTMENT ON COUNTRIES IN CENTRAL AND EASTERN EUROPE

9 Supply-Side Strategy for Productivity, Competitiveness and Convergence for the EU and the CEECs

CHRISTOS N. PITELIS[1,2]

Introduction

We claim that international trade and foreign direct investment (FDI) by transnational corporations (TNCs) need not automatically lead to increased global competitiveness and convergence. Supply-side (competitiveness) policies may facilitate this process provided they address the problem of the apparent absence of a generally agreed upon framework, which recognizes that government measures may impact differently on different groups within and between countries and that they may have different short, medium and longer term effects. This necessitates focusing on global welfare and convergence-enhancing policies in the short and longer term. We suggest productivity-enhancing measures to be the best approximation available for this purpose. We move on to present a model of the determinants of productivity and competitiveness. We then propose a competitiveness strategy in line with the above, paying particular attention to the role of firm clusters, institutions and institution building.

The issues of competitiveness, employment and convergence are at the forefront of economic debate. In Europe, particularly, the economic integration of the European Union (EU), the convergence between the European south and north, and between Europe and the Central and Eastern European countries (CEECs), is arguably the single most important challenge it faces.

Despite the unquestionable potential benefits from integration for the CEECs but also Europe, integration may not come costlessly. A problem facing Europe today concerns convergence between the European north and south. One can hardly escape the question whether the integration of the CEECs - including the enlargement of the EU to include these countries - will facilitate or hinder the process of convergence. A related question is whether and to what extent government policy towards the supply-side of the economy can influence the process of integration and enlargement, preferably in a way which simultaneously achieves convergence between the CEECs and the existing EU, but importantly also within the existing members of the EU.

Given the at least theoretical possibility that integration between the CEECs and the EU may hinder convergence between the current European north and south, it becomes crucial to address the issue of devising and implementing supply-side strategies (SSSs) at the European, member state, and CEECs level which achieve improvements that render a particular member state better off, without, however, reducing the welfare of other member states and even preferably which close the 'gap', namely lead to convergence.

In view of recent developments in the theory and practice of SSS, we also address the question whether institution building can be (part of) such an approach to SSS. The importance of institutions and firm clusters is widely recognized in the economic literature, and it is important to enquire as to whether (and how) these may contribute to the type of SSS required for convergence.

There are four major strands of economic literature relating to our concerns: the theory of international trade and (regional) convergence; the theory of FDI, TNCs and competitive bidding; the theory of SSS, the theory of firms clusters and that of institutions, institutional change and economic development.

In brief, we suggest that integration and inward investment need not lead automatically to convergence. Supply-side measures may assist, but they need not benefit all parties involved groups within and/or between countries and also their short-term effects may differ from the medium and long term effects. This raises the need for a criterion, which, if satisfied, leads to first best outcomes (it improves the welfare of all in the short and long run) and also leads to convergence. We suggest productivity to be the best approximation we have to such a criterion. We then move on to analyze the nature of supply-side strategy, which can lead to global productivity, competitiveness and convergence, paying attention to the role of clusters, institutions and institution building.

Firstly, we assess critically existing literature and debate on international trade, FDI by TNCs, 'competitive bidding' and convergence. Afterwards we provide a model of competitiveness and the determinants of productivity. Then the issue of supply-side strategy is addressed. It is followed by a discussion of the role of firm clusters and institution building within this framework. Summary and concluding remarks follow in the concluding part of the chapter.

International Trade, Foreign Direct Investment and Convergence

Going back to Ricardo's 'comparative advantage theory', it was widely believed until recently that trade between countries can be beneficial to all parties involved, provided they specialized in products where they faced the least comparative disadvantage. Few exceptions for protectionism were allowed, notably in cases of 'infant industries'. In more recent years the 'static' comparative advantage theory has been attacked on various grounds. First, the economic development of Japan has been based on building competitive advantages (dynamic comparative advantage theory) rather than relying on existing ones. This raised questions on the appropriate policies of both the EU (notably the southern part of the EU) and the CEECs. Importantly it raised concerns on the implications of such potential policies for all parties involved (Pitelis, 1994).

A second attack to the 'Ricardian perspective' has come from the 'new international trade theory'. The traditional theory of international trade is based on the assumption of perfectly competitive markets. Under this assumption, markets can allocate resources efficiently without state intervention. However, more recent developments in the theory of international trade explicitly recognize the existence of imperfectly competitive markets and increasing returns. Under these conditions, it is possible that countries with high-return industries can do better than others, raising the possibility for strategic trade policies by governments. Such policies can take the form of subsidies, tax relieves and more generally protectionism. In the face of imperfect markets, government action in support of some firms - the activities of which, for example, generate *positive externalities* (e.g., research and development useful to other firms, customers, suppliers, etc.) - can generate systemic benefits, which can justify such intervention. On the other hand, support by governments for individual firms could alter the expected pay-offs of undertaking an action for these firms, for example, by increasing their expected profits. This can assist domestic firms to compete with rivals on better terms and thus possibly deter foreign firms from competing. The result can be higher market shares and profits for domestic firms. As Krugman (1986: 13-14), a leading proponent of new ideas, points out

> ... once we begin to believe that substantial amount of rents are really out there, it becomes possible, at least in principle, for trade policy to be used as a way to secure more rent for a country ... Common sense and mathematical theorizing confirm that subsidies or protection can in fact be used to encourage external-economy-producing activities.

He concludes that 'the extreme pro-free-trade position ... has become untenable' (p. 15).

However, Krugman (1983, 1994) is cautious about actual policy, given the difficulties associated with identifying strategic sectors and the possibility of government failures and of retaliation by other governments. An implication may be that the pursuit of a rule of conditional cooperative trade initiatives, which will discourage rival countries from free-riding against a committed free-trader.

The new theory of international trade has further implications on the issue of convergence and the potential cost of enlargement. It is widely recognized that imperfect competition can result in adverse effects, namely an uneven distribution of the benefits from trade, including the possibility of some countries being net losers (Krugman, 1989). This uneven distribution of benefits can come about through the existence of excess returns in imperfectly competitive industries. Countries with high-return industries can benefit at the expense of others. Although the possibility of some parties suffering actual losses is small, according to Krugman (1989), the conflict over the division of benefits is important. It can lead to strategic trade policies (European integration itself conceivably being such a policy against third parties) to secure national advantages in oligopolistic industries. Indeed, all parties concerned could in principle become worse off, if they all pursue such policies.

Further problems identified by Krugman (1994) include adjustment costs and income distribution problems, the latter arising, for example, when trade leads to increases in unemployment in some countries. Moreover, Krugman suggests, such problems are likely to be accentuated as a result of enlargement. The original EU member states were very similar, with trade being mainly intra-industry. Such trade is characterized by small adjustment costs. Enlargement has given rise to inter-industry trade, with a more conventional specialization in labor-intensive, low-technology production, on the one hand, and high-technology, capital-intensive or skill-intensive industries on the other. This is likely to be associated with substantial adjustment costs, and implies the possibility of significant costs in terms of unemployment for some partners.

An important force in the process of integration is FDI by TNCs. In principle, TNCs can create markets, transfer technology, management skills, entrepreneurial skills, international networks, culture. TNCs can be a vehicle for industrial restructuring, for privatization and generally for economic reform and integration. FDI may also have undesired effects; to the home countries, the host countries, but also the firms involved in FDI and/or 'competitors' (including TNCs) in host countries. Perceptions of potential undesired effects can be a hindrance to the process of integration[3].

The theory of FDI and TNC involves Hymer's (1976) original doctoral thesis on ownership advantages and conflict reduction as a (market) power induced reason for TNCs. Hosts of related oligopolistic interaction theories and 'global reach' theories have developed these ideas, see Vernon (1971). The internalization theory has emphasized transaction costs related market failures, notably in intangible assets, such as know-how, managerial skills etc, which can be avoided by internalizing (international) markets, see Buckley and Casson (1976), Williamson (1981). Dunning's (2000) eclectic theory or paradigm, most recently recast in terms of Ownership, Location, Internalization (OLI), points to an integrative framework that views all these factors mentioned as important for the process of FDI. Detailed exposition of these and other theories, including resource-based, distributional and macroeconomic considerations, are discussed by their main proponents in Pitelis and Sugden (2000).

In general, these theories point to efficiency (transaction costs reducing and productivity enhancing) and inefficiency (market power enhancing) aspects of FDI and TNCs.

Looking particularly at the impact of FDI on home countries (our concern here being the EU and the CEECs), the literature is mixed. In their concern with international competitiveness, popular authors and management gurus, such as Krugman (1986) and Porter (1990) have assumed a one to one correspondence between a country's TNCs and international competitiveness. Porter has gone as far as proposing outward investment as the measure for national competitiveness. However, others, notably Dunning (1992), have questioned this link. In some cases, outward investment has been seen as a reason contributing to 'de-industrialization' and the 'relative decline' of countries such as the United Kingdom (Coates and Hillard, 1986; Cowling and Sugden, 1987; Pitelis, 1991 and 1994) for critical surveys[4]. In a carefully argued paper, Dunning (1992) makes a convincing case and provides a critical summary of the literature and arguments for the idea that outward investment need not always be beneficial to home countries. It is crucial to identify the conditions for and the types of investments, which enhance welfare.

Similar considerations apply for the case of inward investment. In general, such investment can generate employment, transfer technology and skills, and have beneficial impact on productivity and balance of payments (Dicken, 1992). Particularly in CEECs, additional benefits can relate to the transfer of entrepreneurial skills, culture, marketing and strategic management, a vehicle of restructuring and privatization, increased competitive environment for local firms and, importantly, all these in a package (Buckley and Ghauri, 1994; Radice, 1994). All these would point to the essential need for attracting FDI in CEECs. However, Dunning's (1992) careful account also highlights numerous instances where inward investment can harm the economy of the host country. These are particularly evident if one distinguishes between short-run and long-run effects. While in the short run, for example, it is arguably the case that any FDI particularly in today's CEECs can only be beneficial, in the longer term it may have harmful effects. Such, Dunning notes, include the possibility of TNCs competing out of existence a local competitor with higher overall domestic value added per resource used. Importantly, FDI may also preclude the consideration of potentially alternative paths to development for CEECs[5].

The problems of potential long-term effects from FDI may be accentuated by virtue of the increasing bargaining power of TNCs vis-à-vis states, related in part to their locational flexibility of operations. This problem has been noted by authors from different perspectives and traditions, notably Vernon (1971) and Kindleberger (1984). It is arguable that today's relationship between TNCs and states (including the EU) is one of 'competitive bidding', namely countries and regions having to compete in order to attract FDI, by means of offering 'best deals' to TNCs (ul Haque, 1990). In such a game countries with better overall infrastructure (including the institutional framework) may fare better. 'Strong' states could bargain from a better position, a case in point being past threats by MEPs to withdraw support from car manufacturers were they to proceed with transferring production to India and China[6].

To summarize, imperfect competition and strategic trade policies, as well as competitive bidding by states to attract investment by TNCs are all factors, which, in principle at least, may operate in ways that hinder convergence within Europe. The effects of these factors can be more pronounced if the EU chooses to adopt protectionist policies, which insulate 'its' TNCs from outside competition. Such (fortress Europe) policies may tend to create 'sleepy giants' within the EU who will focus their operations on the captive European market. This may create (facilitate or simply not ameliorate) a tendency for de-industrialization of the Union as a whole. Furthermore, a fortress Europe may tend to increase the incentives for strategic trade policies of European states and also for intra-EU competitive bidding to attract investment by European TNCs. This may result in a deterioration of the position of the relatively worse-off in the Union (who will have a weaker bargaining position) thus hindering the process of convergence.

The question raises concerns about the extent to which and how, the EU, its member states and the CEECs, can help to avoid such potential problems.

Arguably, the CEECs are not in a good bargaining position. Problems relate to uncertainty, unclear rules of the game, bureaucratic constraints, inadequate infrastructure (physical, human and institutional), non-existent or conflicting laws, delays, problems related to the implementation of reforms and restructuring, including privatization, work culture, and potential political instability. Moreover, CEECs do not boast better infrastructure and industrial performance than most middle-level developing countries and have a central government, which 'absorbs' two to three times their GNP. On the other hand, most CEECs are, with few exceptions, better educated, medically cared for and housed for than even the most prosperous developing countries (Dunning, 1994).

A big advantage CEECs possess is their emerging huge market. The creation and nurturing of this market is a fundamental incentive for the EU, the TNCs and the CEECs to devise policies, which allow for the smooth realization of this objective. However, the objectives of states, the EU, the CEECs and the TNCs (EU and CEECs) and local enterprises need not coincide. This renders essential the derivation of feasible strategies for the EU and for the CEECs, ideally compatible with corporate strategies, all leading to Pareto-efficient outcomes.

The state of play on the role of FDI in the integration of the CEECs at the moment can be described as a wealth of theory and a paucity of evidence. Given the significance of the issue at hand, a substantial literature exists on the topic of FDI and integration in general, but also more recently for the CEECs in particular. However, the complex set of problems relating to collection and interpretation (including comparability) of data, has limited the process of empirical investigation if not the very process of FDI and integration itself. This is highlighted by the fact that by the mid-90s CEECs with a total population of more than 400 million had attracted FDI stocks comparable to those of small European countries such as Ireland, Norway and Austria.

To summarize and conclude, FDI by TNCs need not automatically lead to convergence. If anything, in an era of competitive bidding, the opposite could be true, i.e. cumulative success on the one hand versus cumulative failure on the other. It is critical in this framework to address the issue of the potential role by the government and (in its interrelationship to) (the private sector) in preventing this outcome, and instead facilitate policies, which could lead to global Pareto efficiency.

Competitiveness, Productivity and Convergence

Despite the longstanding and increasing interest in, and the continuous discussions concerning competitiveness, there is no generally accepted definition of it. From the many definitions of competitiveness that have been suggested the best known is probably the one adopted by the OECD.

According to the OECD competitiveness is the degree to which a state can, under free and fair market conditions, produce goods and services, which successfully pass the test of international markets while at the same time maintaining and increasing the real incomes of its citizens in the long run. This definition is rather limited and vague. For example, may a country not be interested in its performance in the absence of fair and free markets? Must we only be interested in the real incomes of citizens? Among the many definitions to be found in the literature, Porter (1990) suggests the substitution of the notion of national competitiveness with that of firms and/or sectors. Within this framework, he adopts the view that a country is competitive when a concentration of competitive firms and sectors exists on its territory. The criteria with which to assess their competitiveness are, according to Porter (1990), FDIs made by such firms and/or sectors. An important problem this definition poses is that the competitiveness of firms is not necessarily translated into an improvement of economic welfare within the country itself. A typical, although possibly extreme, case is that of the United Kingdom. This country is the basis of seven of the ten most successful EU multinationals (Kay, 1993). Despite this fact, its relative position in terms of per capita income has declined over time[7].

The emphasis on (real and/or per capita) incomes may be a symptom of economic narrow-mindedness. An improvement of (per capita) real income can reflect an increase in the unequal distribution of income. On the other hand, it is recognized by many economists today that some not strictly economic criteria can better reflect the total welfare (of the citizens) of the country. Among such criteria an important one is life expectancy.

On the basis of the above literature analysis the definition adopted in this chapter is that competitiveness is the improvement of a subjectively defined welfare indicator for a country, over time and/or in relation to other countries. This definition avoids some of the problems of other definitions. However, it does not solve the problem of (how to choose) a generally accepted welfare criterion. A well-known problem of welfare economics is the difficulty of making interpersonal comparisons of welfare and of finding a way of aggregating individual (or community) welfare functions into a social welfare function. Given that the preferences of people, countries, communities, regions, firms, etc. can differ, it is necessary to refer to some criterion whose improvement tends to imply an increase in the welfare of all, at least in absolute terms. In other words, we need a criterion which can lead to systemic benefits, which leads to a positive- rather than zero- or negative-sum game. Our suggestion here is that this criterion could be the (total) productivity of an economy.[8] To the extent that an improvement in productivity is not achieved solely through an increase in the duration and/or intensity of labor, an improvement in competitiveness tends to improve total economic welfare, through an increase in efficiency. Such an improvement tends to have systemic benefits, which can filter out to the whole of the domestic and/or international economy on condition that the firm or country improving its competitiveness is not in a position to increase (and abuse) its monopolistic power as a result of this increase.

The above two conditions are neither trivial nor necessarily probable[9]. They raise potential government competition policy issues to which we shall return later. For the moment it is sufficient to note that, despite its imperfections, this indicator, i.e., productivity, appears to be the best tool we have. It is no coincidence that a number of researchers and international organizations attribute a significant importance to it[10]. Furthermore, it is not by chance that per capita income (which can be considered as the macroeconomic near-equivalent of productivity) is often considered as an indicator of competitiveness.

Despite the recognition of the role of productivity as an important determinant (and/or indicator) of competitiveness, there has been less progress in the analysis of the determinants of productivity[11]. Such an analysis is both useful and necessary as it could lead to the discovery of the subjects and the possible ways and means to influence these factors positively, in order to improve productivity and competitiveness.

There are many factors that could affect productivity, either positively or negatively. Thus, one should concentrate on the most important ones and/or those which appear to directly affect productivity and not indirectly, i.e. through other (direct) factors. On the basis of these criteria, we adopt the following as the main determinants of productivity: human resources, technology and innovation, unit cost economies, infrastructure. Furthermore, these factors operate both in a macroeconomic framework and an institutional one. As a result, macroeconomic policy and the institutional framework can also affect productivity. The model of the determinants of productivity is shown in Figure 9.1.

Human resources, first, include all the people involved in the production process: workers, entrepreneurs and administrative staff, mainly managers. The quantity (working hours, intensity) of labor is important, but more so is its quality. One of the most important themes in political economy is the observation that in the production process one does not buy work, but working potential. The inducement to work is a more complex matter, which requires, among other things, the existence of incentives and disincentives (carrots and sticks). It follows that the quality and intensity of work does not necessarily affect productivity positively, as, for example, when it reduces incentives and thus the quality of work[12]. Furthermore, workers are not the only human resources.

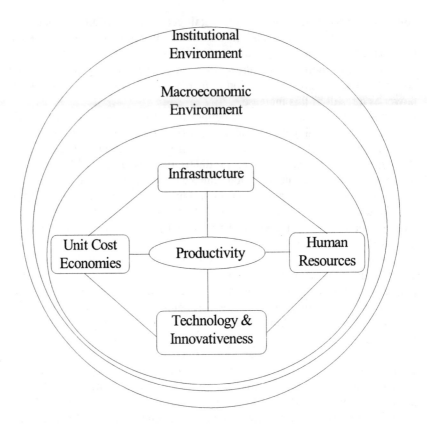

Figure 9.1   The productivity - competitiveness wheel

The quantity and quality of entrepreneurs and managers are extremely important determinants of productivity, given their ability to manage and mobilize other employees. Furthermore, they also influence productivity autonomously, through their contribution to the production process. This contribution is universally acknowledged today as being extremely important[13].

An issue related to the coexistence of groups in the production process is the question of their relations, in other words, the problem of industrial relations and more generally of the 'business climate'. Through incentives, disincentives, strikes, etc, the quality of employment relations can act as a catalyst on productivity[14].

A second important determinant of productivity is technology and innovation. The latter refers to anything new, in other words, new ideas, products, forms of organization, administration of human resources, stocks, etc. The role of technology and innovation is one of the most researched topics in economic theory. They are universally acknowledged as important determinants of productivity (European Commission, 1996b), thus we shall not further discuss this topic here.

A third determinant of productivity are unit cost economies. These are economies of scale, of scope, of growth, of learning, of time, transaction cost economies and external economies. As a whole, we can term them 'transformation economies'. They affect productivity positively by increasing the efficiency of the production process as a whole. The importance of their role is recognized in all economic theory and in strategic management (Best, 1990; Best and Forrant, 1996).

The fourth important determinants of productivity are infrastructure and wealth-producing resources. The terms usually refer to both material and intangible infrastructure and resources. Here we focus on the former. In this category, telecommunications, transport and energy are important. Intangible infrastructure usually relates to human factors and issues concerning public administration. Wealth-producing resources also usually refer to both human and other resources. The material refers to underground and overground (for example, climate) resources, but also to the geographical position of a country or region. These factors, in other words the material infrastructure and the wealth-producing resources, affect the cost and the efficiency of the production process as a whole, and are universally recognized today. See, for a recent example, European Commission (1994, 1996a) and (in relation to productive resources) Porter's (1990) well-known work on the competitive advantage of nations.

These four main, in our opinion, factors affect productivity both autonomously and through the influence each has upon others. For example, both infrastructure and technology and innovation affect unit costs. Furthermore, infrastructure can also affect innovation and vice versa (e.g., mobile telecommunications). Both through their mutual influence and independently, all these factors affect labor and capital productivity in important ways, and thus also the competitiveness of firms and countries as a whole[15].

Competitiveness (and productivity), however, are also influenced by macroeconomic policy and the institutional framework. The view adopted here is that macroeconomic policy produces mainly short-term results, whereas in the long run the most important factor is the productive base of the economy (see, for example Porter, 1998). We simply note that such a policy must be in accordance with, and friendly to supply-side policies (Michie and Pitelis, 1998).

Finally, a factor which influences and embraces all the others is the institutional framework. This refers to the role of the state and public administration and constitutes one of the main interests of economists of all schools. Despite many clashing views there is consensus that the state, its policy, the legal and regulatory framework, the size, quality and efficiency of the public sector, the ability to enforce laws, all influence the factors we have referred to. They also influence the competitiveness of the economy as a whole, mainly though not exclusively, through their influence on transaction costs. From the enormous literature on this topic, a typical view is that of Douglass North (1991), the economics Nobel prize winner, who claims that institutions constitute the main explanatory factor for the development and underdevelopment of countries[16].

The usefulness of the analysis of the determinants of productivity and competitiveness, consists among other things, in its ability to answer certain important questions concerning both the agents and the means of influencing productivity and competitiveness. As far as the agents are concerned, it is clear that labor, firms and the state all play a very important part. For example, the state influences not only the institutional framework and infrastructure of a country, but also its business climate, employment relations, etc. Thus, the issue is not whether the state should intervene, but what is the best possible way to do so. As far as the issue of the extent and intensity (and thus cost) of labor is concerned, this constitutes a subset of the factors influencing competitiveness. Given its potentially negative correlation with incentives, it also influences the quality of the work produced[17]. This observation leads to the conclusion that consensus on the issue of productivity is possible and useful, to the degree that productivity is not mainly achieved (preferably not at all) through an increase in hours worked and/or the intensification of work.

It is worth emphasizing that it is in this direction that the enormous existing literature on the role and importance of the human factor is tending today (Pitelis, 2002). Furthermore, the literature recognizes the existence of a 'high' and a 'low' road towards competitiveness (the former through an emphasis on innovation, the latter on the intensification of work) and places special emphasis on the first road (see, for example, Best, 1990; Humphrey and Schmitz, 1995).

An increase in productivity, however, can lead to an accumulation of market power and/or be accompanied by price collusion[18]. This can hinder the positive effects of productivity (it also negatively affects distribution between firms and consumers) and lead to a reduction in efficiency and productivity in the medium run through a reduction of the competitive pressures on firms, which constitute an important incentive for innovation. Thus, (the consensus for) the existence of a regulatory framework (competition policy) is also necessary, a framework favoring market contestability, and thus not allowing the accumulation and exploitation of oligopoly power in the market (and more generally in the economy-society, through, for example, acquaintances, 'intertwined interests', etc.).

Real convergence can be attained through a differential increase in productivity and competitiveness. In the medium term, there is no other way. Macroeconomic policy can only contribute in the short run. A nominal convergence can contribute to macroeconomic stability, by putting things into place. However, it is insufficient, virtually by definition[19]. The attainment of nominal convergence by all parties, implies a comparative advantage for no-one. This emphasizes the importance of supply-side policies for productivity, competitiveness and convergence.

Supply-side Strategy for Productivity, Competitiveness and Convergence

The implementation of (supply-side) policy measures is the responsibility of government, for example here the (countries of the) EU and the governments of the CEECs. The role of government in general and supply-side strategies (SSS) for development in particular has historically been a most debated subject in economics and management, see Shapiro and Taylor (1990). In recent years debates on SSS have become most topical in partial response to the arguable success of the Far Eastern economies to implement strategies, which facilitated growth, see e.g. Dutt *et al.* (1994). In both the case of Japan, see Dunning (1994), and the 'Four Tigers', see Pitelis (1994), the exploitation of the benefits from technology transfer, often through FDI, were crucial. These economies moved gradually from import substitution to export promotion, to high-return, advanced technology sectors (supported by high wages) to a nurturing of local enterprises, themselves emerging TNCs. The state has played an important role in the process, by pursuing created comparative advantages and by focusing on managed competition (mainly domestic) and managed trade, including protectionism. Recent theories of international trade (Krugman, 1986) and analyses of 'New Competition' (Best, 1990) and the 'Competitive Advantage of Nations' (Porter, 1990) appear to have provided some theoretical support for the Far Eastern perspective. Moreover, such debates have revived interest on SSS, including governments' attitudes to FDI and TNCs, see Cowling (1990), Cowling and Sugden (1992), Pitelis (1992, 1994).

The terms 'industrial policy' (IP), 'industrial strategy' (IS), 'competitiveness strategy', and more generally supply-side strategies have acquired substantial currency in recent years, particularly through their linkage with the topical concerns of 'international competitiveness' and 'de-industrialization', see for example Pitelis (2001). Logically, competitiveness and/or de-industrialization can, at the most, be sufficient conditions for (the need for) SSS, but they are not necessary. SSS need not be concerned with competitiveness and/or be used in countries which experience no symptoms of de-industrialization. However, as Krugman (1994) has aptly observed, concern with competitiveness can provide urgency and popularity to the notion that somehow government policy in general and SSS in particular can help to enhance the country's international competitiveness. Given their wide use, the terms SSS, competitiveness and de-industrialization are often taken for granted today. There is no widely acceptable definition for any of these, this being particularly true for IP and IS. We do not intend to provide an account of existing definitions here, but rather propose our own, which is going to inform the rest of the discussion.

Industrial policy in its more general sense can be any type of government policy, which affects industry. This would evidently encompass all types of government policy, including macro-economic. While the latter may strongly influence industry, here it will be taken as the background against which IP can be applied. In this setting we can define IP as the government policies intended to affect industry directly and specifically towards achieving a particular objective. Usually this objective is the increase in consumers' per capita incomes. Within the context of IP, *competition policy* will be taken to be that subset of IP which is exclusively concerned with the degree of competition in industry. Industrial strategy will be taken as the existence, or otherwise, of a well-thought out and reasonably consistent and coherent set of industrial policies (along with the required resources and mechanisms for implementation) which aim at the realization of a long-term objective concerning industry in particular and, through it, the nation more generally. Lastly, competitiveness strategy and SSS are measures aimed at improving the determinants of productivity of a country.

One way in which growth can be affected is through international trade. The international competitiveness of a country can be defined as the degree to which this country can improve on an index (subjectively chosen) of national welfare in a sustainable way, in the international stage. Government policy in general, and SSS in particular, may influence competitiveness positively or negatively, which renders important the link between SSS and the nature of a nation's attitude to trade. An erosion in a country's relative standing could be the result of a decline in manufacturing employment or output, which is not explicable purely in terms of a country's 'maturity' or of a change in its trade specialization. This can be defined as '(negative) de-industrialization', see Rowthorn and Wells (1987).

Based on an extensive coverage of the existing theory and international experience on IS and SSS, it has been suggested that a country could potentially behave opportunistically, adopting a Machiavellian approach, see Pitelis (1994). In particular a nation state may improve its relative standing if it gains at the expense of others (in a zero-sum game world) or if it receives a larger share of the benefits of growth (in a positive-sum game world). It is possible, and has been widely observed historically, that nation states can unite behind such an objective. For example, the analyses of Bowles *et al.* (1983, 1986) suggest that US post-war growth might have been based on a growth accord between US capital and labor. Similarly, the wide consensus between social groups, or put differently, the corporatist nature of, for example, Japan, the 'four tigers' and Germany, could be seen as a factor contributing to growth.

Assume for the moment that for example the EU decides to adopt such a strategy, one that need not aim exclusively at enhancing productivity, but may generate distributional benefits. Such a strategy could incorporate the following elements. First, build the institutions and mechanisms which guarantee acceptance of the objective of growth - given distribution (consensus) between partners with potentially different interests, notably TNCs, labor and the state (personnel). Second, given consensus (e.g. corporatism), adopt suitably modified policies of selective protectionism, managed trade and controlled liberalization, while relying on domestic firms. Third, make sure that her competitive firms, notably TNCs, are playing the game, i.e. investing at home, repatriating profits and, more generally, abiding by the rules of the accord in behaving nationalistically. Fourth, play the competitive bidding game with foreign TNCs in order to attract them away from rival sites/nation states. Fifth, support (clusters of) small and medium sized enterprises (SMEs) in order to exploit their relative advantages and the synergies between them and large firms, and potentially provide a pool of domestic competitors for existing TNCs and a source of new knowledge and potentially new TNCs. Sixth, provide suitable and stable institutional and macro-economic environment and policies, appropriate infrastructure, including investments in 'human capital' (skills, education, training) and support for R&D, particularly of the type favoring (any) targeted sectors and firms. Seventh, ensure that any benefits from growth are distributed fairly within the nation, to ensure cooperative 'industrial relations' and thus a favorable business climate.

This strategy would apply in the case of the EU. For a country within the EU, some of these policies such as protectionism and managed trade are severely constrained. However, it is possible for a country within the EU to attempt to receive a disproportionate share of the possible benefits accruing to the EU from the above policies, for example by seeking exceptions assisting its firms (allowed in exceptional cases by the EU) and applying R&D policies in a way which discriminates in favor of its own firms and sectors targeted for support, and/or by seeking exceptions from rulings (such as the Social Chapter) which would allow it to receive a disproportionate share of inward investments.[20]

This Machiavellian scenario bears close resemblance to what has already happened in Japan and the Far East, but also in many Western countries throughout their history (see notably the Congress of the US OFTA, 1992 report; Shapiro and Taylor, 1990; Best and Forrant, 1996). There are various demands that, suitably modified, such scenarios are adopted in the West to face the problem of competitiveness, as we have already discussed. Interestingly, critics of such demands focus primarily on the theoretical and/or practical difficulties of applying these in the West (see for example Norton, 1986). Never questioned is the very objective.

However, one could question the *objectives* of the Machiavellian scenario for reasons not only of ethics, but also of long-term interest, including sustainability, see Pitelis (1994). These relate to international distributional considerations. Failure by less-favored regions to converge could generate problems for developed countries too, through, for example, inability to repay loans, but importantly by not facilitating the process of global productivity, and (therefore) wealth, increases. From a dynamic perspective, the main issue is how to generate wealth, compared to how to redistribute it. Arguably an SSS should have this as a prime concern. This takes us back to the productivity-increasing measures discussed in the previous section.

An SS strategy should try to encourage inter- and intra-firm competition so as to nurture conditions favorable to the creation of new ideas, techniques, products, processes, organizational and institutional forms, and, moreover, to best exploit for this purpose the information-providing (and enhancing) attributes of economic organizations, notably markets, firms, states and people at large. A strategy of this type should provide incentives, support, mechanisms and institutions for achieving productivity and competitiveness.[21] Conditions necessary for it are addressing state "capture" by sectional interests (Pitelis, 1994) - in part through striving for conditions of contestability in private and (up to a point) political markets[22] and a plurality of institutional and organizational forms, including, for example, support for (clusters of) SMEs, see below.[23] Pluralism can also enhance the generation and use of new knowledge (see e.g. Simon, 1991, on the coordinating efficiency of organizations).[24]

In line with our discussion, adopted measures should strive to help the EU (to) help the CEECs (to) help the private sector, including the TNCs, to devise strategies which are feasible, consistent, sustainable in terms of distributional (and environmental) considerations and beneficial to all parties at least in the long run. This may well not be possible in all cases, or even in most. A notable case in point is the apparent contradictory pressures governments of CEECs receive from international organizations, such as the IMF and the World Bank (to privatize, liberalize and open their economies to international trade) and some TNCs (which sometimes request monopolistic access to markets and related protectionism as part of a package which will attract them in the region). Devising feasible, consistent, sustainable strategies which nurture dynamic efficiency and enhanced welfare is therefore a challenge we need to tackle.[25]

The exact measures that need to be taken to achieve global Pareto-efficient welfare improvements and convergence can vary according to the conditions prevailing in every country. There is need for international cooperation to make sure that (inter)national policies are not inconsistent and mutually offsetting. In this framework any policy which improves productivity is useful: such policies can be horizontal measures (such as tangible and intangible infrastructure, education, skills, technology and innovation, public sector efficiency improvements, etc). The need to ensure competition also suggests the need to support SMEs. In order to achieve economies of transformation, often related to large size, there should be measures facilitating the 'clustering' of SMEs, see Best (1990), Best and Forrant (1996). 'Clusters' of SMEs can also be a potent source of indigenous development for local financial resources, countering a dependence on TNCs. Technology transfer through FDI should be pursued in conjunction with 'clustering'.

A third way, through which the above can be achieved is through the support of firms' policies to achieve 'optimal size' (subject, however, to this being done through efficiency and innovation, not market power motivated strategies). The role of 'optimal size' in the historical development of capitalism is far too well documented to require further discussion here, see for example Chandler (1986).

Horizontal measures, optimal size, and clusters of SMEs are linked to the competitiveness wheel, through the determinants of productivity. Indeed, to varying degrees, all four influence positively the four determinants of productivity, in rather straightforward and too obvious ways to require further elaboration. Worth noting, instead, is the derivation of policy measures from first principles, namely a model of productivity and competitiveness. This hopefully addresses a major problem in theory, the absence of a generally agreed-upon framework from which supply-side policy measures can be derived.[26]

Regional Clusters and the Role of Institutions and Institution Building

As already noted, the size of firms and the organization of industry are two important factors that impact upon the determinants of productivity. Historically, the quality of firm infrastructure, human resources, technology and innovativeness as well as the existence of unit cost economies, were all felt to be positively linked with large size and oligopolistic industry structures. Indeed the history of capitalism was felt to be the history of large firms, operating in oligopolistic industries (see Chandler, 1990). This author exemplifies the concept of declining unit cost economies through economies of scale and scope in large, growing firms.

In more recent years there has been a realization that advantages of large size can be achieved by smaller firms, operating in less oligopolistic, more competitive environments, but in the form of networks or clusters. Clusters represent agglomerations, usually of SMEs, with horizontal and/or vertical linkages, intra- and/or inter-sectorally, usually within a specified geographical dimension, in a facilitatory institutional setting, which compete and cooperate (compete) in (inter)national markets. It has been found out that the aforementioned characteristics of clustering can lead to increased firm and regional competitiveness, by impacting positively on the determinants of productivity. For example, clusters promote innovation, the quality of human resources, firm management and organization, and also reduce unit costs (mainly through external economies, economies of learning, transaction costs and diversity economies) but also economies of scale (through co-operation), usually attributed to large size.

Clustering is related to another very topical issue: location. In recent years, there has been a revival of interest in locational factors in explaining both agglomerations such as clusters, and innovative activities; see for example Krugman (1998). The new literature provides reasons why local proximity can help clustering. One such reason is that knowledge generation and transmission can be facilitated by geographical proximity (see Audretch, 1998).

A way through which regions and countries have often tried to acquire competitive advantage is through inward investment by transnational corporations (TNCs). Dunning (1998) has, for many years, been a rather lonely champion of the role of locational factors in explaining the spatial choices by TNCs. In recent years his patience has been rewarded, in the recognition afforded to the role of location; see also Porter (1998). It is arguable that clusters are a better alternative to inward investment and, relatedly, large size. Clusters are less mobile, characterized by competition and cooperation (co-petition), and generally are more closely embedded in the local community. In addition, clustering and inward investment are linked. As explained in Pitelis (2000), regional clusters can be a factor attracting inward investment.

It follows from the above that geography, clustering and inward investment can be interrelated and lead to a virtuous circle of regional development.

The policy implications from the above are that countries and regions should try to achieve and maintain competitiveness through combining the inter-related benefits of clustering, inward investment and large size. To do this, clusters need to be identified and facilitated. Large size should be promoted through mergers and acquisitions when conditions for clustering are absent. Inward investment should be attracted and embedded within the regional context, through active measures.

There is no need to focus on particular industries or sectors. Competitiveness, through productivity improvements, can be acquired in every industry or sector. It is mainly a matter of firm strategy, including clustering. Having said this, one cannot build on anything. One has to build foundations, preferably strong ones. This requires an analysis of the competences and opportunities, as well as the weaknesses and threats of a region.

In the context of the 'Future of Greek Industry Project' (Pitelis *et al*, 1997) we identified such foundations in various sectors of Greece: in particular, wine, furniture, textiles, marble, metals and software are among the activities where strengths were identified as well as a basis for clustering. Facilitating clusters, in such and other activities, can help enhance productivity and competitiveness, as explained. Importantly, improving the conditions for entrepreneurship more generally helps local firms, sectors and clusters, and the attraction of inward investment. In general, activities that are chosen by the market, are characterized by the existence of history and competences, and are, or can be, knowledge-intensive, can be prioritized.

Facilitating clustering, 'optimal' size, and attracting inward investment requires both the private and the public sector. Infrastructure, the legal and institutional context, education and health, even culture and attitudes depend largely on government actions. The government may also help in facilitating clustering. However, it cannot be an entrepreneur. The best the government can do is to provide an environment supportive of entrepreneurship. This means a stable macroeconomic environment, clear rules of the game, transparency, efficient bureaucracy, a level playing field and no corruption, and more generally a supportive institutional context, to include institution building.

The institutional environment encompasses and affects all determinants of productivity.[27] As North (1991, p. 98) observes, 'the central issue of economic history and of economic development is to account for the evolution of political and economic institutions that create an economic environment that induces increasing productivity'. Also, the analysis of institutions and institutional change 'offer the promise of dramatic new understanding of economic performance and economic change' (North, 1991, p. 111). This is particularly important for the 'south', for countries experiencing problems of institutional sclerosis, notably Britain, and for the CEECs. It is interesting to note that, in his 1991 Nobel lecture on 'The Institutional Structure of Production', Coase refers twice to Eastern Europe, as follows, 'These ex-communist countries are advised to move to a market economy and their leaders wish to do so, but without the appropriate institutions, no market of any significance is possible... It makes little sense for economists to discuss the process of exchange without specifying the institutional setting within which the trading takes place, since this affects the incentives to produce and the costs of transacting. I think this ... has been made crystal clear by what is going on in Eastern Europe today' (Coase, 1991).

Examples of institutional measures include the delineation and enforcement of property rights, a regulatory environment, which promotes healthy competition, and a pluralism of organizational forms and ownership structures which exploit existing and generate new knowledge. Most important is also an attempt to promote attitudes, values and generally culture conducive to dynamic competitiveness through innovativeness, thus to productivity, growth and convergence. Evidently all these are easier said than done. A way through which these can be achieved is with the government assuming the role of a catalyst, by identifying and implementing in close co-operation with the private sector, changes proposed by those nearer the action, e.g., the private sector itself. Such bottom-up policies exploit dispersed knowledge and also promote subsidiarity and democracy. Exact actions, however, should be based on an analysis of each particular case. This is beyond the scope of this chapter, but the following methodology can be proposed:[28] first, a consensually agreed upon theoretical framework; second, an audit of the external (international) environment; third, an audit of the internal (national) environment; fourth, deciding the direction of the strategy; fifth, its dimensions; sixth, the required actions; seventh, addressing the issues of prerequisites, resources and mechanisms for implementation; eighth, feasible actions; ninth, control-evaluation; and tenth, new actions for implementation.

To conclude, a new supply-side strategy should focus on the nurturing of institutions, mechanisms and organizations, which foster dynamic efficiency, productivity and growth. Our analyses point to the importance of competition facilitated through a plurality of organizational and institutional forms as a *sine qua non* for the realization of such policies. In our epoch, this entails support for new and potential competition and a focus on dynamic competitiveness through innovation.[29] The development of firm clusters can be a potent means of achieving these objectives.

That increases in productivity and competitiveness will, *ceteris paribus*, lead to global welfare improvements is self-evident. That it will lead to convergence is less self-evident, yet straightforward. It is the CEECs, which suffer disproportionately from the lack of institutions, which provide incentives for productivity enhancements. Accordingly, improvements on this front in CEECs can be proportionately larger than in countries which have already established an institutional setting conducive to productivity and growth. This can lead to proportionately higher rates of growth, thus to convergence.

Concluding Remarks

Recent developments in the theories of international trade and (regional) convergence, supply-side strategy, regional clusters, institutions and institutional change and notably their links, seem to cast new light on our important concerns here and seem to provide some promise towards the possibility of developing a strategy to integration and convergence which maximize the net benefits to all parties involved.

Such a strategy involves a focus on productivity, dynamic efficiency and competitiveness through the nurturing of a pluralism of institutional and organizational forms, the development of clusters and the building of institutions and incentive structures that lead to reduced transaction and transformation costs and (thus) productivity, growth and convergence.

Overall in their complex interrelationships, the exploitation of knowledge through the existence of a plurality of institutional and organizational forms, the benefits of competition also arising from these (and appropriate competition policies) the related amelioration of the problem from state capture, technology (and skills) transfer through FDI and the parallel exploitation of the benefits of clustering, can lead to both global Pareto enhancements and convergence. Exact policies would vary from country to country. It is argued, however, that if seen in the required perspective, suggested here, they will be tending to lead to the desired outcome, global integration, growth and convergence.

Notes

1   An earlier version of this chapter has been presented at the International Conferences on Restructuring of South and Eastern Europe, in Volos, Greece (May 2001). I am grateful to participants for comments and discussion. I am particularly grateful to K. Cowling, G. Petrakos, A. Pseiridis and R. Sugden. All errors are mine.

2   Author's affiliation Judge Institute of Management Studies and Queens' College, University of Cambridge, United Kingdom, and Department of Economics, University of Athens, Greece.

3   More generally, the issues involved here concern the role of TNCs and FDI in economic development of home and host countries in general and Europe in particular; relatedly the role of FDI and TNCs on international competitiveness of the EU and/or the CEECs; their impact on subsidiarity and convergence; the role of government policy in achieving its objectives through FDI and TNCs, and relatedly the link between TNCs, nation states and international organizations such as the EU; the benefits of FDI to TNCs and host country enterprises, namely competitive and corporate strategy; and the conditions facilitating compatible SS strategies by countries and business strategies by firms. This is not straightforward. The multiplicity of the actors involved and the complexity of the relationships point to the need for an analysis which makes explicit, first, the standpoint one is adopting, namely the home nation, the 'host' nation, the foreign TNC, the local firms; in the short run, or in the long run. Importantly, all these standpoints may be satisfied simultaneously, but they need not. Most useful, therefore, is being able to identify conditions, mechanisms and institutions that can favor the first best scenario; enhance the welfare of all involved. Our aim should therefore be to help Europe, help the CEECs to devise strategies for FDI that lead at the very least to Pareto-efficient welfare improvements. Essential for this purpose is a theoretical analysis-framework highlighting issues and conditions favorable to the success of the desired objective. This is attempted in the next sections.

4   Work by Iammarino and Pitelis (2000) on outward investment by Greek firms in CEECs is a case in point. Should such investments be seen as a sign of competitiveness and relative to whom CEEC enterprises or advanced countries' TNCs. Is such investment beneficial for Greece? The same questions apply for the case of the EU as a whole.

5   In concluding his analysis, Dunning observes that 'In answer to the question: will foreign inward and outward investment improve the competitive advantage of host or home countries?, the answer that is too frequently (but justifiably) given by economists is "it all depends". The most (but this should not be belittled) an economist can do is first to set out the conditions under which, and the ways in which, domestic or foreign TNCs are likely to benefit national competitiveness (either in an industry or in an economy) in the short and/or long run; and second, to indicate what might be done (and at what cost) to optimize the impact of outward and inward investment (and associated activities, for example, strategic alliances) on that competitiveness' (p. 165).

6   Competitive bidding can take place, and be fierce too, even within a country, a notable case in point being United Kingdom, especially Scotland and/vs. Wales; see

The Economist, June 8-14, 1996, 'Inward Investment Bribing for Britain'. This is likely to be true. It is observed today that the key to competitiveness is to produce goods which are better, cheaper and are produced faster and more flexibly. Labor costs considerations lose part of their importance (see for example Best and Forrant, 1996). This may tend to reduce the attractiveness of lower labor costs to TNCs vis-à-vis other factors. As lower labor costs are typically the characteristic of relatively less-developed countries, the emerging new 'rules of the game' may tend to remove a source of competitive advantage from such countries. This, moreover, may tend to reduce their bargaining power vis-à-vis TNCs. Overall, these factors may tend to imply fewer investments by TNCs in such countries and/or more 'bad deals' over such investments.

7   Second in 1950, 7th today among OECD countries, on the basis of *per capita* income, see Kitson and Michie (1996).

8   The precise definition and measurement of labor productivity and especially of capital productivity is not devoid of problems. However, such problems are beyond the scope of this paper. For discussion and data see European Commission (1996a) and Nolan and O'Donnell (1995). For comparative data on labor productivity see European Commission (1996b).

9   There is an extensive discussion in economic theory on the relation between efficiency and (monopoly) power in the market, see Pitelis (1994) for an overview.

10   For example see Krugman (1994), Porter (1990), European Commission (1996).

11   For discussion see European Commission (1996a) and European Commission (1996b).

12   The importance of the human factor is universally acknowledged today as an important determinant of productivity, see Nolan and O'Donnell (1995) and below.

13   For example, 'the entrepreneur' constitutes the most important figure in the production process in the Schumpeterian and Austrian approach to economics,. The importance of the role of managers was initially emphasized by Penrose (1959), and is nearly universally accepted today. According to Penrose, the quality and quantity of managers is the main factor limiting the rate of increase of the size of a firm, see Pitelis (2002) for more.

14   See the analysis by Nolan and O'Donnell (1995), who also have a particularly interesting discussion on the role of employment relations in productivity and competitiveness.

15   For the important role of infrastructure see European Commission (1996a, b).

16   For overviews of this literature see Pitelis (1991, 1994), among others.

17   We note that we are not adopting the view that the extent, intensity and cost of labor do not influence productivity, but that it is not a clearly important factor (especially if one considers the incentives problem) except possibly in some sectors (based on unskilled labor) and then only *ceteris paribus* (assuming that all the other factors are present and are of a degree which is satisfactory and/or comparable to other countries).

18   I am grateful to A. Pseiridis for pointing this out to me.

19   It may also hinder real convergence, see Michie and Pitelis (1998) for a discussion on this issue, which, however, goes beyond the scope of this chapter.

20   For more on this, including more possibilities of this type, see Pitelis (1997).

21   Such ideas draw on the works of Schumpeter (1942), Hayek (1945) and Penrose (1959). Recent appreciation of their ideas can be seen in the literature on the "endogenous growth theory", see, for example Aghion and Howitt (1988) and Fine (2000) for a critique.

22   There can be too much contestability in public sector markets, in that it can increase the dependence of politicians, bureaucrats, etc. to pressures by organized interest groups, leading to regulatory capture.

23   Seen in this light, EU recognition of the need for education and skills, technology, infrastructure and support for SMEs should be welcome. Similarly welcome are steps to reduce state involvement in certain cases to the extent that this favors contestability (reduced centralization) of the market for government.

24   Supply-side strategy need not be in line with competitive strategy (see Pitelis, 1996). When this happens, governments can be called to undo what firms do. It is best if, when possible, this is avoided. This is particularly true given that firms, including TNCs, are most directly involved in the process of integration and do so for their own benefit. As the Prince of Wales business leaders' forum observed in adverts throughout the national press in Britain in reference to CEECs: 'The key trend which links ... "corporate citizens" is a strategy enhancing their core business in emerging markets, not traditional corporate philanthropy or altruism. ... The stakes for international companies operating in the region are high.'

25   Within this framework, an important decision for CEECs is their route to development and integration. Available routes include for some commentators the neo-liberal path akin to Western-type policies, the protectionist path and the state developmental path, see Radice (1994). For other, notably Dunning (1994), available models include the developing country model, the reconstruction model and the systemic model. These scenarios suggest potentially different rules for, and attitudes to, FDI. The choice will depend, among other factors, on the prevailing special conditions of the economy in hand. This necessitates detailed country case study analyses.

26   Here we limit ourselves to general policy measures or dimensions, without going further to specific actions. The derivation of operational measures from the above framework is possible, but beyond the scope of this chapter.

27   The other factor, the macroeconomic environment falls outside the scope of this particular chapter. Suffice it to note here that macro policies should be supply-side friendly.

28   This is based on the author's own experience with policy making in Greece, where he has coordinated the 'Future of Greek Industry Project', a consensus-based, bottom-up industrial strategy, orchestrated by the government and supported by the major social partners.

29   This need not exclude (threats to) protectionism either, both in support of such players and as a means of ensuring fair and open trade.

References

Aghion, P. and Howitt, P. (1988), *Endogenous Growth Theory*, Cambridge, Mass.: The MIT Press.

Audretch, D.B. (1998), 'Agglomeration and the Location of Innovative Activity', *Oxford Review of Economic Policy*, vol. 14, no. 2, pp. 18-29.

Best, M. (1990), *The New Competition: Institutions for Industrial Restructuring*, Polity Press.

Best, M. and Forrant, R. (1996), 'Creating Industrial Capacity: Pentagon-Led versus Production-Led Industrial Policies', in J Michie (ed.) *Creating Industrial Capacity*, New York: Polity Press.

Bowles, S., Gordon, D. and Weisskopf, T. (1983), *Beyond the Wasteland: A Democratic Alternative to Economic Decline*, New York, NY: Anchor Doubleday.

Bowles, S., Gordon, D and Weisskopf, T. (1986), 'Power and Profits: The Social Structure of Accumulation and the Profitability of the Postwar UK Economy', *Review of Radical Political Economics*, Spring and Summer, vol. 18, nos 1 and 2, pp 132-167.

Buck. y, P and Ghauri, P. (eds) (1994), *The Economics of Change in East and Central Europe*, London: Academic Press.

Buckley, P and Casson, M. (1976), *The Future of Multinational Enterprise*, London: Macmillan.

Buigues, P.-A. and Jacquemin, A. (1997), 'Structural Interdependence between the European Union and the United States: Technological Positions', Paper presented at the International Conference on *Industrial Policy for Europe*, Royal Institute of International Affairs, London, 26-27 June 1997.

Chandler, A.D. (1986), 'Technological and Organisational Underpinnings of Modern Industrial Multinational Enterprise: The Dynamics of Competitive Advantage', in A. Teichova, M. Levy-Leboyer and H. Nussmaum (eds), *Multinational Enterprise in Historical Perspective*, Cambridge: Cambridge University Press, pp. 30-54.

Chandler, A.D. (1990), *Scale and Scope: The Dynamics of Industrial Capitalism*, Cambridge, Mass: The Belknap Press of Harvard University Press.

Coase, R. (1991) 'The Institutional Structure of Production', Nobel Prize Lecture, www.nobel.se/economics/laureates/1991/coase-lecture.html.

Coates, D. and Hillard, J. (1986), *The Economic Decline of Britain*, Brighton: Wheatsheaf.

Congress of the US OFTA, 1992 Report.

Cowling, K. (1990), 'A New Industrial Strategy: Preparing Europe for the Turn of the Century', *International Journal of Industrial Organization*, vol. 8, no. 6, pp. 68-79.

Cowling, K. and Sugden, R. (1987), *Transnational Monopoly Capitalism*, Brighton: Wheatsheaf.

Cowling, K. and Sugden, R. (1992), *Current Issues in Industrial Economic Strategy*, Manchester: Manchester University Press.

Dicken, P. (1992), *Global Shift*, London: Paul Chapman.

Dunning, J.H. (1991), 'The Eclectic Paradigm in International Production' in C.N. Pitelis and R. Sugden (eds), *The Nature of the Transnational Firm*, London: Routledge.

Dunning, J.H. (1992), 'The Competitive Advantage of Countries and the Activities of Transnational Corporations', *Transnational Corporations*, vol. 1, no. 2, pp. 135-68.

Dunning, J.H. (1994), 'The Prospects of Foreign Direct Investment in Central and Eastern Europe' in P. Buckley and P. N. Ghauri (eds), *The Economics of Change in East and Central Europe*, London: Academic Press.

Dunning, J.H. (1998), 'Location and the Multinational Enterprise: A Neglected Factor?' *Journal of International Business Studies*, vol. 29, no. 1, pp. 45-66.

Dunning, J.H. (2000), 'The Eclectic Paradigm of International Production: A Personal Perspective', in C. N. Pitelis and R. Sugden (eds) *The Nature of the Transnational Firm*, 2nd Edition, London: Routledge.

Dutt, A. *et al.* (1994), *Markets, States and Development*, Cheltenham: Edward Elgar.

European Commission (1994a), *Greece: Community Support Framework 1994-99*, Luxembourg: Office for Official Publications of the European Communities.

European Commission (1994b), *Integrated Programmes in Favour of SMEs and the Craft Sector*, Competitive (94)207 Final 3.6.1994, Luxembourg: Office for Official Publications of the European Communities.

European Commission (1994c), *Return to Growth, Full Employment and Convergence*, Luxembourg: Office for Official Publications of the European Communities.

European Commission (1996a), 'Benchmarking the Competitiveness of European Industry III', Commission Communication, Luxembourg: Office for Official Publications of the European Communities.

European Commission (1996b), 'The Competitiveness of European Industry', Working Document of Commission Services, November, Luxembourg: Office for Official Publications of the European Communities.

Fine, B. (2000), 'Endogenous Growth Theory: A Critical Assessment', *Cambridge Journal of Economics*, vol. 24, pp. 245-265.

Hayek, F.A. (1945), 'The Use of Knowledge in Society', *American Economic Review*, vol. 35, pp. 519-30.

Hayek, F.A. (1978), *New Studies in Philosophy, Politics and the History of Ideas*, London: Routledge and Kegan Paul.

Humphrey, J and Schmitz, H. (1995), 'Principles for Promoting Clusters and Networks of SMEs', Paper commissioned by the Small and Medium Enterprises Branch of World Bank.

Hymer, S.H. (1976), *The International Operations of National Firms: A Study of Foreign Direct Investment*, Cambridge, MA: MIT Press.

Iammarino, S. and Pitelis, C.N. (2000), 'Foreign Direct Investment and Less Favoured Regions: Greek Foreign Direct Investment in Bulgaria and Romania', *Global Business Review*, vol. 1, no. 2, pp. 62-83.

Jenkins, R. (1987), *Transnational Corporations and Uneven Development*, Methuen.

Kay, J. (1993), *Foundations of Corporate Success*, Oxford: Oxford University Press.

Kindleberger, C.P. (1984), *Multinational Excursions*, Cambridge, Mas.: MIT Press.

Kitson, M. and Michie, J., (1996), 'Does Manufacturing Matter?', Paper presented at the Eighth Annual Conference of the European Association for Evolutionary Political Economy (EAEPE), Antwerp, Belgium.

Krugman, P.R., (1983), *Targeted Industrial Policies in Theory and Evidence*, Federal Reserve Bank of Kansas City, pp. 123-55.

Krugman, P.R. (1986), 'Introduction: New Thinking about Trade Policy' in P.R. Krugman (ed.), *Strategic Trade Policy and the New International Economies*, Cambridge, Mass.: MIT Press.

Krugman, P.R. (1994), 'Competitiveness: A Dangerous Obsession', *Foreign Affairs*, vol. 73, no. 2, pp. 28-44.

Krugman, P.R. (1989), 'What's New about the New Economic Geography?', *Oxford Review of Economic Policy*, vol. 14, no. 2, pp. 7-17.

Michie, J. and Pitelis, C.N. (1998), 'Demand and Supply-Side Approaches to Economic Policy', in J. Michie and A. Reati (eds), *Employment, Technology and Economic Needs Theory, Evidence and Public Policy*, Cheltenham: Edward Elgar, pp. 42-57.

Nolan, P. and O'Donnell, K. (1995), 'Industrial Relations and Productivity', mimeo, University of Leeds.

North, D.C. (1981), *Structure and Change in Economic History*, London & New York: Norton.

North, D.C. (1991), 'Institutions', *Journal of Economic Perspectives*, vol. 5, no. 1, pp. 97-112.

Norton, R. (1986), 'Industrial Policy and American Renewal', *Journal of Economic Literature*, vol. XXIV, pp. 1-40.

Penrose, E. (1959), *The Theory of the Growth of the Firm*, Oxford: Basil Blackwell.

Pitelis, C.N. (2002), 'On the Garden of Edith', in C.N. Pitelis (ed.) *The Theory of the Growth of the Firm: The Legacy of Edith Penrose*, Oxford: Oxford University Press.

Pitelis, C.N. (2001), 'Privatisation, Regulation and Domestic Competition Policy', in G. Wignaraja (ed.) *Enterprise Competitiveness and Public Policy*. London: Routledge.

Pitelis, C.N. and Sugden, R. (eds) (2000), *The Nature of the Transnational Firm*, 2nd Edition, London: Routledge.

Pitelis, C.N. (1991), *Market and Non-Market Hierarchies*, Oxford: Basil Blackwell.

Pitelis, C.N. (1992), 'A Competitive Strategy for Britain' in K. Cowling and R. Sugden (eds), *Industrial Strategy*, Manchester: Manchester University Press.

Pitelis, C.N. (1992), 'A Competitive Strategy for Europe' in K. Cowling and R. Sugden (eds), *Current Issues in Industrial Economic Strategy*, Manchester: Manchester University Press.

Pitelis, C.N. (1992), 'Towards a Neoclassical Theory of Institutional Failure', *Journal of Economic Studies*, vol. 19, no. 1, pp. 69-86.

Pitelis, C.N. (1994), 'Industrial Strategy: for Britain, in Europe and the World', *Journal of Economic Studies*, vol. 21, no. 5, pp. 2-92.

Pitelis, C.N. (1997), 'Transaction Costs and the Historical Evolution of the Capitalist Firm', mimeo, University of Cambridge.

Pitelis, C.N. (1998), 'Productivity, Competitiveness and Convergence in the European Economy', *Contributions to Political Economy*, vol. 17, pp. 1-20.

Pitelis, C.N. (2000), 'A Theory of the (Growth of the) Transnational Firm: A Penrosean Perspective', *Contributions to Political Economy*, vol. 18, pp. 87-105.

Pitelis C.N., Antonakis, N., Kaloghirou, Y., Katsoulacos, Y., Lyberaki, A., Paraskevopoulos, D., and Tsipouri, L. (1997), *Competitiveness and Industrial Strategy for Greece*, Ministry of Development, Athens, Greece (in Greek).

Porter, M.E. (1990), *The Competitive Advantage of Nations*, Basingstoke: Macmillan.

Porter, M.E. (1998), 'The Adam Smith Address: Location, Clusters and the 'New' Microeconomics of Competition', *Business Economics*, vol. 3, no. 1, pp. 7-13.

Radice, H. (1994), 'Global Integration, National Disintegration?', University of Leeds, Discussion Paper.

Rowthorn, R.E. and Wells, J. (1987), *Deindustrialization and Foreign Trade*, Cambridge: University Press.

Schumpeter, J. (1987), *Capitalism, Socialism and Democracy*, 5th Edition, London: Unwin Hyman.

Shapiro, H. and Taylor, L. (1990), 'The State and Industrial Strategy', *World Development*, vol. 18, no. 6, pp. 861-878.

Simon, H.A. (1991), 'Organizations and Markets', *Journal of Economic Perspectives*, vol. 5, no. 2, pp. 25-44.

ul Haque, R. (1990), 'International Competitiveness: Interaction of the Public and the Private Sectors', *EDI Seminar Series*, Washington DC: The World Bank.

Vernon, R. (1971), *Sovereignty at Bay*, Harlow: Longman.

Williamson, O.E. (1981), 'The Modern Corporation: Origins, Evolution, Attributes', *Journal of Economic Literature*, vol. 19, no. 4, pp. 1537-1568.

10 On the Path of Poland's Globalization

MARIAN GORYNIA, JAN NOWAK and RADOSLAW WOLNIAK

Introduction

Globalization is not a precise term that can be easily and consistently defined (Brown, 1992; Dicken, 1992; Ohmae, 1995; Parker, 1998). In fact, literature supplies a variety of definitions of globalization. In his recent book on globalization, Streeten (2001) provides a sample of 35 different definitions of the term. For the purpose of this paper globalization will be defined as a worldwide integration of societal and economic activity leading to an increased interdependence between countries and regions. Such process is usually characterized by intensification of cross-border trade and capital flows, driven largely by liberalisation of trade and investment regimes and by advances in information and communication technologies. This, in turn, they lead to a greater integration of national economic systems within the world economy.

The scope of these phenomena is reflected in a given economy's share of world trade and foreign investment. A recent publication of the World Bank (2001) even reduces globalization to only one of these two dimensions, measuring the progress in globalization by a change in the ratio of trade to national income. However, looking at both dimensions – international trade and foreign investment – provides a more balanced picture of a country's level of globalization in its economic aspect.

Since 1990, Poland has been going through the process of systemic transformation. As part of that process, Poland has sought to integrate itself with the world economy. Through its closer integration with the world economy, the country has been trying to accelerate GNP growth and to reduce the economic gap separating it from the European Union (EU), to which Poland is applying for full membership.

Before 1990, Poland was a much less open economy and missed out on many of the benefits of globalization. After the transition process was initiated, the country faced the challenge of how to take advantage of globalization to accelerate the introduction of the necessary changes. It liberalized prices and market regimes, privatized most of the state-owned enterprises, re-directed its trade from the Soviet Union-dominated former COMECON trading bloc towards the EU and opened up its market to foreign investment (Ali, Nowak and Pöschl, 2001).

The purpose of this analysis is to determine whether Poland's integration with the world economy has kept pace with the general rate of globalization during the last decade and where it currently stands. Investigation is confined to two dimensions of such integration – world trade and foreign direct investment. These two dimensions are of critical importance as far as Poland's participation in the global economy is concerned. In a wider context, the role of foreign capital and the country's share in international trade have always been the key development issues for all the transition economies of Central and Eastern Europe (CEE).

The analysis first focuses on the evolution of world trade over the decade of 1990 - 2000. Then, Poland's share in world trade over the same period is assessed, using both per capita and total trade volume data, as well as trade to GDP ratios. Thereafter, the analysis moves to foreign direct investment. FDI trends are investigated in the context of different country groups and Poland itself. One of the analytical instruments used in that context is the transnationality index developed by UNCTAD. The subsequent section investigates Poland's external equilibrium. Economic policy implications stemming from the observed trends in foreign trade and FDI constitute the last section of the paper.

Growth Trends in World Trade

The impressive trade growth of the last decade has undoubtedly fuelled the globalization of economic activity. Table 10.1 shows the growth of world merchandise exports and imports in comparison to the growth of GDP during the 1990 - 2000 period. The export volume grew by 96 percent, whereas real GDP growth over the same period was only 25 per cent. In other words, exports increased almost four times as much as the GDP. Although comparable import volume indices for the entire period under investigation are not available, the average growth rate for imports is reported to have been similar to that of exports (WTO, 2001).

Faster growth of world exports compared to world GDP is not a new phenomenon. In fact, the last 50 years have seen trade expand faster than output by a significant margin, increasing the degree to which national economies rely on international trade (WTO, 1998). However, one can observe some acceleration of export growth in recent years. For example, in 2000 exports grew by 12 percent, which is a substantially higher growth rate than the average for the whole decade.

In terms of current prices, the value of world exports amounted to US$ 6,364 billion in 2000, as compared to US$ 3,442 billion recorded at the beginning of the decade. The figures for imports are US$ 6,669 and US$ 3,542 billion, respectively.

Table 10.1   Growth of world merchandise exports, imports and GDP, 1990 - 2000

	Exports			Imports		
Year	US$ billion (Current prices)	Volume Index (Constant prices)	US$ per capita	US$ billion (Current prices)	US$ per capita	GDP (real) index
1990	3,442	100	650	3,542	673	100
1991	3,509	104	660	3,626	682	101
1992	3,759	109	666	3,880	692	102
1993	3,747	113	655	3,859	669	103
1994	4244	124	736	4,369	752	105
1995	5,079	136	861	5,218	876	107
1996	5,347	143	895	5,525	919	110
1997	5,537	158	884	5,720	894	114
1998	5,447	166	857	5,667	902	117
1999	5,662	175	897	5,899	924	120
2000	6,364	196	1051	6,669	1101	125

Note: Per capita figures: own calculations based on population data derived from the World Bank's World Development Indicators databases.

Source: WTO, 2001 (various pages).

When exports of goods are combined with those of services (estimated at US$ 1,435.4 billion), the ratio of world trade to world GDP goes up to 29 percent in 2000. Since 1990, this ratio has increased by 10 percentage points, more than in the two preceding decades combined (WTO, 2001). This represents a further indication of the strengthening of global economic integration in the last decade.

Poland's Position in World Trade

A significant sign of Poland's increased openness to the world after 1989 was its dramatic increase in its foreign trade. As Table 10.2 indicates, Poland's exports grew by an impressive 127 percent between 1990 and 2000 (in real terms). Imports grew even more dramatically (by 426 percent), leading to serious foreign-trade imbalances, compensated for, however, by substantial capital inflows. The growth of exports and, to a smaller degree, imports fluctuated from one year to another. For example, exports grew by more than 25 percent in 2000, but only by 2 percent in 1999.

Table 10.2   Volume indices of imports and exports for Poland, 1990 - 2000*

	1990	1991	1992	1993	1994	1995	1996	1997	1998	1999	2000	2000
	Previous year = 100											1990=100
Exports	100	98	98	99	118	117	110	114	109	102	125	227
Imports	100	138	114	119	113	121	128	122	115	104	111	526
Terms of Trade	100	91	110	108	101	102	97	99	104	101	96	108

Note: *Calculated on the basis of data expressed in Polish zlotys in constant prices.

Source: Central Statistical Office, Poland, 2000 and 2001.

Terms of trade were, for the most part of the decade, favorable for Poland, with the index of 108 for 2000 (as compared to the base year 1990), indicating that the prices of exported goods grew more than those of imported goods.

In reference to the trends in world trade described in the previous section, Poland's share in world exports increased by only 0.1 percent point from 0.4 percent in 1990 to 0.5 percent in 2000. This seemingly insignificant increase translates however into a 25 percent improvement in Poland's position in world trade on the export side. On the import side, the change was much more dramatic. Poland's share increased from 0.3 percent in 1990 to 0.7 percent in 2000. Parallel to that was an increase in the value of exports and imports per capita. The value of exports per capita increased from US$ 376 in 1990 to US$ 820 in 2000, and that of imports grew from US$ 250 to US$ 1268, respectively. In terms of exports per capita, Poland was slightly below the world average, but its imports per capita exceeded the world average (see Table 10.3).

Table 10.3   Poland's Gross Domestic Product (GDP), imports and exports (current prices)

Years	GDP US$ mln[a]	GDP US$ per capita[a]	Imports US$ mln	Imports US$ per capita	Imports % share of world total	Exports US$ mln	Exports US$ per capita	Exports % share of world total	Ratio between exports and GDP
1990	58976	1547	9528	250	0.3	14322	376	0.4	24.3
1991	72924	1998	15522	406	0.4	14903	390	0.4	20.4
1992	84326	2198	15913	415	0.4	13187	344	0.4	15.6
1993	85853	2232	18834	490	0.5	14143	368	0.4	16.5
1994	117978	3057	21569	559	0.5	17240	447	0.4	14.6
1995	126348	3086	29050	753	0.6	22895	593	0.5	18.1
1996	134550	3484	37137	962	0.7	24440	633	0.5	18.2
1997	143066	3702	42308	1094	0.7	25751	666	0,5	18.0
1998	157274	4068	47054	1217	0.9	28229	730	0.6	17.9
1999	155151	4014	45911	1188	0.8	27407	709	0.5	17.7
2000	158839	4110	48940	1268	0.7	31650	820	0.5	19.9

Note: [a] According to official exchange rate.
The exports/GDP ratio: own calculations based on the figures given in the table.

Source: Central Statistical Office, Poland, 2000 and 2001.

However, it would be unjustified to conclude about the seemingly excessive import intensity of the Polish economy. The problem seems to lie more in insufficient exports and less in excessive imports. For example, in 1999 the value of imports per capita in the Czech Republic and Hungary amounted to US$ 2803 and US$ 2782, respectively. The respective figures for exports per capita were US$ 2612 and US$ 2484. It is therefore evident that the gap between exports and imports was not unique to Poland. It also existed in the other two key Central European economies. However, it must also be noted that exports per capita were 3.7 times higher in the Czech Republic and 3.5 times higher in Hungary than they were in Poland. Similar comparisons for imports per capita show that the Czech Republic had a ratio that was 2.4 times higher than Poland, and Hungary had a ratio 2.3 times higher than Poland. One implication of these comparisons is that the relative gap in export performance was much more acute in the case of Poland than it was in the other two transition economies.

Another indicator requiring comment is the export/GDP ratio. The trend here is not clear. No significant increase of that ratio can be observed when both GDP and export values are expressed in current prices and when the official exchange rates are used. The ratio was the highest in 1990. It decreased substantially in 1992 and 1994 and then stabilized at around 18 percent until last year when it grew to almost 20 percent, due to a sharp increase in the value of exports. However, the latest ratio is still far from its 1990 level. Apparently, currency exchange rate fluctuations at the beginning of the transition period played a role in shaping this unusual trend. Also, a relatively high GDP growth has prevented the ratio from increasing substantially.

In conclusion, one can state that save for the unclear picture with respect to the exports/GDP ratio, all the other indicators were pointing to Poland's continuing integration with the world trade system, after the country initiated its transition to an open market economy. However, integrating with the world economy has so far progressed much faster on the import side than on the export side. Thus there seems to be much room for improvement in the area of Poland's export performance.

World-wide Trends in Foreign Direct Investment

Foreign direct investment (FDI) inflows and outflows indicate the extent of host country participation in and contribution to the globalization process. Over the last decade the world has witnessed a tremendous growth in FDI. FDI inflows reached a record US$ 1.27 trillion level in 2000. Compared to US$ 204 billion a decade ago, it represents over 600 per cent increase in the nominal value of FDI (Table 10.4). Of the major country groups shown in the table, Central and Eastern Europe has experienced the most dramatic increase in FDI inflows (approx. 8,500 percent).

FDI inflows into developing countries increased by 700 percent and FDI into developed countries grew by almost 600 percent. The dominance of developed countries in FDI inflows (accounting for 80 percent of the total) has been a constant trend since the end of World War II.

Table 10.4   Inflows and outflows of foreign direct investment in the years 1990-2000 (in US$ billion)

Year	Developed countries		Developing countries		Central-Eastern Europe		All countries	
	Inflow	Outflow	Inflow	Outflow	Inflow	Outflow	Inflow	Outflow
1990	169.8	222.5	33.7	17.8	0.3	0.04	203.8	240.3
1991	114.0	201.9	41.3	8.9	2.5	0.04	157.8	210.8
1992	114.0	181.4	50.4	21.0	3.8	0.1	168.2	202.5
1993	129.3	192.4	73.1	33.0	5.6	0.2	208.0	225.6
1994	132.8	190.9	87.0	38.6	5.9	0.6	225.7	230.1
1995	203.5	305.8	113.3	49.0	14.3	0.5	331.1	355.3
1996	219.7	332.9	152.5	57.6	12.7	1.0	384.9	391.6
1997	271.4	396.9	187.4	65.7	19.2	3.4	477.9	466.0
1998	483.2	672.0	188.4	37.7	21.0	2.1	692.5	711.9
1999	829.8	945.7	222.0	58.0	23.2	2.1	1,075.0	1,005.8
2000	1,005.2	1,046.3	240.2	99.5	25.4	4.0	1,270.8	1,149.9

Source: UNCTAD, 1992, 1996, 1999 and 2001.

The unprecedented growth of FDI inflows into Central and Eastern Europe can be explained by the fact that these inflows were negligible at the beginning of the decade. But even after such a tremendous growth, Central and Eastern Europe's share in the total inflow of foreign direct investment in 2000 amounted to a mere 2 percent. This share has been showing an overall unfavorable trend in the last years decreasing from a high of 4.3 percent in 1995.This might be a reflection of foreign investor perception that until new factors (like the accession of some countries of the region to the EU) are activated the peak of the region's relative attractiveness for FDI has already been reached It should also be noted that the inflows into Central and Eastern Europe were very unevenly distributed across the region, with three countries, Poland, the Czech Republic and Russian Federation (in that order), absorbing two-thirds of the region's total FDI inflows (UNCTAD, 2001).

As far as FDI outflows are concerned, the dominance of developed countries is even more evident. In 2000, these countries accounted for more than 90 percent of the total outflows. Central and Easter Europe's outflows were only US$ 4 billion, also an insignificant 0.3 percent of the total.

However, it is argued that the latter figure is grossly underestimated, as much of the FDI outflow from the Russian Federation goes unreported (UNCTAD, 2001).

Polish Economy and Foreign Direct Investment

The data concerning the value of the inflow of foreign direct investment into Poland are presented in Table 10.5. These data show that in the first half of the nineties the volume of such investment in Poland was not very impressive. In recent years however Poland has become a leader among the countries of Central and Eastern Europe in inward foreign investment. In 2000, Poland attracted over US$ 9 billion in FDI, which represented 37 percent of all the FDI inflows into Central and Easter Europe in that year. The second largest recipient of FDI in the region, the Czech Republic, attracted US$ 4.6 billion (UNCTAD, 2001). The surge of FDI inflow into Poland in 2000 was partly associated with the US$ 4 billion purchase of a majority share in Telekomunikacja Polska S.A. by France Telecom. This purchase is regarded as the region's largest privatization and largest FDI transaction to date.

Table 10.5   Inflow of foreign direct investment into Poland in the years 1990 - 2000 (in US$ million)

FDI Inflow	1990	1991	1992	1993	1994	1995	1996	1997	1998	199	2000
Current Year	88	359	678	1715	1875	3659	4498	4908	6365	7270	9342
Cumulative	88	447	1125	2840	4715	8374	12872	17780	24145	31415	40757

Source: National Bank of Poland, 2000 and 2001.

The comparison of Tables 10.5 and 10.4 makes it evident that the growth rate of the FDI inflows into Poland was considerably higher than that for the global FDI inflows in the years 1990 - 2000. In fact, Poland's FDI growth substantially outstripped the average for Central and Eastern Europe, increasing by a whopping 10,600 percent over the same period. Such significant progress in the dynamics of the inflow of foreign direct investment into Poland was above all possible due to the very low initial values at the beginning of the nineties. Poland's share in the world FDI inflow in 1990 amounted to 0.04 percent, but by 2000 it grew to 0.74 percent. It should be noted that in 2000 that indicator exceeded the indicators of Poland's share in the world exports and imports. The latter observation leads to the conclusion that the Polish economy has been globalizing faster in the FDI dimension than in that of international trade.

Polish Economy and the Transnationality Index

To gauge national economies' level of international openness, UNCTAD uses the transnationality index. The index is calculated as the average of the following four indicators: FDI inflows as a share of gross fixed capital formation; FDI inward stock as a percentage of GDP; value added of foreign affiliates as a percentage of total national value added; and employment of foreign affiliates as a percentage of total employment (UNCTAD, 2001). The transnationality index essentially measures the relative significance of FDI in a given economy. For the 30 developing countries, for which the transnationality index was calculated, it ranged between 3 and 54 percent in 1998, with Hong Kong, China being the most transnationalized country. Among the developed countries, New Zealand held the first position. Seven countries, two developed and five developing ones, had the index value exceeding 30 percent. In Central and Eastern Europe, for which the transnationality index (published in the 2001 World Investment Report) was calculated for the first time, the average index was slightly above 10 percent, lower than the averages for both developed and developing countries. However, this average conceals wide differences between CEE countries. In Estonia and Hungary, the index was close to 25 percent, and in the Czech Republic and Latvia it exceeded 15 percent, indicating a high degree of internationalization of these economies. On the other hand, the index was below 5 percent in one third of the region's countries.

Poland occupied the eighth position among CEE countries, with the transnationality index of about 12 percent, slightly above the regional average (UNCTAD, 2001). One of the reasons for this rather low transnationality index for Poland was the country's very low share of FDI in the gross fixed capital formation in the period for which the index was calculated.

While not undermining the validity of the transnationality index, one cannot help noticing that it is sensitive to the size of the economy. As a rule, although there are exceptions to this rule, smaller countries tend to have higher transnationality indices and bigger ones tend to occupy the bottom of the list. The United States, for example, has the third lowest transnationality index among developed countries. It seems that adjusting the index for the size of the economy could have produced less biased results.

Table 10.6   Current account and merchandise payments, 1991 - 2000 (in US$ million)

Specification	1991	1992	1993	1994	1995	1996	1997	1998	1999	2000
1. Current account	-2596	-1515	-2868	677	5310	-1371	-4309	-6862	-11558	-9946
2.Merchandise payments										
Revenues from exports	13355	14039	13598	17024	22878	24453	27229	30122	26347	28256
Payments for imports	13077	13573	16080	17919	24709	32632	38549	43842	40727	41424
3.Merchandise trade balance	278	466	-2482	-895	-1912	-8179	-11320	-13720	-14380	-13168

Source: Central Statistical Office, Poland, 2000 and 20001.

Globalization and Poland's External Equilibrium

Poland's rapid integration with the world economy has not been free from macroeconomic management challenges. One such challenge was to maintain external economic equilibrium. This becomes evident in Table 10.6, which presents Poland's current account and trade balance in the years 1990 - 2000.

The foreign trade deficit was the main factor influencing the current account balance. In 1997, the deficit on the current account amounted to US$ 4.3 billion, which constituted 3.0 percent of the GDP: in 1998 it amounted to US$ 6.9 billion (4.4 percent of the GDP), whereas in 1999 it increased to US$ 11.6 billion (7.5 percent of the GDP). In 2000, the deficit eased somewhat, amounting to 6.3 percent of the GDP.

Factors that tended to neutralize the influence of the high deficit in foreign trade balance were FDI inflows and revenues from the so-called cross-border trade. In spite of a high current account deficit, the balance of payments was positive during most of the decade under consideration.

The phenomenon of cross-border trade consisted of foreigners (mostly Germans on Poland's western border and Russians, Ukrainians and Byelorussians on Poland's eastern border) visiting Polish cities close to the border and buying cheaper food products and manufactured goods. However, there has been a decrease in the volume of such transactions in recent years, mainly due to administrative restrictions (stringent visa requirements) introduced by Polish authorities and designed to curb the illegal influx of immigrants seeking employment in Poland and subsequently in the countries of Western Europe.

As the role of cross-border trade in compensating for the current account deficit tended to diminish towards the end of the decade, the slack was being picked up by the FDI inflows. In 2000, the FDI filled the current account gap in 94 percent, as opposed to only 55 percent in 1999 (Ali, Nowak and Pöschl, 2001). FDI inflows can also have an indirect compensating effect on the current account deficit by stimulating exports in the long run through helping to upgrade the country's international competitiveness.

The negative trade balance was generated mainly by exchange with the countries of the European Union. According to customs statistics, registering the flow of commodities and not payments actually made, the deficit of trade with the EU increased from US$ 7.3 billion in 1996 to US$ 10.5 billion in 1997 and to US$ 12.9 billion in 1998. Thereafter, i.e. from 1999 to 2000, a decrease in the said deficit was observed. In 1999 it amounted to US$ 10.5 billion and in the year 2000 it went down to US$ 7.8 billion. It should also be noted that a significant factor influencing Poland's trade balance was foreign trade conducted by foreign-owned firms operating in Poland. This, in turn, was due to considerable import requirements of these firms resulting from modernization of their production capacity (investment imports) and from a high demand for supply imports (Olesinski and Pac-Pomarnacki, 1998). However between 1999 and 2000 a much faster growth of exports than imports of these firms was observed which led to a considerable decrease of their negative trade balance: from US$ –11.5 billion in 1999 to US$ –8.7 billion in 2000 (Durka and Chojna, 2001).

A high deficit on the current account may have created a serious threat to a further stable economic growth of Poland. There is much evidence in related literature that countries, which opened their economies and joined the then existing EEC (Spain, Portugal and Greece) also experienced considerable worsening of the current account balance but they financed it with a surplus on the capital account (Nowicki, 1997). In such a situation, it was necessary to implement an appropriate macroeconomic policy in order to prevent overheating of the economy and increased inflationary pressures.

Another potential danger lies in the loss of confidence of foreign firms undertaking direct investment in Poland due to the perceived excessive deficit on the said current account. Just at what point in relation to the country's GDP can such deficit be considered as being excessive is another issue, but once it is reached it may be very difficult to redress the situation since foreign firms may begin to pull out of the country in increasing numbers.

Conclusions and Policy Implications

The process of integrating Poland's transforming economy with the world economic system can be summarized by the following points:

- Poland took advantage of its opening to the world after 1989 by both increasing its participation in world trade and world FDI;
- Both the value of exports from Poland and imports into Poland grew faster than the corresponding worldwide figures, thus increasing the country's level of integration with the world trade system over the last decade. However, the growth of imports substantially outstripped the growth of exports, leading to serious current account imbalances;
- FDI inflows into Poland grew by an unprecedented 10,600 per cent between 1990 and 2000, with the bulk of this growth occurring in the second part of the decade. This phenomenal growth in FDI was not only faster than the worldwide trend, but also substantially outstripped

the average growth of FDI inflows into the Central and Eastern Europe. As a result, Poland's share in world FDI increased dramatically, from 0.03 per cent in 1990 to 0.75 percent in 2000. By 2000, Poland became the largest FDI recipient in the CEE region in absolute terms;

- The transnationality index, calculated by UNCAD for 1998, which measures the relative significance of FDI in an economy, does not however attest to Poland's strong position in world FDI. The index shows that the country is only slightly above the regional average in terms of its transnationality. One explanation of the discrepancy between the phenomenal growth in FDI inflows into Poland and the country's rather low transnationality index is that the index has a bias in favor of smaller economies. It should also be noted that the growth of FDI inflows started in Poland from a very low level and, in spite of the very high rate of that growth in the last decade, Poland still has a long way to go until it can achieve the transnationality index values comparable to those of the most internationalized economies in the world;

- The much faster growth of imports than exports in the past decade was accompanied by a growing current account deficit that threatens Poland's macroeconomic equilibrium and future growth. So far, the deficit has been financed mainly by FDI inflows and cross-border trade, with the former playing an increasing role over time. As a result, no serious balance-of-payments problems have been experienced yet. However, should FDI inflows slow down, the problems related to the Balance of Payments may become acute. To prevent that from happening, Poland must boost exports and balance its current account. The general problem lies also in finding effective methods of sustaining the growth of FDI;

- The overall conclusion is that over the last decade the Polish economy was rapidly integrating with the world economy, especially on the import and FDI fronts. The growth in exports, although substantially higher than the world average, did not keep pace with the growth in imports and FDI. In this respect, Poland's participation in the globalization process was somewhat unbalanced.

The most important policy implication stems from the last conclusion. However opinions on this issue are not uniform. Two distinct approaches and corresponding economic policy models can be distinguished here (Gorynia, 2000):

- Upgrading the competitiveness of Polish exports on foreign markets (according to the enclave model);

- Moving the whole economy of Poland to a higher competitive level (according to the integral model).

According to the first approach disruptions of the external equilibrium appearing in the process of integrating the Polish economy with its foreign environment justify the use of economic policy measures focused on promoting exports. This also means that the obvious focus of policy makers should be on improving the competitive potential and performance of export industries and firms.

Two basic premises seem to emerge in the context of proposing concrete and desirable policy instruments. Premise number one is that foreign-owned firms do not need direct or indirect support measures designed to boost their competitiveness, as they already have an effective competitive advantage upon deciding to enter the Polish market. At the same time, they play an important, and growing, role in providing export earnings for Poland. Research shows that foreign firms operating in Poland demonstrate better export performance and direct more of their output towards export markets than their domestic counterparts. In 1996, the share of exports in total sales of foreign owned companies was 13.9 percent, whereas for domestic firms it was only 8.8 percent. The share of exports by foreign entrants in the value of Polish exports rose from 25 percent in 1994 to 43 percent in 1997 (Durka and Chojna, 1998). In the following years foreign-owned firms in Poland systematically strengthened their positions in the export sectors. Their share of total Polish exports rose to 52 percent in 1999 and 56 percent in 2000 (Durka and Chojna, 2001).

This came as no surprise. These firms tended to have better quality products, more recognizable brand names, wider access to international distribution channels as well as other advantages not possessed by most of their domestic counterparts. Therefore, foreign firms hardly needed any export-specific policy measures aimed at helping them develop export-orientated products and export markets. Instead, these foreign firms, in order to continue exporting from Poland or to be attracted to invest in Poland, need consistent improvement in the general infrastructure and conditions of doing business in this country. Survey data show that 44.4 percent of foreign-owned firms indicated lack of sufficient infrastructure as an 'important' and 'very important' barrier to establishing successful operations in Poland (Wolniak, 1998).

The second premise, which follows from the first one, is that the focus of export-specific policy measures should be rather on domestic companies, which need to build and upgrade their competitiveness to be able to compete in both domestic and international markets. Expansion of these firms into foreign markets should be supported by education and training, demonstrating the rationale and benefits of exporting and the benefits of engaging into more advanced forms of international business once the export stage is mastered. This training should also show the ways in which export or international business plans can be developed and implemented. Being usually small and medium-sized entities, these firms often do not have sufficient knowledge and research capabilities to collect foreign market information on their own. Therefore, government support is needed in this area as well in the form of financing foreign market intelligence gathering and dissemination. The government should also co-finance the country-image boosting campaigns in order to offset the possible negative country-of-origin effects. Finally, there is a pressing need for measures, again in the form of direct and indirect financial support, that would stimulate Polish-owned firms to innovate and develop their core competencies which can be embedded in new products and technologies and can possibly form a solid base for developing and maintaining their competitive advantage in the domestic and foreign markets.

According to the second approach identified above, the underlying aim of all policy measures in the area of international trade and investment should be to improve the country's overall international competitiveness so that Polish products can more successfully and more rapidly penetrate the export markets, especially in the European Union, which is now, and will be more so in the future, Poland's most important trade partner (Gorynia, 1998). In the integral model the focus is on raising the competitiveness of the whole economy and not just the export-oriented sectors. This is in line with Poland's main strategic challenge to develop goods and services that will be effectively marketed on both the domestic as well as export markets. Thus, two general guidelines can be suggested in this context (Gorynia, 1998):

- Economic policy should support developing and raising company competitiveness;
- Such competitiveness should be achieved integrally, i.e., without unfounded differentiation of policy measures for exporters and for those focusing their business on the open domestic market.

It is essential to stress that the policy implications outlined above only 'scratch the surface' of these important and complex issues. Further research is needed into various policy models, approaches and instruments that might be applicable to the specific situation of Poland and other transition economies as they attempt to embrace and absorb the complex process of globalization.

References

Ali, S., Nowak, J. and Pöschl, J. (2001), 'A Decade of Transition in Central and Eastern Europe: Trends in Foreign Trade and Foreign Direct Investment', in K. Fatemi and E. Kaynak (eds), *Challenges and Opportunities for International Business in the Shifting Global Economic Environment*, Proceedings of the Tenth World Business Congress, International Management Development Association, Zagreb.

Brown, J. (1992), 'Corporations as Community: A New Image for a New Era', in J. Renesch (ed.), *New Traditions in Business,* Berrett-Koehler, San Francisco.

Central Statistical Office (2000), *Statistical Yearbook of the Republic of Poland*, Warsaw.

Central Statistical Office (2001), *Statistical Yearbook of the Republic of Poland*, Warsaw.

Central Statistical Office (2001b), *Yearbook of Foreign Trade Statistics*, Warsaw.

Contractor, F.J. (ed.) (1998), *Economic Transformation in Emerging Countries: The Role of Investment, Trade and Finance*, Elsevier, New York.

Dicken, P. (1992), *Global Shift,* Guilford Press, New York.

Durka, B. and Chojna J. (1998), 'Udzial podmiotow z kapitalem zagranicznym w polskim handlu zagranicznym', in B. Durka (ed.), *Inwestycje zagraniczne w Polsce,* Instytut Koniunktur i Cen Handlu Zagranicznego, Warszawa.

Durka, B. and Chojna J. (2001), 'Udzial podmiotow z kapitalem zagranicznym w polskim handlu zagranicznym', in B. Durka (ed.), *Inwestycje zagraniczne w Polsce,* Instytut Koniunktur i Cen Handlu Zagranicznego, Warszawa.

Gorynia, M. (1998), 'The Polish Economy's International Competitiveness and Economic Policy', *Russian and East European Finance and Trade*, vol. 34.

Gorynia, M. (2000), 'Polityka prokonkurencyjna w warunkach integracji z Unia Europejska i globalizacji', *Gospodarka Narodowa*, vol. 11-12.

National Bank of Poland (2000), *Bilans platniczy na bazie transakcji*, National Bank of Poland, Warsaw.

National Bank of Poland (2001), *Bilans platniczy na bazie transakcji*, National Bank of Poland, Warsaw.

Nowicki, N. (1997), 'Bilans platniczy w warunkach integracji', in *Polskie przedsiebiorstwa a Jednolity Rynek Unii_Europejskiej. Korzysci i koszty*, Committee for European Integration, Warsaw.

Ohmae, K. (1995), *The End of the Nation State*, Free Press, New York.

Olesinski, Z. and Pac-Pomarnacki, R. (1998), 'Dzialalnosc duzych inwestorow zagranicznych w Polsce', in B. Durka (ed.), *Inwestycje zagraniczne w Polsce,* Instytut Koniunktur i Cen Handlu Zagranicznego, Warszawa.

Parker, B.B. (1998), *Globalization and Business Practice. Managing Across Boundaries*, Sage Publications, London.

PAIZ (2002), *Press release: 8 April 2002,* State Agency for Foreign Investment, Warsaw.

Streeten, P. (2001), *Globalisation: Threat or Opportunity?*, Copenhagen Business School, Copenhagen.

UNCTAD (1992), *World Investment Report*, Geneva.

UNCTAD (1996), *World Investment Report*, Geneva.

UNCTAD (1999), *World Investment Report*, Geneva.

UNCTAD (2001), *World Investment Report*, Geneva.

Wolniak, R. (1998), 'Ocena funkcjonowania w Polsce przedsiebiorstw z udzialem kapitalu zagranicznego', in Z. Sadowski (ed.), *Kapital zagraniczny w Polsce*, Uniwersytet Warszawski, Warszawa.

World Bank (2001), 'Globalization, Growth and Poverty', *World Bank Policy Research Report*, World Bank, December, New York.

WTO (1998), *International Trade Statistics*, Geneva.

WTO (2001), *International Trade Statistics*, Geneva.

11 Foreign Capital and Economic Development in Hungary

VALÉRIA SZEKERES[1]

Introduction

A great deal of interest is devoted to how foreign enterprises produce and how they perform in various respects in Hungary, yet the number of papers and evidence on these matters are still scanty leaving demand for further investigation.[2] In the economic literature, a number of authors emphasized the need to study both domestic and foreign enterprises in order to properly grasp the effect of foreign direct investment on the local economy. This approach puts great emphasis on the 'domestic alternatives' of foreign firms. From the viewpoint of evaluating the impact of foreign firms on various parameters of development, the examination of the aspects that distinguish them from their local counterparts is important. Differences between foreign and domestic enterprises stem from the fact that multinational enterprises operate in a global network extending into many countries, which most certainly exerts influence on all aspects of their production activity.[3]

The eclectic theory of Dunning (1993) suggests that multinationals have ownership-specific advantages that allow them to produce and successfully compete with domestic producers in a host country, which enjoy certain advantages vis-a-vis them, as far as familiarity with the local legal or business culture is concerned. Dunning points out that these firm-specific advantages mainly include physical as well as intangible assets embodied in managerial capabilities, marketing or engineering. Advantages also arise from common governance, which are related partly to economies of scale on the firm level, partly to market power, technology accumulated worldwide and other attributes caused by multinationality. Operating in a number of countries stimulates the development of specific competencies, which are not available to purely national firms.[4]

This paper presents a comparative analysis of performance of domestic and three types of foreign enterprises in the Hungarian economy. We assume that the performance of foreign firms varies according to the size of the foreign share. We examine the total factor productivity, factor intensity, wages, export intensity, profitability, as well as the rate of tax.

247

Empirical research on the topic indicates that distinctive characteristics between domestic and foreign firms usually include all kinds of aspects of production, but the direction and extent of differences revealed greatly vary. Evidence is extensively found for the more intensive export activity of foreign firms, but the results on higher capital intensity, productivity and profitability are more diverse. Wages, however, are reported in almost all cases to exceed those paid at domestic firms, even with many variables controlled.[5] The results of the research in this chapter are more or less in line with these findings.

Methodology commonly used in empirical research includes discriminant and regression analysis, Wilcoxon tests, or simply comparisons of indicators for foreign and domestic firms. Research is often carried out for the economy as a whole, at the level of industries or on a firm-by-firm basis for a given size and product line. Here, we apply the combined tools of comparison and regression analysis for indicators of firm groups in different ownership. The analysis is based on data of the whole economy of Hungary, making a distinction between 25 sectors.

The chapter is divided as follows. The next section introduces the production indicators investigated. The following section is dedicated to the description of the firm groups and methodology applied. The next section presents a comparison of the productivity, factor intensity, wages, export activity, profitability, and the rate of tax of domestic and the formation of three types of foreign enterprises in Hungary. The results are compared to those of other authors. The comparative section is followed by analysis of the theoretical and policy implications followed by conclusions. The Appendix includes the description of data.

Production Indicators under Analysis

The scope of indicators in the analysis was chosen according to whether or not they reflect some contribution of foreign capital to parameters of economic development. Constraints of the data have made limitations to the choice. We examine the relative performance of foreign firms in respect of productivity, factor intensity, wages per labor, export, profitability, and rate of tax.

Total factor productivity (TFP) is revealed in order to grasp the impact of foreign capital on the efficiency of the economy. Related to the indication of technology, we investigate factor intensity with the assumption that the equity/labor ratio shows somewhat of the capital power of firm groups. Wages per labor is examined for the effect on demand and consumption. Exports are shown to investigate the competitiveness of firm groups as well as the degree to which they may help solve the balance-of-payments problem. Profitability and the rate of tax are also included in the analysis, because they may be considered as indicators of the potential contribution of firms to filling the budgetary gap.

Definition of Firms and Methodology

We make a distinction between three groups of foreign enterprises (FEs) according to the size of the share foreign investors hold of the nominal capital of a firm. FEs1 (Foreign enterprises 1) will include those firms at which the foreign share in nominal capital is below 25 percent, but more than 0 percent. FEs2 will indicate enterprises, where foreign share is between 25 percent and 50 percent. Majority-foreign enterprises (FEs3) will refer to firms in which the foreign share of nominal capital is above 50 percent. Domestic enterprises (DEs) will include state-owned companies and private enterprises owned entirely by Hungarian nationals. In 1994, the number of firms was 170,240, which increased remarkably to 227,064 by 1997. FEs3 accounted for 19,636 enterprises, while FEs2 only accounted for 4,502 and FEs1 for 1,583 companies in 1997.

In the empirical analysis total factor productivity assesses the economic and technical efficiency with which resources are converted into products at firms. It is usually expressed in terms of output per unit of total factor inputs in a function of quantities or prices of output and inputs, scale elasticity and output and input elasticity. Due to the necessary simplification of production and markets, TFP measures not only the 'level of technology', but also the issues influencing production inside and outside the firm. By measuring only the inputs and output, the sole possibility is to treat engineering knowledge, plant organization or disruptions in market affecting production process, as a whole.[6] The Cobb-Douglas production function is applied in the analyses and specified as:

$$Q = A\,L^a\,K^b, (A{>}0,\ a{>}0,\ b{>}0).$$

Q, L and K denote output, labor and capital input respectively. A is a parameter representing the level of technology at time t. Parameters a and b are the output elasticity with regard to labor and capital respectively.

The model is assumed linearly homogenous ($a + b = 1$); in that case it has constant returns to scale, which means that if both inputs are multiplied by any positive constant, output changes by the same factor. If the Cobb-Douglas production function is not linearly homogeneous and $a + b > 1$, the function exhibits increasing returns to scale. While in the case of $a + b < 1$, it has decreasing returns to scale.

Regression equation of the Cobb-Douglas function is written as follows

$$\ln Q = \alpha + a \ln L + b \ln K, \qquad (\alpha \ (constant) = \ln A).$$

Models in the next section analyzing productivity at foreign and domestic firms in Hungary from various aspects take this equation as a base. The method of ordinary least squares is chosen to calculate regression.

Values of performance indicators for the four firm groups are displayed in box plots in Figures 11.1 – 11.5. The box plots are simple graphical representations of distribution by sectors of the indicators, showing the center and spread as well as unusually deviant data points, called outliers. To gain a better visualization of distribution in big enough figures, we omit outliers and will only refer to them in the text. The horizontal line in the interior of the box indicates the center of distribution for the data, which is the so-called median. The height of the box is equal to the interquartile distance, that is the difference between the third and first 'quartile of the data, indicating the spread or width of the distribution for the data. The whiskers, the dotted lines extending from the top and bottom of the box reach to the extreme values of the data or a distance 1.5 x height of the box from the center, whichever is less. The minimum and maximum values as well as the median and mean of the distribution by sectors of production indicators will also be referred to in the text. The figures are given for each category of enterprise for both years, after deflating the 1997 figures by an inflation rate of 1.87 to the 1994 basis.

We will also refer to results of regression tests that examine whether or not the average of indicators of firm groups significantly differs from each other. The method of ordinary least squares is applied to the calculations. The results of Wilcoxon signed-rank nonparametric tests are also introduced to explore whether the changes in production indicators between 1994 and 1997 are significant. Wilcoxon test is applied because it has an advantage of not assuming any specific distribution of the data under analysis. Thus, it can well be used even if the distribution for the data is not normal. It is assumed, however, that the figures compared have similar distribution. Showing the combined effect of the signs and ranking of the differences of each pair, it utilizes information on both the direction and the magnitude of the differences. In the Wilcoxon signed-rank test, signed (positive or negative) differences between two sets of matched samples are calculated by pairs, which are ranked by increasing absolute values from 1 to N. There are 2^N possible orders of the signs, thus the probability of a given distribution is 2^{-N}. The ranks belonging to one of the signs are summed up (v). The probability (P) that the rank sum is equal to a given value (V) can be gained by dividing the number of cases #(v;V) resulting the same rank sum by 2^N.

$$P(V = v) = \#(v;V)/2^N .$$

The significance of the difference between two samples can be gained by adding up the probabilities of rank sums, which are at least or more extreme than that was calculated.[7] Wilcoxon matched pairs test shows, through its p-values, whether the null hypothesis about no difference in the values of indicators can be rejected. If the null hypothesis is rejected, the alternative hypothesis proves true, which is given according to the positive or negative sign of the difference in the median values of the production indicators. Thus, for example, if the median value in 1997 is higher than in 1994, then the alternative hypothesis is that the difference in the indicators between the two years is greater than zero. The test made is one tailed test, because we seek to find out both the direction and the significance of differences in pairs.[8]

Results of Empirical Analysis

Productivity

Models are estimated with figures for the whole economy given by 25 sectors between 1994 and 1997. Since logarithms cannot be taken if figures are zero or negative, the database of each model is adequately adjusted to exclude those sectors, in which some of the figures cannot be interpreted. As with the results of TFP analyses for other countries, foreign firms are found more productive also in Hungary.

The first model is a cross-section model, analyzing the difference in the level of TFP at firms for every year between 1994 and 1997.

$$\ln VA = \alpha + \beta_1 \ln L + \beta_2 \ln EQ + \beta_3 DFE1 + \beta_4 DFE2 + \beta_5 DFE3 \qquad (1)$$

Here, VA represents value added, α indicates the constant element, L is number of employees, EQ denotes equity, and DFE1, DFE2 and DFE3 are dummies for FEs1, FEs2 and FEs3 respectively. The productivity level of DEs is expressed by the constant element α, and those of each foreign firm are represented by the sum of α and the corresponding coefficients of dummies. β_1 and β_2 indicate the degree of scale for the whole economy by years. This equation is estimated for each year.

Figures in Table 11.1 are the estimation results for model (1). They suggest that constant returns to scale prevailed in the economy during the four-year period, since $(\beta_1 + \beta_2)$ was 1.08 in 1994, 0.99 in 1995 as well as in 1996, and 1.04 in 1997.[9] Thus, the Cobb-Douglas production function with constant returns to scale can be justified as a proper model for the aggregate production in the Hungarian economy. Coefficients of the dummies for foreign firms show that they have substantially higher TFP. Among them, FEs2 and FEs1 amounted to the highest values in 1994, which were taken by FEs3 and FEs2 in the following two years. Fit of the model is proven by the values of both F statistic and R squared.

The following model is the basic regression equation of the Cobb-Douglas production function, estimated for four categories of firms with 1997 data.

$$\ln VA = \alpha + \beta_1 \ln L + \beta_2 \ln EQ \tag{2}$$

The most important finding that emerges from the examination of Table 11.2 is the increasing returns to scale at FEs3. On the contrary, FEs1 show decreasing returns to scale, while DEs seem to have rather constant scale. The t statistics of $(\beta_1 + \beta_2)$ for FEs3 and FEs1 also prove at a 5 percent significance level that their returns to scale are different from unity. Due to the difference in the returns to scale, we cannot interpret the lower constant terms as indications of lower efficiency.

It may be claimed that there exists the problem of multicollinearity between equity and labor in both models above, although its possibility is low due to that the analysis was cross-section. In addition, the values of the correlation coefficients between equity and labor extend only from 0.48 to 0.81.

Sun (1998)[10] estimated the Cobb-Douglas production function for data of state-owned and foreign firms in Chinese industries in 1995. Using in a regression equation the figures of value added, net value of fixed capital used directly in production, and the number of employees on a yearly average, he found that the level of technology was higher at foreign enterprises. Agarwal (1979) calculated the total factor productivity in the Indian industries by the ratio of value added to the sum of capital and labor, given by the product of capital and opportunity cost, and labor and average wage rate, respectively. For the manufacturing average, TFP of foreign firms exceeded that of domestic ones by 55 percent.

Table 11.1 Estimation results for equation (1)

Variables (Coefficients)	1994	1995	1996	1997
Employee (β_1)	0.740 [a]	0.587 [a]	0.601 [a]	0.665 [a]
	(6.67)1	(9.48)	(8.75)	(9.61)
Equity (β_2)	0.336 [a]	0.406 [a]	0.393 [a]	0.371 [a]
	(3.57)	(8.64)	(6.82)	(6.68)
Constant (α)	-1.230 [b]	-0.172	-0.142	-0.416
	(-2.53)	(-0.59)	(-0.51)	(-1.32)
Dummy for FEs1 (β_3)	0.554 [b]	0.201	0.206	0.469 [b]
	(2.10)	(1.17)	(1.29)	(2.59)
Dummy for FEs2 (β_4)	0.557 [b]	0.399 [b]	0.497 [a]	0.542 [a]
	(2.28)	(2.53)	(3.27)	(3.19)
Dummy for FEs3 (β_5)	0.488 [b]	0.367 [b]	0.525 [a]	0.598 [a]
	(2.04)	(2.49)	(3.69)	(3.89)
R squared adjusted	0.915	0.967	0.967	0.961
F statistic	178.05	523.87	525.70	432.23
Number of observations	89	91	89	91

Notes: Figures in parentheses are t statistics.
[a] Significant at 1% level (two-tailed test).
[b] Significant at 5% level (two-tailed test).

Table 11.2 Estimation results for equation (2)

Variables (Coefficients)	DEs	FEs1	FEs2	FEs3
Employee (β_1)	0.699 [a]	0.608 [a]	0.511 [a]	0.560 [a]
	(11.390)	(5.050)	(3.240)	(3.160)
Equity (β_2)	0.312 [a]	0.239 [b]	0.537 [a]	0.552 [a]
	(5.540)	(2.870)	(4.430)	(3.600)
Constant (α)	-0.126	1.463 [a]	-0.171	-0.764
	(-0.450)	(3.290)	(-0.410)	(-1.460)
R squared adjusted	0.984	0.908	0.957	0.951
F statistic	727.750	99.88	243.950	216.360
Number of observations	24	21	23	23

Notes: Figures in parentheses are t statistics.
[a] Significant at 1% level (two-tailed test).
[b] Significant at 5% level (two-tailed test).

Factor Intensity

We compare the relative use of the capital of foreign and domestic enterprises on Figure 11.1 that presents the main characteristics of the distribution of the factor intensity, obtained by dividing the equity figures by the corresponding number of labor in each sector, for each of the four groups of firms in Hungary in 1994 and 1997. The findings clearly serve as evidence towards the view that foreign enterprises are more capital-intensive, which is generally suggested by a number of researches carried out for other countries. Moreover, the finding here seems to be true for every industry, although a test of significance was possible only for the economy as a whole.

Figure 11.1 shows that foreign firms, largely in parallel with the increasing ratio of foreign participation, are more capital-intensive than domestic ones. The regression equation proves this for FEs3 in 1994 and for all foreign firms (with FEs1 having the largest average value) in 1997[11]. According to the median values, FEs3 had the biggest amount of equity for an employee in 1997. FEs3 and FEs2 applied around two times as capital-intensive production method as DEs.

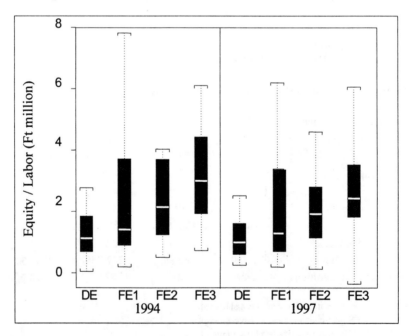

Figure 11.1   Equity/labor

From 1994 to 1997, the sizes of the boxes of FEs3, FEs2 and DEs diminished, which demonstrates that the capital intensity of these firm groups became characterized, in many sectors, by lower equity/ labor ratios. The number of their outliers and large figures significantly decreased. The enlarged size of the boxes of FEs1 in both years is owing to their substantial deviant values in some sectors, which were the electricity, gas, water, and real estate rent in 1997. The p-value of exact Wilcoxon signed-rank test reveals that the capital intensity significantly decreased at both DEs and FEs3 from 1994 until 1997.

It is difficult to find an explanation for the decrease in capital intensity for all types of firms. Regrettably, it cannot be excluded that the consumer price index used as a deflator to the calculation of the 1997 figures made some distortion in the values.

Jenkins (1991) surveyed the empirical literature on the impact of foreign firms in less developed countries with the finding that foreign firms tended to be more capital-intensive than local firms for manufacturing as a whole, but not in all individual industries. Particularly, in the case of matched pairs similar in terms of attributes other than ownership, there was no difference in capital-intensity. According to Hunya (1997), fixed capital per employee was higher in firms with foreign capital than in domestic enterprises in Czech manufacturing. In his 1998 paper, the higher capital endowment of foreign firms was confirmed for Slovakia and Slovenia as well. However, Simoneti *et al.* (1998) found state companies to have an even higher equipment per employee indicator in Slovenia. Kirim (1986) examined the capital intensity of foreign and domestic firms in the Turkish pharmaceutical industry in 1983, but no difference was revealed after controlling for the scale of operations. Solomon and Forsyth (1977) found significant evidence for the much higher capital intensity of foreign firms in the Ghanaian manufacturing sector for 1970, even by using discriminant analysis controlled to give constant product composition of the two ownership groups[12].The relatively higher capital-intensity of foreign enterprises may imply that this group of firms applies production methods of a higher technical level. It may also be indicated that foreign capital is primarily found in sectors and subsectors with a higher intensity of capital in production. For Hungary, a country with abundant labor, this may imply that FDI dynamically fosters the comparative advantages and does not make use of the static ones.

Wages

Here we concern ourselves with the rate of wages paid to employees by firm categories. Regrettably, the lack of information on the skill composition of labor force does not make possible a more exact way of comparison. The research shows a much higher wage per labor for foreign firms, relative to domestic firms. This finding is the same as the general conclusion of other papers on the topic.

Figure 11.2 presents the characteristics of the distribution of the wages/labor ratios at the four firm groups in 1994 and 1997. As shown by every indicator of the distribution, foreign firms pay a remarkably higher salary to their employees than domestic enterprises. The regression test shows the difference to be significant for all foreign firm groups in both years. Foreign firms, among them particularly FEs3, are proved to pay considerably higher salaries than DEs. Foreign enterprise categories are also featured by substantially larger maximum figures, with FEs2 paying as large an amount as 1.31 million Hungarian forints (Ft) per employee in mail and communications.

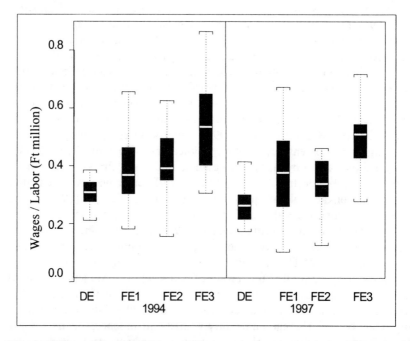

Figure 11.2   Wages/labor

Between 1994 and 1997, the sums of wages per labor became slightly lower at all groups of enterprises, and the relative position of firms considerably changed. The ratios, at least with respect to the median values, were proportionally decreasing from FEs3 towards DEs in 1994. Due, however, to an increase in the ratio of FEs1, unlike in those of other firms, the level of salaries at foreign firm groups became far from those at DEs by 1997.

The survey of Jenkins (1991) confirmed exclusively for less developed countries that wages paid to workers at MNEs were higher than those at local firms, although the difference may have reflected a different skill composition of the labor force. There were cases when no difference was indicated for any disaggregated types of labor or for unskilled labor. Hunya (1997) and Zemplinerova (1997) reported for the Czech economy for 1994 that average monthly wages in foreign firms were almost 20 percent higher than the average of the companies surveyed. Similarly, Hunya (1998) found higher wages on average in manufacturing in Slovakia as well as in Slovenia. According to Aitken *et al.* (1996), however, there was no difference in wages between foreign and domestic firms after controlling for capital intensity and plant size or scale in the US in 1987. On the other hand, applying the same method for Mexico and Venezuela found a considerably higher compensation ratio at foreign enterprises, particularly for skilled workers in Mexico, for the period of 1984 - 90 and 1977 - 89 respectively. Hill (1990) noted that papers on some Asian countries conclusively found foreign firms to pay higher salaries than local firms, even after controlling for their larger average size and distribution towards skill and capital-intensive industries[13].

Results of the analysis here and in other countries support the view that foreign firms tend to employ labor with relatively better skills than domestic enterprises do. This may reflect the presence of advanced technology at foreign firms. It may also be indicated that foreign firms are more able to pay higher wages, which is particularly true in the case of Hungary. Domestic enterprises in a poorer financial situation generally cannot offer wages high enough to attract the most educated part of the labor force.

Export Activity

This subsection investigates some details of export activity by revealing the features of the distribution of export/ sales figures by sectors in 1994 and 1997. The findings are in a sharp contrast with those of most of the research carried out for other countries. Foreign companies, as compared to domestic ones, are clearly found here to export much larger quantities.

As presented on Figure 11.3, foreign firms account for remarkably higher relative export figures than domestic firm groups. The difference was particularly large between DEs and FEs3 as well as DEs and FEs2, in 1997. In fact, regression analysis found it to be significant. FEs3 took huge values in machinery, light industry, furniture and metallurgy, with percentages of around 82 percent, 67 percent, 65 percent and 64 percent respectively. FEs2 also appeared to actively export in light industry and machinery as well as in the transport industry. In 1997, export/ sales values of FEs1 were rather similar to those of DEs, though in some sectors they were much higher. While FEs1 amounted to about 57 percent as a maximum figure, DEs had only around 34 percent, in the furniture and light industries respectively.

The direction of change in export intensity during the four year period varied largely among the enterprise categories. While figures of DEs and FEs2 remained more or less stable, FEs1 accounted for considerably lower values in a number of sectors in 1997. On the contrary, FEs3 were featured by much stronger export intensity than four years before. The positions of the median values in the boxes that had enlarged at all types of firms by 1997, indicate a process towards higher export/ sales values in sectors only for FEs3, whereas the contrary is true for the other firm categories. It may indicate that the production of a number of majority-foreign enterprises, established with the principal aim of export, became full scale by then.

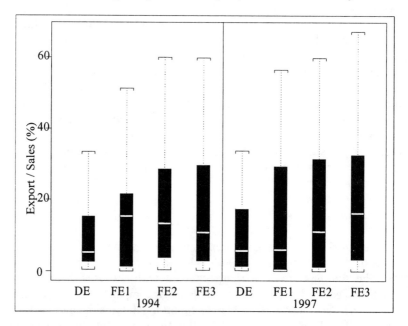

Figure 11.3   Export/sales

According to a summary at Jenkins (1991), only six of the sixteen analyses found foreign firms more export-oriented than local ones, among which not more than merely two cases proved statistically significant. Hunya (1997) reported that exports represented 31 percent of sales in the case of all enterprises and 41 percent for foreign firms in the Czech manufacturing in 1994 Foreign firms were more export-oriented in Poland as well. This was also ι onfirmed by 1996 data for Slovenia and by 1994 data for Slovakia by Hunya (1998). Export share in sales of foreign firms exceeded the average by around 20 percent and 10 percent, respectively. Kumar and Siddharthan (1994) explained the export behavior of 406 Indian enterprises in a Tobit model of many exploratory factors for the 1987 - 88 to 1989 - 90 period, and found a positive impact of foreign ownership, which, however, was significant only in the non-electrical machinery of 13 industries. Lall and Mohammad (1983) also revealed that a foreign presence was positively associated with export propensities in 24 industries of India, though at a low level of statistical significance[14].

Upon theoretical consideration, multinational firms are expected to extensively engage in export. The extent of their export activity relative to that of domestic firms may well be dependent, however, on other factors, such as their distribution among sectors or the competitiveness of local competitors. In Hungary, the much larger share of export in sales at foreign firms may also reflect the fact that during the privatization process, domestic enterprises with established and significant foreign markets became foreign-owned.

Profitability

In this subsection, we investigate the ratio of the net profit before tax to the sales of foreign and domestic firm categories for 1994 and 1997. The slight improvement in the profitability of foreign firms, shown as a result of previous research, is equally true in the present case, due partly to the recent presence of a large volume of foreign capital. Change in the indicators from 1994 to 1997 reveals, however, a considerable improvement.

According to Figure 11.4, foreign firm groups, relative to DEs, seem to have slightly higher profitability. However, regression analysis for average values reveals a significantly poorer profitability for FEs3 and FEs1 in 1994 and for FEs1 in 1997. The form of the box of FEs2, being longer towards the third quartile than below the median value, demonstrates the advantageous position of this group in many sectors in comparison with the others.

By 1997, a remarkable improvement occurred in almost all the indicators of the four firm groups. FEs1 took a huge loss (-52.6 percent) in mail and communications in 1994, but raised a positive return to sales by

1997. They accumulated, however, a considerable amount of loss in the forestry (-89.6 percent) and financial service. Considerable losses at FEs3 in 1994 disappeared or largely decreased four years later, which may reflect an improving profitability situation after setting up production in Hungary at a number of firms of this category. The other two firm groups also showed higher values in 1997, but the huge profit of 144 percent of DEs in the financial service substantially had dropped by 1997. Performance of all the firm groups may have gained from the prosperity of the economy by 1997.

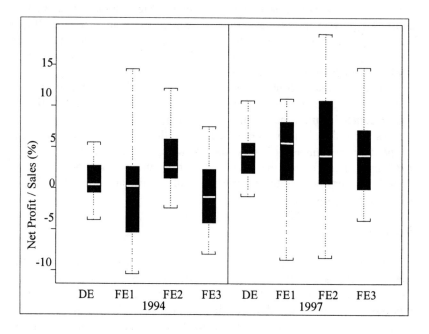

Figure 11.4   Net profit/sales

Researches on the topic do not show clearly a superior performance for foreign enterprises relative to domestic ones. Simoneti *et al.* (1998) reported that foreign companies were behind private domestic ones in respect to net operating profit/loss in Slovenia in 1995. Discriminant analysis in the Indian manufacturing sector in 1980 - 81 by Kumar (1991) resulted in the finding that foreign firms enjoyed significantly higher profit margins than their local counterparts independently of their larger size.[15]

The slightly better profitability of foreign firms is generally explained by their ability to manipulate prices among subsidiaries, which makes it possible to have a profit of a required amount. There are findings which indicate that this is also true for Hungary. However, we may also find that foreign firms, with the recent establishment of the majority of their plants, are not yet able to attain profitable production.

Rate of Tax

The analysis below reveals the rate of tax of domestic and three categories of foreign firms for 1994 and 1997. Figure 11.5 presents the characteristics of the distribution of the average rate of firm groups with bookkeeping by double entry. They reflect a picture that FEs2 and FEs3 affect payments of tax in much less shares in their tax base than other firms in Hungary do. This is confirmed by regression analysis for these foreign firms in both years. An examination of the extreme values reveals that in 1997 foreign firms paid just a few percentages in machinery, while FEs2 and FEs3 paid the same in mail, communications and the food industry as well. Apart from these sectors, FEs3 also amounted to a very low ratio in the chemical industry. At the same time, all the firm groups amounted to a zero tax rate in fishing and repairing, while they had a maximum figure in the financial services.

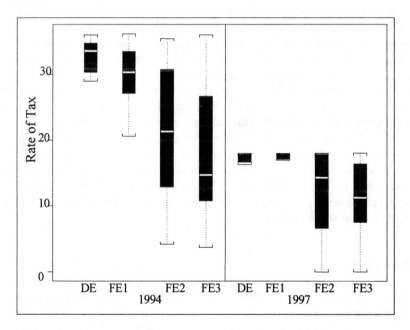

Figure 11.5   Rate of tax

A decrease in the average tax rate at all firm groups by 1997 reflects the fact that the rate of corporate tax was diminished to half as of 1995. Enterprises with the highest and lowest median values in 1994, DEs and FEs3 respectively, paid 33.6 percent and 14.7 percent of the tax base. In 1997, the respective figures at FEs1 and FEs3 were 17.7 percent and 11.2 percent. The big difference in the rate of tax of firm groups reflects the result of the concession policy of the government towards foreign firms.

Theoretical and Policy Implications

The results of the analysis show that the most important differences of performance between foreign and domestic firms seem to be in productivity, wages and the rate of tax in Hungary. These differences may mostly be determined by the nature of foreign capital, but, to a smaller extent, are also influenced by government policy.

Foreign enterprises, as international networks of technological accumulation that is created through a process of innovations, may have a more effective use of labor and capital. Enterprises locating themselves in more than one country can gain easier access to capital abroad and, hence, face different input prices. Capital is abundant and hence cheaper in the investing countries, and much more expensive, due to the shortage, in Hungary. Foreign firms may apply a higher level of technology to the production process and face a lower level of capital prices than DEs. The higher productivity of foreign firms may be caused by their high capital intensity, but it may also imply that they have better trained labor or management more efficient. This entails their paying higher wages.

Those enterprises, which have invested capital of an amount large enough and contributed considerably to an increase in employment in Hungary, are entitled to gain tax allowances of various forms. Foreign firms, having access to abundant capital, are more likely to make such a huge investment, and in fact seem more able to substantially decrease the sum of the taxes to be paid.

Conclusion

In this chapter, we have examined and compared various indicators of the production of domestic and three types of foreign enterprises in the economy of Hungary using 1994 and 1997 figures. The performance of foreign firms in Hungary is largely consistent with those suggested by the literature and observed in other countries. They operate under conditions substantially different from, and generally show production indicators significantly better than those of their domestic counterparts. The way of examination by making a distinction between various types of foreign firms according to the size of foreign ownership share is a rather unusual method of revealing differences from domestic enterprises. The research is intended to contribute greatly to the scarce literature of foreign direct investment in the transition countries.

FEs3 and FEs2 are found to give the best performance in productivity, despite the increase in foreign ownership at firm groups. Foreign firms do not appear to perform much better than DEs with respect to profitability. Data show that capital productivity is superior and improving at domestic firms. Capital intensity seems to be proportionally increasing with the firm groups during the four year period. However, foreign enterprises (FEs3 in particular), are apparently featured by considerably more intensive export activity; an indicator that is really found to improve in parallel with the increase in the share of foreign ownership at firm groups for all the figures, in 1997. A clear-cut difference is also shown to be to the advantage of foreign firms in respect of wages per labor. DEs and FEs1 evidently have a substantially higher rate of tax.

While foreign firms certainly contribute to the revitalization of the economy as far as capital intensity, productivity, export performance and level of wages are concerned, they probably do not yet provide a considerable contribution to the income of government in the form of taxes and do not necessarily improve the current balance of the country[16]. However, it may be argued that the large amounts of both tax allowance and imports are characteristics of only the beginning phase of the inflow of foreign direct investment, which become lower when the production of foreign firms and the concession policy of the government towards them become more established. Thus, the existence of foreign enterprises enhances the chance of an economic take-off in Hungary, if the microeconomic developments are not further hindered by macroeconomic constraints. A longer period of the economic activity of firms is needed to be able to make judgement on whether or not foreign investment will contribute to the relieving of these constraints and will continue to stimulate the firm sector in the future.

Appendix: Data and Measurement

Production figures are derived from the aggregate balance sheet data of all firms in Hungary, which were reported to the Tax and Financial Audit Office in 1994 and 1997. The figures used in the analysis include the output, sales, gross value added, exports, equity, number of employees, wages, net profit before tax and rate of tax by 25 sectors and the four firm groups mentioned in the text. The sectors are the following: agriculture, forestry, fishing, mining, food industry, tobacco industry, light industry, paper industry, chemical industry, non-metal products, metallurgy, machinery, furniture, electricity gas and water, construction, sales, repairing, hotel and restaurant, transport, mail and communication, financial service, real estate and rent, education, health service, and other public services

Sales constitute a considerable part of output, sold on the market, and expressed as total net sales revenue. Conceivably, exports are a part of sales, sold abroad. Gross value added is defined as the total personal costs, excluding the sum of social security contribution, but including the rent of land. Equity includes nominal capital, capital reserves, retained earnings, accumulated losses and consolidated profit. Number of employees is given in a round figure of the annual average number of permanent staff. Net profit before tax implies the net operating profit, net profit on financial transactions and non-recurring receipts. In the rate of tax, the tax to be paid, consisting of calculated and complementary taxes reduced by tax allowances, is divided by the sum of the calculated, specific and complementary tax bases.

While most of the figures are available for firms with bookkeeping by both double and single entry, rate of tax is given only for firms with bookkeeping by double entry. In addition, these figures are missing for both types of enterprises in the sectors of fishing and repairing.

Notes

1   The author works at the Ministry of Education in Hungary. Thanks are given to Professor Yuzo Hosoya (Department of Economics, Tohoku University, Sendai, Japan) for valuable assistance in the econometric analysis. Helpful comments on earlier version of this chapter from Professors Kazuo Yokokawa and Masao Satake (Department of International Economic Relations, Graduate School of International Cultural Studies, Tohoku University, Sendai, Japan) are gratefully acknowledged. Thanks are also due to Mr. Andrew John Barke and Mr. Zsolt Veresegyházy for their technical assistance.
2   Foreign enterprises here indicate those firms, which have some foreign ownership in the par-value capital registered.
3   For references of empirical studies, see, for example, Kumar, N. (1990), *Multinational Enterprises in India*, London: Routledge, p.49 or Newfarmer, R.S. and Marsh L.C. (1981), 'Foreign Ownership, Market Structure and Industrial Performance: Brazil's Electrical Industry', *Journal of Development Economics*, vol. 8, pp. 47-75. Theoretical approach can be found at Dunning, J. H. (1993), *Multinational Enterprises and the Global Economy*, New York: Addison-Wesley, pp.

263-267.

4   Dunning (1993), pp. 80-81.

5   For a review of empirical findings, see Caves, R.E. (1996), *Multinational Enterprise and Economic Analysis*, Cambridge: University Press, pp. 217-231.

6   Problems of TFP measurement are surveyed and discussed by Nishimizu and Robinson (1984).

7   Lehmann and D'Abrera (1975), pp. 123-132.

8   Wilcoxon signed-rank test was applied, e. g., by Kumar (1990), pp. 66-69 and Agarwal (1979) for revealing the significance level of differences in production indicators between foreign and domestic enterprises. However, application of the method must be built on the presumption that the distribution of figures in the two groups is similar. Upon this consideration, in sections 3.5-13 we chose the method to analyze the differences by firm groups only between 1994 and 1997. Further Wilcoxon signed-rank test is used to test the significance of differences in figures between firm groups in the factor analysis in section 14, provided they have similar distribution.

9   This is also confirmed by the t statistics of $(\beta_1 + \beta_2)$, which show that the difference of $(\beta_1 + \beta_2)$ from 1 is not significant.

10   Sun, H. (1998), *Foreign Investment and Economic Development in China: 1979-96*, Ashgate; Blomstrom, M. (1989), 'Labor Productivity Differences Between Foreign and Domestic Firms in Mexico', *World Development*, 16, pp. 1295-1298; Willmore, L.N. (1986), 'The Comparative Performance of Foreign and Domestic Firms in Brazil', *World Development*, 14, pp. 489-501; Asheghian, P. (1982), 'Comparative Efficiencies of Foreign Firms and Local Firms in Iran', *Journal of International Business Studies*, Winter, pp. 113-120.

11   The method of ordinary least squares is applied in calculating regressions. In the regression equations, the constant terms indicate the average indicator for domestic firms, and the coefficients of the dummies, together with the constant figures, give the average values of foreign enterprises for a given year.

[Production indicator] $= \alpha \times$ constant $+ \beta_1 \times$ dummy1 $+ \beta_2 \times$ dummy2 $+ \beta_3 \times$ dummy3.

Dummy 1, 2 and 3 are equal to 1 if the data belong to firm type FE1, FE2 or FE3, respectively, and 0 otherwise. If the t statistic of a dummy proves significant at least at a 10% level, it can be said that the indicators of foreign firms are significantly different from those of domestic ones.

12   Jenkins, R. (1991), 'The Impact of Foreign Investment on Less Developed Countries: Cross-section Analysis versus Industry Studies', pp. 111-130, in Buckley, P.J. and Clegg, J. (eds.) *Multinational Enterprises in Less Developed Countries*, London: Macmillan; Hunya, G. (1997), ibid.; Simoneti, M., Rojec, M. and Rems, M. (1998), 'Enterprise Sector Restructuring and EU Accession of Slovenia', NATO-Economics Directorate, Ljubljana, June 18-19, 1998; Kirim, A.S. (1986), 'Transnational Corporations and Local Capital. Comparative Conduct and Performance in the Turkish Pharmaceutical Industry', *World Development*, Vol. 14, No. 4, pp. 503-521; Solomon, R.F. and Forsyth, D.J.C. (1977), 'Substitution of Labor for Capital in the Foreign Sector: Some Further Evidence', *Economic Journal*, 87, pp. 283-289.

13   Jenkins, R. (1991) ibid.; Hunya, G. (1997), ibid.; Zemplinerova, A. (1997), 'The Role of Foreign Enterprises in the Privatization and Restructuring of the Czech Economy', WIIW Research Report, June, No. 238, Vienna; Hunya (1998), ibid; Aitken, B., Harrison, A. and Lipsey, R.E. (1996): 'Wage and Foreign Ownership. A

comparative study of Mexico, Venezuela and the United States', *Journal of International Economics*, 40, pp. 345-371; Hill, H. (1990), 'Foreign Investment and East Asian Economic Development', *Asian-Pacific Economic Literature*, Vol.4, No. 2, pp. 21-58.

14   Jenkins R. (1991) ibid.; Hunya, G (1997), ibid.; Hunya, G (1998), 'Integration of CEEC Manufacturing into European Corporate Structures via Direct Investment', *WIIW, Working Papers*, May; Kumar, N. and Siddharthan, N.S. (1994), 'Technology, Firm Size and Export Behavior in Developing Countries: the Case of Indian Enterprises', *Journal of Development Studies*, 31, pp. 289-309; Lall, S. and Mohammad, S. (1983-84), 'Foreign Ownership and Export Performance in the Large Corporate Sector of India', *Journal of Development Studies*, 20. pp. 57-67.

15   Simoneti, M. et. al. (1998) ibid.; Kumar, N. (1991), 'Mode of Rivalry and Comparative Behavior of Multinational and Local Enterprises. The case of Indian Manufacturing', *Journal of Development Economics*, 35, pp. 381-392.

16   Hunya, G (1996): 'Foreign Direct Investment in Hungary: a Key Element of Economic Modernization', WIIW Research Reports, February, No. 226, Vienna, drew attention based on 1993 and 1994 figures that foreign firms tended to import more than they export.

References

Agarwal, J. (1979), 'Productivity of Foreign and Domestic Firms in Indian Industries', *Weltwirtschaftliches Archiv*, vol. 115.

Aitken, B., Harrison, A. and Lipsey, R.E. (1996), 'Wage and Foreign Ownership. A comparative study of Mexico, Venezuela and the United States', *Journal of International Economics*, 40, pp. 345-371.

Asheghian, P. (1982), 'Comparative Efficiencies of Foreign Firms and Local Firms in Iran', *Journal of International Business Studies*, Winter, pp. 113-120.

Blomstrom, M. (1989), 'Labor Productivity Differences Between Foreign and Domestic Firms in Mexico', *World Development*, 16, pp. 1295-1298.

Caves, R.E. (1996), *Multinational Enterprise and Economic Analysis*, Cambridge: University Press, pp. 217-231.

Dunning, J. H. (1993), *Multinational Enterprises and the Global Economy*, New York: Addison-Wesley, pp.263-267.

Hill, H. (1990), 'Foreign Investment and East Asian Economic Development', *Asian-Pacific Economic Literature*, Vol. 4, No. 2, pp. 21-58.

Hunya, G (1997), 'Foreign Direct Investment in Hungary: A Key Element of Economic Modernization', WIIW Research Reports, February, No. 226.

Hunya, G (1998), 'Integration of CEEC Manufacturing into European Corporate Structures via Direct Investment', *WIIW, Working Papers*, May.

Jenkins, R. (1991), 'The Impact of Foreign Investment on Less Developed Countries: Cross-section Analysis versus Industry Studies', pp. 111-130, in Buckley, P. J. and Clegg, J. (eds) *Multinational Enterprises in Less Developed Countries*, London: Macmillan.

Kirim, A. S. (1986), 'Transnational Corporations and Local Capital. Comparative Conduct and Performance in the Turkish Pharmaceutical Industry', *World Development*, Vol. 14, No. 4, pp. 503-521.

Kumar, N. (1990), *Multinational Enterprises in India*, London: Routledge.

Kumar, N. (1991), 'Mode of Rivalry and Comparative Behavior of Multinational and Local Enterprises. The case of Indian Manufacturing', *Journal of Development Economics*, 35, pp. 381-392.

Kumar, N. and Siddharthan, N.S. (1994), 'Technology, Firm Size and Export Behavior in Developing Countries: the Case of Indian Enterprises', *Journal of Development Studies*, 31, pp. 289-309.

Lall, S. and Mohammad, S. (1983-84), 'Foreign Ownership and Export Performance in the Large Corporate Sector of India', *Journal of Development Studies*, 20, pp. 57-67.

Lehmann, E. and D'Abrera, H. (1975), 'Comparing Two Treatments or Attributes in a Population Model', in E. Lehmann and H. D'Abrera (eds) *Nonparametrics: Statistical Methods Based on Ranks*, Oakland CA: Holden-Day, pp. 55-119.

Newfarmer, R.S. and Marsh L.C. (1981), 'Foreign Ownership, Market Structure and Industrial Performance: Brazil's Electrical Industry', *Journal of Development Economics*, vol. 8, pp. 47-75.

Nishimizu, M. and Robinson, S. (1984), 'Trade Policy and Productivity Change in Semi-Industrialized Countries', *Journal of Development Economics*, vol. 16, issue 1/2, pp. 177-206.

Simoneti, M., Rojec, M. and Rems, M. (1998), 'Enterprise Sector Restructuring and EU Accession of Slovenia', NATO-Economics Directorate, Ljubljana, June 18-19, 1998.

Solomon, R.F. and Forsyth, D.J.C. (1977), 'Substitution of Labor for Capital in the Foreign Sector: Some Further Evidence', *Economic Journal*, 87, pp. 283-289.

Sun, H. (1998), *Foreign Investment and Economic Development in China: 1979-96*, Aldershot: Ashgate Publishing.

Willmore, L.N. (1986), 'The Comparative Performance of Foreign and Domestic Firms in Brazil', *World Development*, 14, pp. 489-501.

Zemplinerova, A. (1997), 'The Role of Foreign Enterprises in the Privatization and Restructuring of the Czech Economy', WIIW Research Report, June, No. 238, Vienna.

12 Foreign Direct Investment as a Driver for the Restructuring of a Transitional Economy: Internal and Micro-External Change[1]

SONIA FERENCIKOVA

Introduction

This chapter is based on a survey carried out in a group of the largest foreign investors in Slovakia. Its main objective is to identify the internal and external change in Slovak companies, and the impact of foreign direct investment (FDI) on their restructuring. The research studies the impact of FDI on the restructuring of joint ventures and wholly-owned subsidiaries (internal change) and the influence companies with FDI exert on other Slovak firms (micro-external change). The analysis centres around the forms, origin, and development of FDI companies and the benefits these firms bring to the Slovak economy. In addition, the research, being the first of its type in Slovakia, identifies the key success factors of FDI companies in the country and the obstacles to doing business in the Slovak context.

Background of the Study and Method Used

It is no secret that the restructuring of businesses and financial institutions is the basic condition for a successful economic transformation in Slovakia as well as in any other transitional economy. To meet this objective certain capital resources are needed. Businesses and institutions are able to create some of those resources themselves, or they may obtain them in the form of domestic or foreign loans, as assistance from state (government) funds or through foreign direct investment. The contemporary economic conditions in Slovakia are marked by a chronic undercapitalization of businesses and excessive credit rates. State subsidies are not available.

Consequently businesses are looking for capital (this is reflected in the rising external indebtednesses of Slovakia). They will have to search for external financial resources in the forthcoming future. These resources may come as foreign loans or foreign direct investment. Considering the need of Slovak businesses for getting access to foreign markets, to new technologies and know-how in many areas, it can be argued that the capital of foreign firms may be much more important to the restructuring of companies than merely drawing foreign credits. The figures about FDI inflows to Slovakia indicate that the Slovak businesses would be able to profit from the presence of foreign investors in the country to a much greater extent, provided that the overall FDI inflow in the Slovak economy increased.[2]

Viewpoints of macroeconomists, researchers, representatives of governmental and political institutions on the role of FDI in the development of the Slovak economy are frequently published, but there are often considerable differences in their opinions on this issue. At the same time, representatives of firms with FDI do not present their views on the subject in public so often, although their ideas and opinions, which arc based on a real-life experience, could serve as a source of inspiration in many areas.

This fact triggered the launch of this research project studing FDI firms in Slovakia. The survey carried out in 1998[3] covered the following issues: types of FDI companies, their origin, change and development in time, influence (benefits) of FDI on the transformation of local companies recipients of FDI, impact of FDI companies on their environment (including Slovak parent company in case of joint ventures), success factors and factors acting as obstacles to doing business in Slovakia, their economic performance (profit/loss), as well as other economic indicators, such as export, import, local supplies, employment and wages.

The questionnaire format was used to address all the firms with foreign capital investment exceeding the amount of SK 10 million. According to the database[4] provided by the Ministry of Economy of Slovakia, there were 208 FDI firms that had received over 92 percent of all FDI in the country. The remaining 8 percent of FDI inflow was shared among about ten thousand firms. The latter clearly indicates that the attention in this survey was focused on larger and more significant foreign investments. The assumption was that their role and influence on the Slovak economy should be much more remarkable compared to the impact of foreign companies that had small investments of up to SK 100,000.

The questionnaires were distributed to the above identified 208 firms in Slovakia, which were either wholly-owned subsidiaries or joint ventures. The response rate was 56 percent including 117 firms, 67 of which were wholly foreign-owned firms, and 50 functioned as joint ventures. For the sake of clarity and comparison, the research results were analysed separately for those two groups of FDI companies. It is important to stress that all data given in this chapter refer to the sample of businesses that have completed the questionnaire.

Research Results

The research has indicated that the majority of foreign investors who set up joint ventures in Slovakia, came from Germany. In the group of wholly-owned foreign enterprises, Austria enjoyed a leading position with 34.4 percent, followed by Germany with 22.4 percent. As the research results indicate, investors' territorial structure in our sample coincides with that of the major investors in the Slovakia. Our results show that Austrian and US investors prefer wholly-owned subsidiaries to joint ventures, while German and Czech tend to prefer joint ventures (see Figure 12.1 and Figure 12.2).

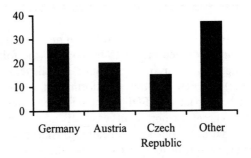

Figure 12.1   Foreign investors in joint ventures by country of origin

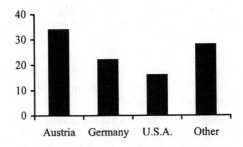

Figure 12.2   Foreign investors in wholly-owned foreign subsidiaries by country of origin

The data indicate that most foreign investors have a majority ownership stake in joint ventures. Foreign investors have majority stakes in 75 percent of all joint ventures studied. The biggest concentration of foreign majority ownership is in the range of 50 – 60 percent of company assets. Most investors consider ownership share of 51 percent or more to be of a critical importance for securing a greater bargaining power in a joint venture in Slovakia and achieving higher capitalization.

In terms of the amount of investment in joint ventures, prevailing were the investments ranging from 10 to 25 million Slovakian korunas (SKK) (17 businesses) and SKK 100 million and above (15 businesses). It is, therefore, interesting that in case of joint ventures foreign investors prefer either the smallest investment on the scale of investments pursued in our research project, or, on the contrary, very big investments exceeding the amount of SKK 100 million. In 43 percent of the wholly owned subsidiaries, the highest volume of investment exceeded SKK 100 million. The latter may be considered as a manifestation of the trend that in case of high investment, foreign investors prefer a 100 percent ownership. The percentage of foreign companies that have invested SKK 10 - 25 million in Slovakia was considerable in the sample investigated. A marked prevalence at the highest investment (over SKK 100 million) in favor of wholly-owned subsidiaries suggests that these firms are larger on average than joint ventures. The share of foreign invesors in joint ventures is presented in Figure 12.3.

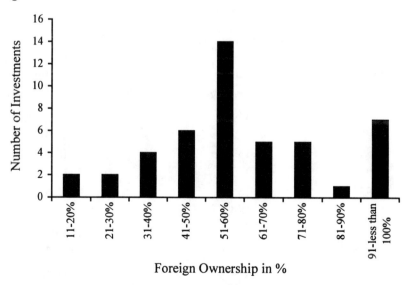

Figure 12.3   Shares of foreign investors in joint ventures

A quarter of the total number of joint ventures were founded in 1991, which may be explained by the initial drive of West European and US companies to test the market after the fall of the Berlin Wall. At the same time, this may have resulted from the policies of the central government institutions, which preferred joint ventures to a complete sell-out of state-owned firms.

On the whole, one-third of joint ventures were founded prior to the establishment of Slovakia; two-thirds came into being after 1993. Out of those, 18 businesses or 76 percent of the companies were set up during the first two years after the establishment of the Slovak Republic. In contrast, during the period 1995 – 1996 very few joint ventures were established.

On the other hand, the majority of foreign-owned businesses, 42 percent, were set up in the first year of Slovakia's independent existence. On the whole, 75 percent of the wholly-owned foreign enterprises were set up since 1993. When comparing these figures with the number of joint ventures, it is obvious that during the period concerned the foreign firms preferred the full ownership, which may be explained in several ways. First, the foreign firms were familiar with the Slovak market and did not need a domestic partner. Second, they protected themselves by takeovers or by setting up firms under their full control in view of the higher degree of political uncertainty. In this way the firms tried to eliminate domestic influence on their business.

The number of FDI companies established in Slovakia in the period 1968 - 1996 is presented in Table 12.1.

Table 12.1   FDI companies established between 1968 and 1996

Year of foundation	Number of joint ventures (%)	Number of foreign-owned subsidiaries (%)
1968	1 (2.0)	0
1969	0	1 (1.6)
1990	4 (8.3)	2 (3.2)
1991	12 (25.0)	7 (10.9)
1992	8 (16.6)	8 (12.6)
1993	9 (18.8)	27 (42.2)
1994	9 (18.8)	6 (9.3)
1995	2 (4.1)	8 (12.5)
1996	3 (6.3)	5 (7.8)

In thirty five joint ventures no changes, either in the form of ownership or organizational structure, occurred in the course of their existence. Some changes took place in 15 joint ventures. In seven of them they were of legal nature. In nine joint ventures the ownership structure changed. In one joint venture radical changes took place. In forty four of the wholly-owned foreign enterprises, 66.7 percent of the total, no changes occurred since their formation. Eighteen businesses (27.2 percent) were transformed from joint ventures into wholly foreign-owned subsidiaries. This is an interesting phenomenon because it shows that over a quarter of wholly-owned foreign enterprises in our sample developed from joint ventures, where Slovak partners had a certain stake of capital. There are several reasons for this phenomenon: the global strategy of large multinational companies, unwillingness or undercapitalization of Slovak parent companies, that were not able to maintain the original share of ownership as investments were rising, readiness to sell one's share especially if Slovak parent companies needed cash, conflicts in management, etc.

Another group of questions deals with the benefits of foreign capital for the transformation of the Slovak economy and implications for local companies. Ninety four percent of joint ventures support the view that FDI plays a positive role in the market development and transformation of the economy on macro and micro level. Only three respondents (6 percent) think that FDI has no effect whatsoever. In the group of respondents - wholly-owned foreign enterprises, all respondents claim that foreign investment has had a favorable influence on the Slovak economy and has had spillover effects on local companies. Table 12.2 presents the range of answers to the question about the dimensions of the favorable influence of the foreign investments on the Slovak economy and local companies. Forty seven joint ventures and 67 wholly-owned foreign subsidiaries provided answers to that question.

The managers of joint ventures and wholly-owned foreign subsidiaries have all emphasised the importance of FDI in ensuring higher quality of goods and services supplied to the Slovak market. They have also underlined that other most important benefits include: growth of employment, capital investment, managerial know-how, and turnover and profit increase. In addition, the enhanced taxation impact was recognised. Differences could be found out in the ranking of those benefits in terms of their importance as listed by different respondents. Foreign-owned businesses see their own favorable role in influencing their environment and micro-external change (development of business activities and local subcontractor channels, know-how transfer). Joint ventures perceive the growth of exports as being slightly more important. Respondents from joint ventures have been positive about the influence of foreign investors on

Slovak firms in terms of their overall competitiveness, as given in Table 12.3.

Table 12.2   Influence of foreign investors on the development of the Slovak economy

Benefits	Joint ventures		WOFS*	
	Number	%	Number	%
1. Higher quality of goods and services supplied	29	61.7	47	70.1
2. Growth of turnover, profit, and taxes	28	59.6	40	59.7
3. Growth of investment	27	57.4	44	65.7
4. Growth of employment	21	44.7	45	67.1
5. Growth of exports	20	42.6	25	37.3
6 Business incentives	19	40.4	29	43.3
- in their own area of business	14	29.8	18	26.9
- in follow-up areas of business	4	8.5	7	10.4
7. Transfer of know-how to other firms	13	27.7	25	37.3
- direct	3	6.4	11	16.4
- indirect	5	10.6	19	28.4
8. Growth of local subcontractor channels	9	19.1	26	38.8
9. In other areas	3	6.4	6	9.0

* WOFS - wholly-owned foreign subsidiaries.

Table 12.3   Influence of foreign investors on joint venture development in Slovakia

Factors	Number	%
1. Technology input	31	62
2. Growth of investment	27	60
3. Training and higher quality of labor force	27	60
4. Modern management implementation	23	51
5. Growth of employment	22	49
6. Modern marketing implementation	18	40
7. Other areas	10	22

The answers indicate that the greatest benefit in the 'hardware' area is seen in technology and growth of investment. Over a half of the firms view 'software' transfer, i.e., an increasing quality of labor force and a simultaneous increase in the managerial standard in the firm, as another most important area. Two-fifths of firms consider transfer of know-how in marketing to be a very significant benefit. The results point to the fact that FDI has caused a crucial internal change in the local companies.

In the part of the questionnaire on the influence of foreign investment on a Slovak parent company, 31 joint ventures (67 percent) indicate that the Slovak parent company has been positively affected by foreign investment; 15 respondents (33 percent) answer that the Slovak company has not been influenced.

The fact that one-third of Slovak parent companies have not been able to profit from the presence of the foreign investor, shows their relatively low bargaining power and lack of experience. On the other hand, this also results from frequent changes in parent companies' ownership structure that have caused those companies to find themselves in a passive position in a joint venture.

Another group of questions has been addressed regarding the fulfilment of business objectives by foreign investors in Slovakia. Sixteen joint ventures (33.3 percent) consider their objectives to have been fully met, 28 firms (58.3 percent) think the objectives have been partially fulfilled, and four firms (8.3 percent) consider their objectives unfulfilled to date, i.e., at the time of completing the questionnaire. While one-third of the joint ventures have expressed significant satisfaction in this respect, less than one-tenth are in 'a waiting position'. The rest are partially satisfied.

Of the total number of 65 respondents representing wholly-owned businesses by foreigners that answered the question on the fulfilment of objectives, 17 companies (26.2 percent) have indicated that their objectives have been fully met, 45 firms (69.2 percent) have considered their objectives to have been partially fulfilled, and three companies (4.6 percent) have not succeeded in fulfilling their objectives. It might therefore be concluded that twenty five percent of the wholly-owned subsidiaries are decidely satisfied on the fulfilment of their objectives, over two-thirds are partially satisfied, while the share of firms whose objectives have not been fulfilled yet is very low.

Generally speaking, the majority of FDI companies in Slovakia (92 per cent of the joint ventures and 95 percent of the wholly-owned subsidiaries) have fulfilled totally or partially their business objectives in Slovakia. Forty eight joint ventures and 64 foreign-owned businesses have indicated the key factors of success for their business operations in Slovakia as presented in Table 12.4.

Table 12.4   Success factors of foreign investors in the Slovak Republic

Success factors	Joint ventures		WOFS	
	Number	%	Number	%
1. Gaining a significant share of the Slovak market	24	50.0	23	35.9
2. The right time of entering the market	23	47.9	41	64.1
3. Choice of the right partner	23	47.9	19	29.7
4. Availability of financial resources	21	43.8	19	29.7
- domestic	7	14.6	4	6.2
- foreign	17	35.4	16	25.0
5. Availability of suitable labor force	19	39.6	21	32.8
6. Successful penetration of foreign markets	17	35.4	17	26.6
7. Using suitable marketing methods	15	31.2	29	45.3
8. Low costs	11	22.9	19	29.7
9. Low competition on the Slovak market	8	16.7	11	17.2
10. Favourable investment climate	8	16.7	4	6.3
11. High protection of domestic market	3	6.3	1	1.6
12. Other	3	6.3	4	6.3

Joint ventures ascribe more importance to typical market factors: gaining a market share and the right timing of accessing the market. They view the choice of the right international partner as an important source of success. It is interesting to observe that the firms in our sample do not attach a special importance to cost factors (low costs). This, however, does not mean that a foreign parent company does not keep an eye on cost-minimization when allocating investments. Few of these firms view protectionism and other unspecified factors as the source of their success.

Likewise, in foreign-owned firms, it is market factors that have been assessed as most important, although their ranking is different. The right time of accessing the Slovak market is assessed as the most significant factor. This is interesting in relation to the fact that most of these companies (42 percent) entered the Slovak market in the first year of Slovakia's independent existence. In contrast to joint ventures, these firms attach a great importance to the application of suitable marketing methods. They also realize the importance of winning a substantial share of the Slovak market. In contrast to joint ventures, they consider low costs as an important factor. Only a very small number of respondents assess the investment climate in the Slovak Republic, domestic market protection, and other unspecified factors as sources of their success. On the other hand, 47 joint ventures and 67 foreign-owned businesses identify the major obstacles to conducting business in Slovakia as described in Table 12.5.

Table 12.5   Obstacles to doing business in the Slovak Republic

Factors	Joint ventures		WOFS	
	Number	%	Number	%
1. Unfavorable investment climate	33	70.2	44	66.7
2. Protection of domestic market	29	61.7	41	62.1
3. Unavailability of financial resources	17	36.2	14	21.2
4. Low business ethics	14	29.8	25	37.9
5. Existence of black economy	9	19.7	14	21.2
6. Inadequate business infrastructure	8	17.0	15	22.7
7. Conservatism of Slovak consumers	8	17.0	8	12.1
8. Other	8	17.0	11	16.7
9. Shortage of qualified labor force	7	14.9	8	12.1
10. Shortage of qualified managers	5	10.6	8	12.1
11. Discrimination against foreign companies	5	10.6	12	18.2
12. Conflicts in managing joint ventures	5	10.6		

A majority of two-thirds in both groups agree on the unfavorable investment climate (in particular tax burden and frequent legislative changes) and domestic market protectionist measures (in particular import surchages, deposits and certification) as the most powerful obstacles to their business activities. It is interesting that both groups also view a low business ethics and existence of black economy as strong obstacles. The difference in ranking attached to these factors by the two groups is small. A significant obstacle to joint ventures' business activities is also an unavailability of financial resources. Foreign-owned firms, on the other hand, have expressed more complaints about the inadequate business infrastructure. It is interesting to observe that conflicts in managing joint ventures have been assessed as the smallest threat to success.

    In spite of the fact that the firms were guaranteed anonymity, only few of them were willing to provide data on their performance, turnover and investment. Likewise, few firms answered the question on the share of exports on sales, and the share of local Slovak suppliers on subdeliveries. Firms were most willing to provide data on the number of employees and their average wages. For the sake of illustration, some results of this part of the questionnaire are given below.

Volume of Turnover

Joint ventures   Data have been obtained from 39 respondents. Ten companies (25.6 percent) have achieved largest turnover volume. It amounted to SKK 100 - 150 million. Only 3 businesses (7.6 percent) achieved a turnover volume of SKK 1 - 10 million. The turnover of joint ventures is presented in Figure 12.4

Wholly foreign-owned subsidiaries   Of 51 respondents, 14 businesses (27.5 percent) had a turnover volume that exceeded SKK 1 billion. The turnover of wholly-owned subsidiaries is presented in Figure 12.5.

Profit/Loss

Joint ventures   12 respondents (30.8 percent) indicated loss. The largest profit-making group consisted of 9 businesses, making profits of SKK 1 - 10 million. The profit/loss of joint ventures is given in Figure 12.6, whereas the profit/loss of the wholly-owned subsidiaries can be seen in Figure 12.7.

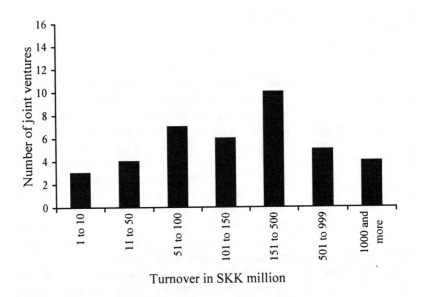

Figure 12.4   Volume of turnover of joint ventures

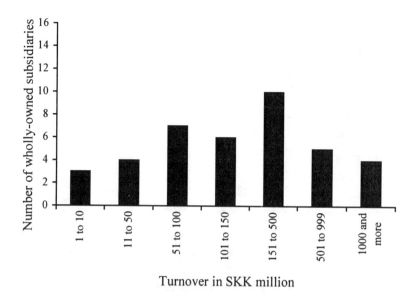

Figure 12.5   Volume of turnover of wholly-owned subsidiaries

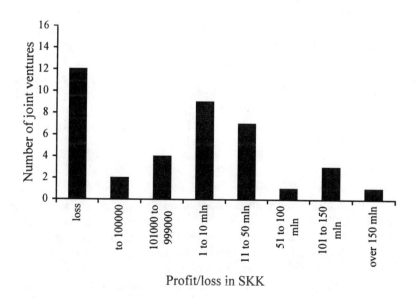

Figure 12.6   Profit/loss of joint ventures

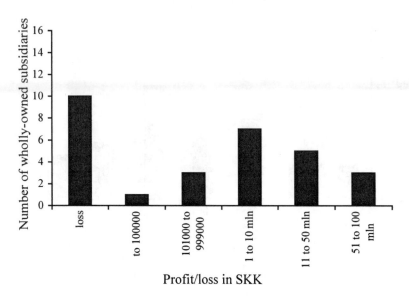

Figure 12.7   Profit/loss of wholly-owned foreign subsidiaries

In spite of the limited number of answers to the question on economic performance (profit or loss), it may be stated that the number of loss-making businesses in both groups is higher than the number of businesses which indicate that their objectives have not been fulfilled. Consequently, a lot of businesses do not consider profit as their priority objective. As our success factors analysis shows, businesses see their priority objectives in gaining a substantial market share in the Slovak Republic. The high rate of loss-making or the low rate of profit-making may have also been brought about by price transfers which occur frequently in the activities of companies operating in international markets.

Share of Exports

Answers to this question are given rather inconsistently, as data have been obtained from 27 joint ventures and 24 wholly-owned subsidiaries. The latter group has achieved a high share of production on exports as in 63 per cent of cases the share of exports exceeds 80 percent. In joint ventures the distribution is more proportionate, in approximately half of the businesses the share is lower than 50 percent. It suggests that these businesses are orientated to the domestic market rather than foreign markets. Only a half of the joint ventures have exports of more than 50 percent. A high pro-export orientation of foreign wholly-owned subsidiaries could possibly indicate that most of these businesses focus on processing and assembling operations employing cheap labor, and a subsequent export, for instance to global networks. However, this assumption has not been confirmed by success factors analysis, where the highest importance is attached to market factors rather than to cost factors even in this group of businesses.

The Share of Slovak Sub-Contractors on Total Supplies

Thirty seven respondents from the wholly-owned foreign subsidiaries and 18 respondents from the joint ventures have not answered the question. The share of Slovak sub-contractors to 53 percent of the joint ventures and 60 percent of the wholly-owned subsidiaries is less than a half of the total deliveries. Consequently, in both types of businesses, foreign suppliers prevail. This is more of a case in wholly-owned foreign subsidiaries.

Conclusions

Having assessed each part of the questionnaire, we have been trying to search for answers to the questions on interdependencies of each of the factors investigated in the questionnaire. We tested a correlation between the size of businesses (amount of capital invested) and their achievements (success). We have arrived at the conclusion that there is no correlation between these two factors. Further, we have investigated the relationship between the volume of capital invested and the share of Slovak sub-contractors. No correlation has been found. We also matched the volume of capital invested against the share of exports on sales figures. No correlation has been found. We have tested the validity of a hypothesis on the existence of relationship between the amount of capital invested and the changeover from joint venture to a wholly-owned subsidiary. However, no relationship of this kind has been found.

In spite of the fact that it is impossible to formulate theses of interdependencies among some of the factors, the research has resulted in some interesting findings. To mention the major one: an overwhelming majority of the firms in the sample view FDI as a significant factor for changes in the transitional economy of Slovakia. This has been justified by the firms mainly by referring to the impact of FDI on the increase in the quality of goods and services supplied to the domestic market; to growth of investment, employment, turnover, profit, and taxes to the state budget. Most of these firms consider their business operations on the Slovak market to be partially successful. It is however, interesting to observe that a quarter or even a third of them consider their business objectives to have been fulfilled in the course of their short-term operations on the Slovak market. They see the source of their success in particular in market factors: winning market share and the right timing of accessing the market. The costs factors have been less emphasized. Only a small number of firms have failed to achieve their objectives on the Slovak market. The firms indicate that the most powerful obstacles to their business activities have been the changing market environment (taxes and legislation), and domestic market protectionist measures.

The conclusions of the research indicate that most firms view as positive the internal changes brought by FDI into local companies in the implementation of new technologies, growth of investment, increasing the quality of labor force, and in know-how transfer, in particular, the managerial know-how. They considered the micro-external change brought to other Slovak companies as important too. According to the research results, two-thirds of local parent companies were positively influnced by their participation in an international joint venture. Our research shows that investors are relatively satisfied with the achievements in the Slovak market place, that is, in the future the internal and micro-external impact of FDI may be accelerated. FDI has brought a positive change in the companies and has caused some positive transformations.However, despite the guarantee of anonymity, many firms were not willing to provide essential statistics which is a certain limitation for the validity of the findings.

Notes

1   This research was undertaken with support from the European Union's Phare ACE programme 1997. The content of the publication is the sole responsibility of the author and in no way does it represent the views of the Commission or its services.

2   According to the latest figures FDI stock in Hungary reached US$ 19.4 bn in December 1998, in Poland US$ 30.7 bn, in the Czech Republic US$ 7.6 bn as of June 1998 and in Slovakia US$ 1.7 bn in October 1998.

3   The author disseminated questionnaires in 1998 according to her ACE PHARE research proposal.

4   It was the only database available in Slovakia and it comprised all FDI companies as of January 1997.

Further Readings

Balaz, P. *et al.* (1998), *Podpora rastu exportnej výkonnosti: základ hospodárskej stratégie transformácie slovenskej ekonomiky (Promoting the Growth of Export Efficiency:*

Basis of Economic Strategy in Restructuring Slovakia's Economy), Bratislava, IAMEX.
Business Central Europe (1996), 'Foreign Investment Survey: Thinking global', April, pp. 39-40.
Dunning, J. (1993), 'The Prospects for Foreign Direct Investment in Eastern Europe', in Artisen, P. *et al.*, *Foreign Investment in Central and Eastern Europe*, London: Macmillan.
Ferencikova, S. (1997), 'East-West Joint Ventures in a Transitional Economy: The Case of Slovakia', *The Davidson Institute Working Paper Series*, University of Michigan Business School.
Ferencikova, S. and Smith, A. (1997), 'Regional Transformation and Foreign Investment on the Road to Capitalism in Eastern Europe: Case Studies from the Manufacturing Sector in Slovakia', *Research Papers in Geography*, University of Sussex.
Fogel, D.S. (1995), *Firm Behaviour in Emerging Market Economies*, Brookfield: Ashgate Publishing Company.
Hoskova, A. (1997), 'Rezervy vo všetkých oblastiach (Reserves in All Areas)', Hospodárske noviny (Economic Paper), p. 1.
Kita, J. (1996), 'Súcasné tendencie vo vývoji marketingu, (Contemporary Trends in Marketing Development)', *Ekonomický casopis (The Economic Journal)*, vol. 44, nos.7-8, pp. 505-516.
OECD (1996), OECD *Economic Surveys: the Slovak Republic*, Paris, OECD.
Penrice, D. (1995), 'The Post-Communist World: The Obstacles to Change', *Harvard Business Review*, vol. 73, no. 1.
Springer, R. (1993), 'Market Entry and Marketing Strategies for Eastern Europe', in Chadraba, P. and Springer, R. *Proceedings of the Conference on Marketing Strategies for Central and Eastern Europe*, Paper 1.
Shuh, A *et al.* (1996), 'Marketing Strategies for East Central Europe: A Balancing between Globalization and Local Market Responsiveness', in Chadraba, P. and Springer, R. *Proceedings of the 4th Annual Conference on Marketing Strategies for Central and Eastern Europe*, Paper 1.
Šaková, B. (1995), 'Motivácia alebo demotivácia zahranicných investorov u nás? (Motivation or De-motivation of Foreign Investors in Our Country?)', *Ekonomické rozhlady (Economic Review)*, vol. 24, no. 4, pp. 26-31.
Review of Statistics: Slovak Republic, (1997, 1998).
Trend (1997), 'Top 100', A special section, 7, 4 June.
UNCTAD (1996), *World Investment Report 1996: Investment, Trade and International Policy Arrangements*, New York, United Nations.
Zorkociova, O. (1999), *Vplyv transformacneho procesu ekonomickych systemov statov strednej Europy na zmeny v oblasti vonkajsich ekonomickych vztahov Ekonomické rozhlady*, vol. 28, no. 3., pp. 63-71.

PART IV

FORMS OF FOREIGN DIRECT INVESTMENT IN CENTRAL AND EASTERN EUROPE

13 Strategic Orientation of Finnish Investors in Russia

INKERI HIRVENSALO and PIIA HELISTE

Introduction

After the collapse of the Soviet Union and the introduction of a market based economic system in Russia, Finnish companies have been interested not only in increased trade with Russian companies but also in direct investments in the country. During the Soviet era bilateral trade relations between the two countries were mostly in the hands of relatively large organizations, large Finnish companies on the one hand and Soviet foreign trade organizations, which had monopoly rights over the range of goods that they were trading, on the other hand. The 1990s saw the entry of medium sized and small Finnish companies first as exporters and later also as direct investors in Russia.

From a strategic point of view the operations of large Finnish companies and those with previous experience in Russia have generally, with very few exceptions, involved small, even marginal investments when compared to the overall scope of the activities of the investing companies. For medium sized and small companies, who often are newcomers to the market and have less experience from international operations in general, the activities in Russia have in turn, been much more significant. However, for both groups of Finnish companies the investments in Russia have generally been small in absolute terms as well as in international comparisons.

There have not been very big differences in the strategic orientation of large and small Finnish companies in the Russian market. The problems they have faced on the market are largely the same and the approaches to solve them have been quite similar, which indicates that the companies are resorting to strategies aimed at solving the peculiarities of the Russian market rather than each trying to pursue a distinguished strategy adapted to the Russian conditions.

This chapter draws upon earlier research (Heliste, 2000; Hirvensalo 1996, 1999) on the strategies of Finnish companies in Russia and aims at relating the findings to some general concepts and theories in the strategy literature. The summaries of the earlier research findings are first presented and then the chapter proceeds with a discussion of the implications from a theoretical point of view, followed by hypotheses and suggestions for further research.

The Underlying Empirical Research

The empirical research is based on case studies, which comprise 12 enterprises with Finnish ownership. Geographically, most of the enterprises are concentrated in northwest Russia. Two-thirds of the companies started Russian operations in St. Petersburg but branched out also to other regions, notably Moscow and its surroundings. The majority of the enterprises are manufacturing units. The lines of industry cover pulp and paper industry, automobile industry (an assembly plant and a tire factory), construction (steel roofs, roof supporting structures, windows, paints, sawing timber), food industry (brewery), and consumer goods (head gear, foot wear). Enterprises, which specialize in services concentrate on transportation (forwarding and transportation, warehousing and gasoline station services). Two of the enterprises are local sales offices.

Eight of the companies are 100 percent foreign owned and in most joint ventures foreign investors own the majority of shares, as the major trend in the ownership structure has been towards fully owned or very close to fully owned subsidiaries. The size of the enterprises varies greatly: the biggest employs hundreds of workers and the smallest has only one local employee.

The investments made by Finnish companies in Russian subsidiaries have generally been relatively small, particularly in relation to the size of the parent companies. In many cases the bulk of the initial investments were made as contributions in the form of used equipment. In addition, the foreign parent has often financed part of the working capital of the subsidiary by granting trade credits for the supplies delivered to the subsidiary. In the wholesale and retail sectors the parent companies have also financed a great part of the inventories or stocks needed in the business. Investments in new machinery and equipment or premises have been relatively small.

As the empirical research is of a case study nature, it is not possible to make strong generalizations on the basis of the findings however, as the findings are very similar among the companies, the authors propose some hypotheses, which could be tested with a larger sample of companies in follow-up research projects.

Summary of Empirical Findings on Strategic Orientation of Finnish Investors in Russia

Motivation for Entry

The most common motivation of the investors to enter the Russian market has been the attraction of the huge mostly untapped market. Companies set up subsidiaries in Russia in order to benefit from the first-mover-advantage already in the beginning of the 1990s although the market was still seen as unstable and the business environment was perceived as very difficult and risky. The driving forces behind this behavior are the small size and limited growth potential of the Finnish market as well as the harsh competition in the West European markets. For many Finnish investors the Russian market is the only market relatively close to Finland, which has a huge market potential and can be profitable in the medium to long term. This view is counterbalanced by the recognition of the still small purchasing power of the market and its relative instability coupled with high macroeconomic and political vulnerability.

The second most common motivation to set up production subsidiaries has been the low factor costs in Russia. The labor costs, in particular, have been very low in comparison to their Finnish level. That also applies to highly educated and qualified employees. The benefits from the cheap labor force in Russia are reflected in the generally small number of Finnish expatriates working for the Russian subsidiaries. Only a few key positions in the general management, marketing or production have usually been filled in with Finnish expatriates. All other employees have been local Russians. However, the low labor costs have often been undermined by the low productivity of labor and the great number of employees that the Russian companies usually have.

A third major motivation for establishing Russian subsidiaries has been the high level of Russian import tariffs. Exporting to Russia becomes often too expensive due to high import tariffs, which has in many cases triggered the decision to commit more substantial resources and make a direct investment in Russia.

Although the motivations for entry are generally clearly explained by Finnish managers, the business strategy for the Russian market seems to be somewhat vague for many Finnish investors. Companies have made the decision to enter the Russian market for various reasons but they have not necessarily worked out exact plans on how to develop the operations in the long run. They seem to be acting more on an ad hoc basis reacting to the changing domestic and regional business environment.

Corporate Governance

There seems to be a clear trend towards majority ownership among Finnish investors in their Russian subsidiaries. One important reason for this is the implementation of effective corporate governance right from the beginning of the operations. When a Finnish investor has decided to join forces with a Russian partner, the partner has been seen to bring more value to the venture than the Finnish counterpart or the Finnish partner has not had much experience in business operations in the Russian context. However, the role and the ownership share of the Russian partner have often been decreased as the operations have developed. The reasons behind this are twofold.

Firstly, the financing needs of the joint venture have usually been covered by the Finnish partner in the form of increased equity, which has driven up the percentage of shares owned by the Finnish partner.

Second, there is often a difference between the Finnish and the Russian ownership strategy, which has resulted in the Finnish partners buying up the Russian shares.

The differences in the strategic emphasis often arise from different time perspectives of the partners. The Finnish investors have generally made the investment with a long-term vision, whereas the Russian investor's time horizon is much shorter. The Finnish partner does not necessarily expect the investment to be profitable in the short run, while the Russians often have such expectations from the very beginning. Similarly, the Finns prefer to reinvest the potential profits in the subsidiaries, whereas the Russian partners prefer to receive dividends, which can be invested in some other businesses.

However, some Finnish companies have also favored a strategy based on partnership, which stresses the local ownership as a significant motivating factor. This strategy is successful when both sides have ascertained that they have a similar understanding of the long-term goals of the mutually beneficial business venture.

The importance of control has also been strongly emphasized in the Russian subsidiaries. There are some examples of cases where the Finnish parent company has suddenly noticed that the Russian unit has been entirely transferred under the ownership of the Russian management.

Organization of the Value Chain

Most Finnish companies have started their operations in Russia via exporting and even after setting up a production subsidiary they often import a relatively big share of their production factors. In many cases this is due to the low quality of the Russian local production or to the unreliability of their deliveries. Usually, the Finnish companies start using more and more Russian production as they develop their operations. Many of th·m also train and educate local companies to perform up to the West rn standards.

Management of the Subsidiary

Finnish companies use quite a lot of Russian managers in their subsidiaries. At the beginning of the operations the manager of the subsidiary has often been Finnish but in many cases he has later been changed to a Russian manager. However, the Finnish companies have experienced substantial problems with the management of their Russian subsidiaries. In many cases the first choice of a manager has been a failure and they have had to substitute him.

Operational Problems

The most common experiences among the Finnish investors include difficulties in dealing with the local administration. Most common are problems incurred with the bureaucracy and the constantly changing regulations. In particular, the tax administration is found very complex and the decisions of the tax police are seen as arbitrary and often depending on the person in charge. Additionally, foreign investors feel that the requirements to them are much more severe than those set to local companies.

Most of the Finnish companies trade against prepayment, almost all of them have also extended small trade credits to certain customer groups. In a number of cases there have been some complications with such receivables but large credit losses seem to have been avoided. Problems with trade credits are mostly due to the different perception of the nature of these receivables. In many cases the Russians do not even consider them as credits that have to be paid back within a certain period of time.

Discussion

Market Entry and Competitive Strategies

As the study focuses on direct investment strategies of Finnish companies, it does not directly deal with the initial entry mode and development of the strategy in Russia over a long period of time. However, it is clear from the research that the operations strategy of the investors is very closely related to the exporting strategy of the companies. Most companies had served the market as exporters for years before making the direct investment, but a few had started their involvement in the Russian market by first setting up a joint venture or a subsidiary. The predominant motivation for foreign direct investment entry among Finnish companies is the Russian market potential. The relatively small investments in sales and marketing units often serve as support to the exporting strategy rather than as an entirely new approach to the market. The few manufacturing operations have been established to serve more as a test base rather than a serious new venture.

Formal, Flexible and Ad Hoc Planning

As summarized above Finnish companies seem to have followed an ad hoc-based strategy in Russia often without a clearly expressed strategic orientation other than avoidance of large and risky operations in the rapidly changing markets. The motivation has often been to have 'the foot in the door' and to be on the spot when the investment environment becomes more favorable.

In the strategic literature Mintzberg (1994a, b) is known as an advocate of incremental and emerging strategy particularly in rapidly changing and unstable circumstances. The Russian market in the last decade has been an extreme example of profound institutional and market changes and therefore Finnish companies have been opting for an incremental approach to Russian investment strategies. As there is much uncertainty about the stability of the legislative framework to which business operations in Russia are subjected, the companies' managers feel they cannot really plan much ahead.

On the other hand, Brews and Hunt (1999), based on empirical research, have recently argued that the environment does not really moderate the need for formal planning but does moderate the firm planning capabilities and planning flexibility. According to their findings planning capabilities are far better developed and formal plans are easier to amend to change in unstable than in stable environments. In the turbulent Russian environment this would imply that the companies operating there would be likely to develop their planning skills and flexible planning, in particular. However, there seems to be very little evidence of such behavior among the Finnish companies in the formal planning processes. The Russian market is considered a potentially important market and this positive long-term view of the companies is the basis of operation in many companies. However, Finnish companies claim that formal strategic planning for the Russian market would be directly related to the development of a more stable legislative and political environment. The ad hoc strategic planning is mostly influenced by the rapid and often unexpected changes in legislation and administrative regulations. On the other hand, those companies who are operating in such circumstances have truly developed their skills in acting rapidly and responding even to unexpected new regulations.

There are two kinds of hypotheses that can be formulated for strategic planning in unstable transition markets:

- Formal (long-term) planning is virtually meaningless in markets with rapid institutional changes, such as frequent changes in the legislative framework;
- In unstable transition markets companies are developing their skills to adapt quickly to rapid, even unexpected changes in the environment.

Both hypotheses are supported by the view of Mintzberg (1994a, b) and the second is also in line with the findings of Brews and Hunt (1999).

'Dominant Logic' of Doing Business in Russia

Prahalad and Bettis (1986) and Bettis and Prahalad (1995) have introduced the concept of dominant logic defined as the way managers conceptualize their business and make critical resource allocation decisions. It is a useful concept when analyzing the experiences of Finnish companies in the Russian markets. Most Finnish direct investors in Russia argue that the dominant logic of doing business there and making critical investment decisions has differed a great deal from that of the Finnish market. An example quoted above refers to the differences in attitudes to the reinvestment of profits gained by Finnish-Russian joint ventures. This seems to indicate a radically different approach towards the longevity of the operations in Russia among the two business communities. Russian managers tend to focus more on the short-term profitability whereas the Finns prefer to emphasize the long-term development of the ventures established in Russia.

In addition to differences in the time horizon, there are many other significant differences in the dominant logic as uncovered by the research on Finnish foreign direct investments, such as attitude towards corporate governance arrangements in general, attitude towards credit and relations to authorities. Thus, there are significant differences in the dominant logic of doing business in Russia as manifested in the management practices of Russian and Finnish managers, which in turn reflect the institutional differences between the two countries.

It is likely that the dominant Russian business logic has its roots both in the legacy of the socialist planning system and in the Russian cultural characteristics. In addition it can be hypothesized that:

The way economic reforms have been introduced in Russia have increasingly influenced the dominant business logic and, among others, strengthened short-term profit orientation.

Implications for Further Research

The hypotheses presented above on competitive strategies and strategic planning in changing market conditions would need to be tested by further empirical research involving a larger group of investors than those interviewed for the purposes of this study. This kind of research would also benefit from an international comparative approach that would allow analyzing the Russian market characteristics from diverse international perspectives. On the other hand it would allow testing the universality of strategic theories developed by western scientists in a different and rapidly changing institutional setting.

Further research should also focus on the various manifestations of the dominant business logic of Russian companies to unravel its dynamics in the changing contextual characteristics of the Russian economic policy.

References

Bettis, R.A. and Prahalad, C.K. (1995), 'The Dominant Logic: Retrospective and Extension', *Strategic Management Journal*, vol. 16, pp. 5-14.

Brews, P.J. and Hunt, M.R. (1999), 'Learning to Plan and Planning to Learn: Resolving the Planning School/Learning School Debate', *Strategic Management Journal*, vol. 20, pp. 889-913.

Campbell-Hunt, C. (2000), 'What Have We Learned about Generic Competitive Strategy? A Meta Analysis', *Strategic Management Journal*, vol. 21, pp. 127-154.

Heliste, P. (2000), 'Foreign Direct Investment in the Vyborg District – A Multiple Investor Study of a Single Investment Target', Master's Thesis in International Business, Helsinki: Helsinki School of Economics and Business Administration.

Hirvensalo, I. (1996), *Strategic Adaptation of Enterprises to Turbulent Transitionary Markets. Operative Strategies of Finnish Firms in Russia and the Baltic States during 1991-1995*, Publications A-120, Helsinki: Helsinki School of Economics and Business Administration.

Hirvensalo, I. (1999), *Sijoitukset Venäjälle; Kokemuksia Venäjälle Tehtyjen Sijoitusten Rahoituksesta*, ETLA B 150, Helsinki. English summary: *The Operational and Financial Strategies of Finnish Companies in Russia in the 1990s*, available on request from the author.

Kosonen, R. (2000), 'The Russian Market Economy in the Making: Institutions, Networks, and Regulation of Post-Socialism in Vyborg', in M. Kangaspuro (ed.) *Russia: More Different than Most. Articles of the Research Programme for Russia and Eastern Europe of the Academy of Finland*, Helsinki: Kikimora Publications.

Mintzberg, H. (1994a), 'Rethinking Strategic Planning, Part I: Pitfalls and Fallacies', *Long Range Planning*, vol. 27, no. 3, pp.12-21.

Mintzberg, H. (1994b), 'Rethinking Strategic Planning, Part II: New Roles for Planners', *Long Range Planning*, vol. 27, no. 3, pp. 22-30.

Nieminen, J. and Larimo, J. (2000), 'Market Strategies and Performance of Finnish Companies in Central and Eastern Europe', *Proceedings of the University of Vaasa*, Vaasa, Finland, Discussion Papers 264.

Porter, M. (1980), 'Competitive Strategy, Techniques for Analyzing Industries and Competitors', New York and London: The Free Press.

Prahalad, C. and Bettis, R. (1986), 'The Dominant Logic: A New Linkage between Diversity and Performance', *Strategic Management Journal*, vol. 7, pp. 485-501.

Törnroos, J.-Å. and Nieminen, J. (eds) (1999), *Business Entry in Eastern Europe. A Network and Learning Approach with Case Studies*, B-4, Helsinki: Kikimora Publications.

14 Organizational Learning as a Solution for Partner Conflicts in Russian-Foreign Joint Ventures

JARMO NIEMINEN

Introduction

Joint venture instability has been studied in different contexts by many researchers (e.g., Gomes-Casseres, 1987; Harrigan, 1988), who indicate a high mortality rate for equity joint ventures. In addition, several researchers have addressed the problems and mistakes occurring in joint ventures (Lyles, 1988; Simiar, 1983). The majority of these problems are based on partner differences. Research on East-West joint ventures has increased considerably in the 1990s. This is due to the opening of the East European markets for foreign investors and the major role of joint ventures in the investment activity of foreign firms in the region. Although joint ventures have been replaced by other forms of foreign investment in the fastest growing economies like the Czech Republic, Hungary and Poland, they still remain the major form of foreign investment in Russia. The increased popularity of East-West joint ventures, their substantial failure rate, and particularly their managerial complexity suggest a closer examination of their management issues.

The previous empirical studies on Russian-foreign joint ventures indicate that these partnerships have to operate in a complex and fast changing environment, which sets particular demands on the management of the venture (see e.g., Nigh *et al.*, 1990; Hertzfeld, 1991; Liuhto, 1991; Lawrence and Vlachoutsicos, 1993; Fey, 1995). The premise of this study is that in order to minimize partner conflicts and reach harmony in managerial decision-making, both joint venture partners have to adopt the concept of learning. This means knowledge transfer from one partner to another, its cognition and consequent change in behavior. This, in turn, is expected to lead to higher trust and organizational performance (Sullivan and Peterson, 1982). Unlike in other forms of interorganizational exchange, joint ventures provide each partner with access to the embedded knowledge of the other partner, which creates the potential for firms to internalize partner skills and capabilities – not just an access to them. This study examines how joint venture partners learn or why they do not learn in Russian-Finnish joint ventures. A theoretical framework for learning is constructed from the works of Argyris and Schon (1978), and Child and Marcóczy (1993).

Framework for the Study

The concept of organizational learning has been a major topic for scholars in strategic management for a long time. The concept was addressed by Cyert and March (1963) over 30 years ago as a process by which the actions of an individual lead to organizational interactions with the environment, the environment responds, and environmental responses are interpreted by individuals who learn by updating their beliefs about cause-effect (i.e., action-response) relationships (Lee *et al.,* 1992). Among others, Morgan and Ramirez (1983) argue that organizational learning occurs when companies act together to solve problems as equal 'co-learners'. Firms build up knowledge through which relationships with other companies can be enriched and expanded. Interaction with the cooperation partners creates actual experience to refer to, thus adding to the knowledge supply.

In management literature learning is seen as a purposive quest to retain and improve competitiveness, productivity, and innovativeness in uncertain technological and market conditions. The greater the uncertainties, the greater the need for learning. The goals of learning in these circumstances can therefore be seen as a response to the need for *adjustment* in times of great *uncertainty* (Dodgson, 1993). Given the high degree of environmental complexity and uncertainty in Russia, learning is expected to play a substantial role in the survival of Russian-foreign joint ventures.

Learning in joint ventures and strategic alliances has been studied by many researchers in different contexts (e.g., Lyles, 1988; Hamel, 1991; Parkhe, 1991; Inkpen, 1992). In the East-West context only a few studies have tried to approach joint ventures from the viewpoint of learning.

Child and Marcóczy (1993) examined the role of managerial learning in Hungarian and Chinese joint ventures. Although Child and Marcóczy (1993) emphasize the role of the Western partner in transferring new insights and knowledge to the East European counterpart in order to enhance local managers' behavioral change, it is argued that learning is crucial also for the Western partner, who has to learn about the new business conduct in a complex and fast changing environment. They have to understand the factors that affect the behavior of their partners and the stimuli provided by the external environment in order to be able to achieve optimal performance (see also Tesar and Nieminen, 1994).

Argyris and Schon (1978) use the concept of organizational learning as a metaphor to describe behavioral and cognitive changes within organizations. This is also emphasized by Crossan and Inkpen (1992) and Garvin (1993). According to Garvin (1993) cognitive detection of new information and/or knowledge is the first phase of learning. This means that individuals are exposed to new ideas and gradually begin to think differently. Consequently, in this study learning is concerned with understanding the new system in Russia and how to do business within it.

The second phase of learning is change in behavior. People internalise their cognitive insights and alter their behavior. The behavioral change leads to the adoption of more effective practices such as accepting decision-making responsibility, communicating information, and introducing performance-related personnel practices (Child and Marcóczy, 1993).

Although the concept of learning has been emphasized in many studies, it is worth noting that 'unlearning', or forgetting past behaviour is often redundant or unsuccessful. Firms that can unlearn and reframe their past success programs to fit with changing environmental and situational conditions will have a greater likelihood of survival and adaptation (Hedberg, 1981; Starbuck, 1983; Lyles, 1988).

Understanding involves both learning new knowledge and discarding obsolete and misleading knowledge. The discarding activity, 'unlearning', is as important a part of understanding as is adding new knowledge. Nieminen and Törnroos (1997) found that in East-West business relationships both parties need to unlearn their past behavioral patterns in order to advance knowledge transfer between the companies under the requirements of the fast changing environment.

Based on the above presented theoretical framework a typology of cognitive and behavioral changes was constructed. It consists of four blocks, including:

- inability to learn;
- resistance to learn;
- imitation;
- learning.

This typology is presented in Figure 14.1.

Change in Behavior

		No	Yes
Change in Cognition	No	Inability to learn	Imitation
	Yes	Resistance to learn	Integrated learning

Figure 14.1   Learning: A typology of a firm's responses to cognitive and behavioral changes

Inability to Learn

This behavior implies that the joint venture partner has not undergone any cognitive or behavioral changes. Inability to change implies that the venture partner is unable to change its past behavioral patterns. In this case the partner does not understand the stimuli for change that come from the external environment or from the other partner, and thus, is unable to change his behavior accordingly. For example, the Western partner may not see any need to adapt to local circumstances (e.g., by changing decision-making systems or management approaches) so that they would comply with accepted Russian behavioral norms. On the other hand, the Russian partner may lack the competence of implementing changes needed in a market economy.

Resistance to Learn

In this block, a joint venture partner understands the need for change, but refuses to act accordingly. The phenomenon of resistance to change has been well documented in organizational literature and it appears to be particularly entrenched in public bureaucracies where existing practices may have been preserved over a long time. In this case Child and Marcóczy (1993) refer to forced learning, which indicates that the joint venture manager does not accept the change, although the need is understood.

Imitation

Imitation occurs when a joint venture partner changes his behaviour, but does not understand the underlying rationale for this behaviour. Child and Marcóczy (1993) noted that '...in several of the Hungarian joint ventures the previous dependence of managers on higher government authorities was transferred to a new dependence on the foreign "expert" partner in which his instructions were followed but without much apparent new understanding'. Such a situation is very common in East-West joint ventures and primarily occurs when the Western partner requests some actions to be taken by his East European partner. The risk in imitation is that it may have positive short-term effects on the relationship, but if the Russian partner is not convinced why certain measures have to be taken, he may change his position to 'resistance to change'. On the other hand, imitation may also take the form of experimental learning, if the manager gets positive feedback of the changed behavior.

Integrated Learning

As indicated above, in order to take place, learning needs both cognitive and behavioral changes from the joint venture partners. Child and Marcóczy (1993) label this phenomenon as integrated learning. This implies that the partners willingly receive new insights from each other and finally accept the need to change. As learning is suggested to be the underlying concept to avoid partner conflicts and finally improve the joint venture performance, this should be that form of learning the joint venture managers should aim at.

Methodology

The questions this study seeks to investigate are difficult to study using quantitative research method due to the complexity of issues involved. Thus, case study methodology (Yin 1989) was chosen for this study since the research in the area of Russian-foreign joint ventures is not well developed. It can also enable us to obtain a richer understanding of the situation.

This study is based on two in-depth case studies of Russian-Finnish joint ventures using qualitative analysis of primary data collected through personal interviews conducted with key managers at the joint venture organization and with key managers of the Finnish partner. Fifteen hours of interviews were conducted at each joint venture resulting in 40–50 pages of narrative data. In addition, archival documents like company records, strategic plans, protocols and other internal documentation were used.

Two cases were chosen to illustrate the occurrence of learning among joint venture partners, one case representing the food industry and the other the paper industry. The following criteria were used when choosing the cases:

- the joint venture had to be engaged in production because it was anticipated that the coordination of the management would be much more complex than in the case of service sector companies;
- the joint ventures needed to have been operating for several years in order to have enough experience of the exchange relationships between the venture partners. The basic characteristics of the case companies are presented in Table 14.1.

Table 14.1   Characteristics of the case companies

Characteristic	Firm A	Firm B
Field of industry	Food	Paper
Annual sales (US$ million)	1900	3900
Previous experience in Russia	More than 50 years	More than 100 years
Major field of business	In non-related business to the joint venture	In related business to the joint venture
Initiation	Soviet/Russian partner	Finnish partner
Reasons for JV formation	Market expansion	Acquisition of raw material
Year of establishment	1988	1988
Present position of the JV	Not active	Active

As a limitation to the study it should be emphasized that the results only reflect the opinions and perceptions of the Finnish parent companies' managers. However, to increase the reliability of the results, the raw data and two manuscripts of the text were checked by the interviewed managers.

Analysis

The empirical analysis is based on the above presented framework (cognitive and behavioral changes among joint venture partners) and is based on the experiences of Finnish managers in two Russian-Finnish joint ventures (to be labelled from here on as Firm A and Firm B). The aim of this section is to analyze the Finnish managers' perceptions of the factors which prohibit learning in a joint venture.

Inability to Learn

The Finnish partner   Both Finnish firms had extensive previous experience in the Russian market, which was expected to have positive effects on learning. The recent changes in Russia, along with the abolition of the clearing system in trade between Finland and Russia, were expected to increase the need for learning in the new environment. The Finnish managers claimed to have difficulties in trying to find out the logic of the fast environmental changes. Like one manager in Firm B pointed out, '...doing business in the present environment (in Russia) is like being in a labyrinth and trying to find your way out of it'. However, the role of the Russian partner proved out to be crucial in interpreting the environmental changes to the Finnish managers. In partner relations the Finnish managers showed high levels of flexibility, which is discussed in more detail below.

The Russian partner   The two cases have a lot of evidence which shows the inability of the Russian partner to learn. In these cases, it is often a matter of lack of understanding or misinterpretation of the signals given by the Western partner. This is partly a question of the lack of managerial competence in Russia and misunderstanding of the basic management terminology. These issues are relics of the past command economy era and this lack of understanding can be reduced by more intensive training programs in management and cross-cultural issues.

Firm A, for example, launched an extensive training program covering all levels of the organization, including employees. This proved to be successful because both companies indicated that the local managers were well educated and extremely willing to learn. In this respect it is important for the Western manager to identify the gaps that prohibit the understanding of the need for change. Although the accumulation of knowledge may take a long time in order to affect behavior, learning can be achieved if the partner does not have any negative attitudes towards change as in the block 'resistance to learn'.

However, in case the Russian managers do not get enough positive feedback for their altered behavior, this pattern may lead to pure 'imitation' and finally to 'resistance to learn'.

Resistance to Learn

The Finnish partner   The Finnish partners have shown very little resistance to learn both from their Russian partners and from the external environment. However, earlier studies have shown that some companies tend to overlook their partners and ignore their knowledge and skills (Tesar and Nieminen, 1994). In our cases resistance occurred only in cases where the Russian partner suggested action the outcomes of which were expected to be negative for the joint venture (e.g., product diversification; extensive investments prior to cash flow availability). These were solely related to extremely high risks that could have been fatal to the venture.

The Russian partner   In our study the Russian partners showed some degree of reluctance to change. This was mainly connected with the resistance to learn new management practices. For example, Firm A appointed a Russian general manager to the joint venture, but he proved to be very reluctant in taking responsibility for the management decisions. This kind of behavior was somewhat typical of managers in the command economy era, but it did not work anymore in the new context. The change seems to be especially difficult for older managers. They appear to be concerned more with getting a high position in the organization, but are not quite ready to work towards achieving pre-set objectives and positive performance outcomes.

In order to improve the motivation among the Russian managers, the Finnish partners have used higher result related rewards (e.g., higher salary, business trips to other countries, healthcare services, and bonuses, etc.). Firm A reduced the decision-making power of some managers who showed resistance to learn. As these managers often tried to disassociate themselves from decision-making responsibility, they were left out of the important, strategic decisions for the company but were still paid the contractually agreed salary. It appeared that everybody was happy with this solution.

It is obvious that many Russian managers are not able to get rid of their old habits and beliefs. As previous studies of managers in other transition economies show, see for example Child and Marcóczy (1993), Russian managers also seem not to express openly their opinions when communicating with their Western joint venture partners. This is a question of corporate, social and group culture, as well as it takes time to introduce and trust new ideas.

Commitment to the joint venture goals was another determinant explaining the resistance to change. Firm A was mainly interested in selling its output in the local market, while the Russian partner wanted to earn hard currency from export operations. This reduced the local partner's commitment to the venture and finally resulted in resistance to the changes suggested by the Finnish partner. In Firm B it became soon evident that in order to make things done in the best possible way, written communication and documents were required by the managers (and employees in some cases) to implement the job.

Imitation

The Finnish partner   Among the Finnish managers imitation took place in the sense that certain behavioral changes were first tested, and if the outcome was positive, the new actions became patterns. This is synonymous with experimental learning in which behavioral change occurs prior to cognitive change. This pattern was supposed to be beneficial in the early stages of the joint venture: increasing resource commitments were made only after the firms gained more experience and knowledge of the local conditions.

The Russian partner   Imitation seems to occur much more often among the Russian managers. Training and education are factors that can enhance the learning of the Russian partner. Although the Russian managers appear to be eager to learn new things, sometimes their inability to understand the rationale behind the needed changes may also have a reverse outcome. Unless the Western partner is able to convince the Russian partner of the positive results of the changed behavior, the local managers may move to the block 'resistance to learn'.

On the other hand, imitation seems to be the most common way to enhance learning among Russian managers. Certain actions are repeated long enough to ensure their cognitive detection.

Integrated Learning

The Finnish partner   The concept of learning was regarded among the interviewed Finnish managers not only useful, but also necessary. One manager from Firm A was convinced that '...without a deep interaction with our Russian colleagues, it would be impossible for us to manage in this environment'.

Equality between the partners was emphasized, despite the huge differences. Positive attitudes and understanding of the partner's different background create a favorable climate for learning. As one manager of Firm B pointed out, 'They have their own culture and traditions, which must not be criticized. The poor economic situation is not their fault, and we want to be a part of the society's development process in local terms'.

Local presence is also regarded as an outcome of learning: in order to acquire first hand knowledge of the market and prepare for the future, a company needs strong presence in the market.

Finnish managers have spent considerable time in learning about the Russian managers' way of thinking; not only inside the company, but also in their leisure time. This decreases the possible negative attitudes, helps to understand the cultural differences that shape the behavior of Russian managers and finally, creates trust between the partners.

Flexibility was also emphasized 'If you want to do things exactly in the way they are done in Finland, you will get nowhere. You cannot act arrogantly and say that we should do it the Finnish way because we know more about these things than our Russian counterparts. You cannot usually do things in a straight-forward way even if you were right.'

Although the autonomy of the joint ventures has gradually increased, joint venture experience has been educational for the Finnish partners in their other business development plans in Russia.

The Russian partner   The cases show that learning has taken place in the partnership, although usually it is preceded by the above presented blocks of 'inability to learn', 'resistance to learn', and 'imitation'. As indicated previously, younger managers are often well educated and eager to learn new things. Learning takes place through individuals, but especially the Russian partners seem to have problems in the integration of learning to the parent organization. New knowledge has been internalized by individuals surprisingly well, but at the same time Russian managers show reluctance in transferring the new knowledge to other members of the organization. This indicates that new knowledge plays a crucial role in the power relations between individuals of the host organization. Another important factor is the personal changes in the structure of the Russian partners in the joint venture organizations, which weakens the learning experience and reduces its long-term value added.

Conclusions

This chapter has addressed the importance of learning among joint venture partners in Russian-foreign joint ventures. Although little evidence is available about the applicability of organizational learning to the development of East-West joint ventures, it is assumed that the presented framework could be useful in analyzing the change patterns of joint venture partners in other transition economies as well. It helps managers to identify those critical areas in joint venture management which complicate the learning patterns of the East European partners.

It seems evident that learning can be achieved by Russian partners (in terms of both cognitive and behavioral change), but it is often preceded by some degree of resistance to learning. Training and education programs are regarded useful among the Finnish managers, but the truth is not that simple. The atmosphere for learning must be created in a way that makes the Russian partner motivated and willing to act in the expected way.

The results also indicate that learning is a mutual process. It is not a case of one-sided transfer of knowledge and skills from one parent organization to another. The Finnish managers emphasized that their Russian partners have acted as change agents while interpreting the complex environment. Thus, the market knowledge and skills of the Russian managers should not be ignored or underestimated.

Among the Finnish joint venture partners, successful learning is strongly influenced by their ability to interpret the cultural and managerial differences between the parent firms. Flexibility, equality and sensitivity were other important issues emphasized in partner relations.

In the two cases there seems to have been lack of trust between the joint venture partners, although the partners had long been doing business together in a buyer-seller relationship. This was also partly due to the lack of authority given to the Russian partners to do some things they were expected to do (e.g., acquisition of raw material, distribution). However, trust-building is a key element also in learning and it should be given a high priority from the very start of the relationship.

The study has several implications for future research. First, as the Russian managers seem to have difficulties in integrating their knowledge in their own organization, one future direction would be to investigate how new knowledge and skills can be transferred more effectively to the Russian partner organization. Second, the results show that the Finnish parent companies have had extreme difficulties in trying to adapt to the changing environment. Company adaptation and learning from the external environment should be of greater interest to the practitioners as well. Third, learning patterns in other exchange relationships than joint ventures should be given special attention in future management research and publications.

References

Argyris, C. and Schon, D. (1978), *Organizational Learning*. London: Addison-Wesley.
Child, J. and Marcóczy, L. (1993), 'Host-Country Managerial Behaviour and Learning in Chinese and Hungarian Joint Ventures'. *Journal of Management Studies*, vol. 30, no. 5, pp. 613–631.

Crossan, M.M. and Inkpen, A.C. (1992), 'Organization Learning: An Exploration of the Learning Concept and Evidence from the Case of Joint Venture Learning', *Working Paper Series* No. NC 92-009-K. National Centre for Management Research and Development, Western Business School, University of Western Ontario, Canada.

Cyert, R.M. and March J.G. (1963), *A Behavioral Theory of the Firm*, Englewood Cliffs, NJ: Prentice Hall, Inc.

Dodgson, M. (1993), 'Organizational Learning: A Review of Some Literatures', *Organization Studies*, vol. 14, no. 3, pp. 375–394.

Fey, C. (1995), 'Important Design Characteristics for Russian-Foreign Joint Ventures', *European Management Journal*, vol. 13, no. 4, pp. 405–415.

Garvin, D.A. (1993), 'Building a Learning Organization', *Harvard Business Review*, (July–August), pp. 78–91.

Gomes-Casseres, B. (1987), 'Joint Venture Instability: Is It a Problem?', *Columbia Journal of World Business*, vol. 22, no. 2, pp. 97–102.

Hamel, G. (1991), 'Competition for Competence and Inter-Partner Learning within International Strategic Alliances', *Strategic Management Journal*, vol. 12, pp. 83–104.

Harrigan, K.R. (1988), 'Strategic Alliances and Partner Asymmetries', *Management International Review*, vol. 28, pp. 53–72.

Hedberg, B. (1981), 'How Organizations Learn and Unlearn', in P. Nystrom and W. Starbuck (eds) *Handbook of Organizational Design*, Oxford: Oxford University Press, pp. 68-97.

Hertzfeld, J.M. (1991), 'Joint Ventures: Saving the Soviets from Perestroika', *Harvard Business Review*, (January–February), pp. 80–91.

Inkpen, A.C. (1992), *Learning and Collaboration: An Examination of North American – Japanese Joint Ventures*, PhD thesis, University of Western Ontario, London, Canada.

Lawrence, P. and Vlachoutsicos, C. (1993), 'Joint Ventures in Russia: Put the Locals in Charge', *Harvard Business Review*, (January–February), pp. 69-78.

Lee, S., Courtney, J.F. and O'Keefe, R.M. (1992), 'A System for Organizational Learning Using Cognitive Maps'. *OMEGA International Journal of Management Science*, vol. 20 (Spring), pp. 23–36.

Liuhto, K. (1991), 'The Interaction of Managerial Cultures in Soviet-Finnish Joint Ventures – Including Estonian-Finnish Joint Ventures', *Publications of the Institute for East-West Trade*, B 10/1991. Turku School of Economics: Turku, Finland.

Lyles, M.A. (1988), 'Learning among Joint Venture Sophisticated Firms', *Management International Review*, vol. 28, pp. 85–98.

Morgan, G. and Ramirez, R. (1983), 'Action Learning: A Holographic Metaphor for Guiding Social Change', *Human Relations*, vol. 37, pp. 1-28.

Nieminen, J. and. Törnroos, J.-Å (1997), 'The Role of Learning in the Evolution of Business Networks in Estonia: Four Finnish Case Studies', in M. Forsgren and I. Björkman (eds) *The Nature of the International Firm*, Copenhagen: Copenhagen Business School Press, pp. 164-185.

Nigh, D., Walters, P. and Kuhlmann, J.A. (1990), 'Soviet-USSR Joint Ventures: An Examination of the Early Entrants', *Columbia Journal of World Business*, vol. 25 (Winter), pp. 20–41.

Parkhe, A. (1991), 'Interfirm Diversity, Organizational Learning, and Longevity in Global Strategic Alliances', *Journal of International Business Studies*, vol. 22, no. 4, pp. 579–602.

Simiar, F. (1983), 'Major Causes of Joint Venture Failures in the Middle East: The Case of Iran', *Management International Review*, vol. 23, no. 1, pp. 58–68.

Starbuck, W.H. (1983), 'Organizations as Action Generators', *American Sociological*

Review, vol. 48, pp. 91–102.

Sullivan, J. and Peterson, R.B. (1982), 'Factors Associated with Trust in Japanese-American Joint Ventures', *Management International Review*, vol. 22, no. 2, pp. 30–40.

Tesar, G. and Nieminen, J. (1994), 'Managerial Conflicts in East-West Joint Ventures – A Bilateral Perspective', in P. Chadraba and R. Springer (eds) *Proceedings of the Conference on Marketing Strategies for Entering Central and Eastern Europe*, Vienna, December 3-6, pp. 38-52.

Yin, R.K. (1989), *Case Study Research: Design and Methods*, Newbury Park, CA: Sage Publications.

15 Foreign Market Expansion in Newly Emerging Markets: Finnish Companies in the Visegrád Countries

ZSUZSANNA VINCZE

Introduction

The importance of the emerging markets in the world can hardly be underestimated nowadays. Researchers, as well as practitioners, realize the need for tools to address challenges posed by the emerging markets. Critical thinking is needed about important issues in emerging markets, as well as in bridging the gap between theory and practice.

During the last decade, the Central and Eastern European (CEE) business environment and organizations have been going through profound changes. The Visegrád countries, the Czech Republic, Hungary, Poland and the Slovak Republic, are the fastest developing, most industrialized and westernized among the newly emerging country markets of Central and Eastern Europe. Companies from those economies have been actively involved in the process of attracting foreign direct investment (FDI), as well as trying to internationalize their own activities. It can be assumed that companies operating in the Visegrád markets would not necessarily follow the prescribed stepwise foreign market expansion. Rather, they have to find out and implement alternative responses to unpredictably occurring opportunities and problems. In dealing with those challenges companies may find collaboration with local companies the most valuable source of tacit knowledge and experience.

Context and Purpose of the Study

It is often suggested that countries which have started their industrialization after World War II could be considered as emerging markets. This rather general definition includes almost all states outside the 'triad powers'. However, those countries have quite divergent social, political and economic systems. They differ very much in their approaches to economic development. The Central European (CE) countries are in the group of industrializing countries, which have the state apparatus under challenge. Another distinction between different emerging markets is that they are either export-oriented or follow import substitution policies. The export-oriented markets are opening up and growing fast. Rapid growth characterizes the earlier closed economies of Asia, Latin America and, since the early nineties, Central Europe (Aulakh *et al.*, 2000). Looking back in history from the point of view of western companies the most severe obstacle to doing business in Central Europe, apart from the political system, was the deficient information restricting collaboration between companies from the East and West.

In addition, even though the Visegrád countries are presented as a regional economic bloc often evaluated as a group of countries rather than as independent entities (Lavigne, 1995; Borish and Noël, 1997), their transition process in terms of initial conditions varied a lot. The transition process is complex and certain elements of change do not happen at the same time and in the same way. After a decade of experience with those economies academic research and business experience have come to acknowledge that the transition to market-led is more than just economic reforms. Market and structural economic reforms are underpinning fundamental social, political and institutional changes (North, 1997; Naim, 2000). The systemic approach to understanding change in Central Europe is a prerequisite for any company intending to operate in those markets.

This chapter aims at understanding and explaining foreign market entry and expansion of two Finnish middle-sized manufacturing companies. During the last decade, 1990 - 2000, the two companies entered and expanded their operations in the markets of the Visegrád countries (Figure 15.1; six entries and further expansions comprise the six cases presented in the analysis). The companies had relatively little previous experience in foreign markets before they entered the Visegrád countries. The two companies started operations on those markets as pioneers in their own field. In spite of the fact that other Finnish companies had tried to enter those markets previously, less than a dozen companies invested enough resources to be able to sustain organizational growth and realize significant profit. The companies analyzed in this study were among the few who took the risk and the challenge to conquer the unknown. Those firms have committed resources, which allowed them to experience sustained performance improvement and achieve profitability in the volatile and ever changing business conditions of the Visegrád countries.

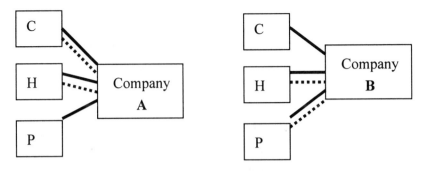

••••••   The unit of analysis: Inter-organizational relationship

————   Personal relationship in employee-employer context

Figure 15.1   Investments analyzed in the study
                 (C = Czech Republic, H = Hungary, P =
Poland)

When analyzing the cases we will try to answer the following research questions:

• How did the two Finnish companies expand their businesses in the Visegrád markets during the period 1990 - 2000?
• How did the companies develop strategies in the seemingly similar country markets?
• What was the role of long-term business relationships with local partners in the expansion of business operations?

Our initial assumption was that there were crucial differences within the Visegrád markets, which the two companies had to understand and learn how to deal with. The two firms selected for the study are middle-sized companies that tried to gain first mover advantage (Ansoff, 1957; Baker and Becker, 1997) in the Visegrád country markets. We have also assumed that previous experience and established business relationships would significantly influence the operations in the Visegrád markets. That is why the focus of this study is on the interdependent processes of foreign market expansion and development of business relationships.

The opening of the CE market was a strategic opportunity for the Companies A and B. In spite of that fact, it should be suggested that developing a strong competitive position in emerging markets entails more than just transferring a successful domestic strategy to new markets. The environmental characteristics, timing of market entry, strategic priorities, partner selection and managing a unique combination of marketing mix elements play a decisive role in a successful foreign expansion.

Theoretical Background

Welch and Luostarinen (1988) define the process of internationalization as 'the increasing involvement of a company in international operations'. Foreign market expansion can be viewed in terms of business growth, increased sales volume, growing turnover and profitability in particular country markets. It should be noted, however, that growth in one market has direct impact on the overall growth of a company. This leads to ever growing complexity of business operations.

Studies that focus on the process of internationalization are central to the analysis in this research. A number of published papers on internationalization apply a perspective, which is processual, dynamic and holistic. First, the stages-models of internationalization (e.g., Bilkey and Tesar, 1977) describe the changes companies adopt as measures of their commitment to the internationalization process. Second, for example, Johanson and Wiedersheim-Paul (1975), Johanson and Vahlne (1977), Welch and Luostarinen (1988) explain the logical development of the internationalization process. The process of internationalization is viewed as founded on two major concepts, 'psychic distance' and the increased experiential knowledge of a foreign market. These concepts can be used to explain how companies commit resources to international markets over time. In other words, the focus is on the processual determinants of companies' increased involvement in foreign market operations. Third, the contingency approach claims that firms' international development depends upon a wider range of external and internal factors (Turnbull, 1987; Fletcher, 2001). The assumption is that companies do not necessarily follow a step-wise linear expansion that is suggested in the aforementioned two processual models. Finally, internationalization from a network perspective (Johanson and Mattsson, 1988; Axelsson and Johanson, 1992) focuses on the firm's position in a foreign market underpinned by relationships of various degree of importance. Thus, the network perspective puts the market and the relationships of the firm into focus, rather than concentrating only on internal development.

In summary, internationalization is seen as a process of international business expansion based on experience and learning about foreign markets, cultures and institutions. However we argue that apart from learning about foreign markets, internationalization is also learning about the internal resources and capabilities of the firm (Christensen, 1991; Eriksson *et al.*, 1997). Market knowledge and market commitments affect both commitment decisions and the way current decisions are performed. These, in turn, change market knowledge and commitment (Johanson and Vahlne, 1977). In the network approach, internationalization is often described as being a set of connected learning processes (Axelsson and Johanson, 1992).

Today, process-models of internationalization are frequently criticized as being too deterministic, putting too much emphasis on perceived psychic distance (e.g., Holmlund and Kock, 1998). The psychic distance concept (O'Grady and Lane, 1996) might lead to a paradox. Furthermore, the concept is not sufficient to elaborate on the environmental influence enhancing the interdependence between an operating company and its business environment. Furthermore, a move in a particular market should be seen more as a part of the overall growth process of the company. Although commitment decisions are related to the learning, we should recognize that learning is not a linear process. The network perspective enriches the understanding of the learning process arguing that knowledge is gained after a transaction, or after decision has been implemented. Network researchers (Ford, 1990; Majkgård and Sharma, 1998) argue that some loss of independence and revenue sharing is inherent in networking but it is assumed that inter-firm cooperation enables a firm to position itself in a foreign market quickly. The cumulative nature of network processes leads to the arguments developed by network theorists about the sequential order of internationalization (Johanson and Mattsson, 1988; Christensen and Lindmark, 1991). In addition, the understanding of the internationalization process as a set of learning processes supports the research based on the network perspective. However, the timing of internationalization is still not easy to incorporate into the analysis.

We argue that the linear sequential model of development is sometimes inadequate to deal with the complexities of internationalization. It assumes invariance between and within all organizational units, thus, following a prescribed order of developmental phases, one is locked after another (Van de Ven, 1992). In agreement with Van de Ven (1992), we believe one could further the understanding of the internationalization process by applying a more teleological process theory to the research process. According to the ideas of the teleology process theory one should know the desired outcome from the internationalization of a particular company that is the profitable growth of the company in a foreign market. What we need to understand better is how managers identify the options they have and how they decide which option is the best one to achieve that desired performance outcome (Julien *et al.*, 1997). Therefore, we have to unveil the specifics of that mechanism in order to understand the internationalization process in more depth.

Methodological Issues

In order to apply a teleological perspective, we have collected longitudinal processual data, both retrospective and in real-time. In all cases, the managers in charge of implementing strategic decisions were chosen to be the main source of information (Table 15.1). Both the managers from the internationalizing Finnish companies and those from the host-country intermediaries in each Visegrád market have discussed and evaluated the ten years of business expansion. We have evaluated those key relationships with host-country intermediaries using the approach of Eriksson and Chetty (1998) in presenting the concept of bridgehead relationship.

Table 15.1   Key features of the research design

Research Area	Business expansion in emerging market
Context	Finnish companies in the Czech Republic, Slovakia, Hungary and Poland
Number of Cases	2 x 3
Levels of Analysis	Company level of relationships
	Personal level of relationships
Time Frame	1990 - 2000, almost 10 years (longitudinal)
Data Sources	Introductory questionnaire
	Interviews (retrospective and real-time)
	Archives
	Observations
Research Output	A substantive theory of foreign market expansion process. Central is the process of creating organizational momentum. It can explain variations in lower level processes

The data collection and analysis were guided by the grounded theory methodology (Glaser and Strauss, 1967; Eisenhardt, 1989; Strauss and Corbin, 1990; Pettigrew, 1990, 1997; Glaser, 1992; Langley, 1999; Partington, 2000).

As this study investigates the strategic behavior, i.e., actions and experiences of managers in newly emerging markets, we believe that grounded theory approach offers the best potential for this research. We have incorporated a variety of variables that impact on foreign market expansion. The chosen methodology utilizes the breath and depth of the data in order to incorporate the variety and range of variables.

The theory generation process can be usefully conceptualized in three major phases (Edwards, 1998): a descriptive phase, a theoretical-heuristic or theory-development phase and a theory-testing phase. These phases are in accordance with the dual nature of scientific knowledge creation, namely, the use of both inductive and deductive thinking, within the same study. Each phase represents a different aspect of the research process. The phases have specific aims and suggest particular strategies. Even though those phases are useful for structuring a case study research, particularly with grounded theory methodology, this is not a linear process.

There is always a need for iteration between the steps. Glaser (1992) suggests that the grounded theory method he and Strauss developed in 1967 is particularly useful for researchers concerned with issues relating to human behavior in organizations, in groups or in any other social configuration. Furthermore, grounded theory methodology is important for processual case studies (Pettigrew, 1990), in moving from analytical chronology and diagnosis of cases towards interpretative/theoretical output. However, grounded theory in a well-researched field like the internationalization of the firm does not necessarily generate new concepts. Rather, it can be used to unravel the basic social process conceptually, which is often missed by researchers.

There are problems within the grounded theory being applied to management problems. The latter are linked to the symbolic interactionist roots of the universal grounded theory developed by Glaser and Strauss (1967). Those have a purpose different from creating knowledge directly applicable to managerial situations (Partington, 2000). It is mostly interested with the symbolic interactions and their importance in relationships. The type of qualitative data used in management research is also different. The data consists mostly of retrospective accounts, documentary records and interviews, which have an ontologically different status than the observation data used in the universal grounded theory methodology. Partington (2000) suggests a simpler analytic framework within the critical realist perspective (Bashkar, 1975). In the interview-based causal theory building, the aim is to build causal theory while acknowledging the lack of absolute causal certainty. Management actions are not always easy to observe and evaluate in an objective way. Furthermore, social processes are rarely reducible to absolute laws. Reality here is socially constructed and consists of individuals' interpretations. Context/stimuli, meanings/cognitive processes and responses/behaviors are real. However, some of the elements are revealed as observable events, some are accessible through the subjective accounts of the managers and other organizational actors. Some are uncovered through speculation of the researcher over apparent causal tendencies, which need further inquiry and verification.

This study mainly analyses recollection of past events, recorded in interview data. There is an emphasis on tacit knowledge. The grounded theory analysis has been conducted using a simplified paradigm model and a conditional matrix (see Partington, 2000).

Analysis and Discussion

The process analysis involves in-depth examinations and incorporations of changed action/interaction in response to changes in conditions as these vary over time.

Table 15.2   Steps of analysis

Steps	Where to find?	Abstraction level
Data split	Appendix	Level 0
Data reduction	Analysis	
Open coding		
Axial coding		
Selective coding	Description	Level 1
Selection of the main processes	Implementing the theory of the business (X)	Level 2
	Adaptation to external environment (Y)	
	Internal re-organizing (Z)	
Cross-case analysis	Variations	
Identify case results (Test the findings)	Figures	Level 3
Conclusions	Reflection against previous knowledge	

In accordance with grounded theory methodology (Table 15.2), the open coding[1] procedures helped us to extract several sub-processes within cases. With axial and selective coding, first within cases, then across cases, we have identified three main processes as pillars of the substantive theory.

The main processes (See Figure 15.2) are:

- Implementing the theoretical views of doing business in a foreign environment, in terms of the companies' assumptions of the business they are in. What are the companies' objectives? How do they define the expected results? In other words, these are the companies' perceptions of who their customers are and what those customers value and pay for. The key category is the core competence in relation to the product quality, capacity and processes;
- The second, simultaneously pursued, is the process of adaptation to the external environment. Here, the moves of the potential customers and competitors, as well as the macro level changes, are most important. The bridgehead relationship dyads (Eriksson and Chetty 1998) have a central role in this adaptation process as macro and market changes are filtrated through them;
- The reorganization of internal structure, both in the Finnish headquarters and in the relationship dyads, comprises the third pillar of the substantive theory.

These processes are relevant in answering the three specific research-questions of this study, yet only partially. Through constant comparisons between the categories and these three processes, we have arrived at the core finding of this study which identifies that the basic social process is the creation of organizational momentum.[2] With this basic social process one is able to tackle the variation between cases. Creation of organizational momentum, either deliberately or spontaneously, is unique for every company.

The creation of organizational momentum underlies the complex, non-linear organizational growth process (Figure 15.2). In this study we have focused on business expansion in newly emerging markets, which is one of the possible strategies pursued by a company in order to grow. However, in creating an organizational momentum other strategies are used in parallel (i.e., new product development, sustaining the positioning in the domestic market, etc.).

Organizational momentum originates from two sources. One is rooted in what the expanding company took from its past and the other in what the partner brought to it. Undoubtedly, at the beginning of the internationalization process the Finnish company brought into the host countries of CE its product, technology and the capacity it had to produce. It also had managerial know-how and an adequate organizational structure for entering a new market area. The Finnish market at the time was shrinking. The CE potential partner had to have the ability to provide the

Finnish company with market access, as well as to collect and disseminate reliable CE market information. However, as the venture developed the CE country partners had to develop their capabilities in raising resources, acquiring new technology and exploiting internal and external networks. At the same time, the Finnish company had to reorganize its structure and develop more non-traditional and creative approaches to doing business allowing for a higher degree of flexibility. These new developments cannot be detached from the past expansion behavior of those companies.

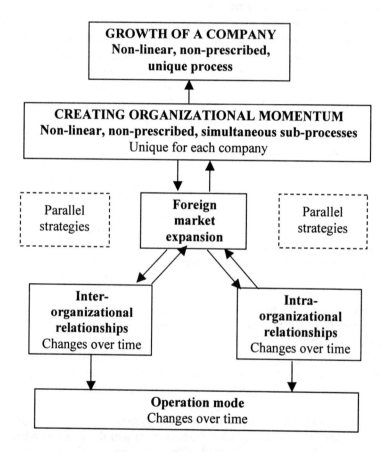

Figure 15.2   Sustaining growth by the case companies

As Figure 15.3 shows, the two sources add to both tangibles and intangibles. Continuous creation of organizational momentum prepares the company to be ready to take opportunities and avoid threats. We believe that the concept has the potential to explain the crucial role of the host-country business partners. In the analyzed cases, that were most successful, the momentum for further expansion was created exactly with first mover advantage in one of the Visegrád markets.

Based on the on-going cross-case analysis, we could introduce examples showing how some concepts extracted by the grounded theory analysis fit the concept of organizational momentum. We recognize that by no means these can be considered entirely new concepts. However, evaluating them in the specific context of the Visegrád countries, and in relation to the basic social process identified here we might facilitate a fresh insight in the process of internationalization.

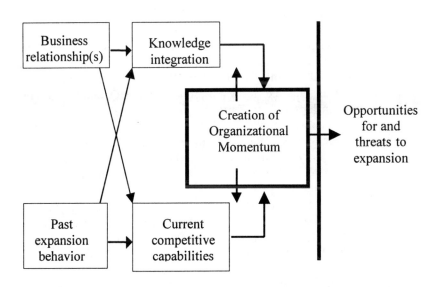

Figure 15.3   **Creation of organizational momentum in foreign market expansion**

The successful business dyads developed together parallel with commitment to the joint business. In these cases trust developed early in the relationship. When the business grew in complexity and importance, trust in the partners was further strengthened by relationship-specific investments on both sides. However, a calculated commitment characterized more the evolving relationships rather than the initial commitment. In the cases when partners did not like each other from the onset of the relationship, trust could not develop. Thus, other relationship specific investments were neglected. The outcome was that these partnerships were dissolved.

In bridgehead type of relationships the role of relationships was to filtrate market information (intangibles) towards the Finnish company. Therefore, they have had major importance to the adaptation processes (Y processes in Table 15.2).

The tangible resources were shared according to joint interest between the partners. From the point of view of the Finnish companies this was evaluated as resource saving exchanges. Using the tangible and intangible benefits from the collaboration with the host partners, the Finnish investors found it easier to expand in the other Visegrád countries on a later stage. The timing of expansion was central to the implementation of the business idea (X processes in Table 15.2) and to any further expansion. The decisive role of bridgehead partners was to provide market access and customer base for the Finnish companies in the host-country markets. As businesses grew in volume and complexity, the Finnish companies wanted to take more control. This required reorganization of the HQ and within the bridgehead relationships as well (Z process in Table 15.2).

Initially, the Finnish companies evaluated their host country partner according to their success in gaining long-term market position in the respective country market. Later on, as the relationship developed, the cost effective capability of the host partners to carry out other tasks (functions) became very important.

Organizational inertia is a processual phenomenon. The cases in each group (relating to Company A and B) are interrelated. The concept of organizational inertia fits to the 'Past expansion behavior' block in Figure 15.3. Once the Finnish companies managed to establish successful operations in one Visegrád country, they tried to transfer the business idea in its either identical or similar format to the other countries. Two types of rather negative consequences from the actions of the Finnish investors could be identified. One was market divestment and the other, a relatively slow speed (muddling-through) in the expansion process. Inertia could be detected when the Finnish company chose a partner in the second or third Visegrád country market. In later entries, trust was based on previous experience from a successful investment in one of the Visegrád markets involving a different partner. However, one should take into account that the key role of the host country partner was to provide market access and customer base for the Finnish company. Within the fairly similar environment of the Visegrád countries companies will face somewhat different external forces when they enter any particular country market or expand operations in the other Visegrád states.

Throughout the analysis we had to make a clear distinction between own investments and relation-specific investments. Relation-specific investments are not always easy to calculate by numbers. However, those are significant. The early expansion of the two Finnish companies was characterized more by relation-specific investments. In the most successful cases, the bridgehead partner took a significant part from these types of investments (i.e., saved resources for the Finnish company). With the relationship-specific investments the businesses were set up and grew. Following that, the Finnish companies started to implement strategies for own investment. It should be noted that all cases started with more complex market entry modes than exporting. This indicates that timing was more important for the case companies than learning of and gaining experience in those markets. In the cases where a real bridgehead partner from the host-country market facilitated the process of internationalization of the Finnish company, the latter managed to achieve better timing and was fast to learn. The cost of investment for the Finnish companies in the first years of transition in the Visegrád economies was relatively low compared to entry into Western markets. Visegrád markets were also attractive for competitors because of their customer base and relatively low factor costs. The Finnish companies assumed that positioning themselves in the market and building consumer awareness was the first step to achieving control over the market gradually establishing direct relationships with customers.

Conclusion

There are discussions about the importance of history, the embeddedness and the overall complexity of the internationalization process. Furthermore, some studies admit that many winning strategies exist (e.g., Julien *et al.*, 1997). Others discuss different determinants of the internationalization process. There are arguments that internationalization with gradually evolving stages would be more applicable to the early phases of a company's international expansion and, probably, easier to be adopted by small and medium-sized companies (Johanson and Mattsson, 1988). This study has some similarities with the findings of strategic management research; particularly Weick's concept (1988) of enacted environment, as well with Mintzberg's views on intended and realized strategy. This is rarely a linear process (e.g., Mintzberg and Waters, 1982). The Austrian approach of entrepreneurship is also relevant here. With the concept of entrepreneurial discovery it is able to tackle an essential part of the dynamics of the competitive market process (Kirzner, 1997). Organizational change literature has developed the concept of 'organizational momentum' (Mahajan, Sharma and Bettis, 1988), which refers to organizational structure at one point of time. Nevertheless, these similarities certainly help to prove the conceptual validity of the theory generated in our study.

In summary, this study has shown that creating organizational momentum is central to the growth process of a company, whatever strategy it chooses[3]. With this concept one can analyze companies' behavior in a foreign market over a long period of time. The theory can be applied simultaneously to environmental, strategic and operational issues explaining variations in the actions/interactions pursued by the case companies. When creating an organizational momentum a company creates options for the future that would allow its management to grasp opportunities and avoid unpredictable threats.

Notes

1   Coding is the actual analysis of the data. In the analysis using the procedure of open coding one breaks down, examines, compares and conceptualizes the data. It is the initial stage of constant comparative analysis. With axial coding one identifies connections between categories extracted by open coding (based on conditions, action/interactions and consequences). Selective coding is the part of the data analysis process when one identifies the core category(s), and to that systematically relates the other categories thus he/she constructs the main story line.

2   Our preliminary definition is that when timing cannot be carefully planned the company needs to prepare itself to undertake strategic actions requiring rational allocation of resources.

3   In the empirical cases, the central strategy was expansion in foreign markets in the period of time 1990 - 2000.

References

Ansoff, H. I. (1957), 'Strategies for Diversification', *Harvard Business Review*, September-October, pp. 113-124.

Aulakh, P. S., Kotabe, M. and Teegen, H. (2000), 'Export Strategies and Performance of Firms From Emerging Economies: Evidence from Brazil, Chile, and Mexico', *Academy of Management Journal*, vol. 43, no. 3, pp. 342-361.

Axelsson, B. and Johanson, J. (1992), 'Foreign Market Entry - The Textbook vs. the Network View', in B. Axelsson and G. Easton (eds) *Industrial Networks - A New View of Reality*, London and New York: Routledge, pp. 218-234.

Baker, M. J. and Becker, S. H. (1997), 'Pioneering New Geographical Markets', *Journal of Marketing Management*, vol. 13, no. 1/3, pp. 89-104.

Bhaskar, R. (1975), *A Realist Theory of Science*, Leeds: Leeds Books.

Bilkey, W and Tesar, G. (1977), 'The Export Behavior of Smaller-Sized Wisconsin Manufacturing Firms', *Journal of International Business Studies*, vol. 8, no. 1, pp. 93-98.

Borish, M. and Noël, M. (1997), 'Privatization in the Visegrád Countries: A Comparative Assessment', *The World Economy*, vol. 2, pp. 199-219.

Christensen, P. (1991), 'The Small and Medium-Sized Exporters' Squeeze: Empirical Evidence and Model Reflections', *Entrepreneurship and Regional Development*, vol. 3, no. 1, pp. 49-65.

Christ nsen, P. and Lindmark, L. (1991), 'In Search of Regional Support of Small and Medium-Sized Firms – A Network Perspective', Paper presented at the 38th North American Meeting of the Regional Science Association, in New Orleans, Louisiana, U.S.A., November 7-10.

Edwards, D. (1998), 'Types of Case Study Work: Conceptual Framework for Case-Based Research', *Journal of Human Psychology*, vol. 38. no. 3, pp. 36-70

Eisenhardt, K. (1989), 'Building Theories from Case Study Research', *Academy of Management Review*, vol. 14, no. 4, pp. 532-550.

Eriksson, K. and Chetty, S. (1998), 'The Development of Experimental Knowledge in Internationalization through Customer-Supplier Relationship', *Proceedings of the 27th EMAC Conference, Track 2: International Marketing*, Stockholm, Sweden, December 8-10.

Eriksson, K., Johanson, J., Majkgård, A and Sharma, D. (1997), 'Experimental Knowledge and Cost in the Internationalization Process, *Journal of International Business Studies*, vol. 2, pp. 337-360.

Fletcher, R. (2001), 'A Holistic Approach to Internationalization', *International Business Review*, vol. 10, pp. 25-49.

Ford, D. (ed.) (1990), *Understanding Business Markets*, London: Academic Press.

Glaser, B. and Strauss, A. (1967), *The Discovery of Grounded Theory, Strategies for Qualitative Research*, Chicago: Aldine Publishing Company.

Glaser, B. (1992), *Emergence Vs. Forcing: Basics of Grounded Theory Analysis*, Mill Valley, CA: Sociology Press.

Holmlund, M. and Kock, S. (1998), 'Relationships and the Internationalization of Finnish Small and Medium-Sized Companies', *International Small Business Journal*, vol. 16, no. 4, pp. 46-63.

Johanson, J. and Mattsson, L.-G. (1988), 'Internationalization in Industrial Systems - A Network Approach', in N. Hood, and J.-E. Vahlne (eds) *Strategies in Global Competition*, London: Routledge, pp. 287-314.

Johanson, J. and Vahlne, J.-E. (1977), 'The Internationalization Process of the Firm - A Model of Knowledge Development and Increasing Foreign Market Commitments', *Journal of International Business*, vol. 8, no. 1, pp. 23-32.

Johanson, J. and Wiedersheim-Paul, F. (1975), 'The Internationalization of the Firm – Four Swedish Cases', in P. Buckley and P. Ghauri, P. (1994) *The Internationalization of the Firm*, London: The Dryden Press, pp. 16-31.

Julien, P.-A., Joyal, A., Deshaies, L. and Ramangalahy, C. (1997), 'A Typology of Strategic Behavior among Small and Medium-Sized Exporting Businesses: A Case Study', *International Small Business Journal*, vol. 15, no. 2, pp. 32-46.

Kirzner, I. (1997), 'Entrepreneurial Discovery and the Competitive Market Process: An Austrian Approach', *Journal of Economic Literature*, vol. 35, March, pp. 60-85.

Langley, A. (1999), 'Strategies for Theorizing from Process Data', *Academy of Management Review*, vol. 24, no. 4, pp. 691-710.

Lavigne, M. (1995), *The Economics of Transition from Socialist Economy to Market Economy*, Basingstoke: Macmillan.

Mahajan, V., Sharma, S. and Bettis, R. (1988), 'The Adoption of the M-Form Organizational Structure: A Test', *Management Science*, vol. 34, no. 10, pp. 1188-1201.

Majkgård, A. and Sharma D. (1998), 'Client-Following and Market-Seeking Strategies in the Internationalization of Service Firms', *Journal of Business-to-Business Marketing*, vol. 4, no. 3, pp. 1-41.

Mintzberg, H. and Waters, J. (1982), 'Tracking Strategy in an Entrepreneurial Firm', *Academy of Management Journal*, vol. 25, no. 3, pp. 465-499.

Naim, M. (2000), 'Washington Consensus or Washington Confusion?', *Foreign Policy*, Spring, pp. 86-98.

North, D. (1997), 'The Contribution of the New Institutional Economics to an Understanding of the Transition Problem', *WIDER – Annual Lectures 1*.

O'Grady, S. and Lane, H. (1996), 'The Psychic Distance Paradox', *Journal of International Business Studies*, vol. 2, pp. 309-326.

Partington, D. (2000), 'Building Grounded Theories of Management Action', *British Journal of Management*, vol. 11, pp. 91-102.

Pettigrew, A. (1990), 'Longitudinal Field Research on Change: Theory and Practice', *Organization Science*, vol. 1, no. 3, pp. 267-292.

Pettigrew, A. (1997), 'What is a Processual Analysis?', *Scandinavian Journal of Management*, vol. 13, no. 4, pp. 337-348.

Strauss, A. and Corbin, J. (1990), *Basics of Qualitative Research: Grounded Theory Procedures and Techniques*, New York: Sage Publications.

Turnbull, P. (1987), 'A Challenge to the Stages Theory of the Internationalization Process', in P. Buckley and P. Ghauri (eds) (1994), *The Internationalization of the Firm*, London: The Dryden Press, pp. 172-185.

Van de Ven, A. (1992), 'Suggestions for Studying Strategy Process: A Research Note', *Strategic Management Journal*, vol. 13, pp. 169-188.

Weick, K. (1988), 'Enacted Sense-Making in Crisis Situations', *Journal of Management Studies*, vol. 25, no. 4, pp. 305-317.

Welch, L. and Luostarinen, R. (1988), 'Internationalisation: Evolution of a Concept', *Journal of General Management*, vol. 14, no. 2, pp. 34-64.

Name Index

Subject Index

cross-border trade, 230, 240, 242
Cuba, 145
cultural proximity, 181, 185, 186,
    191, 195, 196, 198
currency board, 67
currency crisis, 67
current account, 17, 22, 23, 24,
    240, 241, 242
Cyprus, 147, 148
Czechoslovakia, 12, 19, 38, 45,
    137, 157, 158, 161, 162
Czech Republic, 1, 4, 5, 6, 7, 8,
    12, 13, 14, 15, 16, 17, 18, 19,
    20, 21, 22, 23, 24, 25, 26, 27,
    28, 29, 30, 32, 33, 34, 36, 40,
    41, 45, 48, 50, 51, 52, 54, 55,
    60, 63, 65, 66, 68, 69, 71, 72,
    73, 74, 75, 79, 80, 81, 82, 87,
    88, 89, 91, 96, 134, 142, 146,
    147, 157, 158, 160, 161, 162,
    163, 164, 165, 168, 169, 172,
    173, 174, 175, 176, 177, 181,
    189, 234, 236, 237, 238, 296,
    309, 311, 314

Daewoo, 33, 87, 101
Daihatsu, 166, 167, 168, 170, 176
De Beers, 144
debt service, 194
Demirbank, 193
Derzhkomstat, 120, 122, 125,
    127
Denso International Europe B.V.,
    174
Denso Manufacturing, 174, 175
Deutsche Telekom, 33
developed countries, 235, 236,
    238
developing countries, 181, 182,
    183, 184, 185, 187, 198, 209,
    235, 238

East Asia, 188
eclectic paradigm, 182, 185
eclectic theory, 247
Economic Commission for
    Europe, 12, 26, 36
economic growth, 1, 17, 24, 34,
    63, 64, 65, 76, 91
Efes Beverage Group, 192, 195
Egypt, 141, 142
Elektrim, 33
Enka, 192
Erdemir, 193
Eridania Beghin-Say, 33
Estonia, 1, 4, 5, 12, 13, 15, 18,
    26, 27, 28, 29, 30, 31, 32, 41,
    43, 45, 60, 63, 65, 66, 67, 68,
    69, 71, 72, 73, 74, 75, 80, 82,
    96, 140, 238
Esztergom, 171
Euro-Asia, 185
Euro-Matsushita, 162
Europe, 38, 40, 41, 45, 54, 57, 58
European Bank for
    Reconstruction and
    Development (EBRD), 12,
    27, 29, 31, 33, 35, 36, 40, 41,
    54, 57, 173
European Central Bank (ECB),
    67
European Union (EU), 15, 18,
    19, 20, 22, 28, 29, 30, 31, 32,
    34, 35, 39, 42, 44, 45, 62,66,
    76,82,89, 95, 117, 123, 124,
    134, 137, 148, 152, 166, 188,
    195, 198, 203, 204, 205, 206,
    207, 208, 209, 210, 215, 217,
    219, 224, 225, 226, 230, 240,
    244
European Commission, 213, 225,
    227, 228
Exedy Corporation, 159